AF651310

THE STATE OF CHILDREN IN INDIA

Promises to Keep

THE STATE OF CHILDREN IN INDIA

Promises to Keep

A. B. BOSE

MANOHAR
2003

First published 2003

© A.B. Bose, 2003

All rights reserved. No part of this publication may be reproduced or transmitted, in any form or by any means, without prior permission of the author and the publisher

ISBN 81-7304-474-0

Published by

Ajay Kumar Jain for
Manohar Publishers & Distributors
4753/23 Ansari Road, Daryaganj
New Delhi 110 002

Typeset at

Digigrafics
New Delhi 110 049

Printed at

Print Perfect
New Delhi 110 064

Contents

Tables

Figures

Abbreviations

ANM	Auxiliary Nurse Midwife
ARI	Acute respiratory infection
CBHI	Central Bureau of Health Intelligence
CEDC	Children in specially difficult circumstances
CHC	Community Health Centre
CINI	Child in Need Institute
CLASP	Child Labour Action and Support Programme
CLPR Act	Child Labour (Prohibition and Regulation) Act
CSWB	Central Social Welfare Board
DPEP	District Primary Education Programme
DW & CD	Department of Women and Child Development
EPI	Expanded Programme of Immunization
ICDS	Integrated Child Development Services
IIPS	International Institute for Population Sciences
IMR	Infant Mortality Rate
IPECL	International Programme on the Elimination of Child Labour
MCH	Maternal and child health
MOHFW	Ministry of Health and Family Welfare
MSJE	Ministry of Social Justice and Empowerment
NCLP	National Child Labour Projects
NFE	Non-formal education
NFHS	National Family Health Survey
NICD	National Institute of Communicable Diseases
NIHFW	National Institute of Health and Family Welfare
NIN	National Institute of Nutrition
NLI	National Labour Institute
NNMB	National Nutrition Monitoring Bureau
NPCB	National Programme for Control of Blindness
NPCL	National Policy on Child Labour
NPE	National Policy on Education
NSS	National Sample Survey
NSSO	National Sample Survey Organization

ODA	Overseas Development Agency
OPV	Oral polio vaccine
ORS	Oral rehydration solution
PEO	Programme Evaluation Organization
PHC	Primary Health Centre
PNDT Act	Prenatal Diagnostic Techniques (Regulation of Misuse) Act
PROBE	Public Report on Basic Education
RCH	Reproductive and child health
SIDA	Swedish International Development Agency
SLL	Special and Local Laws
SRS	Sample Registration System
TT	Tetanus toxoid
TT2	Two doses of tetanus toxoid vaccine
UIP	Universal Immunization Programme
WWCDN	Women's Work and Child Development Network

Preface

Children are a nation's 'supremely important asset', declared the National Policy on Children (1974), while stating the goals and outlining the policies and measures. It went on to add: 'their nurture and solicitude are our responsibility' and 'equal opportunities for development to all children during the period of growth should be our aim, for this would serve our larger purpose of reducing inequality and ensuring social justice'. Earlier, the Constitution of India gave directions to the State on specific child development concerns and granted them protection. More recently, India has ratified the United Nations Convention on the Rights of the Child (1989), signifying India's commitment to meet the protection, survival, and development needs of children.

In 1951, India's nascent asset comprised 137 million children aged 0–14 years. This increased to 317 million in 1991, and is estimated to have reached 352 million at the start of the twenty-first century (2001). The developmental needs of these children, nearly half of whom are from lower income groups and three-fourths of whom live in rural areas, call for strong political and administrative commitment, integrated policies, coordinated action, and an effective delivery system.

At the dawn of the twenty-first century it is necessary to take stock of what has been achieved and what is yet to be achieved, so that the child development goals set by the nation can become a social reality. The present study is an attempt in this direction. It gives an overview of the current state of India's children after nearly five decades of independence. Official statistics on programmes tend to overwhelm the reader with schemes and the monies spent on them, and virtually ignore the outcome, which is the real aim of public spending and should have occupied the centre stage of official reports on progress. The present study, by contrast, focuses mainly on the outcomes as reflected by various key indicators of child development.

Most studies on child development pick up specific areas. The need for an effort which brings together different sectors of child development has been voiced at many forums. The present study is an attempt to fill this gap, and is of the nature of an overview of the current state of India's children. The first chapter gives a brief description of the setting in the context of which child development issues become important. Subsequent chapters take up the major child development concerns, identify the main outcome indicators which describe the current state, and analyse the trends on the basis of data. The main child development concerns covered in the different chapters are child survival, nutrition status, educational status, child abuse as reflected in child labour and in sexual abuse, severely disadvantaged children, and children who come in conflict with law. Mention has been made of new and emerging problems such as drug abuse and AIDS. The chapters indicate the promises that were made and the goals that were set, so that the progress achieved can be assessed in the light of these solemn declarations of commitment. The unfinished agenda in each area of social concern has been indicated. The text is meant for the general reader interested in social development, and aims at communicating with a wide audience, so as to share with persons of diverse educational backgrounds the key child development issues.

The study is based on secondary data generated by Census operations, the Sample Registration System, National Sample Surveys and other national surveys, and multi-centre studies. Use has also been made of data available from micro-studies published in journals and reports of surveys. There are some problems in using secondary data, apart from the considerable time lag in publication, as has been the case with the 1991 Census. Concepts and definitions of terms used in different studies vary. The tabulation framework is not the same even in multi-centre studies, making comparisons difficult. Some of the micro-studies do not indicate the period when data collection was done. A fairly large number lack the rigour of competently done research. Most evaluation studies funded by official agencies are not published. They are kept in safe bureaucratic custody and are not available even for consultation by researchers under the dispensation that they are intended for official use only. These reports become untraceable after a couple of years or so. Official policy in this matter must change so that the outcomes of intervention strategies and programmes are shared and useful data on change and development becomes available to a much larger audience and can be used for designing new programmes, or even for training as 'lessons learnt'. For a number of emerging areas of vital concern, hardly any data are available, except on expenditure and persons benefited which are of little help in analysing the situation. The unfortunate reality is that on most of the child development goals mentioned in the policy statements, no worthwhile attempt has been made to set up data collection systems to monitor the progress in the attainment of these goals. This is a pressing need and calls for focused data collection endeavours. The assessment presented here differs from the picture painted in official reports. It is the author's firm belief that an objective analysis of the situation, indicating both failures and achievements in giving a better deal to children, is necessary so that the next two decades see positive steps and not rhetoric.

A study of this nature would not have been possible without the assistance, insights, and encouragement of a large number of professional colleagues. I am particularly thankful to Shri S.K. Sinha for his encouragement and help. I am grateful to Professor S.N. Ranade for suggesting ways in which the presentation could be enriched. I have been amply assisted in my endeavour by my wife, Enakshi Bose, who helped in the compilation and tabulation of data, and preparation of notes. I am thankful to Shri Ankush Singhal for diligently typing the manuscript. I am deeply indebted to the Gram Niyojan Kendra for sponsoring the study, and particularly Professor K.K. Mukherjee and Dr. Sutapa Mukherjee for making the study possible. Without the help unhesitatingly given, the study would not have seen the light of day. I shall feel amply rewarded if the major concerns identified in the document are addressed with seriousness of purpose and commitment so that in the coming years children receive a much better deal than they have in the past.

December 2001
New Delhi

A.B. BOSE

1 The Setting

The development status of children is affected by some key social and economic factors. Some of these are briefly discussed in the paragraphs that follow.

India is the world's largest democracy. It has a federal system of government, with the states having their own democratically elected governments. The relative jurisdiction of the central and state governments over different matters has been indicated in the Seventh Schedule of the Constitution of India under the Union, Concurrent and State Lists. Social services fall either in the Concurrent or in the State list. However, the implementation of schemes, including those of the central government, is done by the states. The seventy-third and seventy-fourth constitutional amendments have recognized a third tier, below that of the state government, viz., panchayati raj institutions, given them financial and administrative powers, and listed the subjects falling in their area of activities, a number of which relate to those social services which have a direct bearing on children.

Development programmes in the country, including those for children, are carried out within the framework of the five-year plans. Some of these programmes are wholly funded by the central government, some by both central and state governments, and some entirely by the state government, depending on whether the programmes are classified as central, centrally sponsored, or state sector schemes. In addition, a wide variety of programmes are being implemented by non-governmental organizations, which are now growing as a vibrant sector in social development.

Population

From 548 million persons in 1971, the population of India crossed the billion mark officially on 11 May 2000. The 2001 Census gives the provisional population total for the country as 1,027 million persons. The population is expected to reach 1,264 million in 2016.

Figure 1.1 gives the growth curve of the population. More than 150 million persons are likely to be added to India's population in each of the next two decades as Table 1.1 indicates. Such a massive increase in numbers will, to a large extent, offset the gains of economic development and require massive inputs for social services, civic amenities, and infrastructure development. A positive sign is

TABLE 1.1: GROWTH OF POPULATION, INDIA, 1971 TO 2016

	1971	1981	1991	2001	2011	2016
Total population (in million)	548.160	683.329	846.387	1027.015	1178.889	1263.543
Decadal increase (in million)	108.925	135.169	163.059	180.627	151.874	84.654*
Decadal growth rate	24.80	24.66	23.86	21.34	14.79	7.18*
Annual exponential growth rate	2.20	2.22	2.14	1.93	1.38	1.39

* Quinquennial increase/growth rate.

Sources: *Census of India*, 1991. Population of 1981 includes interpolated population of Assam and that of 1991 includes interpolated population of Jammu & Kashmir.

Census of India, 2001, Provisional Population Totals.

Population Projections for India and States 1996–2016, Registrar General, India, for population in 2011 and 2016.

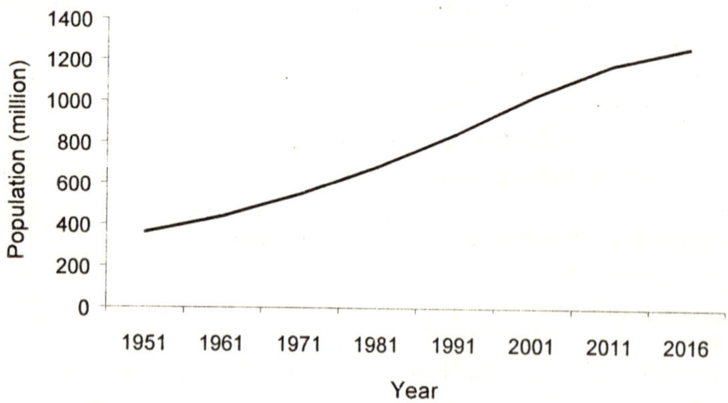

FIG. 1.1: POPULATION OF INDIA, 1951 TO 2016.

the evidence of the slowing down of the population growth rate since 1981.

The population of states constituting the Indian Union varies considerably in size as evident from Table 1.2. Figure 1.2 gives in graphic form the population of the 16 bigger states (states with a population of more than 5 million) in 2001. Uttar Pradesh, the biggest state, had a population of 139 million in 1991. It retained its position with a population of 166 million in 2001 even after a separate state (Uttaranchal) was carved out of it in 2000. Eighteen states had a population of more than 10 million in 2001, while two states (Himachal Pradesh and Uttaranchal) had a population of more than 5 million but less than 10 million. The two undivided states of Uttar Pradesh and Bihar together had 27 per cent of the country's population in 1991. In 2016, their share (including the two new states of Uttaranchal and Jharkhand carved out of them in 2000) is expected to be 30 per cent. This indicates how critically important it is to improve the child development profile in these states if the national aggregate of child development indicators is to show a significant improvement. Currently, several states are lagging behind on social as well as economic development indicators. Their economic growth rates have been lower than that of the other states and, given their current political and administrative situation, the position is unlikely to change much in the near future. The children

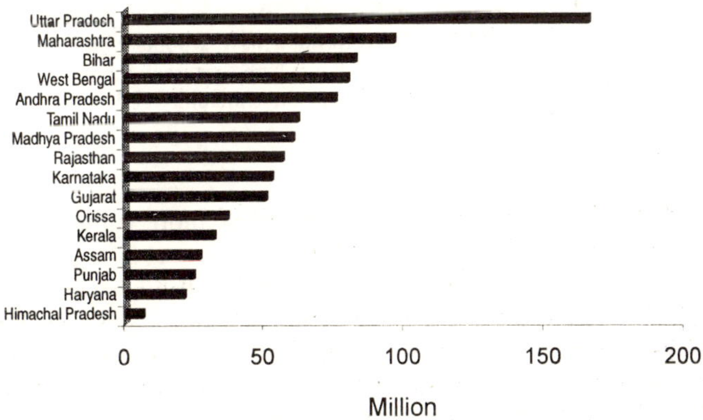

FIG. 1.2: POPULATION OF STATES, 2001.

TABLE 1.2: POPULATION OF INDIA AND STATES, 2001 TO 2016

(in million)

India/State	2001	2011	2016
INDIA	1027.015	1178.889	1263.543
Uttar Pradesh	166.053	217.053*	242.861*
Maharashtra	96.752	102.563	107.802
Bihar	82.879	121.319**	132.305**
West Bengal	80.221	90.836	96.231
Andhra Pradesh	75.728	84.801	88.623
Tamil Nadu	62.111	67.562	69.866
Madhya Pradesh	60.385	96.583***	105.155***
Rajasthan	56.473	65.307	71.413
Karnataka	52.734	59.615	62.783
Gujarat	50.597	56.061	59.338
Orissa	36.707	39.475	41.023
Kerala	31.839	35.647	36.877
Assam	26.638	30.468	32.502
Punjab	24.289	26.728	28.045
Haryana	21.083	23.451	25.173
Himachal Pradesh	6.077	7.958	7.945

* Includes Uttaranchal
** Includes Jharkhand
*** Includes Chhatisgarh

Source: *Census of India*, 2001, Provisional Population Totals. *Population Projections for India and States, 1996–2016*, Registrar General, India, for population in 2011 and 2016.

Note: States have been arranged in descending order of their Census 2001 population. Only bigger states, i.e. those states which have a population of more than 5 million have been included here. The states of Jharkhand, Chhatisgarh and Uttaranchal came into existence in November 2000. These states, and Jammu & Kashmir have a population of more than 10 million but have not been shown here because in the subsequent text they could not be included due to non-availability of data on most child development indicators.

of these states will, therefore, continue to be more vulnerable than those in most other parts of the country.

India's massive population problem arises from its inability to sufficiently bring down the birth rate, although it adopted family planning as a key instrument of population control as early as the 1950s, and huge investments were made from the central budget. Table 1.3 which gives the birth rate and death rate shows that between 1951–61 and 1999 the birth rate declined from 41.7 to 26.1, a difference of 15.6 points or a decline of 37 per cent. In other words, on an average, there has been a decline of about one point every three years. During the same period, death rate declined by 62 per cent. Projections made by the Technical Group on Population Projections indicate that the birth rate will come down to 21.4 in 2011–16 and the death rate to 7.5 (Registrar General India 1996). A lot of wishful thinking had gone into the projections made in the 1960s and 1970s on decline in the birth rate on the assumption that fertility was all about technology and supplies, underplaying the behavioural dimensions of the problem and the impact that factors like education of women, child survival, standard of living, and user friendly and efficient service delivery systems have on fertility. The

TABLE 1.3: BIRTH AND DEATH RATE, INDIA, 1951–61 TO 2011–16

	1951–61	1961–71	1975	1980	1985	1990	1995	1999	2001–6	2006–11	2011–16
Birth rate	41.7	41.2	35.2	33.3	32.9	30.2	28.3	26.1	22.8	22.3	21.4
Death rate	22.8	19.0	15.9	12.5	11.8	9.7	9.0	8.7	8.3	7.8	7.5
Natural growth rate	18.9	22.2	19.3	20.8	21.1	20.5	19.3	17.3	14.5	14.5	13.9

Source: Sample Registration System.
Population Projections for India and States, 1996–2016, Registrar General, India.

Note: Figures from 2001–6 onwards are projections made by the Technical Group on Population Projections.

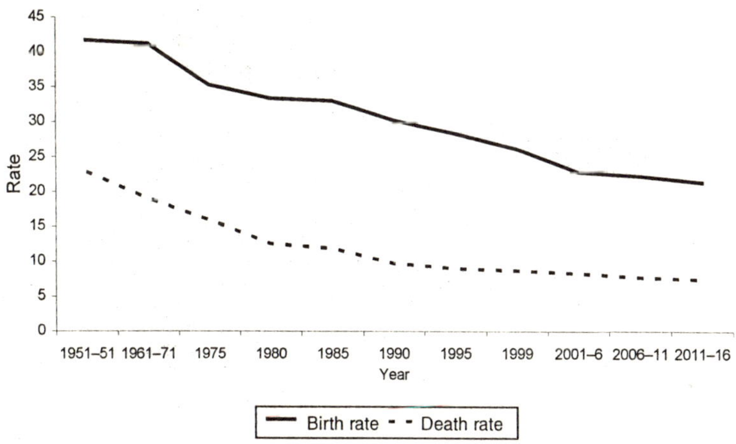

FIG. 1.3: BIRTH AND DEATH RATE, INDIA, 1951–61 TO 2011–16.

relative movement of birth and death rates between 1951–61 and 2011–16 given in Figure 1.3 shows that the gap between birth and death rates is getting narrowed, indicating a lowering of the natural growth rate of population.

The more populous and backward states have higher birth rates. The 1999 birth rate was the highest in Uttar Pradesh (32.1), followed by Bihar (31.5), Rajasthan (31.1), and Madhya Pradesh (31.1). At the other end of the spectrum are Kerala, where the birth rate in 1999 was 18.0 and Tamil Nadu where it was 19.3. Projections for 2011–16 indicate that Uttar Pradesh will continue to have a high birth rate (29.8) even in 2011–16 while the national birth rate figure is projected at 21.4. Bihar, Madhya Pradesh and Rajasthan, too, are expected to have birth rates of 25 and above in 2011–16. Massive increase in numbers projected in these states which not only have a large population but are also economically backward, have slower economic growth rates, and are faced with a huge backlog of social services, has serious economic implications for social development in these states and puts at risk the development opportunities of children, particularly from the lower income groups.

Rural-Urban Distribution

India's population is predominantly rural. In 1951, only 17 per cent of the population was urban which increased to 26 per cent in 1991. The projected urban population in 2001 is 28 per cent. Even in 2016, the urban population is projected to be only 34 per cent (see Table 1.4). Figure 1.4 gives in graphic form the percentage of urban population in the country between 1951 and 2016.

The percentage of rural population varies in different states. There are several large states in the country which, in 1991, had more than 80 per cent rural population, prominent among them being Bihar (87 per cent), Orissa (87 per cent), and Uttar Pradesh (80 per cent).The projected rural population of these states in 2001 are 85 per cent, 83 per cent, and 77 per cent respectively.

Urbanization is often equated with development. However, one of its visible negative consequences has been the tremendous increase in slum population in all cities, estimated to be between 25 to 45 per cent of the city's population, mainly due to the non-availability of affordable housing for the large number of poor migrants from rural areas who come to the cities in search of employment. Slums are very poorly served by civic amenities, resulting in an extremely

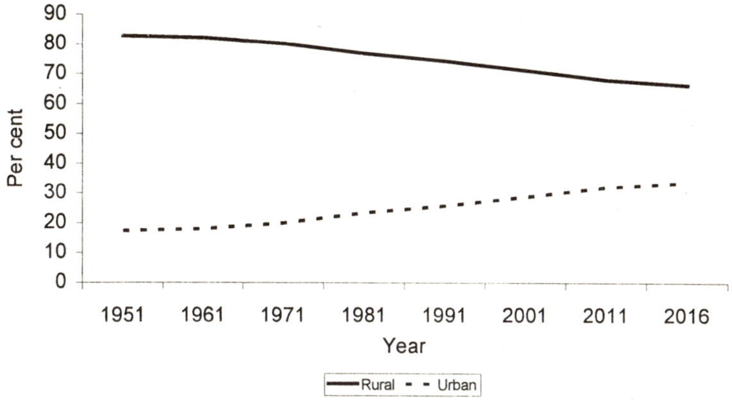

FIG. 1.4: PERCENTAGE OF RURAL AND URBAN POPULATION, INDIA, 1951 TO 2016.

TABLE 1.4: PERCENTAGE OF POPULATION IN RURAL AND URBAN AREAS, INDIA, 1951 TO 2016

	1951	1961	1971	1981	1991	2001	2011	2016
Rural	82.71	82.03	80.10	76.66	74.29	71.23	68.01	66.33
Urban	17.29	17.97	19.90	23.34	25.71	28.77	31.99	33.67

Sources: *Census of India*, 1991.
Population Projections for India and States, 1996–2016, Registrar General, India.

Note: Figures from 2001 to 2016 are projections made by the Technical Group on Population Projections.

unhealthy living environment which affects children the most. The compensatory factor, however, is that there is greater availability of social services in urban as compared to rural areas, which gets reflected in wide disparity on all social development indicators between rural and urban areas at the national and state levels.

ADMINISTRATIVE UNITS

The geographical area of different states, too, shows considerable variation. Rajasthan now has the largest area (342,239 sq km), pushing Madhya Pradesh, which had the largest area (443,446 sq km) before the creation of Chhatisgarh, to second place. Table 1.5

TABLE 1.5: AREA, DENSITY, AND NUMBER OF DISTRICTS IN STATES, 2001

State	Area (sq km)	Density (pop. per sq km)	No. of districts
Rajasthan	342,239	165	32
Madhya Pradesh	308,245	196	45
Maharashtra	307,713	314	35
Andhra Pradesh	275,069	275	23
Uttar Pradesh	240,928	689	70
Gujarat	196,022	258	25
Karnataka	191,791	275	27
Orissa	155,707	236	30
Tamil Nadu	130,058	478	30
Bihar	94,163	880	37
West Bengal	88,752	904	18
Assam	78,438	340	23
Himachal Pradesh	55,673	109	12
Punjab	50,362	482	17
Haryana	44,212	477	19
Kerala	38,863	819	14

Source: *Census of India*, 2001, Provisional Population Totals.
Note: States have been arranged in descending order of their area. Data for 16 bigger states are given here.

gives the area, number of districts, and population density of the bigger states. It is evident that there is a very wide range not only in terms of population and geographical area but also in number of districts. The area of Rajasthan is nearly nine times the area of Kerala, the smallest of the 16 states listed in the Table, whose area is almost equivalent to that of Jaisalmer district of Rajasthan. Uttar Pradesh, Madhya Pradesh and Bihar, even after their division to form new states, have 26 per cent of the total number of districts in the country. A big population, a large area, and a large number of administrative units (districts, blocks and villages) make the task of coordination of development administration difficult, specially when these happen to be states backward on social and economic development indicators, have a poor infrastructure, weak administration, and ineffective governance.

SEX RATIO

The sex ratio in India, 933 females per 1,000 males in 2001, is adverse to females. In 1901, the sex ratio was 972 females per

TABLE 1.6: SEX RATIO, INDIA, 1901 TO 2016

	1901	1911	1921	1931	1941	1951	1961	1971	1981	1991	2001	2011	2016
Sex ratio (no. of females per 1,000 males)	972	964	955	950	945	946	941	930	934	927	933	943	947

Source: *Census of India*, 2001, Provisional Population Totals.
Population Projections for India and States, 1996–2016, Registrar General, India.

Note: Figures of 2011 and 2016 are projections made by the Technical Group on Population Projections.

1,000 males. A hundred years later it is lower by 39 points. The sex ratio has shown a consistent decline since 1901, except for a small rise in 1981, followed by a decline and then again a rise as Table 1.6 shows. The first half of the twentieth century (1901 to 1951) witnessed a decline of 26 points in the sex ratio, and in the next half (1951 to 2001) a further decline of 13 points. From 2011 onwards, the projections on sex ratio indicate a tendency to improve but the sex ratio will still be adverse to females. Figure 1.5 depicts the changes in sex ratio between 1901 and 2016.

The adverse sex ratio and its decline has caused great concern to demographers, social scientists, and policy makers. Attempts to draw

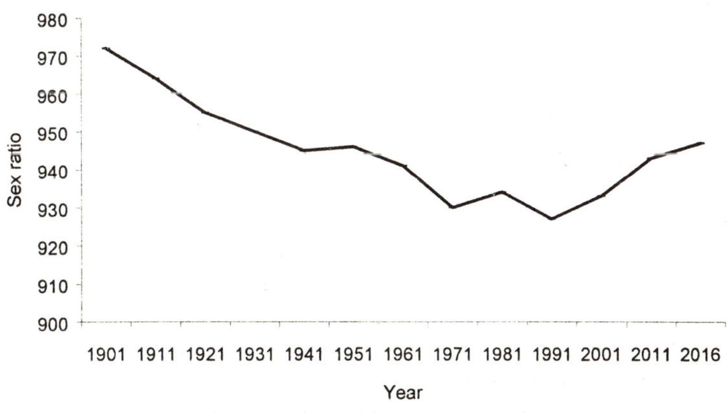

FIG. 1.5: SEX RATIO, INDIA, 1901 TO 2016.

attention to the phenomenon have been captioned by catchy phrases such as 'endangered sex' and 'missing females', 32 million lesser females in 1991, 35 million in 2001, about the same number in 2011, and 34 million in 2016. Women's groups invariably cite this indicator as an evidence of gender based discrimination and high female mortality.

The sex ratio of a population is determined by several factors, and not just the mortality differential between males and females. Sex ratio at birth is an important factor which needs to be given due weightage in explaining sex ratio. The 1921 Census reported that the number of females born per 1,000 males averaged 933 in the decade ending 1921. However, the sex ratio varied in the different provinces, the sex ratio at birth being the highest in Madras Province (956 females per 1,000 males), and the lowest in Punjab (906 females per 1,000 males) and United Provinces (919 females per 1,000 males). A study by the Demographic Training and Research Centre, Bombay covering about two million live births in hospitals and health centres throughout India during 1949–58, found a sex ratio of 940 females per 1,000 males at birth for the country as a whole (Ramachandran and Deshpande 1964). A study by the Registrar General and Census Commissioner which covered six million live births during 1981–91 in hospitals, health centres, and institutions located mostly in urban areas found a sex ratio of 891 females per 1,000 males at birth (Registrar General and Census Commissioner, 1993). Data on sex at birth in India collected by the Sample Registration System (SRS) indicated a range in sex ratio between 905 (1988–92) and 913 (1982–6). In Haryana, Punjab, Rajasthan, and Uttar Pradesh, the sex ratio at birth did not exceed 900 females per 1,000 males.

Data from countries where registration of births is fairly complete shows that male births outnumber female births, the ratio being 950 to 960 female births per 1,000 male births. This is reported to be nature's way of ensuring a balanced sex ratio as the female newborn infant is biologically stronger and better equipped by nature for survival. However, Indian data, even though partial, shows a far more adverse sex ratio at birth that cannot be explained by the phenomenon of female foeticide, which is a more recent phenomenon, the magnitude of which is difficult to estimate.

An explanation sometimes given for the better sex ratio in the earlier part of the twentieth century is that the presence of adverse survival conditions in that period, due to the poor availability of medical facilities, resulted in deaths of more male than female children, the latter being biologically stronger. The situation began to reverse later due to the availability of improved health care which was more accessible to the male than the female child due to discriminatory practices. Hence, the decline in sex ratio in the population is due to greater male survival disadvantage in the earlier part of the century and greater female disadvantage in the later years. Sample Registration System data available from 1970 indicate that from 1970 to 1987, the female death rate was only marginally higher than that of males. In 1988, there was no difference in the male and female death rate. From 1989 to 1999 the male death rate, except for one year, has been higher than the female death rate. The 1999 death rate is 9.0 for males and 8.3 for females. Age specific death rates for 1998 indicate that from the age group 0–4 years to the age group 20–4 years female death rates exceed male death rates. In the age group 25–9 years the death rate is the same. From the age group 30–4 years onwards, the trend is reversed.

Migration does not appear to be a plausible explanatory factor of the adverse sex ratio because more males than females go out of the country for employment or studies. The effect of illegal migration from across the borders is indeterminate as the sex composition of such migration is not known.

Under-enumeration of females or double counting of males in census operation as a factor has been raised by some demographers but not accepted by others as there is little reliable evidence of lapses or bias at the level either of the enumerator or the respondent. The issue of sex ratio, therefore, needs serious probing by biologists and demographers for a rigorous examination of different factors. In the first place, accurate data on sex at birth, both community and hospital based, needs to be collected systematically from different parts of the country on a regular basis. The Civil Registration System has to be strengthened so that there is complete recording of all vital events, which unfortunately is not the case at present though the Registration of Births and Deaths Act, 1969 makes registration of all vital events compulsory. Data on sex ratio at birth has assumed much greater importance now and will help in getting indirect evidence on female foeticide, which appeared on the demographic horizon in the 1970s and has continued despite its legislative ban in 1994. Female disadvantage in survival is now feared to be starting earlier, shifting from childhood stage to the womb, due to foeticide.

It extends to the neonatal stage, due to infanticide, and post-neonatal stage, due to discrimination in health and nutrition care.

EXPECTATION OF LIFE AT BIRTH

The expectation of life at birth has gone up from 32.5 years for males and 31.7 years for females in 1941–51 to 59.7 years for males and 60.9 years for females in 1991–5. SRS quinquennial estimates from 1970–5, given in Table 1.7, indicate that from 1981–5 onwards female life expectancy exceeds male life expectancy at birth. In 1991–5 it was higher by 1.2 years. In 2011–16, female life expectancy is projected to be higher than male life expectancy by 1.9 years.

The difference in expectation of life at birth in rural and urban areas is quite large as evident from Figure 1.6. In 1991–5, expectation of life at birth was 58.9 years in rural areas but in urban areas it was 65.9 years, a difference of 7 years. In 1970–5, the difference was 10.9 years, the expectation of life at birth being 48.0 years in rural areas and 58.9 years in urban areas. This shows that rural areas, where three-fourth of the population lives, continue to be at a survival disadvantage, even though there has been some improvement in this regard. For instance, in rural areas the expectation of life at birth improved between 1970–5 and 1991–5 by 22.7 per cent, while in urban areas it improved by 11.9 per cent during the same period. Decline in infant and early childhood mortality rates is

TABLE 1.7: EXPECTATION OF LIFE AT BIRTH, INDIA, 1970–5 TO 2011–16

	1970–5	1976–80	1981–5	1986–90	1991–5	1996–2001	2001–6	2006–11	2011–16
Male	50.5	52.5	55.4	57.7	59.7	62.4	64.1	65.6	66.9
Female	49.0	52.1	55.7	58.1	60.9	63.4	65.4	67.2	68.8
M-F	0.5	0.4	-0.3	-0.4	-1.2	-1.0	-1.3	-1.6	-1.9

Sources: *SRS Based Abridged Life Tables 1990–94 and 1991–95*, Registrar General, India.
Population Projections for India and States 1996–2016, Registrar General, India.

Note: Figures from 1996–2001 onwards are projections made by the Technical Group on Population Projections.

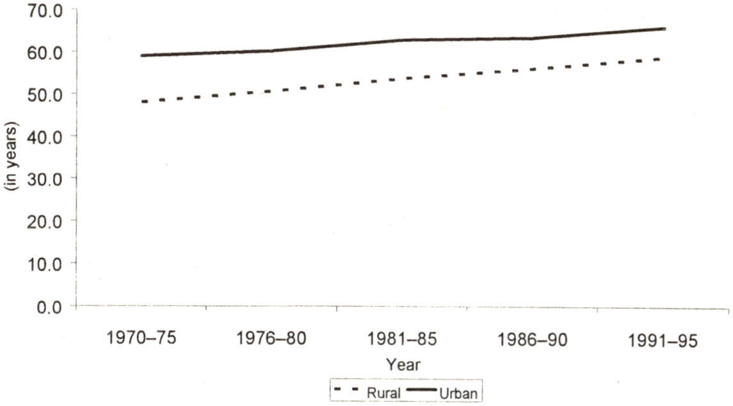

FIG. 1.6: EXPECTATION OF LIFE AT BIRTH IN RURAL AND URBAN AREAS, INDIA, 1970–5 TO 1991–5.

expected to bring about further improvements in life expectancy in the coming years in both rural and urban areas.

AGE COMPOSITION

The age structure of a population is a function of the birth rate, death rate in different age groups, and migration (which is age selective), assuming there is no enumerator bias in the collection and recording of age related data. India's population, even though comparatively young, is demographically ageing as is the case with the rest of the world, with the percentage of population aged 60+ increasing and the percentage of population 0–14 years going down progressively. The trend is evident from Table 1.8. and will continue in later years due to the lowering of fertility rate and longer life expectancy. The number of children (0–14 years) which in 1991 numbered 317 million is projected to increase to 348 million in 2001 and 350 million a decade and a half later (2016).

Sub-classification of children according to various stages of the life-cycle is useful for planning and programming and gives a better picture of the scale of efforts involved. Table 1.9 gives the statistical dimensions in the coming years. Focal social service concerns vary according to the age group of the child. For instance, in 2001 about

TABLE 1.8: AGE DISTRIBUTION OF POPULATION, INDIA, 1971 TO 2016

(percentage)

Age (in years)	1971	1981	1991	2001	2011	2016
0–14	42.03	39.57	37.46	34.33	28.48	27.73
15–34	30.58	32.27	33.72	35.16	36.81	35.46
35–59	21.43	21.67	22.03	23.54	26.57	27.87
60+	5.97	6.49	6.80	6.97	8.14	8.94
Total	100.00	100.00	100.00	100.00	100.00	100.00

Sources: *Census of India*;
Population Projections for India and States, 1996–2016, Registrar General, India.

Note: Figures from 2001 onwards are projections made by the Technical Group on Population Projections.

TABLE 1.9: NUMBER AND PERCENTAGE OF CHILDREN AT DIFFERENT STAGES, INDIA, 2001 TO 2016

Age (in years)		2001	2006	2011	2016
<1 (infants)	No.(in million)	21.706	24.855	24.294	24.918
	%	2.14	2.27	2.06	1.97
1-2 (toddlers)	No.(in million)	43.084	45.865	48.177	49.357
	%	4.26	4.19	4.09	3.91
3-5 (pre-school)	No.(in million)	66.065	63.731	70.034	72.498
	%	6.53	5.82	5.94	5.74
6-10 (primary school)	No.(in million)	118.256	106.945	109.131	115.801
	%	11.68	9.77	9.26	9.16
11-13 (middle school)	No.(in million)	74.468	69.364	62.520	66.398
	%	7.36	6.34	5.30	5.25
14-15 (high school)	No.(in million)	47.269	48.397	43.607	42.51
	%	4.67	4.42	3.70	3.36

Sources: *Census of India*;
Population Projections for India and States 1996-2016, Registrar General, India for figures from 2001 onwards.

Note: Figures are based on projections made by the Technical Group on Population Projections. Percentages have been calculated from the total population.

22 million infants need immunization services, and their mothers maternal health services. In 2016, the number is expected to be 25 million. Pre-school services have to be provided for 66 million

TABLE 1.10: PERCENTAGE DISTRIBUTION OF WORKERS AND NON-WORKERS AGED 15–59 YEARS IN RURAL AND URBAN AREAS, INDIA, 1991

Area	Sex	Main workers	Marginal workers	Main + Marginal workers	Non-workers	Total
Rural	Male	84.65	0.89	85.54	14.46	100.00
	Female	30.53	13.11	43.64	56.36	100.00
	Total	58.30	6.84	65.14	34.86	100.00
Urban	Male	75.45	0.49	75.94	24.06	100.00
	Female	12.89	1.61	14.50	85.51	100.00
	Total	46.40	1.01	47.41	52.59	100.00
Total	Male	82.03	0.78	82.81	17.19	100.00
	Female	25.82	10.04	35.86	64.14	100.00
	Total	55.01	5.23	60.24	39.76	100.00

Source: *Census of India*, 1991.
Note: Main workers are those who had worked for the major part of the year (six months or more). Marginal workers are those who had worked for less than six months in the year.

children in 2001 and 72 million children in 2016. Primary schools will be required for 118 million children in 2001 and 116 million in 2016.

WORK PARTICIPATION

The 2001 Census figures on work participation are not yet available. According to the 1991 Census, 60 per cent of the population aged 15–59 years were workers (see Table 1.10). In rural areas, 65 per cent of the population aged 15–59 years in 1991 were workers—58 per cent were main workers (those engaged in a productive economic activity for six months or more in a year) and 7 per cent marginal workers (those engaged in a productive economic activity for less than six months in a year). In urban areas the percentage of workers was lower at 47 per cent (46 per cent main workers and 1 per cent marginal workers). Among males aged 15–59 years, work participation rate is more than 75 per cent in both rural and urban areas. Among females it is only 36 per cent—15 per cent in urban areas as compared to 44 per cent in rural areas. The percentage of female non-workers aged 15–59 years is very high in urban areas (86 per cent) and is about one and a half times the percentage in rural areas.

POVERTY

Poverty exercises an adverse influence on the health and nutrition status of children. Inadequate and irregular earnings affect the quantity and quality of food that a family can consume throughout the year, its standard of living, and access and use of health care.

Removal of poverty has been a central concern of Indian planners, and its reduction a key indicator of success in implementation of policies and programmes, particularly those aimed at alleviating poverty of the rural and urban poor. Data in Table 1.11 indicate that in two and a half decades (1973–4 to 1999–2000) the percentage of population below poverty line has come down from 55 per cent in 1973–4 to 36 per cent in 1993–4, and further down to 26 per cent in 1999–2000. The decline in percentage of the poor has taken place in both rural and urban areas. The number of persons below poverty line fell in rural areas by 68 million in this period, but in urban areas it has increased by 7 million. On the whole, there has been a decline of 61 million persons.

The extent of poverty varies considerably between states. Table 1.12 gives the number and percentage of population below the poverty line in 1999–2000. Figure 1.7 gives the comparative position relating to the percentage of the poor in different states in graphic form. The data show that in 1999–2000, among the bigger states, Orissa had the largest percentage of population below the poverty line, followed by Bihar. In numbers, Uttar Pradesh and Bihar together had 96 million persons below the poverty line or 37 per cent of the country's poor. Bihar (undivided) also had 38 districts, the largest number in the list of 100 most backward and poorest districts in the

TABLE 1.11: NUMBER AND PERCENTAGE OF POPULATION BELOW POVERTY LINE, INDIA, 1973–4 TO 1999–2000

Year	Number of persons (in million)			Percentage of persons		
	Rural	Urban	Total	Rural	Urban	Total
1973–4	261.290	60.046	321.336	56.44	49.01	54.88
1983	251.957	70.940	322.897	45.65	40.79	44.48
1993–4	244.031	76.337	320.368	37.27	32.36	35.97
1999–2000	193.243	67.007	260.250	27.09	23.62	26.10

Source: Planning Commission.

Note: Figures in brackets give the percentage.
The 1999–2000 estimates followed a different methodology and may not be fully comparable with earlier estimates.

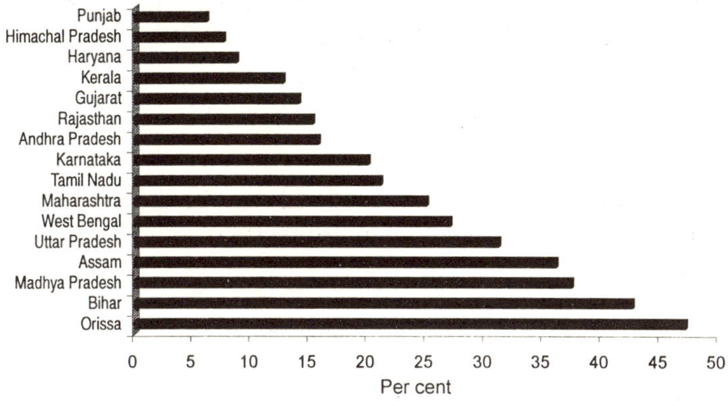

FIG. 1.7: PERCENTAGE OF POPULATION IN STATES BELOW POVERTY LINE, 1999–2000.

TABLE 1.12: PERCENTAGE OF POPULATION BELOW POVERTY LINE IN STATES, 1999–2000

State	Population below poverty line	
	Percentage	No. (in million)
Orissa	47.15	16.909
Bihar	42.60	42.564
Madhya Pradesh	37.43	29.854
Assam	36.09	9.455
Uttar Pradesh	31.15	52.989
West Bengal	27.02	21.349
Maharashtra	25.02	22.799
Tamil Nadu	21.12	13.048
Karnataka	20.04	10.440
Andhra Pradesh	15.77	11.901
Rajasthan	15.28	8.813
Gujarat	14.07	6.789
Kerala	12.72	4.104
Haryana	8.74	1.734
Himachal Pradesh	7.63	0.512
Punjab	6.16	1.449

Source: Planning Commission.

Note: States have been arranged in descending order of percentage of population below the poverty line. Data for 16 bigger states given here. Figures of Bihar include Jharkhand, of Madhya Pradesh include Chhatisgarh, of Uttar Pradesh include Uttaranchal.

country identified in 1997, followed by Madhya Pradesh (undivided) with 19 districts and Uttar Pradesh (undivided) with 17 (Ministry of Rural Areas and Employment 1997).

LITERACY

The level of education, particularly of a woman, exercises a strong influence on her own health and nutrition status as well as that of her children.

India's achievements in the spread of literacy have been very modest as the data in Table 1.13 indicates. In 1991, the literacy rate of persons aged 7 years and above was 52 per cent. In 2001, this rose to 65 per cent. It is true that when India became free the spread of literacy was very low, particularly in rural areas, as evident from the 1951 census figures. After almost five and a half decades of independence, nearly one-third of the population aged 7 years and above is still illiterate. The gender difference in literacy rate 7+ in 1991 was about 25 per cent. In 2001, there was a modest decline, but was still 22 per cent. The rural urban difference in literacy rate 7+ continues to be large; it was about 28 per cent in 1991. The 2001

TABLE 1.13: LITERACY RATE, INDIA, 1951 TO 2001

Year	Rural			Urban			All areas		
	Male	Female	Total	Male	Female	Total	Male	Female	Total
1951	19.02	4.87	12.10	45.06	22.33	34.59	23.54	7.63	15.83
1961	29.09	8.55	19.01	57.49	34.51	46.97	34.46	12.96	24.04
1971	33.76	13.17	23.73	61.27	42.14	52.44	39.45	18.69	29.45
1981	40.79	17.96	29.65	65.83	47.82	24.82	46.89	24.82	36.23
	(49.69)	(21.77)	(36.09)	(76.83)	(56.37)	(67.34)	(56.50)	(29.85)	(43.67)
1991	47.07	24.85	36.31	68.74	53.84	61.70	52.74	32.17	42.84
	(57.87)	(30.62)	(44.69)	(81.09)	(64.05)	(73.08)	(64.13)	(39.29)	(52.21)
2001	Not available			Not available			64.13	45.84	55.30
							(75.85)	(54.16)	(65.38)

Source: *Census of India*.

Note: The census has defined a literate as a person who can both read and write with understanding in any language. To enable comparison, the literacy rate given here is inclusive of all age groups as the earlier censuses gave literacy rates inclusive of all age groups. Figures in brackets give, in addition, the literacy rate 7+ in 1981, 1991 and 2001. Figures for 1981 do not include Assam and for 1991 do not include Jammu and Kashmir as census was not undertaken.

TABLE 1.14: NUMBER OF ILLITERATE PERSONS AGED 7 YEARS AND ABOVE IN RURAL AND URBAN AREAS BY SEX, INDIA, 2001

Illiterate (in million)			Literate (in million)		
Male	Female	Total	Male	Female	Total
108.216 (36.05)	191.927 (63.95)	300.143 (100.00)	339.969 (59.99)	226.746 (40.01)	566.715 (100.00)

Source: *Census of India*, 2001, Provisional Population Totals.
Note: Figures of 2001 do not include a district and a few talukas in Gujarat, and a district in Himachal Pradesh, where census could not be undertaken.

Census figures of literacy rate in rural and in urban areas are still not available. The difference in female literacy rate 7+ between rural and urban areas was 33 per cent in 1991. Urban female literacy rate 7+ was higher than rural male literacy rate 7+, indicating that the rural urban divide constitutes a bigger disadvantage than gender in the spread of literacy. However, within rural and urban areas gender becomes an important factor.

In 2001, there were 300 million illiterate persons aged 7 years and above in India (see Table 1.14). Of these, 64 per cent were females. Between 1991 and 2001, the number of illiterate persons (excluding Jammu & Kashmir) was lower by 32 million or 10 per cent. The decline was 17 per cent in the case of males and 5 per cent in the case of females.

There is considerable inter-state variation in literacy rates. In 1991, six states, viz., Bihar, Rajasthan, Uttar Pradesh, Andhra Pradesh, Madhya Pradesh and Orissa, had more than half the population aged 7 years and above illiterate. In 2001, only Bihar remained in this category (see Table 1.15). At the other end of the spectrum is Kerala where only 9 per cent of the population aged 7+ was illiterate in 2001. Uttar Pradesh and Bihar, together, accounted for nearly one-third of the country's illiterate population.

Female literacy is a critically important factor in child development. Bihar, Uttar Pradesh, and Rajasthan each had more than half the females aged 7 years and above illiterate in 2001. Andhra Pradesh, Orissa, and Madhya Pradesh too, had nearly half the females aged 7+ illiterate. At the other end of the spectrum is Kerala where only 12 per cent females aged 7 years and above were illiterate. Bihar and Uttar Pradesh, together, had 30 per cent of the total illiterate females

TABLE 1.15: NUMBER AND PERCENTAGE OF ILLITERATE PERSONS AGED 7 YEARS AND ABOVE IN STATES, 2001

State	Percentage of illiterate persons 7+	No. of illiterate persons 7+ (in million)	Percentage of illiterate females 7+	No. of illiterate females 7+ (in million)
Bihar	52.47	34.969	66.43	21.169
Uttar Pradesh	42.64	57.811	57.02	36.504
Rajasthan	38.97	17.936	55.66	12.309
Andhra Pradesh	38.89	25.690	48.83	15.965
Orissa	36.39	11.473	49.03	7.635
Madhya Pradesh	35.89	17.861	49.72	11.840
Assam	35.72	7.961	43.97	4.712
INDIA	34.62	300.143	45.84	191.927
Karnataka	32.96	15.133	42.55	9.596
Haryana	31.41	5.599	43.69	3.620
West Bengal	30.78	21.267	39.78	13.235
Punjab	30.05	6.380	36.45	3.636
Gujarat	30.03	12.469	41.40	8.267
Tamil Nadu	26.53	14.669	35.45	9.763
Himachal Pradesh	22.87	1.195	31.92	0.827
Maharashtra	22.73	18.998	32.49	13.030
Kerala	9.08	2.559	12.14	1.770

Source: *Census of India*, 2001, Provisional Population Totals.
Note: Data given for 16 bigger states, arranged in descending order of percentage of illiterate persons.

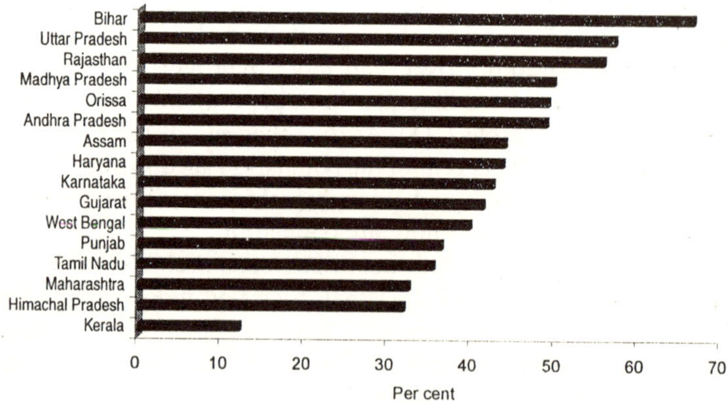

FIG. 1.8: PERCENTAGE OF ILLITERATE FEMALES 7+ IN STATES, 2001.

7+ in the country in 2001. Figure 1.8 gives the comparative position in female illiteracy 7+ in different states.

HOUSING AND AMENITIES

One-third rural households and 10 per cent urban households were found by the 1991 census to be living in kutcha (not durable) houses, 36 per cent rural households and 18 per cent urban households were found living in semi-pucca (semi-durable) houses, while 31 per cent rural households and 73 per cent urban households were found living in pucca (durable) houses (see Table 1.16). Most houses have limited accommodation and are overcrowded. For instance, 40 per cent urban households were living in single rooms in 1991, which, though an improvement over 1961 when 50 per cent households were living in single rooms, indicates nevertheless that the urban stock of affordable housing needs to be considerably augmented. In rural areas, too, 41 per cent households were found in 1991 to be living in single rooms which is, again, a reflection of their inability to afford more rooms even though space *per se* is not generally a problem in rural areas. A large number of urban pucca houses are of poor quality, built in unauthorized colonies and congested neighbourhoods, and suffer from poor civic amenities. Slums, which now cover a large part of every city's landscape, continue to grow at a fast pace, adversely affecting the city's quality of life and putting considerable pressure on the civic services.

Basic civic amenities, particularly in rural areas, are lagging far behind. Safe drinking water and toilet facilities have a direct bearing on morbidity. In rural areas safe drinking water was available in

TABLE 1.16: PERCENTAGE OF HOUSEHOLDS LIVING IN PUCCA, SEMI-PUCCA AND KUTCHA HOUSES, INDIA, 1991

Area	Year	Pucca	Semi-pucca	Kutcha
Rural	1981	22.53	36.93	40.55
	1991	30.59	35.65	33.76
Urban	1981	64.70	21.80	13.50
	1991	72.75	17.69	9.56
Total	1981	32.67	33.29	34.04
	1991	41.61	30.95	27.44

Source: *Census of India*, 1991.
Note: Figures exclude Jammu & Kashmir.

1991 to only 56 per cent households as determined by source (tap or handpump/tube well). Thus, a basic need like access to safe water inside the home or near it was not available to 44 per cent of the households. The situation aggravates during years of drought and during the summer months causing distress to rural women who have to travel long distances in heat and dust to collect drinking water. Even where water is available their potability is rarely tested at regular intervals. Some parts of the country have belts which have excess levels of fluoride and arsenic. Contamination of underground water from human wastes and from chemicals, pesticides, heavy metal, hazardous wastes, and other pollutants are being increasingly reported from rural and urban areas. Contamination of municipal water supply lines due to seepage of sewerage water occurs in cities and towns, particularly during the summer and rainy seasons, due to faulty laying of pipes and poor maintenance. The absence of a functional network of water testing laboratories to serve the needs of rural and urban areas for regular monitoring of the situation has aggravated the dangers from the problem.

Less than 10 per cent households in rural areas had toilet facilities in 1991. Defecation in the open is not only a major cause of contamination of surface water and poor environmental sanitation, but is also instrumental in spreading disease.

The National Family Health Survey 1998–9, which followed a different categorization of amenities, gives more recent data on availability of water, electricity and toilet facility to households. Survey data indicate an improvement in the situation since 1991. Piped water or water from hand-pumps was available to 72 per cent households in rural areas and 93 per cent in urban areas. However, sanitary disposal of human waste continues to be a greatly neglected matter in rural areas, with only 19 per cent rural households reporting the availability of toilet facility.

Summing Up

The development status of Indian children is affected by some key social and economic factors. Prominent among these are the massive population and its high rate of growth, widespread illiteracy, poverty of large segments of the population, backwardness of rural areas, unsatisfactory level of development of infrastructure, and the poor state of public social services and civic amenities.

The population of India rose to 1,027 million in 2001 and is expected to reach 1,264 million in 2016. A positive development is the evidence of slowing down of the population growth rate since 1981. In 2001 India was expected to provide immunization services to 22 million infants, pre-school services to 66 million children, primary schools to 118 million children and middle/upper primary schools to 74 million children.

India's population is predominantly rural—74 per cent in 1991. Projections made by the Technical Group on Population Projections indicate 71 per cent of the population resident in rural areas in 2001. In 2016, the rural population is expected to be 66 per cent. In view of the backwardness of the rural population on social development indicators and the generally poor state of social services in rural areas, the state of children will, to a large extent, be affected by the development status of rural areas. Even in urban areas, the tremendous increase in population living in slums which have an unhealthy environment and are very poorly served by civic and social services, adversely affects the development of children.

The two undivided states of Uttar Pradesh and Bihar, had 27 per cent of the country's population in 1991. In view of the higher birth rates in these states, they (including Uttaranchal and Jharkhand which were carved out of them) are projected to have 30 per cent of the country's population in 2016. These states not only have a large population. They are also very backward on social and economic development indicators. It is, therefore, of critical importance to improve the child development profile of these states if the national aggregates are to show a significant improvement.

Poverty and massive illiteracy are major factors affecting the development of the country and also of children. Even after more than five decades of independence 26 per cent of the population was below the poverty line in 1999–2000. Orissa had the largest percentage of population below the poverty line (47 per cent). Undivided Uttar Pradesh and Bihar together had 96 million persons below the poverty line or 37 per cent of the country's poor in 1999–2000. They figure at the bottom in per capita income. More than half of the country's hundred most backward and poorest districts were identified in 1997 in these two, then undivided, states.

India has a rather poor record on the literacy front. In 2001, that is nearly five and a half decades after independence, 35 per cent of the population aged 7 years and above was still illiterate. This is undoubtedly an improvement over the situation in 1991 when 48 per cent of the population 7+ was illiterate. Female literacy rate

7+ was 54 per cent in 2001. Bihar had two-thirds of its females 7+ illiterate. Uttar Pradesh and Rajasthan, too, had more than half the females 7+ illiterate.

Housing in both rural and urban areas inhabited by low income groups is of poor quality with basic civic amenities in an unsatisfactory state. Only 9 per cent rural households in 1991 had toilet facilities, 30 per cent had electricity, and 56 per cent safe drinking water (source tap/handpump/tube well). Only 4 per cent rural households had all the three facilities while 31 per cent had none. The National Family Health Survey 1998–9 showed some improvement, but the availability of these basic amenities, so vital for the health of children, are still lacking for large segments of the poor in rural areas and urban slums. The destiny of India's children is closely linked to the tackling of these basic factors which have a vital bearing on their growth and development, particularly in the states of Uttar Pradesh, Bihar, Jharkhand, Rajasthan, Madhya Pradesh, Chhatisgarh, and Orissa, and in the backward regions of other states.

2 Struggle for Survival

Health is a key factor in a nation's growth and development. Public health in India has been a subject of national attention, public debate, and government intervention for several decades, and a number of national programmes were launched in the past to control and eradicate the major diseases. While there has been success in some areas, in general, public health services have been characterized by poor performance. The burden of disease has fallen disproportionately heavily on the poor, the worst affected being children. Frequent episodes of disease have not only caused pain and suffering to children, but also affected their growth and development and influenced performance in school.

Child health indicators now find a regular place in the measurement of development. Health planners of developing countries are now increasingly focusing on child survival strategies and endeavouring to ensure that the benefits of advances in medical science and technology can reach the poor through an integrated approach to health care and a well-designed and efficiently implemented health delivery system. Commentators on the health status of children use a number of standard child survival indicators that are relatively simple to compute and comprehend and are useful for monitoring progress. These indicators have the additional benefits of acceptability and use by health planners and health administrators throughout the world, permitting thereby comparison over time and across countries. The more commonly used indicators among them for which data are available will be used here to reflect the extent of success of public health policies and the health care system in dealing with factors which affect morbidity and mortality of children in India. It is important to remember, however, that child survival is not synonymous with child health, and that morbidity data are also very important. Unfortunately, the collection of morbidity data is not done systematically, particularly community based data. Also, due to the absence of standardization in the presentation of data, making a comparison of findings of different studies over time or across regions is often rendered difficult.

THE MANDATE

Right to health is a basic human right and flows from the right to life. The Constitution of India under Article 21 makes right to life a Fundamental Right. Article 47, a Directive Principle of State Policy, lays down that 'raising the level of nutrition and the standard of living of its people and the improvement of public health' is among the primary duties of the State. The National Policy for Children, 1974, the National Health Policy, 1983, the National Nutrition Policy, 1993, the National Plan of Action on Children, 1992, the National Plan of Action on Nutrition, 1995 and the five year development plans lay down the goals and targets to be achieved to raise the health and nutrition status of children.

The Universal Declaration of Human Rights, 1948, which India has ratified, proclaims that every person has a right to a standard of living adequate for the health and well-being of himself and of his family, including medical care, and the right to security in the event of sickness. It also states that motherhood and childhood are entitled to special care and assistance. The United Nations Convention on the Rights of the Child, 1989 which, too, India has ratified clearly states that every child has the inherent right to life and, to the maximum extent possible, the survival and development of the child has to be ensured by the State. The Convention enumerates the measures that the State is required to take for the full implementation of this right. These include reduction of infant and child mortality, provision of medical assistance and health care to all children, combating disease and malnutrition, prenatal and postnatal health care to mothers, preventive health care, nutrition and health education, clean drinking water, protection from the risks of environmental pollutants.

The pages that follow give an indication of the extent to which children have benefited from the implementation of these instruments of public health policy.

DEATHS IN INFANCY

Infant deaths (deaths below age one year) are indicative of wastage of human life. They reflect the state of maternal and child health services, access to them, and extent of utilization. In 1998, infant

TABLE 2.1: PERCENTAGE OF INFANT DEATHS TO TOTAL DEATHS, INDIA, 1976 TO 1998

Area	Percentage of infant deaths							
	1976	1979	1982	1985	1988	1991	1994	1998
Rural	30.5	32.2	30.6	28.1	28.3	25.2	23.9	22.4
Urban	23.9	24.3	24.6	21.4	21.3	18.0	18.0	14.3
All areas	29.6	31.1	29.8	27.1	27.2	24.1	22.8	21.0

Source: Sample Registration System.

deaths constituted 21 per cent of total deaths, down from 30 per cent in 1976, but still an unacceptably high figure (see Table 2.1). In some states and in rural areas the incidence is much higher, as the data in subsequent tables will show. Unfortunately, this scale of loss of human life soon after birth does not draw public or even media attention as it happens within the four walls of homes in widely dispersed settings. The silver lining in an otherwise dark scenario is that the percentage of infant deaths to total deaths has declined by 29 per cent over a 22 year period since 1976. In urban areas this percentage declined by 40 per cent, and in rural areas by 27 per cent. The percentage of infant deaths to total deaths was 57 per cent higher in rural areas in 1998 as compared to urban areas, reflecting the difference in survival conditions and the differential availability and use of health care facilities in rural and urban areas. Figure 2.1 gives the relative situation on infant deaths in rural and urban areas.

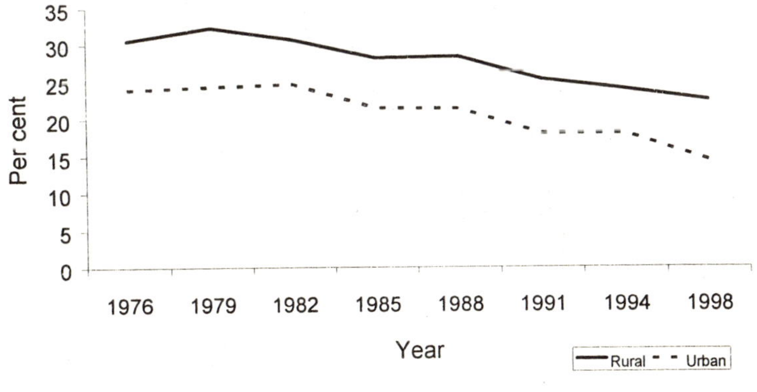

FIG. 2.1: PERCENTAGE OF INFANT DEATHS TO TOTAL DEATHS IN RURAL AND URBAN AREAS, INDIA, 1976 TO 1998.

TABLE 2.2: PERCENTAGE OF INFANT DEATHS TO TOTAL DEATHS IN STATES, 1998

<15	15–19	20–4	25+
Kerala (4.4)	West Bengal (15.1)	Gujarat (20.8)	Uttar Pradesh (26.4)
Tamil Nadu (12.0)	Punjab (15.8)	INDIA (21.0)	Madhya Pradesh (26.8)
Maharashtra (14.2)	Karnataka (16.2)	Assam (21.2)	Rajasthan (29.9)
	Andhra Pradesh (16.8)	Bihar (22.2)	
	Himachal Pradesh (19.8)	Orissa (22.6)	
		Haryana (23.5)	

Source: Sample Registration System.
Note: Data for 16 bigger states given here.

Disaggregation of national level data by states brings out the difference in the situation in different parts of the country. Table 2.2, which gives the percentage of infant deaths to total deaths in sixteen states, shows a wide range. In Kerala, 4 per cent of the total number of deaths in 1998 was that of infants. In Rajasthan, the incidence was as high as 30 per cent, in Uttar Pradesh 26 per cent, and in Madhya Pradesh 27 per cent, indicating the unsatisfactory state of affairs on health matters in large parts of the country and the loss of precious human life. The relative situation in different states is presented graphically in Fig. 2.2.

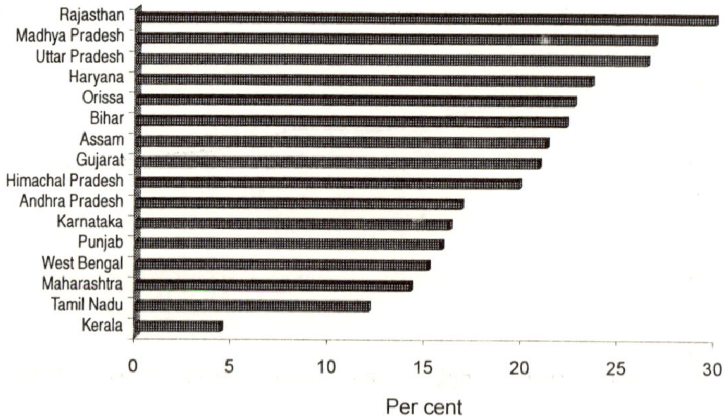

FIG. 2.2: PERCENTAGE OF INFANT DEATHS TO TOTAL DEATHS IN STATES, 1998.

TABLE 2.3: INFANT MORTALITY RATE, INDIA, 1970 TO 2000

	1970	1973	1976	1979	1982	1985	1988	1991	1994	1997	2000
IMR	129	134	129	120	105	97	94	80	74	71	68

Source: Sample Registration System.

INFANT MORTALITY RATE

The most widely used indicator of child survival is infant mortality rate (IMR), which measures the number of infant deaths per 1000 live births during the year. In India, the infant mortality rate is still very high, at 68 in 2000 (see Table 2.3). It has, however, been declining since 1978, after a fluctuating trend between 1970 and 1977 when it varied between 140 and 126. The decline in IMR between 1970 and 1980 was 11.6 per cent, between 1980 and 1990 it was 29.8 per cent, and between 1990 and 2000 it was 15.0 per cent. In the 30 year period 1970 to 2000, IMR has declined by 47 per cent. The National Health Policy (1983) target for the year 2000 is an IMR below 60. There is thus a slippage in the attainment of the target, mainly because of poor performance in some of the bigger states like Uttar Pradesh, Madhya Pradesh, Orissa, and Rajasthan.

Disaggregation of infant mortality data by its components gives a better understanding of the phenomenon. The important disaggregated indicators are neonatal mortality rate (NNMR), post neonatal mortality rate (PNMR), still birth rate (SBR), and perinatal mortality rate (PMR). Table 2.4 gives the data on these disaggregated infant mortality indicators for the period between 1970 and 1998.

TABLE 2.4: INFANT MORTALITY RATE, NEONATAL MORTALITY RATE, POST NEONATAL MORTALITY RATE, STILL BIRTH RATE, AND PERINATAL MORTALITY RATE, INDIA, 1970 TO 1998

Year	Infant mortality rate (IMR)	Neonatal mortality rate (NNMR)	NNMR as % of IMR	Post-neonatal mortality rate (PNMR)	PNMR as % of IMR	Still birth rate (SBR)	Perinatal mortality rate (PMR)	SBR as % of PMR
1970	129	68	52.7	61	47.3	17	45	37.8
1980	114	69	60.5	45	39.5	11	56	19.6
1990	80	53	66.3	27	33.7	12	48	25.0
1998	72	45	62.5	27	37.5	9	42	21.4

Source: Sample Registration System.

Neonatal mortality rate measures the number of deaths in the first four weeks after birth per 1,000 live births during the year, and PNMR measures the number of deaths in the subsequent 48 weeks of an infant's life per 1,000 live births during the year. The sum of these two components gives the IMR. The neonatal mortality rate declined from 68 in 1970 to 45 in 1998, a fall of 34 per cent, while the post neonatal mortality rate declined from 61 to 27 during the same period, a fall of 56 per cent. Thus, the decline in PNMR was far grater than that of NNMR. This trend is also evident if one considers the proportion of NNMR in IMR. In 1970, NNMR was 53 per cent of the IMR. In 1998, this rose to 63 per cent. For the same reference period, PNMR fell from 47 per cent of IMR in 1970 to 37 per cent in 1997. This shows that there has been less success in reducing mortality in the first four weeks of an infant's life, which are critically more important for survival, than in the subsequent 48 weeks.

Still birth rate, which measures the number of still births per 1,000 live plus still births during the year, declined from 17 in 1970 to 9 in 1998, a fall of 47 per cent in the 28 year period.

The perinatal mortality rate (PMR), which measures the number of still births plus infant deaths within a week of birth for every 1,000 live plus still births during the year, is a sensitive indicator of the availability, accessibility, and use of maternal and neonatal health care services and their quality. It is also an indicator of the extent of pregnancy wastage. Empirical studies have shown that the perinatal period is a critical time (Chandrasekhar, et al. 1998). During the period 1970 to 1998, PMR has shown a fluctuating trend. Between 1971 and 1984, it fluctuated between 51 and 67. Between 1985 and 1998, it fluctuated in the range of the 40s. On the whole, during the period 1970 to 1998 the gains in bringing down PMR have been small, as is evident from Table 2.4. The National Health Policy PMR target of 30–5 in 2000 will, thus, not be reached.

The percentage of still birth rate (SBR) to perinatal mortality rate (PMR) has declined significantly between 1970 and 1998, indicating that the first week of the infant's life continues to be an area of considerable concern and needs to be specifically addressed to bring down NNMR and PMR in any significant measure.

Sample Registration System (SRS) data on early neonatal mortality corroborate the critical role of the first week in an infant's life. Early neonatal mortality rate (ENNMR), which measures the number of deaths within a week of birth per 1,000 live births during the year,

TABLE 2.5: EARLY NEONATAL, NEONATAL AND POST NEONATAL MORTALITY RATE, INDIA, 1998

Early neonatal mortality rate			Neonatal mortality rate			Post neonatal mortality rate		
Rural	Urban	Total	Rural	Urban	Total	Rural	Urban	Total
37	22	34	49	27	45	28	18	27

Source: Sample Registration System.

was 34 in 1998, while late neonatal mortality rate (LNMR) which measures the number of deaths of infants of age one to four weeks per 1,000 live births during the year, was 11, making neonatal mortality rate 45 (see Table 2.5). In other words, ENNMR was more than three-fourths of NNMR. The critical nature of the first week in the life of an infant is also evident from the fact that early neonatal deaths constituted 47 per cent of infant deaths in 1998. The early neonatal mortality rate (ENNMR), as well as NNMR, in rural areas is considerably higher than in urban areas, reflecting the difference in availability and use of antenatal and neonatal health care services. Figure 2.3 gives the percentage share of ENNMR, LNNMR, and PNMR in IMR in 1998.

Neonatal mortality shows considerable variation not only between rural and urban areas, but also between different states, reflecting the extent of availability and use of neonatal care services.

Table 2.6 gives the percentage of neonatal deaths in infant deaths in different states in 1998. In some states where there has been greater success in bringing down post neonatal deaths than neonatal deaths, the share of neonatal deaths in infant deaths has gone up.

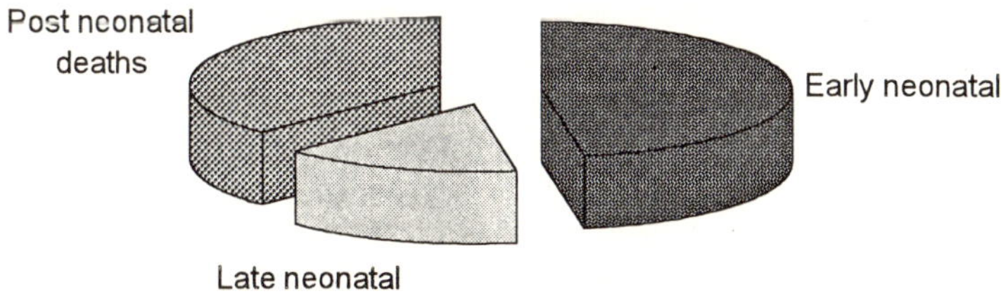

FIG. 2.3: PERCENTAGE DISTRIBUTION OF EARLY NEONATAL, LATE NEONATAL, AND POST NEONATAL DEATHS, INDIA, 1998.

TABLE 2.6: PERCENTAGE OF NEONATAL DEATHS IN INFANT DEATHS IN STATES, 1998

55–9	60–4	65–9	70+
West Bengal (57.0)	Rajasthan (60.0)	Bihar (65.8)	Karnataka (71.2)
Haryana (58.3)	Maharashtra (60.3)	Assam (66.8)	Himachal Pradesh (73.0)
	Punjab (60.4)	Tamil Nadu (66.8)	
	Uttar Pradesh (61.3)	Gujarat (68.0)	
	Orissa (61.9)	Andhra Pradesh (68.9)	
	Madhya Pradesh (62.1)	Kerala (69.9)	
	INDIA (63.0)		

Source: Sample Registration System.
Note: Date for 16 bigger states given here.

Public child health services need to focus their attention on neonatal care, particularly early neonatal care.

RURAL-URBAN DIFFERENCE IN IMR

In 2000, rural IMR was 74 and urban IMR was 43. In other words, rural IMR was 72 per cent higher than urban IMR. The difference in rural and urban IMR is very prominent indicating that the factors which affect infant mortality operate with greater intensity in rural areas. The wide gap between rural and urban IMR, despite both showing a declining trend, has continued for the last two and a half decades, though some narrowing of the gap is now discernible (See Fig. 2.4). Between 1971 and 1981, the difference between rural and urban IMR was more than 50, between 1982 and 1989 it ranged between 40 and 49 and during the period 1990 to 2000 the difference ranged between 28 and 37. In the period 1970 to 2000, rural IMR fell by 46 per cent and the urban IMR by 52 per cent. The rural-urban difference in IMR has to be seen in the context of the fact that three-fourths of the births take place in rural areas, thus indicating the gravity of the situation in rural India.

The difference between rural and urban areas in neonatal mortality rate, post neonatal mortality, perinatal mortality rate, and still birth rate available up to 1998 is given in Table 2.7. The data show that even though there has been a decline in NNMR, PNMR, PMR, and SBR in both rural and urban areas, the difference is still very large. In 1998, NNMR was higher in rural areas by 81 per cent, PNMR by 56 per cent, and PMR by 55 per cent.

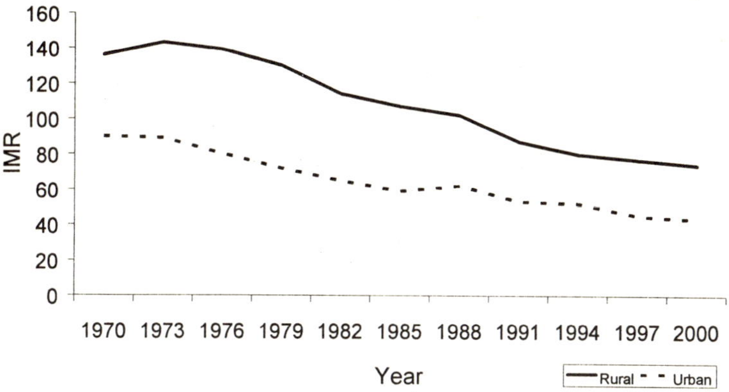

FIG. 2.4: INFANT MORTALITY RATE IN RURAL AND URBAN AREAS, INDIA, 1970 TO 2000.

TABLE 2.7: INFANT MORTALITY RATE, NEONATAL MORTALITY RATE AND POST NEONATAL MORTALITY RATE IN RURAL AND URBAN AREAS, INDIA, 1970 AND 1998

Area	Year	Infant mortality rate (IMR)	Neonatal mortality rate (NNMR)	NNMR as % of IMR	Post neo-natal mortality rate (PNMR)	PNMR as % of IMR	Still birth rate (SBR)	Perinatal mortality rate (PMR)	SBR as % of PMR
Rural	1970	136	72	52.9	64	47.1	18	46	39.1
	1998	77	49	63.6	28	36.4	9	45	20.0
Urban	1970	90	46	51.1	44	48.9	14	34	41.2
	1998	45	27	60.0	18	40.0	8	29	27.6

Source: Sample Registration System.

INTERSTATE VARIATION IN IMR

The interstate variation in IMR is very marked. Infant mortality rate data for 2000, given in Table 2.8, shows that Kerala is far ahead of the other states in terms of a positive environment for infant survival. While Kerala had an IMR of only 14, in Orissa the IMR was 96, almost seven times the IMR in Kerala. This shows how disadvantaged infants are in the high mortality states in the matter of basic right to life. Figure 2.5 gives the relative position in different states.

TABLE 2.8: INFANT MORTALITY RATE IN STATES, 2000

< 20	40–59	60–79	80+
Kerala (14)	Maharashtra (48)	Himachal Pradesh (60)	Uttar Pradesh (83)
	Tamil Nadu (51)	Bihar (62)	Madhya Pradesh (88)
	West Bengal (51)	Gujarat (62)	Orissa (96)
	Punjab (52)	Andhra Pradesh (65)	
	Karnataka (57)	Haryana (67)	
		INDIA (68)	
		Assam (75)	
		Rajasthan (79)	

Source: Sample Registration System.
Note: Date for 16 bigger states given here.

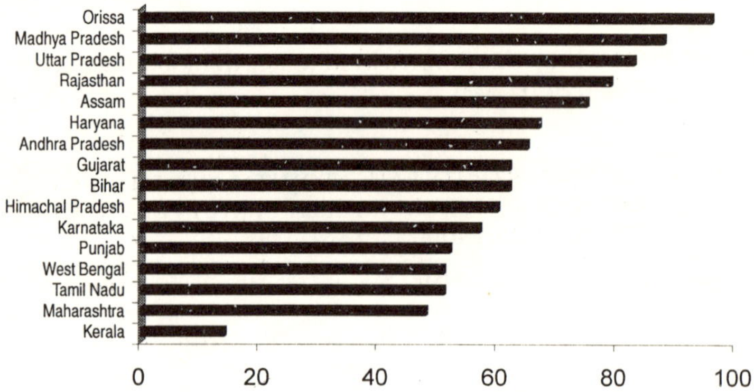

FIG. 2.5: INFANT MORTALITY RATE IN STATES, 2000.

GENDER DIFFERENCE IN IMR

Before birth and immediately thereafter, when nature rather than nurture plays the predominant role, male mortality is higher. Some hospital based studies have reported male preponderance in perinatal deaths (Aras, Pai and Purandare 1990). Data from the Sample Registration System available for the period 1990–3 indicate the same trend. Table 2.9, which gives the still birth rate and perinatal mortality rate by sex, shows higher male mortality as compared to female mortality.

After birth, socio-cultural determinants begin to exercise their influence on the nurturing of the child. The birth of a male infant is a joyous event for not only the parents and relatives, but also the

TABLE 2.9: STILL BIRTH RATE AND PERINATAL MORTALITY RATE BY SEX IN RURAL AND URBAN AREAS, INDIA, 1990–3

Residence	Still birth rate				Perinatal mortality rate			
	Male	Female	Total	M-F	Male	Female	Total	M-F
Rural	12.5	10.2	11.5	2.3	40.4	37.0	38.8	3.4
Urban	10.8	9.1	10.1	1.7	25.8	20.3	23.2	5.5
Total	12.2	10.0	11.3	2.2	37.6	33.7	35.8	3.9

Source: Sample Registration System.

birth attendant and servants attached to the household (because more and better gifts will be received), as well as neighbours and well-wishers. Strong preference for the male child cuts across caste and class barriers. The woman's status in the family enhances if she gives birth to a male child. Such a discriminatory attitude has accounted for the neglect of the female child where she is not the first or only girl child, resulting in higher female mortality.

The gender difference in IMR, given in Table 2.10, shows that female IMR is mostly higher than male IMR. The female infant being biologically stronger should, other things being equal, have better chances of survival. However, as stated earlier, socio-cultural factors operate to negate the biological advantage.

A close look at the components of IMR by gender, given in Table 2.11, shows that while at the neonatal stage male mortality is higher because the female child is biologically stronger, the position is reversed at the post neonatal stage where female mortality is higher, indicating that the female infant receives less health and nutrition care and medical attention and has a higher risk of not surviving at the post neonatal stage, more so in the rural areas.

The degree of gender bias in different states is reflected in a higher female PNMR. Table 2.12 gives the difference between female and

TABLE 2.10: INFANT MORTALITY RATE BY SEX, INDIA, 1979 TO 1998

Sex	1979	1981	1983	1985	1987	1989	1991	1993	1995	1998
Male	119	110	105	96	95	92	81	73	73	70
Female	121	111	105	98	96	90	80	75	76	74
Total	120	110	105	97	95	91	80	74	74	72
M–F	–2	–1	0	–2	–1	2	1	–2	–3	–4

Source: Sample Registration System.

TABLE 2.11: NEONATAL AND POST NEONATAL MORTALITY RATE BY SEX IN RURAL AND URBAN AREAS, INDIA, 1990–3

Residence	Neonatal mortality rate				Post neonatal rate			
	Male	Female	Total	M-F	Male	Female	Total	M-F
Rural	56.5	52.6	54.7	3.9	27.2	33.0	26.9	– 5.9
Urban	33.9	27.9	31.1	6.0	17.0	21.1	19.0	– 4.1
Total	52.2	47.9	50.2	4.3	25.2	30.7	27.9	– 5.5

Source: Sample Registration System.

male NNMR and PNMR in 1990–3 in the sixteen bigger states. The data show that in Uttar Pradesh, Punjab, Haryana, Madhya Pradesh, Orissa and Rajasthan, female PNMR is much higher than male PNMR. Only in Kerala is the male post neonatal mortality rate moderately higher. Punjab and Haryana have a progressive economy with the highest per capita income. However, they seem to be regressive in matters affecting gender equality.

TABLE 2.12: SEX DIFFERENTIAL IN INFANT MORTALITY RATE, NEONATAL MORTALITY RATE AND POST NEONATAL MORTALITY RATE, INDIA AND STATES, 1990–3

India/States	Infant mortality rate (M-F)	Neonatal mortality rate (M-F)	Post neonatal mortality rate (M-F)
INDIA	– 1.2	+ 4.3	– 5.5
Andhra Pradesh	+ 7.1	+ 7.7	– 0.6
Assam	+ 4.4	+ 4.4	– 0.8
Bihar	– 2.5	+ 2.7	– 5.2
Gujarat	+ 0.9	+ 4.6	– 3.7
Haryana	– 7.6	+ 1.4	– 9.1
Himachal Pradesh	+ 5.4	+ 10.7	– 5.2
Karnataka	+ 8.5	+ 9.0	– 0.5
Kerala	+ 5.3	+ 4.1	+ 1.2
Madhya Pradesh	+ 1.2	+ 9.2	– 8.0
Maharashtra	– 0.5	+ 0.7	– 1.2
Orissa	+ 3.7	+ 11.3	– 7.5
Punjab	– 8.7	+ 0.6	– 9.3
Rajasthan	– 3.3	+ 4.0	– 7.2
Tamil Nadu	+ 0.8	+ 3.1	– 2.3
Uttar Pradesh	– 10.6	+ 0.4	– 11.0
West Bengal	+ 2.0	+ 7.5	– 5.4

Source: Sample Registration System.
Note: Data for 16 bigger states given here. Figures give the average of 4 years.

Decreased access of girls to timely medical care has been highlighted in a number of reports based on comprehensive fertility and mortality studies in Punjab in the 1950s. For instance, a study of 615 deaths in villages in Ludhiana district during the three year period 1957 to 1959 found that fewer females received medical care in fatal illness than males and, that too, generally by persons of a lower level of competence (Singh, Gordon and Wyon 1962). The study of Khanna villages in the 1950s reported that by five years of age, survivors from 1,000 live born boys far exceeded the survivors from an equal number of live born girls (Wyon and Gordon 1971). The Narangwal study in 1970–3 reported higher mortality among female infants and female children aged 12–23 months (Kielman, et al. 1978). The restudy in 1984 of eleven villages originally surveyed in the 1950s in the Khanna study showed far higher female post neonatal mortality. Also, much more was spent on medical care of boys than of girls (Das Gupta 1987). A later study covering 2,595 children admitted in 1987 to the Pediatric Ward of Brown Memorial Hospital, Ludhiana reported that three out of four girls ill enough to require hospitalization were denied essential medical care by their household because of their sex (Booth and Verma 1992). Some recent studies from other parts of the country have, however, reported the absence of discriminatory health care by the household on the basis of gender. For instance, a study in Pondicherry region covering children attending the weekly under-fives clinic at six Primary Health Centres in August 1990 did not find any gender bias. The facility was utilized almost equally by boys and girls (Premrajan and Srinivasan 1991). The study by BAIF Development Research Foundation covering sample rural areas in five states in different parts of the country, too, did not find gender difference in the treatment of morbidity (BAIF Development Research Foundation 1997). It is necessary to closely monitor the situation in different parts of the country, particularly among communities where socio-cultural factors strongly discriminate against the girl child, so that programmes to eliminate gender bias can be better targeted.

Female Foeticide

A relatively recent phenomenon is the abusive use of diagnostic technologies (ultrasound, amniocentesis, etc.) for finding out the sex of the foetus, and then aborting it if found to be a female. This morbid expression of discrimination against the girl child began to be increasingly reported from the 1970s. In a study conducted at the All India Institute of Medical Sciences, New Delhi on fifteen pregnant women for prenatal diagnosis of genetic disorders, it was found that seven out of eight patients who had an amniocentesis test carried out primarily for the determination of the sex of the foetus aborted it when it was found to be a female (Verma et al. 1975). Another study conducted in a large hospital during a 12 month period in 1976–7 reported that of the 450 female foetuses predicted as result of antenatal determination of sex, medical termination of pregnancy was done in the case of 430 (Ramanamma and Bambawale 1980). Public attention was drawn to the phenomenon as it became known that an overwhelming majority of couples who come for prenatal diagnostic tests do so to find out the sex of the foetus and abort it if this is found to be female. The government banned the use of these tests in public hospitals for the determination of sex. However, a growing number of private medical clinics began to offer sex determination tests in cities and towns all over the country at an affordable cost. Exploiting the strong desire to have male offspring, they also provided or arranged for facilities to couples who wished to abort the female foetus. Various covert and overt devices were used, including advertisements, handouts, bill-boards, and even agents to get clients (Nanda, Singh and Aggarwal 1993; Sinha 1991; Srinivasan 1992). A semi-clandestine market developed, linking the clients and the service providers through an effective non-formal communication network. Interestingly, some gynaecologists and doctors tended to think that they were doing a service by not bringing into the world an unwanted girl child who would be subject to discrimination and humiliation throughout her life. They also felt they were promoting the cause of family planning by helping families to choose the sex composition of their children and limit the family size.

Some empirical studies on sex ratio of live births have corroborated the strong possibility of the practice of sex selective foeticide. For instance, a study of live births, both hospital based and community based, of villages in Ludhiana district of Punjab betweem 1981 and 1989 showed a declining sex ratio, indicating the possibility of female foeticide (Sachar, Verma, Prakash, et al. 1990; Sehgal, Sachar, Verma et al. 1990). Another study from May 1990 to December 1991 at Brown Memorial Hospital, Christian Medical College, Ludhiana reported evidence of abortion of female foetus following sex determination tests. It found that sex ratio at birth in the hospital declined from 934 females per 1000 males in 1982 to 758 in 1993. Most foetal sex determination tests were done in the case of mothers who already had at least one daughter. The use of foetal sex determination tests was found to increase with rising household income. Among mothers with some education, the frequency of use did not change with increasing education (Booth, Verma and Beri 1994). Yet another study conducted in some villages in neighbouring Haryana in 1996 reported that it found 'incontrovertible evidence of the practice of female foeticide' (George and Dahiya 1998). Civil registration data from Haryana indicates a declining ratio of female births per 1,000 male births. The National Capital Territory of Delhi, which has a fairly complete civil registration system, also shows an adverse sex ratio at birth: over the twelve year period 1984 to 1995 the sex ratio ranged between 842 and 885.

The root causes of female foeticide are the strong preference for male offspring and lower status of girls (and girl's mother). Parents depend on sons to provide support in old age and continuity to the family line. Sons have been assigned by religion and custom certain roles in socio-religious ceremonies and rituals. In rural areas, sons provide muscle power which enhances the capacity of the family to protect its interests. Girls are perceived as an economic liability, especially when the number is more than one. The ever growing menace of dowry, rising expenses on marriage ceremonies and post-marriage expectations and demands, followed by ill-treatment if these are not met, have further lowered the status of girls. The strong preference for male offspring cuts across religious, caste, and socio-economic class boundaries. The acceptance of sex determination tests has been found by some studies to be greater among higher income families and those with larger landholdings. The attitude of even educated couples indicates how desperately the male child is wanted to complete the family when they have only daughters. The adoption of the small family norm by families sometimes works against the girl child as parents wish to choose a family size in which at least one child, if not two, is a son. Birth order and gender of previous offspring, therefore, play an important role in the decision for sex selective abortion (Kaur 1993; Nanda et al. 1993; Nirbhawne et al. 1996; Shah and Taneja 1991).

Women's groups, scientists, and social activists have agitated strongly against the abusive use of prenatal diagnostic technology for the sole or primary purpose of finding out the sex of the foetus, as they consider it to be only unethical but also a lethal blow against gender justice. They protested against the participation of doctors/clinics to tap the highly profitable hidden market for sex determination and sex selective foeticide, and also campaigned for a ban on it by the government. Maharashtra became the first state to prohibit its abuse, when it enacted in 1988 the Maharashtra Regulation of Use of Prenatal Diagnostic Techniques Act. Later, in 1994, the Government of India passed the Prenatal Diagnostic Techniques (Regulation of Misuse) Act (PNDT Act) to 'provide for the regulation of the use of prenatal diagnostic techniques for the purpose of detecting genetic or metabolic disorders or chromosomal abnormalities of certain congenital malformation or sex linked disorders, and for the prevention of misuse of such techniques for the purpose of prenatal sex determination leading to female foeticide, and for matters connected therewith or incidental thereto'. The Act prohibits any person conducting prenatal diagnostic procedures from communicating to the pregnant woman or her relatives the sex of the foetus by words, signs, or in any other manner. Advertisement relating to availability of prenatal determination of sex has been banned. Every offence under the Act has been made cognizable, non-bailable, and non-compoundable. Penal provisions for violation of the Act cover imprisonment and fine, which increase in severity for subsequent convictions. The Act and the Rules framed thereunder came into force on 1 January 1996. During the first few years of the operation of the Act no case of violation of the law was reported from any part of the country (Ministry of Health and Family Welfare, 2000).

To oversee the implementation of the Act, a Central Advisory Board has now been constituted. State Advisory Committees have been constituted in most of the states, and authorities identified for the enforcement of the Act. Responding to a public interest litigation, the Supreme Court has now given direction to state governments to take action to register ultrasound clinics in the states and enforce the Act.

It is too early to say to what extent legislation can eliminate sex determination, significantly reduce it, or make the operations clandestine whereby clinics network with agents to get clients. Media reports indicate that sex determination tests continue in a covert manner as the demand is still very strong, to meet which subtle non-formal but effective marketing techniques are employed. These have penetrated rural areas and have begun to offer services nearer the homes of the clients (Gurung 2000; Krishnakumar 1998, 1999; Mittal

1997; Mukherjee 1996). However, the National Crime Records Bureau reported the incidence of only 45 foeticide cases registered in the country under the Indian Penal Code in 1994, 38 in 1995, 39 in 1996, 57 in 1997, 62 in 1998, and 61 in 1999 which is far removed from the ground reality. After the Supreme Court's directives on enforcement, some cases have been registered under the PNDT Act.

Legislation, though a powerful instrument of the State, cannot by itself curb the evil of foeticide unless the law is strictly enforced. The social factors which propel the demand have to be seriously addressed too. The administrative machinery has to be strengthened. The support of panchayati raj institutions, which have one-third seats reserved for women, needs to be mobilized. Vigilance of non-governmental organizations (NGOs) and their active participation is required to curb the clandestine operation of sex determination tests. Concerted efforts are necessary to bring a change in attitudes which discriminate against the female infant. Cooperation of the medical fraternity is necessary. State Medical Associations are now trying to mobilize the support of doctors to put an end to the morbid practice of sex selective abortion.

Female Infanticide

Reports of female infanticide have surfaced recently in the media. The practice of infanticide drew official attention in India when its presence was reported during the colonial era by British administrators who, during the course of their tours in northern and western India, noticed very adverse sex ratio among children of certain castes in some areas. They were appalled to find that this was the outcome of the practice of female infanticide, primarily due to the acute problems faced by parents in getting a daughter married and the humiliation and suffering often caused to the girl and her family. This led to the passage of Regulation XXI of 1795 and Regulation III of 1804, declaring female infanticide as murder. Since these Regulations had limited coverage and effect, in 1870 the Female Infanticide Prevention Act was passed, penalizing persons responsible for the commission of the offence of murder of a female infant. The Act also covered negligence in the maintenance of the female child in a manner which endangered her life or health. It empowered the magistrate to place such a child under proper supervision and, if necessary, remove the child from the custody of such a person.

Though little was reported about female infanticide for a long period after Independence, recent reports indicate that it is being practised in some castes within the four walls of domestic privacy in some parts of the country. Media accounts and some recent studies have revealed the existence of the phenomenon in some districts of Tamil Nadu, Bihar and Rajasthan (Adithi 1995; Chunkath and Athreya 1997; George, Abel and Miller 1992; Pachauri 1988; Rajaretnam 1992; Srinivasan 1992; Venkatramani 1986; Wadhwa 1995). It is possible that female infanticide is carried out surreptitiously in other parts of the country as well. The National Crime Records Bureau has begun compilation of statistics on female infanticide since 1994. It reported only 131 cases on female infanticide in 1994, 139 in 1995, 113 in 1996, 107 in 1997, 114 in 1998, and only 87 in 1999 in India. These figures are widely believed to under-report the prevalence, indicating how law enforcing agencies are way behind in detecting the crime and the very low priority they accord to this social problem.

Various causative factors have been cited in studies and media reports for the pertinacious existence of the problem. Girls born lower in the birth order in poor families in some communities were found to face the risk of being put to death immediately after birth, or within a week, indicating how gender and birth order interact to decide the probability of survival of the female infant. The pressure of the husband and in-laws silences the mother of the infant since a woman's already low status declines further if the child born is a girl, and especially so if that adds to one or more female children already born to the couple. Other factors pushing the parents to snuff out the life of the new born female infant are the expenses of bringing up a girl who, on marriage, will leave her natal family and give nothing in return to her parents in old age; exorbitant rise in demand for dowry, which families are unable to bear for more than one girl; rising expenses on marriage ceremonies due to social pressures and the pressures of in-laws; the subordination and humiliation of the girl and her parents due to a girl's inferior status; and the harassment, and at times torture, faced by the girl even after marriage due to persistent post-marriage demands and expectations. The step is rationalized as unfortunate but unavoidable to save the girl from a life of deprivation, suffering, harassment, and torture. Female infanticide graphically demonstrates the powerlessness of women and helplessness of the mother, born out of anxiety, fear, loss of status, and scorn on the birth of a female infant. It is a morbid manifestation of gender based discrimination and a gross violation of the right to life, a Fundamental Right guaranteed by the Constitution of India.

Legislation by itself can hardly be expected to make a dent on the problem of female infanticide. Some welfare measures have been suggested to prevent its occurrence. One is that an option should be available to the mother to give the female infant away in adoption or leave it in a cradle of a children's home. The success of such an alternative has to be considered in the context of a situation where female infanticide may have tacit social acceptance in the local community but giving away the infant in adoption does not. The success of government schemes, such as depositing a sum of money on the birth of a female infant of lower birth order to be given to her along with accumulated interest when she reaches the age of 18 years, remains to be seen, especially since such schemes, which are of the nature of relief, take the focus away from the main issues of gender discrimination which need to be seriously addressed. Non-governmental organizations and government agencies have to collaborate, exercise vigilance to detect cases of female infanticide, and take action. Panchayati raj institutions, which now have one-third women members, should generate community pressure against the practice. Strong social and political mobilization is also necessary to stop discrimination against the girl child. The menace of dowry has to be frontally attacked.

EARLY CHILDHOOD MORTALITY

Early childhood deaths continue to be high in India. In 1998, 21 per cent of the total number of deaths were of infants, 8 per cent were of children aged 1–4 years, and 4.5 per cent of deaths were of children aged 5–14 years (see Table 2.13). Thus, even though the post-infancy

TABLE 2.13: PERCENTAGE DISTRIBUTION OF DEATHS BY AGE IN RURAL AND URBAN AREAS, INDIA, 1998

	Age (in years)							
Area	< 1	1–4	0–4	5–9	10–14	15–59	60+	Total
Rural	22.4	8.3	30.7	3.1	1.6	26.6	38.0	100.0
Urban	14.3	5.0	19.3	2.7	1.0	31.5	45.5	100.0
Total	21.0	7.7	28.8	3.0	1.5	27.4	39.2	100.0
R-U	8.1	3.3	11.4	0.4	0.6	– 4.9	– 7.5	

Source: Sample Registration System.

stages (1–4 and 5–14 years) see a lower percentage of deaths, the incidence is still high. In 1998, 29 per cent of the total deaths were of children aged less than 5 years, indicating that infancy and early childhood remain critical areas of concern in child survival, particularly in rural areas. Its incidence indicates weaknesses in preventive and curative health care services for children.

There is considerable interstate variation in the percentage of deaths of children aged 0–4 years to total deaths, as is evident from Table 2.14. In 1998, Rajasthan had the highest percentage of deaths of children aged less than 5 years to total deaths (40 per cent), while Kerala had the lowest percentage (5 per cent). Figure 2.6 presents

TABLE 2.14: PERCENTAGE OF DEATHS OF CHILDREN 0–4 YEARS TO TOTAL DEATHS IN STATES, 1998

< 10	10–19	20–9	30 And Above
Kerala (5.1)	Tamil Nadu (14.0)	Andhra Pradesh (20.3)	Assam (32.4)
	Maharashtra (18.2)	Punjab (20.3)	Bihar (32.8)
	West Bengal (19.6)	Karnataka (20.5)	Haryana (33.0)
		Himachal Pradesh (22.4)	Madhya Pradesh (36.9)
		Gujarat (27.0)	Uttar Pradesh (37.8)
		INDIA (28.8)	Rajasthan (39.7)
		Orissa (29.0)	

Source: Sample Registration System.
Note: Data for 16 bigger states given here.

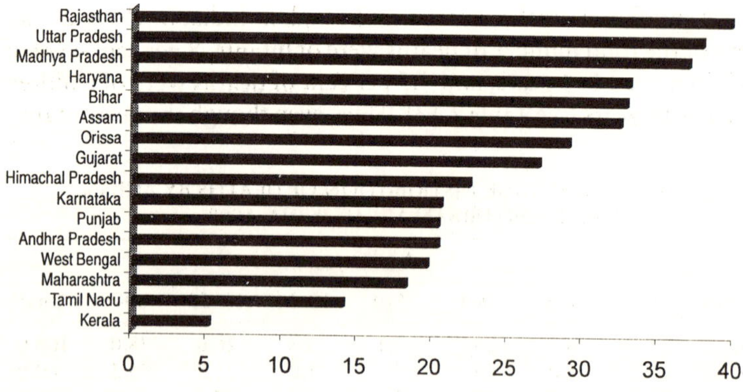

FIG. 2.6: PERCENTAGE OF DEATHS OF CHILDREN AGED 0–4 YEARS TO TOTAL DEATHS IN STATES, 1998.

the data in graphical form. Child survival is at a very unsatisfactory level in a number of states. In five states, one-third or more of the total number of deaths in 1998 were of children aged less than 5 years.

Age specific death rate, which indicates the number of deaths per 1,000 population in that age group, is given in Table 2.15 for the years 1970 and 1998. It indicates the change in mortality pattern in

TABLE 2.15: AGE SPECIFIC DEATH RATE, INDIA, 1970 AND 1998

Age (in years)	1970	1998
0–4	53.0	22.5
5–9	4.8	2.2
10–14	2.1	1.1
15–19	2.9	1.8
20–4	3.6	2.5
25–9	3.9	2.6
30–4	4.5	3.0
35–9	5.1	3.6
40–4	7.3	4.7
45–9	10.5	6.4
50–4	16.0	10.8
55–9	22.2	16.3
60–4	38.2	28.2
65–9	49.0	41.5
70+	111.7	89.0

Source: Sample Registration System.

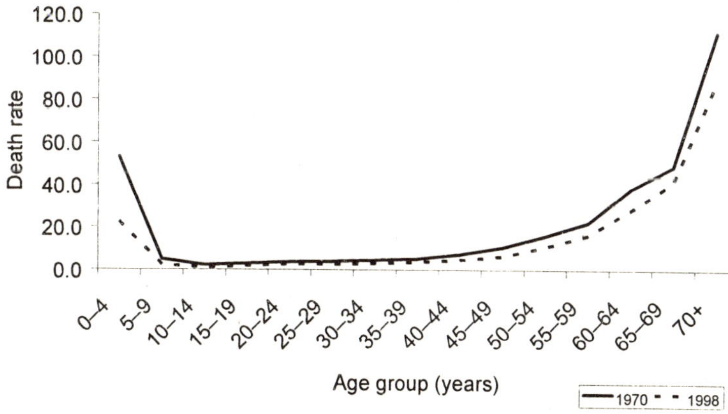

FIG. 2.7: AGE SPECIFIC DEATH RATE, INDIA, 1970 AND 1998.

TABLE 2.16: AGE SPECIFIC DEATH RATE OF CHILDREN, INDIA, 1982–4 AND 1998

Year	Age (in years)			
	<1	1–4	5–9	10–14
1982–4	126.1	15.6	3.6	1.7
1998	74.7	7.7	2.2	1.1

Source: Sample Registration System.
Note: 1982–4 mortality rate is the average of three years.

the 28 year period. Graphical presentation of the data shows a curve with the height of the inverted head still very high in the 0–4 year age group, after which it begins to fall, climbing steeply from age 55 years (see Fig. 2.7). A good national health situation would reflect very low levels of mortality in early childhood which is still not the case in India, though during the period 1970 to 1998 early childhood mortality rates have declined considerably. In the 0–4 year age group as well as the 5–9 year age group, the age specific mortality rate declined by more than 54 per cent between 1970 and 1998 (see Table 2.15).

The break up of 0–4 year age specific mortality data into less than 1 year and 1–4 years data available from 1982 show the critical nature of the first year of life of a child compared to later years. The age specific death rate data indicate a very sharp decline from the less than 1 year age group to the 1–4 year age group. It drops significantly thereafter as well, as is evident from Table 2.16. During the period 1982–4 to 1998, the decline in the 1–4 year death rate has been higher (51 per cent) than in the less than 1 year age group (41 per cent).

RURAL-URBAN DIFFERENCE IN EARLY CHILDHOOD MORTALITY

The rural-urban difference in early childhood mortality is quite marked, as is evident from Table 2.17, indicating that rural areas, where three-fourths of the population lives, lag far behind on survival indicators. In 1998, the age specific death rate in the less than 1 year age group was 74 per cent higher in rural as compared to urban areas. In the 1–4 year age group, it was higher by 105 per cent, and in the 5–9 year age group by 33 per cent. The wide gap between rural and urban areas has not changed much between 1982–4 and 1998, though

TABLE 2.17: AGE SPECIFIC DEATH RATE OF CHILDREN IN RURAL AND URBAN AREAS, INDIA, 1982–4 AND 1998

Area	Year	Age (in years)			
		<1	1–4	5–9	10–14
Rural	1982–4	138.9	17.7	4.1	1.9
	1998	81.0	8.6	2.4	1.2
Urban	1982–4	75.1	8.1	1.8	1.1
	1998	46.5	4.2	1.8	0.6
R–U	1982–4	63.8	9.6	2.3	0.8
	1998	34.5	4.4	0.6	0.6

Source: Sample Registration System.
Note: 1982–4 mortality rate is the average of three years.

there is a fairly large decline in mortality in both rural and urban areas. In the less than 1 year age group, for instance, mortality declined between 1982–4 and 1998 by 42 per cent in rural areas and 38 per cent in urban areas.

GENDER DIFFERENCE IN EARLY CHILDHOOD MORTALITY

The age specific death rate by gender shows a steep decline for both sexes in the age groups less than 1 year as well as 1–4 years between 1982–4 and 1998 (see Table 2.18). In the less than 1 year age group, the decline is 43 per cent in the case of males and 38 per cent in the case of females. In the 1–4 year age group, the decline is sharper. In 1998, female mortality was higher in all the age groups indicating

TABLE 2.18: AGE SPECIFIC DEATH RATE OF CHILDREN BY SEX, INDIA, 1982–4 AND 1998

Sex	Year	Age (in years)				
		<1	1–4	0–4	5–9	10–14
Male	1982–4	128.3	13.1	38.1	3.2	1.6
	1998	73.4	6.2	21.0	2.1	1.0
Female	1982–4	123.9	18.2	40.8	4.0	1.8
	1998	76.3	9.4	24.1	2.4	1.2
M–F	1982–4	4.4	–5.1	–2.7	–0.8	–0.2
	1998	–2.9	–3.2	–3.1	–0.3	–0.2

Source: Sample Registration System.
Note: Mortality rate 1982–4 is the average of three years.

neglect of the female child on health matters. A welcome feature is the narrowing of the gender gap in age specific mortality rates.

INTERSTATE VARIATION IN EARLY CHILDHOOD MORTALITY

There is large variation between states in the 0–4 years age specific death rate (see Table 2.19). In 1998, Kerala had the lowest 0–4 years age specific death rate at 3.6, while Madhya Pradesh, Uttar Pradesh, Rajasthan, Orissa and Assam, had nearly eight times this figure. Incidentally, in 1975, that is 23 years earlier, the 0–4 age specific

TABLE 2.19: AGE SPECIFIC DEATH RATE OF AGE GROUP 0–4 YEARS IN STATES, 1998

< 10	10–19	20–9	30 and above
Kerala (3.6)	Maharashtra (12.7)	Haryana (22.4)	Madhya Pradesh (32.6)
	Tamil Nadu (13.0)	INDIA (22.5)	
	West Bengal (15.0)	Bihar (22.9)	
	Karnataka (16.7)	Assam (27.5)	
	Himachal Pradesh (16.7)	Rajasthan (27.7)	
	Punjab (16.8)	Orissa (29.0)	
	Andhra Pradesh (18.1)	Uttar Pradesh (29.6)	
	Gujarat (19.6)		

Source: Sample Registration System.
Note: Data for 16 bigger states given here.

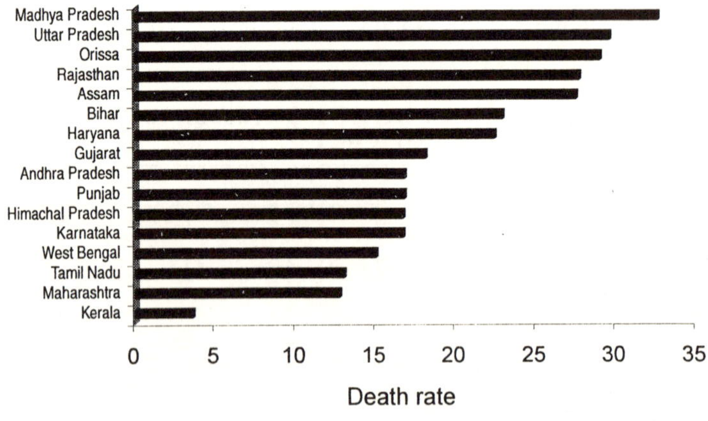

FIG. 2.8: AGE SPECIFIC DEATH RATE AGE GROUP 0–4 YEARS IN STATES, 1998.

death rate in Kerala was 19.7. In 1998, seven states had 0–4 years age specific mortality rate higher than the rate in Kerala in 1975. Figure 2.8 shows in graphic form the relative situation in different states.

CAUSATIVE FACTORS

There are several factors, both medical and non-medical, which affect early childhood mortality. Some of these operate with greater intensity at the perinatal, neonatal, and post neonatal stages.

CAUSES OF PERINATAL, NEONATAL, AND INFANT MORTALITY

Data from hospital based studies in different parts of the country indicate that the most important causes of perinatal and neonatal mortality, often referred to as biological causes, are macerated still births, immaturity-low birth weight, birth asphyxia trauma, congenital malformation, and infection. The relative contribution of each of these and other factors have, however, varied in different studies. (Bhat and Ravikumara 1996; ICMR 1990 b and c; Singh et al. 1988; Singh et al. 1991; Singh and Paul 1988). Respiratory infections and diarrhoeal diseases are important causes of infant morbidity and mortality. The contribution of tetanus and other infections has come down in recent years due to wider coverage of mothers and infants under the maternal and child health services and the universal immunization programme.

The trail of occurrence of these causes leads to the health and nutrition status of the pregnant woman, for it is in her womb that the foetus grows and the outcome of pregnancy is primarily determined. Among the factors which are likely to affect adversely the pregnancy outcome are maternal malnutrition, pregnancy at very young age or late age, low body weight, high parity (birth order more than four), short birth interval (less than 18 to 24 months), and complicated obstetric history. These, in turn, are affected by socio-economic and environmental factors like poverty, occupation, illiteracy, ignorance of nutritional needs during pregnancy, age at marriage, practice of contraception, environmental sanitation and hygiene, and access to safe drinking water. The availability, accessibility, and use of obstetric, antenatal, and neonatal care facilities, the quality of services provided, early registration of pregnancy, iron and folic acid supplementation during pregnancy, selection of high risk cases for hospital delivery, facility for transfer of such cases to the hospital in good time, and safe delivery practices in non-hospital settings help greatly to moderate the effect of the adverse socio-economic situation in which the mother is placed and reduce the incidence of maternal mortality, still births, miscarriage, and neonatal mortality. We shall consider later in the text some of the factors in greater detail.

CAUSES OF EARLY CHILDHOOD MORTALITY AND MORBIDITY

In 1979, the Registrar General conducted a countrywide survey on infant and child mortality. The cause of death as reported by the respondent was noted for each age. The survey found water borne diseases and respiratory infections to be the predominant causes of death among children of age 1–5 years, while among infants tetanus, pre-maturity, and respiratory infections were the primary causes.

Data on causes of death are also available from micro-studies, mainly hospital based. These indicate that diarrhoeal diseases, respiratory infections, and nutritional deficiencies are the most important causes of morbidity and mortality. Among the vaccine preventable diseases, tuberculosis, poliomyelitis, measles, and typhoid are prominent causes. In the newborn, neonatal infections, low birth weight, and pre-maturity are the important causes (Awasthi et al. 1996; Deivanayagam et al. 1987; Reddaiah et al. 1988). There is, however, a lack of data on morbidity patterns in different parts of the country. This is a major lacunae which remains unmet.

LOW BIRTHWEIGHT

Birthweight is an important indicator of chances of survival of the infant and its likely pace of physical growth and development. It is also a useful indicator of maternal health and nutrition status, the state of maternal and child health services, and extent of their use by pregnant women. Often low birthweight babies (birthweight less than 2,500 g.) are malnourished and hence more vulnerable to a variety of infections. Studies have shown that a large percentage of low birthweight babies are born pre-term (Trivedi and Mavlankar 1986). However, even when they are full term infants they are often small for gestational age, indicating intrauterine growth retardation due to poor maternal health and nutrition during pregnancy (Gopalan 1994). The incidence of mortality, particularly perinatal and neonatal deaths, increases when the birthweight is very low (Aras et al. 1990; Ghosh et al. 1979; ICMR 1990b, c; Kaushik et al. 1998; Singh 1986).

An ICMR Task Force collaborative study in 1982–3 of high risk pregnancies and maternal mortality, based on 43,550 women admitted in ten teaching hospitals in different parts of the country, indicated that 26.0 per cent of the new born babies had a birthweight less than 2,500 g. (14.6 per cent below 2,250 g. and 11.4 per cent between 2,250 and 2,499 g.). In 6.8 per cent of babies, the birthweight was below 2,000 g. Low birthweight was found to be more prevalent in babies with mothers of age less than 20 years or more than 35 years, illiterate mothers, and mothers with history of abortion and short birth interval, the factors being more apparent in the case of babies weighing less than 2,250 g. Among working women labourers, too, a large number of new born babies had low birthweight. Among the babies who died during hospital stay, 80.1 per cent were low birthweight, 75.2 per cent weighing less than 2,250 g. (ICMR 1990b).

A five year (1981–5) review of patients of severe anaemia admitted as emergency cases in the labour room in Medical College Hospital, Rohtak indicated that the incidence of low birthweight babies was 61.4 per cent, perinatal deaths were 46.8 per cent, and pre-term deliveries 41.1 per cent (Rathee et al. 1987). Other studies, too, have reported a higher incidence of low birthweight where mothers have poor nutritional status (Gattani and Nimale 1998).

The National Health Policy of 1983 had stated that in India 30 per cent of babies born were of low birthweight. The targets set for reduction of incidence of low birthweight were 25 per cent in 1985, 18 per cent in 1990, and 10 per cent in 2000. However, no countrywide study was conducted to find out the percentage of low birthweight babies in 1985 and 1990, and no data collection system was established to monitor the progress made. No mechanism was put in place even to collect birthweight data from institutional births, assuming there were problems in collecting community based figures. The National Family Health Survey in 1992–3 reported that 79 per cent infants were not weighed at birth. Of the babies whose birthweight was known, 26 per cent babies were found to be of low birthweight, that is, less than 2,500 g. (IIPS 1995). The second National Family Health Survey (NFHS-2) in 1998–9 reported that

70 per cent of the babies were not weighed at birth. Among the babies whose birthweight was known, 23 per cent weighed less than 2,500 g. (IIPS 2000). Thus, the target for 1990 was far from being reached even in 1998–9. Micro-studies carried out in different parts of the country, mostly hospital based, have indicated rates between 19 to 40 per cent (Gattani and Nimale 1998; Hirve and Ganatra 1994; ICMR 1990 b and c, 1994; Makhija et al. 1989). Areas that were well served by maternal and child health services, where a large percentage of pregnant women received good quality antenatal care and nutritional supplementation, and had hospital deliveries, were found to have a lower incidence of low birthweight babies (Antonisamy et al. 1994; Prasad, Rao and Sujatha 1994). The incidence of low birthweight babies among poor pregnant women living in urban slums was found to be higher than the national estimate of 30 per cent (Patel 1989). Apart from medical factors and the extent of availability and quality of maternal and child health services and degree of their use, socio-economic factors such as economic class, occupation, literacy level, age, parity, and birth interval have been found to influence the infant's birthweight.

Low birthweight, especially when the weight is below 2,000 g., imperils the infant's chances of survival when neonatal care facilities of a high order are not available, which is the case for the bulk of the population in both rural and urban areas. The reduction in incidence of low birthweight would depend upon achieving the long term goals of improving the health and nutrition status of the mothers, as well as their socio-economic status. As a short term goal, far better coverage of pregnant women in rural areas and urban slums by antenatal and post-natal care services, early registration of pregnancy, identification of high risk mothers, monitoring their cases, and providing health care services could contribute to a lowering of the incidence of low birthweight babies, while good neonatal care services would improve the chances of their survival.

Maternal Malnutrition

Maternal malnutrition, as reflected in deficiency of iron folic acid, vitamin B-12, and protein, has been and continues to be an area of great concern. From the public health point of view, the most dominant factor is iron deficiency anaemia. An ICMR Task Force Study in eleven states reported that 87.6 per cent pregnant women were anaemic with haemoglobin level below 11 grams/decilitre. In

72 per cent, the g/dl level was below 10, and in 12.6 per cent below 7. It also commented that the prevalence of anaemia during the last three decades has not significantly decreased (ICMR 1989b). Some micro-studies on rural pregnant women have reported similar results (Agarwal, Agarwal and Tripathi 1987; Koen et al. 1992). Another ICMR Task Force Study on high risk pregnancies covering ten teaching hospitals found that the haemoglobin level at the time of admission was less than or equal to 8 g/dl in the case of 4.9 per cent women and less than 10 g/dl in the case of 33.6 per cent women (ICMR 1990c).

The National Family Health Survey, 1998–9 (NFHS-2) reported 36 per cent of ever married women aged 15–49 years with a body mass index below 18.5 indicating a high prevalence of nutritional deficiency. It also found 52 per cent (54 per cent rural women, 46 per cent urban women) with same degree of anaemia (haemoglobin level less than 11 g/dl in the case of pregnant women and less than 12 g/dl in the case of others). There were large interstate variations. Kerala had the lowest percentage of ever married women 15–49 years with anaemia (23 per cent), while in states like Assam, Bihar, Orissa, and West Bengal the percentage was more than 60 (IIPS 2000).

Prevalence of anaemia among Indian females is very high even in adolescence. Many women do not have adequate iron stores when they become pregnant. Anaemia aggravates complications during pregnancy and adversely effects the perinatal outcome in the form of low birthweight, perinatal and neonatal mortality and maternal mortality (Bhat and Ravikumara 1996; Rathee et al. 1987; Roy and Chakravorty 1992).

Severe anaemia is a serious health hazard. Moderate anaemia, too, can cause complications. Anaemia is caused primarily because of insufficient intake of food containing essential nutrients. Iron and folic rich foods often do not find a place in the diet due to poverty, non-availability ignorance and food habits. Even during pregnancy, most poor mothers do not get the additional food and nutrients they need for the healthy growth of the foetus. Added to this is the hard labour that poor women have to put in even in the last days of pregnancy and the need to resume work soon thereafter. Hookworm infestation has also been found to contribute to iron deficiency among rural pregnant women (Koen et al. 1992).

The Government of India launched the National Nutritional Anaemia Prophylaxis Programme (NNAPP) in 1970 to provide iron folic acid supplements to pregnant and lactating women, and children between one and eleven years of age. A comprehensive evaluation in eleven states in 1984–6 reported a dismal picture of implementation of the programme. The survey indicated that 89.3 per cent women in the second trimester, 76.5 per cent women in the third trimester, and 50.6 per cent women at full term had not received any supplement. Overall, 80.2 per cent women did not receive supplementation. There was no difference in mean haemoglobin level between the women with supplementation and without supplementation. Supplementation had made no impact in combating anaemia. The actual delivery of the tablets to the pregnant women was woefully short of the actual target population, and even those who received the tablets did not get adequate supply. Beneficiaries who received the supplements were lower in number than what was shown in the records. Drop-outs occurred due to non-supply of supplements and irregular supply. Low coverage, high rate of discontinuation of supplements, poor quality of tablets, and unsatisfactory state of health service adversely affected the impact of the programme. The educational component received inadequate attention. The medical officer did not have proper knowledge of the programme. Most of the auxiliary nurse midwives (ANMs) were not well aware of the programme. The supply of drugs was not very regular, and the quality of the tablets was found to be very poor on analysis (ICMR 1989 b).

A subsequent evaluation of the programme in 1990–1 in four states indicated the possibility of inadequate doses to beneficiaries, lower potency of the tablets, deficiency in supplies, poor storage facilities, shortcomings in information, education and communication material, and weaknesses in monitoring. It was also observed that 40 per cent of the iron folic acid tablets distributed were not consumed by the beneficiaries (Kapil, Saxena and Nayar 1996).

Further evidence of unsatisfactory performance of the programme is evident from the National Family Health Survey 1992–3, which indicated that in only 50 per cent of the live births during the previous four years did the mothers receive iron folic acid. Here, too, urban women were better served - 68.7 per cent mothers in urban areas as compared to 45.1 per cent in rural areas. The National Family Health Survey 1998–9 (NFHS-2) carried out six years later reported that in the case of only 58 per cent live births in the country in the three years preceding the survey were iron folic acid tablets or syrup received by mothers. The percentage of such mothers in urban areas was 75.7 and in rural areas 52.5. For a programme which has been in existence for nearly three decades, the coverage thus continues to be poor.

Teenage Marriage and Pregnancy

Teenage marriage leads to teenage pregnancies, which put both the mother and the foetus at risk. The National Family Health Survey 1998–9 reported that of the currently married women aged 15–19 years, 52.2 per cent had no child ever born, 34.8 per cent had one child ever born, and 13.0 per cent had two or more children ever born (IIPS 2000). Sample Registration System data for 1998 indicate that the 15–19 year age specific marital fertility rate is very high, at 220. The outcome of teenage pregnancies, especially when accompanied by lack of antenatal care, access to referral services, and moderate to severe anaemia, tends to enhance perinatal mortality, birth of underweight babies, and maternal mortality and morbidity. The national survey of infant and child mortality in 1979 by the Registrar General reported a far higher rate of infant mortality in both urban and rural areas when the age of marriage was below 18 years (Registrar General 1983).

Age at marriage, which is strongly influenced by socio-cultural factors, needs to be raised if teenage pregnancies, and the consequent risks to the mother and the child, are to be reduced. A welcome feature is that age at marriage has been progressively rising in India in both rural and urban areas, though at a rather slow rate. This is evident from a perusal of the percentage of females aged 10–14 years who are married as reported by successive censuses. The incidence of married women in the 10–14 year age group has come down considerably, and was only 4.5 per cent in 1991. Even then, the 1991 census indicated 2.11 million married girls aged 10–14 years in the country (excluding Jammu & Kashmir). In the 15–19 year age group, however, the percentage of married women in 1991 was 35.3 (40.7 per cent in rural areas and 21.3 per cent in urban areas). Even though this is lower than the 1981 figure of 43.4 per cent (48.8 per cent in rural areas and 28.1 per cent in urban areas), it is still very high. In numbers it meant 12.98 million married females aged 15–19 years in 1991 (excluding Jammu & Kashmir). In 1991, 79 per cent of married females aged 10–14 years and 64 per cent of married females aged 15–19 years in India were in the five states of Andhra Pradesh, Bihar, Madhya Pradesh, Rajasthan and Uttar Pradesh.

The 1991 Census reported that in the case of 45 per cent currently married women who married during 1986-91, the age at marriage was below 18 years. Among the bigger states, the highest percentage was in Bihar (65.8 per cent), followed by Rajasthan (60.7 per cent), Madhya Pradesh (59.7 per cent), Andhra Pradesh (58.3 per cent) and Uttar Pradesh (55.9 per cent).

The chief factors which lead to early marriage of girls are family and caste tradition, local custom, illiteracy/low level of literacy of the parents, little or no schooling of the girl, desire to reduce the cost of marriage by performing two or more marriages together, and lower dowry when both the boy and the girl are very young. It is also believed by many parents that the earlier the girl gets married the better it is since it will be easier for the girl to adjust in the husband's family, apart from relieving the parents of a primary duty as early as possible. At some places like Rajasthan and Madhya Pradesh, a large number of child marriages take place on days considered auspicious, as, for instance, *Akha Teej*.

The law on minimum age at marriage (18 years in the case of girls and 21 years in the case of boys) has not had much impact as a large number of parents do not seem to be aware of it, particularly parents who are illiterate or have low levels of literacy. The National Family Health Survey 1992–3 reported that two-thirds of married women aged 13–49 years did not know correctly the legal minimum age of marriage of girls, while 80.2 per cent did not know it correctly in the case of boys. The percentage was much higher in rural areas—three-fourths did not know the correct legal age in the case of girls and 87.0 per cent in the case of boys. Clearly, publicity of provisions of the Child Marriage Restraint Act is poor. Enforcement is virtually non-existent. Even though millions of girls in the country are married before they attain the age of 18 years, the number of cases registered under the Act in the country in the six year period 1994–9 was only 391 (NCRB 2001).

Antenatal Care

Antenatal care is a key factor in child survival and safe motherhood. It plays an important role in improving the nutrition and health status of the mother during pregnancy, in promoting the healthy development of the foetus, and in the pregnancy outcome, thereby reducing maternal mortality and morbidity, and perinatal, neonatal, and post-neonatal mortality and morbidity. Its important components are antenatal check-up from the first trimester of pregnancy, administering iron and folic acid tablets to pregnant women for tackling anaemia, giving tetanus toxoid injections to protect against tetanus infection of the mother and the neonate, advising the mother about food, nutrition, and other matters related to pregnancy, and safe delivery through trained midwife or other health professional. Antenatal check-up helps in early identification of high risk pregnancies and timely referral services which are key elements of a public health system that aims at safe pregnancy outcome and survival of mother and child.

The national review of universal immunization programme in 1989 by the National Institute of Health and Family Welfare reported that in 35 study units out of 43, more than 50 per cent pregnant women reported some contact with health personnel during the antenatal period, and in 22 study units the percentage was more than 75. In 35 study units, more than 50 per cent pregnant women received two doses of tetanus toxoid vaccine booster dose. This included 18 study units where the percentage was more than 75 per cent. There were, however, considerable interstate and inter-district variations. Bihar, Rajasthan, and Uttar Pradesh were the low performing states, while Kerala and Tamil Nadu were the high performing ones (Gupta and Murali 1989).

The National Family Health Survey 1992–3 and 1998–9 give more detailed information on coverage. The data given in Table 2.20 show that in rural areas more than two-fifths of pregnancies were not covered by antenatal care visits in 1992–3. In 1998–9, there was only marginal improvement in the situation. The coverage of TT2, however, has shown an improvement between 1992–3 and 1998–9 in both rural and urban areas. The situation was somewhat better in urban areas. The National Health Policy 1983 had set the target of 60 to 75 per cent mothers receiving antenatal care by 1990, and 100 per cent by 2000. The actual achievement, thus, falls far short of this goal. The National Health Policy 1983 had set the target of 100 per cent women being covered by TT vaccine in 1990. The National Family Health Survey 1992–3 found that only 54 per cent live births were covered by two or more doses of TT to the mother (48 per cent in rural areas and 74 per cent in urban areas). The National Family Health Survey 1998–9 found the coverage to be 67 per cent (63 per cent in rural areas and 82 per cent in urban areas), far short of the target set by the National Health Policy 1983.

There is considerable interstate variation in the extent of reach of

TABLE 2.20: PERCENTAGE OF LIVE BIRTHS BY NUMBER OF ANTENATAL CARE VISITS AND NUMBER OF TETANUS TOXOID INJECTIONS DURING PREGNANCY, INDIA, 1992–3 AND 1998–9

Year	Area	No. of antenatal care visits						No. of tetanus toxoid injections during pregnancy				
		None	1	2–3	4+	Don't know/ missing	Total	None	One	Two or more	Don't know/ missing	Total
1992–3	Rural	42.4	6.7	28.9	21.0	0.9	100	44.7	7.4	47.7	0.1	100
NFHS–1	Urban	17.8	4.1	30.7	46.9	0.5	100	19.4	6.0	74.4	0.3	100
	Total	36.8	6.1	29.3	26.9	0.8	100	39.0	7.1	53.8	0.2	100
1998–9	Rural	39.8	8.8	28.3	22.4	0.8	100	28.2	8.5	62.5	0.8	100
NFHS–2	Urban	13.6	6.0	25.0	54.7	0.7	100	9.9	7.3	81.9	1.0	100
	Total	34.0	8.2	27.6	29.5	0.7	100	24.1	8.2	66.8	0.8	100

Sources: National Family Health Survey, 1992–3.
National Family Health Survey, 1998–9.

Note: In NFHS–1, data relate to live births during the four years preceding the survey. In NFHS–2, they relate to live births during the three years preceding the survey.

antenatal care services. Table 2.21 gives the percentage of live births in various states in the three years preceding the National Family Health Survey in 1998–9 for which mothers received at least one antenatal check-up, at least two doses of TT, and iron and folic acid for three or more months.

The national review of immunization programme, the National Family Health Survey 1992–3, and micro-studies which enquired into reasons for not utilizing antenatal care services or incomplete immunization found that the more prominent among them were lack of awareness of the need, lack of information, and deficiencies in the delivery system (inconvenient place, timings, and distance; absence of vaccinator; and non-availability of vaccine).

Medical Attention at Delivery

Proper medical attention at delivery is a critical factor for safe motherhood and child survival, particularly when antenatal care has not been received or only partly received. India has a high incidence of maternal mortality and morbidity. The National Family Health Survey 1998–9 had estimated the maternal mortality rate (MMR) to be 540 maternal deaths per 100,000 live births. The Sample Registration

TABLE 2.21: EXTENT OF ANTENATAL CARE IN PREGNANCY IN STATES, 1998–9

Percentage of live births during the three years preceding the survey for which mothers received at least one antenatal check-up during pregnancy	Percentage of live births during the three years preceding the survey for which mothers received at least two doses of tetanus toxoid injections during pregnancy	Percentage of live births during the three years preceding the survey for which mothers received iron folic acid tablets or syrup for three or more months during pregnancy
Uttar Pradesh (34.6)	Uttar Pradesh (51.4)	Bihar (19.8)
Bihar (36.3)	Assam (51.7)	Uttar Pradesh (20.6)
Rajasthan (47.5)	Rajasthan (52.1)	Rajasthan (30.6)
Haryana (58.1)	Madhya Pradesh (55.0)	Madhya Pradesh (38.4)
Assam (60.1)	Bihar (57.8)	Assam (45.3)
Madhya Pradesh (61.0)	Himachal Pradesh (66.2)	Haryana (53.3)
Punjab (74.0)	Gujarat (72.7)	West Bengal (56.4)
Orissa (79.5)	Orissa (74.3)	Orissa (62.2)
Karnataka (86.3)	Karnataka (74.9)	Punjab (64.2)
Gujarat (86.4)	Maharashtra (74.9)	Gujarat (66.6)
Himachal Pradesh (86.8)	Haryana (79.7)	Andhra Pradesh (70.7)
West Bengal (90.0)	Andhra Pradesh (81.5)	Himachal Pradesh (70.9)
Maharashtra (90.4)	West Bengal (82.4)	Maharashtra (71.6)
Andhra Pradesh (92.7)	Kerala (86.4)	Karnataka (74.2)
Tamil Nadu (98.5)	Punjab (89.9)	Tamil Nadu (84.1)
Kerala (98.8)	Tamil Nadu (95.4)	Kerala (88.6)

Source: National Family Health Survey, 1998–9.

Note: Data relate to live births during the three years preceding the survey for 16 bigger states.

The states have been arranged in ascending order of coverage. Figure in brackets gives the percentage.

System estimated the MMR to be 407 in 1998. Due to large sampling error, the confidence intervals for these estimates are wide. In India, safe delivery, particularly in rural areas, is still a major problem area. Sample Registration System data for 1998 indicate that only one-fourth of the deliveries were institutional while 29 per cent were attended by trained professionals in non-institutional settings (see Table 2.22). A very high percentage of deliveries continue to be in the hands of untrained professionals and others (*dais* that is, traditional birth attendants, and others, etc.) in rural areas. Though there has been some progress since 1970, the position is still far from satisfactory, particularly in the rural areas where 54 per cent of the deliveries in 1998 were in the hands of untrained professionals and others.

The National Health Policy 1983 had set the target of 80 per cent

TABLE 2.22: PERCENTAGE DISTRIBUTION OF LIVE BIRTHS BY TYPE OF MEDICAL ATTENTION AT DELIVERY, INDIA, 1970 AND 1998

Area	Year	Type of medical attention at delivery			
		Institutional	Trained professional (doctor, nurse, or trained midwife)	Untrained professional (traditional birth attendant)	Relatives or others
Rural	1970	4.2	8.1	61.8	25.9
	1998	18.0	28.2	49.2	4.6
Urban	1970	28.3	21.5	37.0	13.2
	1998	59.6	31.4	7.6	1.4
All areas	1970	10.3	11.4	55.6	22.7
	1998	25.4	28.8	41.8	4.1

Source: Sample Registration System.
Note: Institutional refers to delivery at hospital, maternity home, nursing home, and health centre. Trained professional refers to delivery attended at home by doctor, trained *dai*, trained midwife, trained nurse, etc. Untrained professional refers to delivery by untrained traditional birth attendant (*dai*).

deliveries by trained birth attendants in 1990 and 100 per cent in the year 2000. The target reached in 1998 was only 54 per cent, as the data in Table 2.22 show. In urban areas, however, the coverage was 91 per cent as compared to 46 per cent in rural areas, indicating a very wide difference in access to safe delivery between rural and urban areas. More than half the deliveries that take place in rural India continue to face risk. It is evident, therefore, that the public health care system has only partially met the safe motherhood needs of rural women, even five decades after independence.

There is considerable interstate variation in the percentage of

TABLE 2.23: PERCENTAGE OF LIVE BIRTHS DELIVERED BY UNTRAINED PROFESSIONALS AND OTHERS IN STATES, 1998

Percentage			
Less than 20	20–39	40–59	60 and above
Kerala (1.0)	Karnataka (24.7)	INDIA (45.9)	Orissa (62.2)
Punjab (1.3)	Gujarat (25.4)	Himachal Pradesh (49.1)	Assam (62.8)
Haryana (7.3)	Andhra Pradesh (29.5)	West Bengal (49.9)	Madhya Pradesh (63.2)
Tamil Nadu (13.7)	Maharashtra (31.6)	Uttar Pradesh (50.2)	Bihar (65.2)
			Rajasthan (65.8)

Source: Sample Registration System.
Note: Date for 16 bigger states given here.

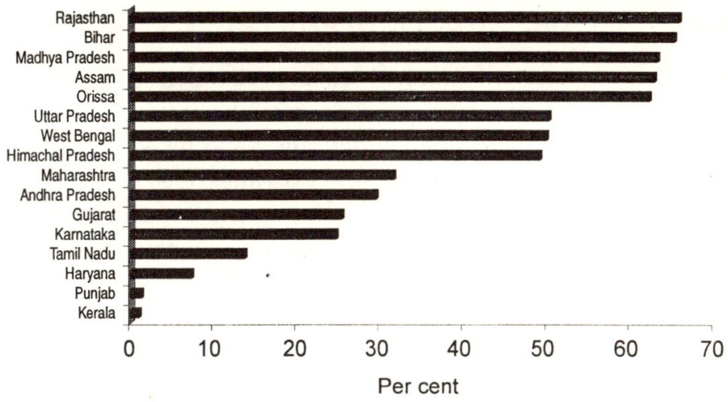

FIG. 2.9: PERCENTAGE OF LIVE BIRTHS DELIVERED BY UNTRAINED PROFESSIONALS AND OTHERS IN STATES, 1998.

deliveries attended by untrained functionaries, as is evident from Table 2.23. In the states of Rajasthan, Bihar, Madhya Pradesh, Orissa, and Assam, the percentage of such deliveries exceeded 60 in 1998. Kerala and Punjab have been able to achieve a very high percentage of deliveries in trained hands, the percentage of babies delivered under untrained functionaries being less than 2. Figure 2.9 brings out the comparative situation in rural and urban areas of states in graphic form.

States where a large percentage of births are attended by untrained functionaries tend to have a higher IMR (see Table 2.24).

TABLE 2.24: DISTRIBUTION OF STATES BY IMR AND PERCENTAGE OF DELIVERIES ATTENDED BY UNTRAINED FUNCTIONARY, 1998

IMR	Percentage of deliveries by untrained functionary			
(1998)	< 20	20–39	40–59	60+
<20	Kerala			
40–59	Punjab Tamil Nadu	Karnataka Maharashtra	West Bengal	
60–79	Haryana	Andhra Pradesh Gujarat	Himachal Pradesh	Assam Bihar
80+			Uttar Pradesh	Madhya Pradesh Orissa, Rajasthan

Source: Sample Registration System.
Note: Data for 16 bigger states given here.

Some Other Factors Associated with IMR

The level of education of women in the reproductive age groups has been found to have a close association with the presence of a more favourable environment for maternal and child health. Education promotes better preventive health practices and much greater use of maternal and child health services. In India, the same trends are discernible. States that have a higher percentage of women aged 20–44 years with level of education primary and above tend to have a lower IMR. This is evident from Table 2.25 which shows higher IMR (1998) in states which have a low percentage of women in the 20–44 year age group with primary and above level of education.

Poverty, too, is a contributory factor of high IMR as it is often associated with illiteracy, bad living conditions, high fertility, poor health and nutrition status, and low utilization of maternal and child health services. The relationship between poverty and IMR is evident from Table 2.26 which gives the percentage of population below the poverty line (1999–2000) and the IMR (1998) in the 16 bigger states. Some states continue to have high IMR despite a low percentage of population below the poverty line.

TABLE 2.25: DISTRIBUTION OF STATES BY IMR, 1998 AND PERCENTAGE OF WOMEN AGED 20–44 YEARS WITH LEVEL OF EDUCATION PRIMARY AND ABOVE 1991

IMR (1998)	Percentage of women 20–44 years with level of education primary and above				
	15–24	25–34	35–44	45–54	55+
<20					Kerala
40–59		Karnataka	Maharashtra Tamil Nadu West Bengal	Punjab	
60–79	Andhra Pradesh Bihar	Assam Haryana	Gujarat Himachal Pradesh		
80–99	Madhya Pradesh Orissa Rajasthan Uttar Pradesh				

Source: SRS for IMR, *Census of India, 1991* for level of education.
Note: Data for 16 bigger states given here.

TABLE 2.26: DISTRIBUTION OF STATES BY IMR, 1998 AND POPULATION BELOW POVERTY LINE, 1999–2000

IMR (1998)	Percentage of population below poverty line				
	< 15	15–24	25–34	35–44	45+
< 20	Kerala				
40–59	Punjab	Karnataka Tamil Nadu	Maharashtra West Bengal		
60–79	Gujarat Haryana Himachal Pradesh	Andhra Pradesh		Assam Bihar	
80+		Rajasthan	Uttar Pradesh	Madhya Pradesh	Orissa

Source: Planning Commission for poverty estimates; Sample Registration System for IMR.
Note: Data for 16 bigger states given here.

Too many births at close intervals contribute to high IMR, especially since high fertility affects the health and nutrition status of the mother. Table 2.27 gives the relationship between the IMR 1998 and the birth rate 1998 in the 16 bigger states.

TABLE 2.27: DISTRIBUTION OF STATES BY IMR AND BIRTH RATE, 1998

IMR (1998)	Birth rate (1998)			
	< 20	20–4	25–9	30+
< 20	Kerala			
40–59	Tamil Nadu	Karnataka Maharashtra Punjab West Bengal		
60–79		Andhra Pradesh Himachal Pradesh	Assam Gujarat Haryana	Bihar
80+			Orissa	Madhya Pradesh Rajasthan Uttar Pradesh

Source: Sample Registration System.
Note: Data for 16 bigger states given here.

DIARRHOEAL DISEASES

Diarrhoea is a major public health problem relating to children. Frequent episodes of diarrhoea cause malnutrition and make the child susceptible to other diseases through reduced body resistance. The 1979 national survey of infant and child mortality by the Registrar General indicated that diarrhoea was one of the major causes of post neonatal and early childhood mortality and morbidity (Registrar General 1983). An ICMR multi-centre study in 1983–5 covering rural and urban centres, too, found diarrhoea to be a leading cause of post neonatal mortality [ICMR 1990c).

In 1985, a national survey of diarrhoeal diseases among children aged under 5 years by the National Institute of Communicable Diseases (NICD) showed that the median biweekly incidence rate during the post-monsoon period September to October was 5.8 per cent in urban areas, 6.1 per cent in urban slums, and 18.0 per cent in rural areas. It found diarrhoea to be an important cause of childhood mortality, and observed that a child aged under 5 years in rural areas has more than two times the risk of not surviving than his counterpart in urban slum areas (NICD 1986). A subsequent survey by the NICD from December 1987 to March 1988 indicated a previous two week incidence rate of 12.7 per cent in the case of infants and 6.3 per cent in the case of children aged 1–4 years, giving a combined rate of 7.5 per cent for children aged under 5 years (NICD 1988). The annual number of episodes in different study centres varied from 1.0 to 4.1, the median being 1.8 (NICD 1988).

A national survey of diarrhoea in February 1987 in rural India reported 28 per cent children aged under 5 years having loose motions during the previous two weeks, and 48 per cent during the previous two months (Viswanathan and Rohde 1990).

A later survey in 1992 by IMRB carried out in 15 districts (one from each state), covering both rural and urban areas, indicated a previous two week incidence rate varying from 8.4 per cent in Mysore to 30.9 in Medinipur among children aged under 5 years. It was higher in rural than in urban areas. The survey found that the incidence rate tended to decline with age—children aged 3 years plus but less than 5 years accounted for less than one-fifth of diarrhoea cases. It also found more male children suffering from diarrhoea, due perhaps to a larger incidence of intake of unprotected food and water due to greater mobility, or better reporting due to greater concern for the health of the male child (IMRB 1993).

The National Family Health Survey 1992–3 reported a previous two week incidence rate of 10 per cent during the same period. There were, however, considerable interstate variations. This, survey, too, found the incidence to decline with age. The incidence was higher among children aged 6–11 months. However, unlike the IMRB study, NFHS found hardly any gender difference (male children incidence rate was 10.3 per cent while for female children it was 9.8). Like the IMRB study, it found a higher incidence in rural areas, but the difference was small (rural 10.4, urban 8.8). The incidence rate declined when level of education of mother of the child was middle school/high school and above (IIPS 1995).

Apart from the national survey, several micro-studies, too, have reported diarrhoea as a major health problem in urban slums and rural communities, and a leading cause of morbidity, with children suffering several episodes per year (Agarwal et al. 1986; Gupta et al. 1998; Sen Gupta et al. 1997; WWCDN 1995). The attack rate in diseases like cholera has been found to be much higher in the case of children. A study of 75 gastroenteritis deaths that occurred in 22 major hospitals in Delhi during 1990 to 1992 showed that nearly half the deaths were of infants and three-fourth of the deaths were of children aged less than 5 years, including infants. Dehydration was the most immediate cause of death (44 per cent), followed by septicemia (28 per cent). Malnutrition was the most common associated cause. The majority of deaths occurred among persons living in slum areas (Kumar et al. 1994).

Among the causes which figure prominently in the occurrence of diarrhoea and other water-borne diseases is non-availability of safe water in adequate quantity. The 1991 Census reported that 55.5 per cent rural households and 81.4 per cent urban households had access to safe drinking water, that is, water supplied from a tap or a hand-pump/tube well situated within or outside the premises. The National Family Health Survey 1998–9 has shown an improvement. The assumption, however, that the source makes the water safe is not necessarily true as the source could and does get contaminated at times by biological and chemical pollutants. Underground as well as surface water in many parts of the country has been contaminated by hazardous industrial wastes, pesticides, and chemical pollutants, and has become an important causative factor in disease

The study in 1992 by IMRB showed a wide variation in the percentage of households having access to safe water (taps/hand-pumps/

tube-wells). The open well, a traditional but unsafe source, was a major source of drinking water for a large percentage of households. Pond and river water was normally used for washing, bathing and other activities. There was seasonal variation in the use of water source for various purposes. Also, more than one source is used in some rural areas (IMRB 1993).

Statistics on the percentage of households having safe drinking water tend to be deceptive and are usually compiled on the basis of lay reporting of source of water, and then categorized as safe or unsafe depending on the source. In rural areas, particularly, water samples are not taken to test for potability. Contamination of drinking water wells and ponds is caused when environmental sanitation and hygiene are poor, open space is used for defecation, and there is indiscriminate disposal of excreta of infants, with the result that any overflow of surface water during the rainy season mixes with the water in wells and ponds and makes the water unsafe. Studies on quality of drinking water in wells in rural areas have indicated contamination from faecal coliform and others agents (Agarwal et al. 1986). Contamination of drinking water in wells, handpumps, or even taps in the summer months and the rainy season is a regular feature. Outbreak of diarrhoeal diseases, including gastroenteritis, due to contamination of drinking water has been reported from Delhi and other cities at fairly regular intervals, particularly during May to September. Water from shallow handpumps, dug near garbage dumps or cesspools of dirty water, and water from taps get contaminated when leaking water pipes are near sewage water.

Ensuring supply of safe water is only one part of the problem. There is always the risk of its contamination when it is being collected or in storage in the house. Several studies have shown that water quality deteriorates when it is not properly stored (Agarwal et al. 1986; Bandopadhyaya et al. 1992; Datta, et al. 1993; Ghosh et al. 1997; Gupta, Murali and Seth 1998). Risks arise due to unclean water container, the way the container is covered, place where the container is kept, extent of use of separate ladle for taking out water, and contact with unclean hands, particularly after using the toilet. Washing hands with soap or ash before eating, before cooking or while serving or feeding, and better personal and domestic hygiene reduces considerably the chances of infection.

Absence of toilet facilities, defecation in the open, and poor personal hygiene are important contibutory factors to diarrhoeal diseases. The 1991 Census reported only 9.5 per cent rural households having toilet facilities. In the case of urban households, the percentage was 63.9. In urban slums, the state of public toilet facilities is dismal. Defecation in the open is common, creating insanitary conditions, thus providing fertile ground for the spread of diseases. Small children tend to defecate close to the house or just outside the compound. Most mothers throw the infant's excreta at some spot near the house, some dispose it in the drain, while some leave it as it is if the defecation is not inside or too near the house. Washing hands with soap or ash after disposing of children's faeces is uncommon.

Awareness of mothers of the causes of diarrhoea of children, particularly in urban slums and rural areas, is poor. Some mothers associate it with teething and the evil eye. The importance of personal hygiene, use of toilets for defecation, and washing of hands with soap or ash after defecation and before eating, cooking, serving food or feeding is either not understood or not taken seriously, especially by illiterate or semi-literate women from poor households. Some mothers tend to reduce the consumption of fluids by children on the assumption that this would reduce the watery discharge. Food consumption is reduced in the belief that the child is incapable of normal digestion. The resultant dehydration and underfeeding affects the child's health and exposes him to risk. Fortunately, the importance of feeding the child and giving adequate liquids is now much better understood, due to sustained campaigns launched through the mass media and health personnel.

Recognizing that diarrhoea is a major contributor to early childhood mortality and morbidity, the Government of India launched in 1986 an oral rehydration therapy programme to prevent diarrhoea associated deaths among children due to dehydration. Under this programme, the use of Oral Rehydration Solution (ORS) is promoted as the first line of treatment by: (i) creating awareness among mothers through mass media, video shows, mothers' meetings; (ii) training of medical and paramedical personnel and mothers; (iii) instructing mothers on the preparation and use of home made solution from sugar, salt, and water; and (iv) ORS supplies (oral rehydration salt packets). Thus, the strategy is to reduce mortality through improved management of diarrhoeal cases in the home and at health facilities, both public and private. Surveillance of outbreak of gastroenteritis and cholera is done through regular reporting of all such cases by hospitals. Some benefits have accrued from the programme, as is evident from lower hospital admission, bed occupancy, and mortality due to diarrhoea.

A national survey of diarrhoea in rural India in 1987 showed considerable inter-state variation in regard to awareness of ORS, ranging from 8 per cent in Karnataka and 11 per cent in Orissa to 40 per cent in Tamil Nadu and 47 per cent in Kerala. Knowledge about how to prepare ORS was found to be not satisfactory. The positive findings were that mothers were aware of diarrhoea as a problem that could have dangerous consequences and that a child should continue to receive fluids during diarrhoea. The study also reported that breastfeeding was continued during diarrhoea; also, food was given as it was felt that this was necessary to give a child energy and strength. However, rural practitioners, though aware of ORS, preferred to use medicinal items and placed major emphasis on administration of drugs, medicines, syrups, and even injections (Viswanathan and Rohde 1990).

The National Family Health Survey 1992–3 found that only 42.7 per cent mothers knew about ORS packets and 25.9 per cent had ever used them. Knowledge and use was higher among urban mothers, and was positively related to the level of education and extent of exposure to mass media. There was considerable inter-state variation in the percentage of mothers who knew about ORS and who used them. The National Family Health Survey 1998–9 showed an improvement in percentage of mothers who know about ORS packets, a difference of 20 per cent. There was also a rise in percentage of children who were treated with a solution made from ORS, 27 per cent in 1998–9 as compared to 18 per cent in 1992–3.

Several micro-studies have reported that while most mothers gave normal quantity of food to the child during diarrhoea, not many increased the quantity of fluids; some even reduced the quantity of fluids given to the child. Though there was awareness of ORS, it was not given by a large proportion of care givers, and knowledge of the preparation of ORS was unsatisfactory. The incidence of correct use is low, often due to failure of paramedical personnel to transmit knowledge to the mother on the manner of the preparation and use of ORS (Bandopadhya, Banerjee and Sharma 1993; Bhatia et al. 1999; Kulashreshtha and Sapru 1991; Sircar et al. 1991).

Acute Respiratory Infections

Acute respiratory infection (ARI) is a common cause of morbidity and mortality among children aged under 5 years. The national survey of infant and child mortality in 1979 by the Registrar General brought out that acute respiratory infections figured prominently among the sicknesses of children (Registrar General 1983). The annual survey of causes of death in rural areas by the Registrar General, India has indicated pneumonia and other respiratory infections among the leading causes of death of children under 5 years. Several hospital based studies have indicated that respiratory infections were a common ailment among children brought to outpatient departments of hospitals for treatment. Community based studies, too, have found ARI to be an important cause of morbidity and mortality (Narain 1987; Patwari et al. 1988, Patnaik 1991; Roy et al. 1991).

Children aged under 5 years tend to suffer from several episodes of acute respiratory infection in a year. The survey in 1987–8 by the National Institute of Communicable Diseases in seven areas in the country indicated a median of 3.5 episodes per child in a year, of which 15.6 per cent were moderate/severe in nature (NICD 1988). The National Family Health Survey 1992–3 reported 7 per cent children under 4 years of age suffering from symptoms of ARI during the two weeks preceding the survey; there were, however, large interstate differences (IIPS 1995). The National Family Health Survey 1998–9 reported a higher percentage. The two surveys were carried out at different times of the year. Both the surveys found the incidence of ARI to be higher among boys than girls. The incidence of ARI has been generally found to be higher in the first year of life (Bhattacharjee et al. 1991; Narain 1987; Patwari et al. 1988; Roy et al. 1991; Singh and Nayar 1996). However, some studies have reported higher rates in post-infancy than in infancy (Patnaik 1991). A higher proportion of male, as compared to female, children are brought to hospitals/ health facilities/health providers. This may be due to greater importance given to treatment of a male child by the family rather than a higher incidence rate among male children (Bhattacharjee et al. 1991; Patwari et al. 1988; IIPS 1995, 2000; Roy et al. 1991). Several community based studies have, however, found no gender difference in incidence (Chhabra et al. 1993, Singh and Nayar 1996).

The prevalence of ARI has been found to be higher among low birthweight babies and malnourished children (Singh and Nayar

1996). Children with vitamin A deficiency tend to suffer from ARI (Pandey and Chakraborty 1996). A number of non-medical factors have been found to be associated with ARI. Among these are factors such as the weather, overcrowding in the home, bad housing, particularly dampness and poor ventilation, type of fuel used for cooking, poor personal and environmental hygiene, socio-economic status of the family, and the level of education of mother. Several studies have reported a higher incidence of severe lower respiratory infection in big cities with higher pollution levels (Narain 1987; Singh and Nayar 1996).

As a part of the public health strategy to reduce mortality and morbidity among children due to ARI, the Government of India launched a national programme in 1991. Under the programme, peripheral level health workers are given training for recognition of pneumonia and its treatment with contrimoxmazole. Parents of patients are given information on home-level care of cough and cold, home-level case management of mild to moderate ARI, recognition of severity of ARI through symptoms, and timely referral of patient to hospital. This has provided some relief. The full impact of the programme is, however, yet to be assessed, but micro-studies indicate a reduction in the number of cases and of case fatality.

POLIOMYELITIS

Poliomyelitis is the primary cause of lameness among children. A national survey organized by the Directorate General of Health Services (DGHS) in 1981–2 reported that the prevalence rate of poliomyelitis per 1,000 children aged 5–9 years was 6.2 in rural areas and 6.5 in urban areas. There were, however, large interstate variations. The survey estimated that 1,67,275 cases occurred annually, which was about ten times the number reported by the Central Bureau of Health Intelligence (Basu and Sokhey 1984).

The national review of immunization programme in India by the National Institute of Health and Family Welfare (NIHFW) in 1989 reported a prevalence rate of lameness due to paralytic polio to be 4.5 per 1,000 children aged under five years. There was, however, wide variation between states (Gupta and Murali 1989). The percentage of lame children due to paralytic poliomyelitis was 66 per cent of the total number of lame children aged under 5 years, almost the same as reported by the DGHS survey in 1981–2. In several districts, the percentage was more than 80 per cent.

The age of onset of paralytic polio cases was reported in the survey by the DGHS in 1981–2. It found that in 9.9 per cent cases it was 0–6 months, in 25.2 per cent cases it was 7–11 months, in 35.1 per cent cases 12–23 months, and in 16.9 per cent cases it was 24–35 months. In other words, in 87.1 per cent cases, the age of onset was less than 3 years (Basu and Sokhey 1984). Several micro-studies have also reported that almost nine-tenths of the cases occur before age 3 years, the bulk between 6 and 35 months (Sharma et al. 1990, Mandke et al. 1994). The national review of immunization programme in India in 1989, too, reported early age of onset of paralytic polio cases. In some parts of the country, more than half the cases reported attacks before one year of age (Gupta and Murali 1989).

Most surveys have reported a higher incidence of paralytic polio cases among boys as compared to girls. Sample surveys in 1981 by State Health Directorates reported 793 cases of girls per 1,000 cases among boys in Gujarat. The Madhya Pradesh survey reported 626 girls per 1,000 boys, while the Tamil Nadu survey reported 802 girls per 1,000 boys. Higher prevalence rates among boys as compared to girls was also reported by the national review of immunization programme in India in 1989 (Gupta and Murali 1989).

In the 1980s, immunization against polio in many parts of the country was characterized by low coverage, incomplete doses, and vaccine failure. The national review in 1989 reported that in some districts about 20 to 30 per cent children suffering from poliomyelitis were reported to have been immunized against polio, some after even three doses of oral polio vaccine (OPV), thus raising questions regarding potency of the vaccine administered, and the adequacy and schedule of number of doses given. A number of later studies on the potency of oral polio vaccine have reported considerable improvement from several areas, with more than 90 per cent of the vaccine samples having retained the minimum required potency. However, several areas still report a lower percentage (Deshpande et al. 1995).

Better immunization coverage of children with polio vaccine has succeeded in bringing down the incidence of polio in several parts of the country. A study based on children admitted in 12 Delhi hospitals between 1975 and 1992 found that the incidence of poliomyelitis in Delhi has decreased from 15.6 per 100,000 population in 1975 to 5.9 in 1992. The authors identified four distinct phases. The incidence was very high (annual average 15.19) during the era before the Expanded Programme of Immunization (1975 to 1978). It showed a moderate decline (annual average 14.01) in the era of the Expanded Programme of Immunization (1979 to 1984). In the Universal Immunization Programme era (1985 to 1988) there was a further decline (annual average 11.01), and in the subsequent period (1989 to 1992) the incidence went down substantially (annual average 4.98). The decline in the incidence of poliomyelitis has been reflected in a significant reduction of incidence of lameness due to poliomyelitis (Bhattacharjee et al. 1994). Similar reports have been reported in studies from other parts of the country (Mandke et al. 1990).

The national review of immunization programme in India in 1989 reported that out of 43 districts/units covered by the survey, over 50 per cent coverage of Polio-3 was achieved in 81.4 per cent units (Gupta and Murali 1989). The National Family Health Survey 1992–3, however, gave a more subdued picture. The national aggregate for Polio-3 coverage of children aged 12–23 months was 53.4. Among the bigger states, the lowest coverage was in Bihar (31.6 per cent) and the highest in Tamil Nadu (85.3 per cent). The National Family Health Survey 1998–9 has reported improved coverage with Polio-3 (62.8 per cent of children aged 12–23 months). However in some states (Assam, Bihar, Rajasthan, and Uttar Pradesh), the coverage continues to be low (less than 45 per cent).

The coverage of children with Polio-3 has to be substantially stepped up, particularly in states which are lagging behind. With better cold chain maintenance and stabilization of the delivery system, vaccine potency loss as a cause of failure will decline in importance. Continuous surveillance will, however, be necessary. Incomplete or non-coverage will require attention implying proper targeting of more vulnerable areas and groups and better scheduling of operations. A substantial reduction in cases of drop-out has to be brought about. The reasons for failure to attain full immunization coverage are mainly administrative—vaccine not available, vaccinator absent, time schedule not kept, place of vaccination inconvenient or too far. There are other reasons as well such as ignorance of mothers about the importance of following the schedule of vaccination, non-availability of time, and fear of reactions (Gupta and Murali 1989).

Delhi began pulse polio immunization with a successful launch in 1994. The strategy was later adopted in other states. Successive pulse polio campaigns have been carried out throughout the country on pre-announced days. These have been characterized by large-scale information, education, and communication support to generate awareness, active community mobilization and participation (including schoolchildren), media publicity, networking, coordinated management, and strong motivation and participation of the medical fraternity and non-officials.

MEASLES

Measles, a highly communicable disease was, for a long time, one of the primary causes of early childhood mortality and morbidity. The national survey on infant and child mortality in 1979 found it to be among the ten primary causes of early childhood deaths (Registrar General 1983). Traditional beliefs in rural areas about the disease being caused due to the wrath of the goddess often resulted in no treatment or delayed treatment, thereby increasing the risks of complications and mortality.

Community based studies on the incidence of measles have generally found it to be the highest among children between 6 and 48 months with a peak at 12–23 months, decreasing progressively thereafter (Agarwal et al. 1976; Garai and Chakravarthy 1980; Lobo et al. 1987; Narain and Banerjee 1989). However, age shifts have been reported in other countries, particularly when the younger population is fully immunized. Incidence rates reported by various community based studies show a wide range, varying from 21 to 175 per 1,000 children below 5 years of age, higher rates occurring mainly in situations of outbreaks of the disease. The incidence rates are very low in areas where children have received the vaccine (Narain and Banerjee 1989; Singh et al. 1994).

Case fatalities have been found to be higher in younger children not given the vaccine. Where health facilities are poor, case fatalities are higher, specially during outbreaks (John et al. 1980; Risbud et al. 1994; Singh et al. 1994). They have been found to be low in areas where medical facilities were available (Lobo et al. 1987; Narain and Banerjee 1989). Most fatalities arise due to complications which develop in some children, more common among them being bronchopneumonia and diarrhoea. The incidence of complications and case fatality is higher among malnourished children.

Data on gender distribution of measles cases and case fatality do not show a consistent trend. Some studies show a higher incidence among females (Narain and Banerjee 1989) while some do not find a gender difference (Singh et al. 1994). A study by NICD of measles outbreak in 1996 in a district in Uttar Pradesh reported that while there was no gender difference in the infection, case fatality was higher among the female children (NICD 1999). Another study in Uttar Pradesh which covered a larger area, too, reported higher case fatality among female children (Singh et al. 1999).

Measles became a part of the universal immunization programme in 1985. Initially, measles coverage was poor and the potency of the vaccine uncertain. The national review of immunization programme in India in 1989 reported that out of 43 districts/units covered by the survey, 11 had less than 25 per cent coverage while in 21 the coverage was between 26 and 50 per cent (Gupta and Murali 1989). The National Family Health Survey 1992–3 reported 42.2 per cent coverage of children aged 12–23 months with measles vaccine, with states like Bihar having a coverage of only 14.6 per cent children and Uttar Pradesh 26.3 per cent children. Measles vaccine coverage has picked up in recent years in some states, reducing morbidity and mortality of children due to measles but it still lags behind the other vaccines. The National Family Health Survey, 1998–9 reported a higher coverage of 50.7 per cent children 12–23 months. Among the bigger states, Tamil Nadu recorded the highest coverage (90.2 per cent), followed by Himachal Pradesh (89.1 per cent), Kerala (84.6 per cent) and Maharashtra (84.3 per cent). However, the coverage continued to be poor in some states (Bihar 16.6 per cent, Assam 24.6 per cent, Rajasthan 27.1 per cent, Uttar Pradesh 34.6 per cent, and Madhya Pradesh 35.5 per cent).There are still large pockets in rural areas of several states where immunization coverage, surveillance machinery, and timely containment measures in case of outbreak are at unsatisfactory levels, resulting in a high incidence of morbidity and case fatality, particularly due to post-measles complications.

TETANUS

Tetanus has been an important cause of morbidity and mortality. The national survey on infant and child mortality in 1979 found tetanus to be the leading cause of death among infants in rural areas (14.2 per cent) and the second largest cause for deaths in urban areas (6.8 per cent) (Registrar General 1983). In some states, fatality from tetanus was much higher (Uttar Pradesh 30.6 per cent in rural areas and 23.2 per cent in urban areas). The incidence of tetanus is higher in rural areas, particularly in states which rank low on health status indicators, because of poorer immunization coverage, unsafe deliveries at home by untrained *dais*, presence of unhygienic and infective conditions, and poor access to antenatal care and medical facilities for diagnosis and treatment.

Neonates are particularly susceptible to tetanus. An ICMR national collaborative study in 1982–4 reported 18.5 per cent neonatal deaths due to tetanus (ICMR 1990c). Sample surveys conducted in 1981 and 1982 by the Directorate General of Health Services, too, found neonatal tetanus to be a major cause of neonatal and infant mortality (Sokhey 1991).

Due to expanded immunization coverage of pregnant women and infants, larger resort to safe delivery practices, and better access to health care service the incidence of tetanus as well as case fatality is on the decline. Data compiled by the Central Bureau of Health Intelligence (CBHI) is indicative of this trend. Some empirical studies have also reported a lower incidence. For instance, a study covering the period 1983–93 in Delhi found a significant decline in neonatal and post-neonatal cases of admission (Talukdar et al. 1994). Other studies, too, have confirmed this trend (Deivanayagam et al. 1991).

The National Family Health Survey 1992–3 had reported that 52 per cent children aged 12–23 months were vaccinated with DPT-3, and in the case of 54 per cent live births the pregnant women had been vaccinated with two doses of TT. The National Family Health Survey 1998–9 reported coverage of 55 per cent, and 67 per cent, respectively. However, some states (Assam, Bihar, Madhya Pradesh, Rajasthan, and Uttar Pradesh) are still lagging in providing vaccine coverage.

IMMUNIZATION

Immunization of children against six vaccine preventable diseases (tuberculosis, diphtheria, tetanus, pertusis, poliomyelitis, and measles) occupies an important place in the National Health Policy. Its crucial role in reducing the incidence of morbidity and mortality of young children and prevention of onset of handicap has long been recognized. Immunization of children was earlier carried out under maternal and child health services. It was given a separate identity when the Expanded Programme of Immunization (EPI) was launched in 1978 for providing vaccination free of cost to cover all eligible children and pregnant women. Immunization against polio was included in the programme in 1979–80. BCG, which was being given since 1962, was included in EPI in 1981–2. A vaccine against measles was also added. The six vaccines became a part of the Universal Immunization Programme (UIP), launched in 1985 covering not only children but also pregnant women with two doses of tetanus toxoid (TT) vaccine or a booster dose, if vaccinated previously. It was given the status of National Technology Mission, one of the seven in the country, to achieve early universal coverage, self-sufficiency in vaccine production, maintenance of cold chain equipment, and smooth functioning of operations so that the implementation of the programme could improve.

The national review of immunization programme in India in 1989 reported that when the programme covering vaccine preventable diseases was launched, some doubts were raised about its ability to reduce mortality since most early childhood deaths were caused by diarrhoeal diseases, respiratory infections, and pre-maturity rather than the six vaccine preventable diseases. It was argued that there was, therefore, little epidemiological justification for allocating huge national resources for the programme instead of first tackling the more important causes of infant and childhood mortality. Doubts were expressed about the dependence on a single vaccine to control a disease. Apprehensions were expressed about production, supply, and delivery schedules, retention of potency of vaccine at point of delivery, compliance with immunization schedule, motivation of personnel, and motivation of the community. The assumption that 85 per cent coverage of infants would provide herd immunity was also questioned (Gupta and Murali 1989). The Government of India, however, decided to move ahead with its programme of universal immunization.

During the early phase, progress in immunization coverage was slow. An ICMR Task Force survey of immunization of children aged 12–23 months in the first half of 1988 in 11 states (two districts in each state covering rural areas) showed considerable variation between states and between districts within the same state. Immunization coverage was found to be better in districts brought under the UIP. The pooled coverage of fully immunized children (all

TABLE 2.28: VACCINE COVERAGE OF CHILDREN AND PREGNANT WOMEN, 1988

	DPT	Polio	Measles	BCG	DPT+ Polio + Measles	BCG + DPT + BCG + Polio	TT2 (pregnant women)
Districts covered under UIP	47.9	47.1	20.7	30.2	13.9	24.2	11.9
Districts not covered	29.3	27.0	7.4	18.9	5.3	12.9	12.0

Source: ICMR, An Assessment Study of Coverage and KAP of Immunization Programmes in Different States of the Country, 1990.

Note: Figures give the pooled percentage coverage for the 11 states covered by the survey.

six vaccines) was, however, only 13.9 per cent in the districts covered by the UIP (see Table 2.28). In Bihar, the coverage was less than 1 per cent, in Orissa 1 per cent, and in Uttar Pradesh 3 per cent. In the districts not covered by UIP, the pooled coverage for the 11 states was 5.3. If measles, which was introduced later in UIP (in 1982) was excluded, the pooled coverage for the eleven states rose to 24.2 per cent for districts covered under UIP, and 12.9 per cent for districts not covered. The Task Force observed that although the programme of providing two doses of tetanus toxoid vaccine to pregnant women was in operation for more than a decade, the pooled coverage was only 12 per cent for the 11 states. In several states, it was far less (ICMR 1990a). These percentages of coverage of children are far lower than the figures reported by vaccination coverage evaluation surveys sponsored by the Government in different states in 1987 (Sokhey and Farley 1990).

A later survey by the National Institute of Health and Family Welfare carried out in 1989 to review the immunization programme found some improvement, but the situation was still unsatisfactory. Out of 43 districts/urban units covered by the survey, the percentage of fully immunized children (all the six vaccines) was less than 25 per cent in 16 districts/urban units, between 26 and 50 per cent in 25 districts/urban units, and more than 50 per cent in only 2 districts/urban units. If measles was excluded, the percentage coverage of immunized children was less than 25 in 9 districts, 26 to 50 per cent in 14 districts/urban units, and more than 50 per cent in 20 districts/urban units (Gupta and Murali 1989).

TABLE 2.29: PERCENTAGE OF CHILDREN AGED 12–23 MONTHS AND PREGNANT WOMEN RECEIVING IMMUNIZATION, INDIA, 1992–3 AND 1998–9

	Percentage vaccinated							
	BCG	DPT-3 (three doses)	Polio (three doses)	Measles	All	None	Pregnant women	
							TT2	None
National Family Health Survey, 1992–3	62	52	53	42	35	30	54	39
National Family Health Survey, 1998–9	72	55	63	51	42	14	67	24
Targets set by Universal Immunization Programme for 1990	80	85	85	85	85	Not given	100	Not given

Sources: *National Family Health Survey 1992–3*, India; *National Family Health Survey 1998–9*, India;
Ministry of Health & Family Welfare, *Towards Universal Immunization*, 1985.

Notes: (i) 'All' refers to fully vaccinated children aged 12–23 months, i.e. those who received all the vaccinations (BCG, measles, and three doses each of DPT and polio vaccine). TT2 (two doses or more of tetanus toxoid injection). Coverage relates to live births during the four years preceding the survey in the case of National Family Health Survey 1992–3 and three years in the case of the National Family Health Survey 1998–9.
(ii) UIP target in the case of DPT is for children less than 3 years; in the case of polio and BCG it is for infants.

The National Family Health Survey in 1992–3 and 1998–9 reported comprehensively on immunization coverage. Table 2.29, which presents the findings, shows that BCG was the best performer in both 1992–3 and 1998–9, while measles lagged behind. An uncomfortable finding was that 30 per cent children received no vaccination in 1992–3. In 1998–9, the percentage of such children came down to 14.

The national immunization targets for 1990 were set by the National Health Policy 1983 and the Universal Immunization Programme (1985). The target for 1990 was set at 85 per cent coverage of infants against vaccine preventable diseases and 85 per cent pregnant women against tetanus (Ministry of Health and Family Welfare 1985). In 1992–3, that is two years later, the ground reality was very different. As against the 1990 target of 85 per cent vaccine coverage of infants against six vaccine preventable diseases, the actual coverage was only 35 per cent in 1992–3. Even six years later (1998–9), the coverage was only 42 per cent, that is, less than half the target. While there has been some progress, the performance is far below the target, and considerable ground remains to be covered before the goal of universal immunization is reached.

RURAL-URBAN DIFFERENCE IN IMMUNIZATION

Lower vaccine coverage in rural areas, particularly in the backward states due to the poor state of public health services, has been brought out by various coverage evaluation surveys (Gupta and Murali 1989; Nagi 1997; Singh 1991). The National Family Health Survey 1992–3 found the difference in percentage of fully vaccinated children between rural and urban areas to be 20 per cent, while the National Family Health Survey 1998–9 found the difference to be 24 per cent (see Table 2.30).

TABLE 2.30: PERCENTAGE OF CHILDREN 12–23 MONTHS RECEIVING VACCINATION IN RURAL AND URBAN AREAS, INDIA, 1992–3 AND 1998–9

Survey	Area	Percentage of children aged 12–23 months receiving					
		BCG	DPT-3	Polio-3	Measles	All	None
National Family Health Survey, 1992–3	Rural	57.6	46.6	48.4	37.7	30.9	34.0
	Urban	77.6	68.8	70.2	57.5	50.7	16.4
	Difference (U–R)	20.0	22.2	21.8	19.8	19.8	–17.6
National Family Health Survey, 1998–9	Rural	67.1	49.8	58.3	45.3	36.6	16.7
	Urban	86.8	73.4	78.2	69.2	60.5	6.4
	Difference (U–R)	19.7	23.6	19.9	23.9	23.9	–10.3

Source: *National Family Health Survey, 1992–3*; *National Family Health Survey, 1998–9.*

Note: 'All' refers to children who are fully vaccinated, i.e. they have received BCG, measles, three doses each of DPT and polio vaccine.

GENDER DIFFERENCE IN IMMUNIZATION

In recent years, vaccination coverage surveys have begun to give the break-up by sex to assess the extent of discrimination against the girl child at the household level. Surprisingly, the official vaccination coverage surveys, both under Expanded Programme of Immunization and the Universal Programme of Immunization, ignored this disaggregation.

Micro-studies in the 1970s and early 1980s indicated more male children being brought for immunization. The ICMR Task Force study carried out in 1988 covering 11 states found that, on the whole, the coverage of male children was moderately higher. In some states, however, the difference was quite marked (ICMR 1990a). An immunization coverage survey of children 12–23 months in four states of north India in April to August 1991 in 175 districts, too, found that the immunization coverage of male children was marginally higher (Singh 1991). A survey of 15 districts in nine states in 1995 pointed in the same direction (Nagi 1997). The National Family Health Survey 1992–3, too, indicated that, on the aggregate, male coverage was moderately higher (difference less than 4 per cent) for all the vaccines, including fully vaccinated children (see Table 2.31). The percentage of female children receiving no vaccination was higher (difference 4.5 per cent). The National Family Health Survey 1998–9, also showed a marginally higher coverage for boys.

TABLE 2.31: PERCENTAGE OF CHILDREN AGED 12–23 MONTHS RECEIVING VACCINATION BY SEX, INDIA, 1992–3

Sex		Percentage of children 12–23 months receiving					
		BCG	DPT-3	Polio-3	Measles	All	None
National Family Health Survey 1998–9	Male	64.0	53.5	55.0	43.7	36.7	27.8
	Female	60.3	49.8	51.7	40.6	34.1	32.3
	M–F	3.7	3.7	3.3	3.1	2.6	–4.5
National Family Health Survey 1998–9	Male	72.8	56.3	63.4	51.6	43.1	13.5
	Female	70.3	54.0	62.2	49.8	40.9	15.3
	M–F	2.5	2.3	1.2	1.8	2.2	–1.8

Sources: *National Family Health Survey, 1992–3*, India; *National Family Health Survey, 1998–9*, India.

Note: 'All' relates to children who are fully vaccinated, i.e. they have received BCG, measles and three doses each of DPT and polio vaccine.

TABLE 2.32: DIFFERENCE BETWEEN PERCENTAGE OF MALE AND FEMALE CHILDREN AGED 12–23 MONTHS FULLY VACCINATED IN DIFFERENT STATES, 1992–3 AND 1998–9

State	Difference in percentage of fully vaccinated children 12–23 months (M–F)	
	1992–3	1998–9
Andhra Pradesh	+3.1	–8.6
Assam	–2.0	+13.1
Bihar	+3.7	+4.0
Gujarat	+3.0	+0.2
Haryana	+6.7	–0.8
Himachal Pradesh	+7.5	+8.3
Karnataka	–3.3	+5.7
Kerala	+2.9	–5.5
Madhya Pradesh	+7.2	+9.4
Maharashtra	–5.9	+4.5
Orissa	+3.7	+0.8
Punjab	+14.7	+5.3
Rajasthan	+5.0	–0.7
Tamil Nadu	+6.4	+1.5
Uttar Pradesh	+5.5	+4.8
West Bengal	–4.7	+0.7

Sources: *National Family Health Survey, 1992–3*; *National Family Health Survey, 1998–9*; *Reports of States.*

The situation, however, varied in different states. Data from State Reports of the National Family Health Survey 1998–9 indicate that in twelve of the 16 bigger states the percentage of fully vaccinated male children was higher, while in four the percentage of fully vaccinated female children was higher. The extent and direction of change from the 1992–3 survey varied in different states (see Table 2.32).

INTERSTATE VARIATION IN IMMUNIZATION

Large variation between states and between districts within the state have been brought out by several surveys on immunization coverage (ICMR 1990a; Singh 1991; Gupta and Murali 1989; Sokhey and Farley 1987). The National Family Health Survey indicates the same pattern. Table 2.33 gives the coverage in 1998–9 by each vaccine as well as all the vaccines in the sixteen bigger states. The percentage of children aged 12–23 months who have received no vaccine is quite high in several states. Tamil Nadu, Himachal Pradesh, Maharashtra,

TABLE 2.33: PERCENTAGE OF VACCINATED CHILDREN AGED 12–23 MONTHS IN STATES, 1998–9

Percentage	Percentage of children 12–23 months who received the vaccine					
	BCG	DPT 3	Polio 3	Measles	All vaccines	None of the vaccines
< 25		Bihar (24.2)		Bihar (16.6) Assam (24.6)	Bihar (11.0) Assam (17.0) Rajasthan (17.3) Uttar Pradesh (21.2) M. Pradesh (22.4)	Tamil Nadu (0.3) Maharashtra (2.0) Kerala (2.2) Himachal Pradesh (2.8) Andhra Pradesh (4.5) Gujarat (6.6) Karnataka (7.7) Punjab (8.7) Orissa (9.4) Haryana (9.9) West Bengal (13.6) Madhya Pradesh (13.9) Bihar (16.8) Rajasthan (22.5)
25–49	Bihar (37.7)	Rajasthan (26.1) Uttar Pradesh (33.9) M. Pradesh (37.0) Assam (37.5)	Assam (37.9) Bihar (41.0) U. Pradesh (42.3) Rajasthan (44.6)	Rajasthan (27.1) U. Pradesh (34.6) M. Pradesh (35.5)	Orissa (43.7) West Bengal (43.8)	U. Pradesh (29.5) Assam (33.2)
50–74	Assam (53.5) Rajasthan (53.9) U. Pradesh (57.5) M. Pradesh (64.9)	West Bengal (58.3) Orissa (61.9) Gujarat (64.1) Haryana (71.1)	M. Pradesh (56.7) West Bengal (61.7) Orissa (68.4) Gujarat (68.6) Haryana (74.3)	W. Bengal (52.4) Orissa (54.0) Gujarat (63.6) A. Pradesh (64.7) Karnataka (67.3) Haryana (72.2)	Gujarat (53.0) A. Pradesh (58.7) Karnataka (60.0) Haryana (62.7) Punjab (72.1)	

75+	West Bengal (76.5)	Karnataka (75.2)	Karnataka (78.3)	Punjab (76.5)	Maharashtra(78.4)
	Gujarat (84.7)	Andhra Pradesh (79.5)	Andhra Pradesh (81.6)	Maharashtra (84.3)	Kerala (79.7)
	Orissa (84.7)	Punjab (82.0)	Punjab (83.6)	Kerala (84.6)	H. Pradesh (83.4)
	Karnataka (84.8)	Kerala (88.0)	Kerala (88.4)	H. Pradesh (89.1)	Tamil Nadu (88.8)
	Haryana (86.8)	H. Pradesh (88.8)	H. Pradesh (89.8)	Tamil Nadu (90.2)	
	Punjab (88.7)	Maharashtra (89.4)	Maharashtra (90.8)		
	A. Pradesh (90.2)	Tamil Nadu (96.7)	Tamil Nadu (98.0)		
	Maharashtra (93.7)				
	H. Pradesh (94.6)				
	Kerala (96.2)				
	Tamil Nadu (98.6)				

Source: *National Family Health Survey, 1998–9.*

and Kerala are the high performing states. In Tamil Nadu, of the children aged 12–23 months, 89 per cent were fully vaccinated, and less than 1 per cent did not receive any vaccine. At the other end are the poorly performing states of Bihar, Rajasthan, Assam, Uttar Pradesh, and Madhya Pradesh.

The percentage of fully vaccinated children aged 12–23 months in different states is given in Fig. 2.10 and the percentage receiving no vaccine is shown in Fig. 2.10. In Fig. 2.11 the states have been arranged in ascending order according to the percentage of children

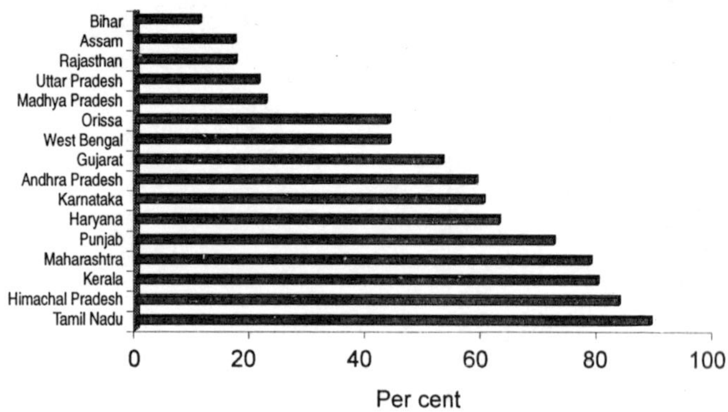

FIG. 2.10: PERCENTAGE OF FULLY VACCINATED CHILDREN AGED 12–23 MONTHS IN STATES, 1998–9.

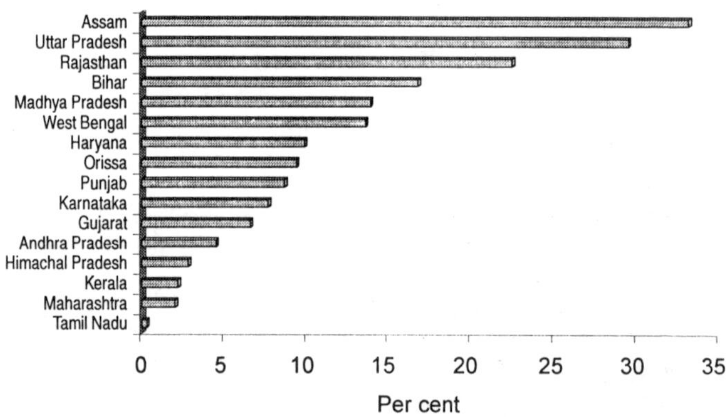

FIG. 2.11: PERCENTAGE OF CHILDREN AGED 12–23 MONTHS IN STATES RECEIVING NO VACCINE, 1998–9.

receiving all vaccines and in Fig. 2.11 in descending order according to the percentage of children receiving none of the vaccines.

DROP-OUT RATE IN IMMUNIZATION

BCG and polio vaccines have to be given thrice to each child as per schedule in order to provide immunity. Failure to do so swells the number of unprotected children. An ICMR Task Force survey in the first half of 1988, which covered 11 states, reported high drop-out rates for both DPT and polio, even in districts which were covered under Universal Immunisation Programme. It found the drop-out rate between the second and third dose to be almost twice that between the first and second dose. It also found considerable interstate variation in the drop-out rate (ICMR, 1990a). The national review of immunization programme a year later in 1989 by the National Institute of Health and Family Welfare, too, brought out the prevalence of high drop-out rates. Out of 41 districts/units for which data were collected, 12 reported a drop-out rate of more than 20 per cent in the case of DPT; in the case of OPV, the drop-out rate was much higher (Gupta and Murali 1989). The survey in 1991 by the Institute for Research in Medical Statistics (IRMS), covering four states in north India, found that high drop-out rates continued to trouble the programme (Singh 1991). The National Family Health Survey 1992–3 showed that the basic reasons for the high drop-out rate had not been sorted out. The national aggregate indicated a drop-out rate of 22 per cent in the case of DPT (first dose to third dose) and 20 per cent in the case of polio (first dose to third dose). The drop-out rate was higher between the second and third dose than between the first and the second dose, and higher in rural than in urban areas. The survey showed variation between states in drop-out rate. There was hardly any gender difference in drop-out rates in the aggregate, but in several states female drop-out rates were higher. The National Family Health Survey 1998–9 indicated similar trends.

Drop-out is basically due to: (i) problems in the delivery system, such as inconvenient location and time; intimation not given widely and in time; vaccination service not available at the scheduled time and place; and vaccine not available; (ii) low level of awareness such as lack of information about number of doses to be given and the interval at which they are to be given; (iii) weak motivation; (iv) absence from the place due to migration for reasons of employment; and (v) other reasons such as illness of the child (Gupta and Murali 1989; ICMR 1990a; IIPS 1995; Singh, 1991).

RURAL PRIMARY HEALTH CARE SERVICES

The official government policy is to set up a rural health care system based on a combination of preventive, promotive, and curative services. The primary health infrastructure comprises a Primary Health Centre (PHC), the norm for which is a population of about 30,000, with sub-centres, the norm for which is a population of about 5,000. The sub-centres have two health workers, one male and one female Auxiliary Nurse Midwife (ANM). A lady health visitor is appointed to supervise the functioning of four to five sub-centres. For four PHCs, a Community Health Centre (CHC) is envisaged to cover a population of about 100,000 in a Block. CHCs are expected to function as a first referral centre and have a 30-bed hospital with provision for specialist doctors in gynaecology, paediatrics, surgery, and medicine. In the primary health care structure, trained manpower has been made available by way of community health guides and trained birth attendants. The growth of the rural health care infrastructure is given in Table 2.34.

Administration of the primary health care system is the responsibility of the State Government. Policy guidelines and directives emanating from the Centre and the five year plans provide the general framework for the functioning of the primary health care structure. There is, however, enough flexibility in the system. In urban areas, local governments, too, provide some primary health care services. The financing of public health care is done by states from their own budgetary resources and from grants by the central government through centrally sponsored and central schemes. In

TABLE 2.34: GROWTH IN PRIMARY HEALTH CARE INFRASTRUCTURE IN INDIA

Year	Primary Health Centre (PHC)	Sub-Centre	Community Health Centre (CHC)	No. of PHCs per CHC
1961	2,565			
1971	5,112	28,489		
1981	5,740	51,405	217	26.5
1991	20,450	130,958	2,071	9.9
1999	22,962	137,271	2,935	7.8

Source: Ministry of Health and Family Welfare.

recent years, a large volume of external aid has been received by states to strengthen and upgrade public sector health services.

Apart from health care services provided by the government, private medical practitioners following different systems of medicine, trusts, charities, NGOs, and private sector health care institutions provide services. In rural as well as urban areas, unqualified medical practitioners, quacks, and faith healers also function, and have a fairly large clientele.

While the provision of a basic health infrastructure in rural areas by the public sector has to be appreciated, major shortcomings in the functioning of the system have been brought out from time to time by empirical studies. Deficiencies have also been extensively reported in the media. These are not universal, but neither are they too localized or of the nature of a minor shortcoming or a one-time occurrence. These are more apparent in the health apparatus of some states as compared to others. The drawbacks are indicative of the deep malaise that has set in, and reflect the lack of political and administrative will to improve the public health care system. Among the weaknesses brought out from time to time are the following:

- Big gap between the norms laid down for the PHC structure and the actual position. An ICMR Task Force Study in 1987–9 covering 398 PHCs in 18 states and 1 union territory found the following position:

Population range of a PHC	PHC	
	No	%
< 40,000	49	12.3
40,000–79,000	63	15.8
80,000–1,20,000	100	25.1
121,000–150,000	93	23.4
More than 150,000	93	23.4
Total	398	100.0

  The data indicate that states are still in the process of implementation of the norm. In 1987–9, 47 per cent of the PHCs were each covering a population of more than 120,000 (ICMR 1991). The position has, however, improved since the time of the survey. In 1999, there were 22,962 PHCs, giving an average of 7.8 PHCs per CHC compared to 26.5 PHCs per CHC in 1981. This is still far below the norm;
- Very poor serving of the gynaecological needs of rural women;

- Very low budgetary provisions, especially in states lagging in health care;
- Big backlog in construction of buildings, shortage of space in existing buildings, and poor maintenance;
- Unsatisfactory locations, long distance (sometimes more than 5 km for remote villages), and inconvenient timings which clash with working hours and mean a loss of wage;
- Shortage of diagnostic tools and equipment; poor maintenance, due to which equipment are often out of order for long periods;
- Suboptimal functioning of the health sub-centres;
- Shortage of essential drugs, delayed supplies, and malpractices in procurement, storage, and dispensing;
- Shortage of specialists in CHCs; vacant posts of Lady Health Visitors and ANMs. For instance, information compiled by the Directorate General of Health Services indicates that in June 2000, out of 2,424 paediatricians required as per norm in 29 states/ union territories, only 1,028 posts (42.4 per cent) had been sanctioned, but only 453 were in position. In other words, only 18.7 per cent of the required number of paediatricians were in position (DGHS, 2000).
- Vacant post of doctors for long periods in remote and backward areas, but doctors in excess of the norm in favourable locations;
- Doctors not available at PHC; when available, considerable time is taken to see a patient; patients are given only prescription and asked to buy drugs from the market; curt behaviour of the medical and paramedical staff; manner of taking the drug or how to take care of the patient is not properly explained; doctors are more concerned with their own convenience and private practice;
- Poor public health administration, particularly in the backward areas; extraneous considerations in postings and transfers; poor staff motivation and self image;
- Poor referral linkages;
- Weak coordination and integration with other services;
- Community perception of functioning of public health infrastructure is unfavourable. Not many have faith in its efficiency. Poor patients feel they are not given the required attention or treatment and that influence or money is needed for proper attention;

- Weak efforts to upgrade the quality of services through motivation and training;
- Total absence of accountability for failure to achieve targets.

A multi-centre collaborative study on the care of mothers and infants with a comprehensive maternal and child health (MCH) care package utilizing a high risk approach strategy at primary health centres in six states (Gujarat, Haryana, Madhya Pradesh, Maharashtra, Rajasthan, Uttar Pradesh) by ICMR in 1986 found that the infrastructure facilities in terms of physical space, equipment, and general supplies, including drugs, were poor, except for facilities for immunization, such as refrigerator and vaccines under universal immunization programme. The manpower position was, however, satisfactory. The study observed:

> The provision of MCH services was limited to providing the Iron Folic Acid (IFA) tablets and Tetanus Toxoid (TT) immunization. There was no concept of detection of high risk factors by Auxiliary Nurse Midwives (ANMs) in pregnant women/new borns or for their better care by having a suitable referral system. The quality of care was poor during antenatal, intranatal (including the use of safe delivery kits) and postnatal periods. Data recording was poor reflecting gross under-reporting of births, deaths and other vital statistics. [ICMR 1994]

The study found significant improvement as a result of the package of interventions for comprehensive health care.

Another ICMR Task Force Study in 1987–9 on the quality of family welfare services at primary health centre level, covering 18 states and 1 union territory found:

> . . . while the resources in terms of physical facilities were comparatively satisfactory at PHCs, these were greatly deficient at the level of sub-centre which is the first contact point for the community; this was specially so with respect to routine antenatal care. With regard to manpower position, there was substantial shortage of ANMs; . . .
>
> The labour room and operation theatre which are essential infrastructure for the delivery of good quality family welfare services were generally observed to be poorly equipped and maintained at PHC level. In nearly half of the sub-centres facilities for normal delivery were absent. . . .
>
> . . . The quality of care administered by the ANM in the field indicated that coverage of antenatal care was inadequate and where the services were provided these were limited to administration of Tetanus Toxoid and distribution of Iron Folic Acid tablets. . . .
>
> . . . The results of the evaluation clearly indicate that the quality and coverage of FW (Family Welfare) services as currently being offered in the

national programme is poor and that the MCH component is substantially weak in most instances. [ICMR 1991]

Evaluation of Community Health Centres, which constitute the third tier in the primary health care system and are expected to function as referral centres for the PHCs under their jurisdiction, was done by the Programme Evaluation Organisation (PEO) of the Planning Commission in 1997–8 and covered eight states. The Report indicates that the lessons from earlier evaluations of public health programmes have not been learnt. Norms regarding population coverage and linkage with PHCs for referral services were far from being achieved. There were wide gaps between norm and ground reality. Most existing CHCs were not equipped to deliver the expected specialized services because of vacant posts (only 30 per cent of the required posts of specialists were in position), non-availability of physical facilities and equipment, or their non-functional state. Of the 31 sample CHCs covered by the study, 5 did not have an Operation Theatre, 5 did not have a Labour Room, 12 did not have a Pathological Laboratory, and 9 did not have safe drinking water. There was a mismatch between medical specialists and the provision of equipments, facilities, and supporting staff. Only 2 of the 31 sample PHCs were found to have been used to some extent as referral centres. Eleven CHCs had not attended any referral cases, while 18 had been used suboptimally, with an average of only 206 cases per year. All the sample CHCs covered by the study were working like PHCs, thus indicating that CHCs were not providing the specialist services expected of them. Of the sample beneficiaries, 57 per cent were either dissatisfied or partially satisfied with the quality of services delivered, the major reasons being non-availability of doctors, indifference and unsympathetic attitude of doctors and paramedical staff, and non-availability of prescribed medicines (PEO 1999).

The poor functioning of the health care system is reflected in the low performance on all the child health indicators, particularly in the backward states where the deficiencies are more prominent. Failings in the public primary health care system hit the poorest the most, as they either have to go without preventive and curative care or, when the ailment is acute, go to private medical practitioners, a large number of whom are unqualified. A number of surveys of rural primary health care have indicated that for curative health care the use of private medical care (including quacks) is fairly widespread, in many places the predominant mode, the reasons being convenience, promptness, availability, and a patient friendly behaviour as compared to the poor services in government institutions (BAIF DRF 1997; Levine et al. 1992; Samuel, Gupta and Wadhwa 1992; Sundar 1994; WWCDN 1995).

If a significant impact on child health is to be made, particularly in the backward states, the health care infrastructure has to be considerably improved through budgetary support, adequate physical infrastructure, a strong and efficient health administration, reforms for a far better health delivery system, accountability, and training of medical and paramedical personnel. Determined efforts, political commitment, and accountability are necessary to reach out the services, particularly to the poor, and provide client friendly health care.

The national programme of Integrated Child Development Services (ICDS), launched in 1975, has among its objectives the improvement of health and nutrition status of children aged 0–6 years, reduction of mortality, morbidity, and malnutrition, and the nutrition and health education of mothers to enhance her capability to look after the normal health and nutrition needs of the child. The village anganwadi worker in an ICDS project area which has the same geographical area as a Community Development Block, facilitates immunization, health check-up, referral, and other services with the help of the PHC network, thus providing a link between the village, the PHC sub-centre, and the PHC. In February 2001, there were 4,384 operational ICDS projects.

The state of functioning of ICDS projects has not been very different from the other social service programmes. Survey data show fairly low levels of achievement in health status in states despite large areas being covered by ICDS projects.

In 1992–3 the Government of India launched the Child Survival and Safe Motherhood Programme for strengthening maternal care interventions (antenatal check-up, immunization against tetanus, safe delivery, anaemia control, safe delivery kits, training of birth attendants, etc.); child survival services (immunization, oral re-hydration therapy, acute respiratory infection control); and prophylaxis schemes for administering iron and folic acid tablets and vitamin A doses. The programme does not seem to have made much impact by way of significant reduction in infant mortality. IMR, which was 74 in 1993, came down to 72 in 1998, a decline of only 2 points.

For the Ninth Plan (1997–2002), the Government of India has formulated a reproductive and child health (RCH) strategy which aims to bring the services within easy reach of the community. It incorporates the components relating to child survival and safe motherhood. Under the programme, general obstetric care and child health facilities will be substantially upgraded in PHCs. The first referral units at sub-district level will provide comprehensive emergency obstetric and neonatal care. The districts have been divided into three categories on the basis of their current reproductive and child health status for deciding the packages of reproductive and child health (RCH) interventions. To what extent the new formulation will succeed in bringing significant improvements in health care delivery systems remains to be seen. The maladies in the public health care system are well known. Higher allocation for the public health care system is an urgent need. Equally important is determined action to reform the functioning of the system and accountability.

MALNUTRITION

Malnutrition is a serious problem affecting Indian children. Because of its low visibility, the damage it causes to a child's healthy growth and development, and the contribution it makes to death, disease, and disability, is often not appreciated. The problem of malnutrition among children was highlighted by the report of the Working Party of the Indian Council of Medical Research which described it as 'the biggest public health problem in the country'. Based on studies in 1971–4 at six centres in different parts of the country, covering 18,356 pre-school children, the report indicated that malnutrition was widespread in the pre-school population. It found extensive protein calorie malnutrition and other nutritional deficiencies. The report pointed out that the intake of calories, vitamins, and minerals by children was deficient and observed that the widespread protein calorie malnutrition was to a considerable extent conditioned by inadequate calorie intake, and what the children were suffering from was really more a food gap than a protein gap (ICMR 1984).

NUTRITION STATUS

The report of the National Nutrition Monitoring Bureau (NNMB), after comparing the results of its repeat survey in 1988–90 in eight states with the 1975–9 survey data, found there was an increase in percentage of normal children; also, there was substantial reduction in percentage of children suffering from severe forms of underweight, stunting, as well as wasting with corresponding increase in the milder forms. Prevalence of severe protein energy malnutrition was lower in the 1988–90 survey data as compared to that in 1975–9. However, nearly one-fifth of the 12,000 pre-school children examined were found to suffer from clinical malnutrition of some kind or the other. Major nutritional deficiency signs encountered were those of protein energy malnutrition, and vitamin A and vitamin B complex deficiency. The report observed that during the previous 10 to 15 years there was no significant change in the consumption pattern of households despite an impressive increase in food production in the country, due to poor access to food and low purchasing capacity (NIN 1991).

The National Family Health Survey 1992–3 provides more recent data on nutrition status as determined by anthropometric criteria, using the measure of number of standard deviations from the median of an international reference population, recommended by the World Health Organization (WHO). The survey found that among children aged under 4 years of age, 53.4 per cent were underweight (weight for age), 52 per cent stunted (height for age), and 17.5 per cent were in the category of wasted (weight for height). The percentage of severely undernourished children was quite high, 21 per cent in the case of weight for age and 29 per cent in the case of height for age. The survey also indicated that with increase in age, there was a marked increase in malnutrition. It was lowest in the below 6 month age group when children are mostly breastfed. The National Family Health Survey 1998–9 found 47 per cent children under the age of three years to be underweight (weight for age) and and 45 per cent to be stunted (height for age). The percentage of severely undernourished children was 18 per cent according to weight for age, and 23 per cent according to height for age (IIPS 2000).

A survey sponsored by the Food and Nutrition Bureau of the Department of Women and Child Development, which covered 18 states and union territories in 1995–6 reported a similar state of nutrition status. The findings, based on measure of standard deviation from the median reference population, indicated that 49 per cent children aged 1 to 5 years were underweight and 56 per cent were stunted (DW&CD 1998). Thus, all the three national surveys found nearly half the children to be undernourished.

Some other studies, too, have brought out the unsatisfactory nutrition status of children. A survey on the impact of women's work on maternal and child health, which covered rural areas and urban slums in five states in 1989–91, found that about one-fifth of the sample children were under three standard deviations from the reference weight for age. Also, the proportion of children malnourished fluctuated with the seasons and reflected varied food availability and illness rates (WWCDN 1995). Studies in tribal areas and urban slums have found the presence of a large percentage of underweight children (Ray et al. 1997; Yadav and Singh 1999).

RURAL-URBAN DIFFERENCE

The National Family Health Survey 1992–3 found undernourishment to be higher in rural areas; 56 per cent children were underweight and 54 per cent were stunted (see Table 2.35). In urban areas, 45 per cent were underweight and the same percentage of children were stunted. The prevalence of severe undernourishment was higher in rural areas. The 1998–9 follow up survey, too, found undernourishment to be substantially higher in rural areas indicating that the causative factors operate with greater intensity in rural areas as compared to urban areas.

TABLE 2.35: NUTRITION STATUS OF CHILDREN IN RURAL AND URBAN AREAS, INDIA, 1992–3 AND 1998–9

	Age	Area	Weight for age		Height for age	
			Percentage below -3 SD	Percentage below -2 SD	Percentage below -3 SD	Percentage below -2 SD
National Family Health Survey 1992–3	Under 4 years	Rural	22.4	55.9	30.9	54.1
		Urban	14.8	45.2	22.0	44.8
		All areas	20.6	53.4	28.9	52.0
National Family Health Survey 1998–9	Under 3 years	Rural	19.9	49.6	25.4	48.5
		Urban	11.6	38.4	15.4	35.6
		All areas	18.0	47.0	23.0	45.5

Sources: *National Family Health Survey, 1992–3*; *National Family Health Survey, 1998–9*.

Note: -2 SD (standard deviation) includes children who are below -3 SD from the International Reference Population median.

GENDER DIFFERENCE

The National Family Health Survey 1992–3 found male and female children aged under 4 years 'about equally disadvantaged nutritionally'. The 1998–9 Survey found the girls to be slightly more likely to be underweight and stunted. This is evident from Table 2.36.

The National Nutrition Monitoring Bureau (NNMB) repeat surveys (1988–90), did not find a sex bias either in terms of nutrient intake or in terms of anthropometry (NIN 1991). The survey sponsored by the Food and Nutrition Bureau, too, found little difference in nutrition status of boys and girls aged 1 to 5 years (DW&CD 1998). However, the situation varied from state to state, and within a state, between different socio-economic groups and geographical areas. The National Family Health Survey (NFHS) 1992–3 while reporting no gender disparity in nutritional disadvantage when the data was aggregated for the country, did find that in 6 out of the 16 bigger states, the percentage of female underweight children was higher (difference Haryana 6.7, Tamil Nadu 6.6, Gujarat 5.1, West Bengal 4.3, Andhra Pradesh 4.0, Punjab 4.0, Karnataka 2.9, and Maharashtra 2.7). Punjab and Haryana are both economically better off states, and yet undernutrition was more common in female children than in male children. Discrimination against the girl child

TABLE 2.36: NUTRITION STATUS OF CHILDREN BY SEX, INDIA, 1992–3 AND 1998–9

	Age	Sex	Weight for age		Height for age	
			Percentage below -3 SD	Percentage below -2 SD	Percentage below -3 SD	Percentage below -2 SD
National Family Health Survey 1992–3	Under 4 years	Male	20.2	53.3	28.1	52.3
		Female	21.0	53.4	29.4	51.7
		Total	20.6	53.4	28.9	52.0
National Family Health Survey 1998–9	Under 3 years	Male	16.9	45.3	21.8	44.1
		Female	19.1	48.9	24.4	47.0
		Total	18.0	47.0	23.0	45.5

Sources: *National Family Health Survey, 1992–3*; *National Family Health Survey, 1998–9*.

Note: -2 SD (standard deviation) includes children who are below -3 SD from the International Reference Population median.

in Punjab in matters affecting nutrition and health status has been reported in several other studies as well. The Khanna study carried out in some villages of Ludhiana district in the 1950s brought out this socio-cultural phenomenon (Gordon, Singh and Wyon 1965; Singh, Gordon and Wyon 1962; Wyon and Gordon 1971). Later studies in Punjab have also indicated discrimination against female children. For instance, Das Gupta in her restudy of 11 villages of the Khanna study observed that sex bias fell more heavily on higher birth order girls and 'are far stronger than those of socio-economic status'. The study found that in the matter of allocation of food, though infant boys and girls had roughly similar calorie intake, girls were given more cereals while boys were given more milk and fats with their cereal. Also, much more was spent on medical care of boys than girls—in fact, here the sex differential was much wider. The study observed that the data suggested that discrimination against the girl child was primarily motivated not by economic hardship but rather by cultural factors. Due to son preference, scarcity of resources could heighten discrimination against females (Das Gupta 1987). Some other studies in Punjab have pointed in the same direction (Sachar et al. 1990).

Micro-studies from other parts of the country on gender difference in nutrition status are not conclusive. They have been carried out at different periods, during which a change in attitudes is likely to have taken place. Also, local factors and socio-cultural values vary among different caste groups and communities. Some studies have reported a gender bias in food and health care and higher incidence of malnutrition among girls (Benjamin and Zachariah 1993; Geetha and Swaminathan 1996; Gupta 1986; Kakker et al. 1987; Khadi, Khateeb and Patil 1996; Rao and Karkhanis 1993; Reddy and Satyanarayana, 1991; Sen and Sen Gupta 1983; Srivastava and Nayak 1995). Some, however, have found little or no gender difference in nutrition status or bias in intra-household distribution of food, though in some instances intake of milk or milk products was higher among boys (Premrajan and Srinivasan 1991; Pushpamma, Geervani and Laxmi Devi 1982; Subrahmanyam and Rao 1995; Varma and Goel 1993). It is necessary, through repeat empirical studies, to identify areas and groups, where socio-cultural factors account for discrimination against the girl child in matters of food, nutrition and health care so that intervention strategies can be planned to ensure that no child suffers because of gender. Gender discrimination needs close monitoring. Parental attitudes need to be influenced to ensure equal treatment of the girl child.

INTERSTATE VARIATION

There is marked variation between states in regard to the state of undernutrition. This was also brought out by the NNMB surveys. The National Family Health Survey 1998–9 points in the same direction. Table 2.37 gives the status of children aged under 3 years based on the anthropometic measure of age for weight. The data show that Kerala, which ranks very high on health and education status indicators, has the lowest prevalence rate of undernutrition. Bihar, Madhya Pradesh, Uttar Pradesh, Rajasthan and Orissa have high prevalence rate of undernourishment. These states rank poorly on health and education indicators and also have a large per cent of population below the poverty line.

TABLE 2.37: NUTRITION STATUS OF CHILDREN UNDER 3 YEARS OF AGE IN STATES BASED ON ANTHROPOMETRIC INDEX OF WEIGHT FOR AGE, 1998–9

Weight for age			
State	Percentage of children -3SD	State	Percentage of children below -2SD
Kerala	4.7	Kerala	26.9
Punjab	8.8	Punjab	28.7
Haryana	10.1	Haryana	34.6
Andhra Pradesh	10.3	Assam	36.0
Tamil Nadu	10.6	Tamil Nadu	36.7
Himachal Pradesh	12.1	Andhra Pradesh	37.7
Assam	13.3	Himachal Pradesh	43.6
Gujarat	16.2	Karnataka	43.9
West Bengal	16.3	Gujarat	45.1
Karnataka	16.5	West Bengal	48.7
Maharashtra	17.6	Maharashtra	49.6
Orissa	20.7	Rajasthan	50.6
Rajasthan	20.8	Uttar Pradesh	51.7
Uttar Pradesh	21.9	Bihar	54.4
Madhya Pradesh	24.3	Orissa	54.4
Bihar	25.5	Madhya Pradesh	55.1

Source: *National Family Health Survey, 1998–9.*

Note: -2 SD (standard deviation) includes children who are below -3 SD from the International Reference Population median. Data for 16 bigger states have been given here. These have been arranged in ascending order.

CAUSATIVE FACTORS

There are several causes of malnutrition. Poverty is undoubtedly a very important cause due to which the family is unable to buy the quantum of food grains and other food items it needs. Most vulnerable are the rural poor, who have no landholding, or have one that is too small to provide sufficient food for consumption. Household food security is to a large extent dependent on a regular income and availability of food at affordable prices. Low and uncertain incomes cause stress, which may aggravate in some seasons and cause household food insecurity (in quantity as well as quality), resulting in inadequate intake of calories, protein, and nutrients. The situation gets aggravated during natural calamities like drought, flood, cyclone, and earthquake, the impact of which on the food security of poor households could spread over a number of years. There is, thus, the situation of laudable increase in the country's food grain production but limited gains in the quantum and quality of food consumed by a large percentage of households due to poor purchasing power. The public distribution system which provides subsidized food grains, leaves a very large number of the rural and urban poor uncovered. Its implementation continues to be very unsatisfactory. There is not only wrong selection of beneficiaries, but also diversion of food grains on a large-scale due to widespread malpractices. There are recurring complaints about the non-availability of the stipulated amount of food grains and their poor quality.

Ignorance and illiteracy of the mother is another important factor which impedes the flow of information and knowledge about diets and feeding practices. It compounds the problem of dietary inadequacy due to: (a) faulty infant feeding and care practices, such as not giving colostrum to the newborn infant; giving pre-lacteal foods, and that, too, in an unhygienic manner; delayed introduction of supplementary food in proper quantity containing required nutrients; (b) deficiency of nutrients in the diet even though they are inexpensive and locally available; (c) cooking methods and practices relating to preservation of food which often result in loss of nutrients; and (d) unscientific beliefs about foods to be consumed or avoided by a pregnant woman and feeding practices to be followed.

Health and nutrition status of pregnant women, care practices during pregnancy, consumption of food in proper quantity containing adequate nutrition, and utilization of antenatal services has a strong influence on foetal outcome and the health and nutrition status of the infant. The unsatisfactory situation in this regard, due to medical and non-medical factors, have been documented in several research studies and reported elsewhere in the text.

Frequent episodes of illness caused by unsafe drinking water, bad environmental sanitation and personal hygiene, poor housing, and worm infestation of children affect adversely the health and nutrition status of children. Poor access to and utilization of medical facilities are other important factors.

BREASTFEEDING

The importance of breastfeeding for the infant's survival and good health has long been recognized. The practice is near universal in India. A large percentage of infants are exclusively or predominantly breastfed at least for four to six months. However, there are some practices relating to breastfeeding and weaning, brought out by various studies, which are matters of concern. Prominent among these are: (a) late initiation of breastfeeding, sometimes 72 hours after birth; (b) discarding colostrum which is not only nourishing but also provides protection against infection, under the mistaken notion that it is not good for the newborn; (c) giving pre-lacteal feeds such as jaggery, honey, herbal concoctions (*ghutti*), sugar water, tea, plain water, and gripe water, which are often prepared and given in unhygienic conditions; (d) giving supplements to the infant even before four months of age; and (e) neglect of breast hygiene. Another major problem area is late introduction of supplementation and weaning food in adequate quantity containing the right nutrients (Bavdekar et al. 1994; Gupta et al. 1979; Gurudeva et al. 1982; Khan 1990; Kumar et al. 1989; Kushawaha et al. 1987; Nagaraj et al. 1997; Prabhakara et al. 1987; Zodpey et al. 1996).

The National Family Health Survey 1992–3 indicated broadly the trend of universal breastfeeding. The study found no difference by sex in the initiation of breastfeeding of the child; however, rural-urban differences did exist. About one-third urban babies started breastfeeding within one day of birth, as compared to one-fourth rural babies. Early initiation of breastfeeding was found to be more common for children whose birth was assisted by health professionals and for children born in a health facility. The medium length of exclusive breastfeeding (only breast milk and no other liquid, including water) was only 1.4 months, but the median length of full breastfeeding was 4.7 months. Male children were breastfed for a slightly longer period than female children (25.3 months, compared to 23.6 months for female children), but exclusive breastfeeding and full breastfeeding was for a slightly longer time for female children because male children started receiving water and supplements at an earlier age. Of children under six months of age, 92 per cent were found to have been breastfed six or more times in the previous 24 hours. There was no difference in this matter between the male and female child. However, more rural women (93 per cent) than urban women reported this practice. Only half the children less than four months old were exclusively breastfed. The introduction of solid or mashed food was late. The survey found that 63 per cent of the mothers discarded the colostrum. The National Family Health Survey 1998–9 reported similar findings. The national survey sponsored by the Food and Nutrition Bureau of the Department of Women and Child Development for the preparation of nutrition profile up to the district level found that 52 per cent of the mothers followed the practice of discarding colostrum (DW&CD 1998).

Breastfeeding is of paramount importance in building the health and nutrition status of the newborn infant. It is, therefore, necessary to build on the strong base of breastfeeding in the country. Nutrition and health education of pregnant women is very necessary, and they must be made aware of the importance of exclusive breastfeeding up to 4–6 months of age and introduction thereafter of complementary foods containing all the required nutrients in adequate quantity. Educated upper and middle class women, too, need to be covered as some studies have shown that duration of breastfeeding is getting shorter in some segments of the population. The National Family Health Survey 1998–9 found that there was complementary feeding only in the case of about one-third breastfeeding infants of ages 6–9 months. Feeding colostrum to the newborn and discarding the use of pre-lacteal feed has to be propagated. Mothers have to be made aware of the dangers of infection from the use of bottle with nipple and of the importance of breast hygiene. Health professionals, both in public and private sectors, need to be trained and instructed to convey to mothers appropriate messages connected with breastfeeding. Area specific awareness programmes are necessary so that they dispel wrong beliefs and practices about breastfeeding. The Infant Milk Substitutes, Feeding Bottles and Infant Foods (Regulation of Production, Supply and Distribution) Act, 1992 needs to be strictly enforced. The World Health Organization has suggested some indicators of breastfeeding, like exclusive breastfeeding rate, predominant breastfeeding rate, timely complementary feeding rate and continued breastfeeding rate. Such standardized data collection, even in micro-studies, will help in the monitoring of trends. Unfortunately, little has been done in this regard to build the database disaggregated by key variables.

Micro-nutrient Deficiencies

Micro-nutrients, though required by the body in minute quantities, are very important for women during the period of pregnancy and breastfeeding of the child. They are also needed by children during the period of their growth and development. Deficiencies in iodine, iron folate, and vitamin A have been recognized for nearly three decades as public health problems in India. Nutritionists are now suggesting that deficiencies in zinc also need public health attention as it affects the growth and development of the child and could result in vulnerability to infectious diseases. Unfortunately, there is hardly any data available on the prevalence of zinc deficiency in the community in different parts of the country. This is an area which needs immediate research attention.

IODINE DEFICIENCY

Iodine deficiency is a serious nutritional problem and could result in impaired mental development and performance, muscular disorders, stunted growth, defects in stance, squint, deaf mutism, and poor muscular coordination. In pregnant women, iodine deficiency could affect the development of the brain of the foetus and result in the birth of iodine deficient babies who may be cretins characterized by physical and mental handicap. It is also a contributory factor in abortion, miscarriage, stillbirth, and neonatal death (ICMR 1989a; UNICEF 1998).

Iodine deficiency disorders affect a fairly large segment of the population, and are not confined to a limited geographical area in the Himalayan and sub-Himalayan region as was the assumption in the past. They are caused by deficiency of iodine in foods and water due to iodine deficiency in the soil arising from thousands of years of iodine leaching. A common visible effect of iodine deficiency is goitre.

The prevalence of goitre has now been reported from almost every part of the country, as is evident from surveys conducted between 1981 and 1993. In several districts, the goitre prevalence rate has been found to be more than 30 per cent (CBHI 2000). Micro-studies on schoolchildren and community surveys in different parts of the country have reported prevalence rates which, in some sample populations studied, exceeded 50 per cent (ICMR 1989a; Pandav et al. 1980).

An ICMR Task Force Study spread over a two-year period 1984 to 1986, covering 14 districts in nine states, reported an overall prevalence rate of 21.1 per cent. There was very large variation between districts. The age specific prevalence rate showed that in children aged less than 1 year it was 2.9 per cent, in children aged 1–4 years it was 9.5 per cent, in children aged 5–9 years it was 26.5 per cent, in children aged 10–14 years it was 37.3 per cent, and in the age group 15–19 years the percentage was 31.4. The prevalence rate declined in the older age groups. Among males it was 15.5 per cent, and among females 26.8 per cent (ICMR 1989a). Several other studies have also reported a higher prevalence rate among females (Bharadwaj et al. 1997; Pandav et al. 1980; Sundaram et al. 1997).

Some later surveys on iodine deficiency have shown that prevalence of iodine deficiency in children continues to be a problem. A study in four states and three union territories showed that in primary schoolchildren, the prevalence rate varied from 2.6 per cent to 20.6 per cent (Kapil and Nayar 1997). A study in Karnataka in 1988–91 found, in several districts, a prevalence rate of more than 10 per cent among children. A survey on urban schoolchildren in Bangalore city reported a prevalence rate of 31 per cent (Sundaram et al. 1997), while a survey in 1993–4 among schoolchildren in the Kashmir valley reported a prevalence rate of 44 per cent in the sample (Zargar et al. 1996). A survey in a community development block in Uttar Pradesh found a prevalence rate of 50 per cent (Lal et al. 1996). These and other studies show that there is no room for complacency, and iodine deficiency continues to be a major nutritional problem.

An easy and inexpensive way to combat the public health problem of iodine deficiency disorders is to add iodine to the salt that is used by households for cooking. In 1962, the Government of India launched a national programme of goitre control. The programme faced severe problems of implementation in the matter of production of iodized salt, its distribution to states, its sale, and its acceptance by households as the cost of iodized salt was higher. The programme limped in the first two decades hardly making an impact, drawing the comment that 'administrative incompetence, lack of co-ordination between various agencies involved, and commercial and vested interests have apparently combined to wreck the programme' (Gopalan 1983). In 1986, goitre control was included in the Prime Minister's 20 point programme.

The programme was modified in 1992 and renamed as the National Iodine Deficiency Disorders Control Programme. Its objectives are universal iodization of salt; its ready availability in all states through enhanced and streamlined iodized salt production facilities with private sector participation; and imposition and enforcement of ban by states on the sale of common salt as a food item. In 1998–9, the production of iodized salt was 4.1 million tonnes against the total requirement of 6.2 million tonnes for human and animal consumption. The sale of non-iodized salt was banned in 31 out of 32 states/union territories (Department of Salt, 1997).

Implementation problems of the programme continue. A survey of salt sold and consumed in different states in the early 1990s showed that iodine content was less than the minimum of 15 parts per million (ppm) in a number of cases. In several states, the salt samples showed 20 or more per cent of salt samples with iodine below the minimum prescribed level of 15 ppm. There were production problems and bottlenecks in the regular supply of iodized salt to the consuming centres. In some states, part of the non-iodized salt meant for industrial use was diverted for home use. Poor packaging, transportation delays, and unsatisfactory storage resulted in loss of iodine content. At the household level, too, iodized salt was not properly stored (Department of Salt 1995).

A study undertaken of sample districts in 10 states and 2 union territories in 1995–7 showed that on the aggregate, two-thirds of the 12,052 salt samples at beneficiary level had an iodine content of 15 ppm plus. However, in Uttar Pradesh, more than 80 per cent of the salt samples indicated iodine content below the minimum of 15 ppm. In several other states/union territories, too, the percentage of salt samples below the minimum level was quite high—Goa 78.0 per cent, Pondicherry 69 per cent, Haryana 46.6 per cent, Kerala 46.2 per cent, Delhi 42.3 per cent, Rajasthan 39.9 per cent, Madhya Pradesh 35.2 per cent, Bihar 28.5 per cent, and Punjab 28.7 per cent. In Rajasthan, 31.9 per cent salt samples, and in Goa 48.9 per cent salt samples had no iodine at all (Kapil and Nayar 1997). The National Family Health Survey 1998–9 found that only 49 per cent households used cooking salt with minimum iodine content of 15 ppm, 22 per cent used salt that was inadequately iodized and 28 per cent used salt that was not iodized at all. The consumption of iodized salt was much higher in urban areas and among households with a higher standard of living.

The Government of India's commitment to universal access of iodized salt by 1995 was not achieved. The new time frame to control iodine deficiency disorders by the year 2000 was also not met. In the meantime, in a highly debatable move, the Government of India, bowing to the pressure of indigenous salt manufacturers, Sarvodaya leaders, and some other groups opposed to the ban on sale of non-iodized salt for human consumption, issued a notification lifting the earlier central notification restricting the sale of non-iodized salt, with effect from 30 Semtember 2000. The arguments given by those advocating withdrawal are that the current ban has adversely affected indigenous salt manufacturers, benefited large manufacturers and multinational companies, and increased the price of salt to the consumer, thus affecting the interests of the poor. It has been further stated that there should be no compulsion in a public health measure of this nature, and it should be left to individuals to consume the type of salt they want. Apprehension has also been expressed about the effect of increase in iodine on the human system as a result of consumption of iodized salt, a fear discounted by nutritionists. The move has been strongly opposed by the medical fraternity and public health experts who are of the firm opinion that such a step will undo the progress painstakingly achieved in the past to contain the problem, reduce its incidence, and ultimately eradicate iodine deficiency disorders. They have argued that the increase in price as a result of iodization is not much and is a small price to pay for protection against iodine disorders. They have strongly advocated that efforts to universalize the consumption of iodized salt of the required potency have to be continued with greater vigour.

The ban on sale of non-iodized salt as a food item should continue and should be strictly enforced. Production and distribution of iodized salt, packaging of salt, and its consumption have to be closely monitored. Testing of iodine content is necessary at not only the production level but also at the retail outlet and household levels. Awareness in the community of the importance of iodized salt is necessary so that only packed iodized salt is purchased and properly stored. To facilitate the availability of iodized salt at a reasonable price the public distribution system should include the sale of iodized salt.

VITAMIN A DEFICIENCY

Vitamin A deficiency is a primary cause of preventable blindness. It also impairs the immune system of the child and the capacity to fight infection. It has been reported as a contributory factor in deaths from diarrhoeal diseases and measles. Low doses of vitamin A supplements have been found to reduce pregnancy related deaths (UNICEF 1998).

The clinical manifestation of vitamin A deficiency in the form of keratomalacia (nutritional blindness) has shown a significant decline in the last two decades. It is currently a relatively unimportant factor in causing blindness in India, and is no longer the public health problem it once was (Gopalan 1993). This has also been reported by the national survey of blindness in India. The main factors contributing to its decline have been general socio-economic development, better health care, availability of medicines to control infection, and the implementation of the national prophylactics programme for prevention of vitamin A deficiency launched in 1970 under which mega doses of vitamin A are administered periodically to children six months to five years of age. However, conjunctival xerosis and bitot spots, despite some decline, still remain a public health problem.

The national survey of blindness by the National Programme for Control of Blindness (NPCB) and the World Health Organization conducted during 1986–9 reported an overall vitamin A deficiency prevalence rate of 6.0 per cent in the age group 0–6 years. It was only 1.7 per cent in the age group less than 2 years but 6.2 per cent (almost four times) in the age group 2–6 years, probably due to the protective effect of breastfeeding in the first two years of the child's life. The survey found that prevalence was higher in the plains of Uttar Pradesh, Rajasthan, Haryana, Madhya Pradesh, and Gujarat. It was relatively lower in the north-eastern states and also in the Deccan plateau (Maharashtra, Andhra Pradesh, Karnataka, Tamil Nadu, and Kerala). It was more prevalent in rural (6.5 per cent) than in urban areas (4.8 per cent). There was hardly any difference in prevalence rates among male and female children (Mohan 1989) The survey, after comparing the results of the 1979–81 survey by the National Nutrition Monitoring Bureau (NNMB) in ten states, and the trachoma control pilot project (1959–64), concluded that vitamin A deficiency still presents a public health problem in many states. The NNMB repeat surveys (1988–90) and the NNMB–NCAER surveys in 1994 in eight states found that vitamin A intake continued to be far below recommended levels (NIN 1991, 1996).

The findings of several micro-studies indicate higher levels of vitamin A deficiency among pre-schoolers and schoolchildren in backward areas, drought prone areas, and urban slums than in the general population. The prevalence has also been found to be more among children of higher birth order in poor families with illiterate parents. Malnutrition, dietary intake low in vitamin A rich foods, and history of diseases such as diarrhoea, measles, worm infestation, and repeated episodes of sickness also lead to the deficiency. Deficiency of vitamin A does not appear to be gender related. Some studies have reported a higher prevalence rate among males, and some among females, while some studies have found only a marginal difference (Dwivedi et al. 1995; Fakhir et al. 1993; Katiyar et al. 1988; Pratinidhi, Bapat and Shah 1984; Sampathkumar and Abel, 1993; Sharma et al, 1987).

A primary cause of vitamin A deficiency in childhood is to be found in the poor vitamin A nutrition status of the mother during pregnancy and lactation, and inadequate inclusion of foods rich in vitamin A and carotene in the diet. The ICMR study in 1971–4 on pre-school children had pointed out that their diets were grossly inadequate in vitamin A (ICMR 1984).

A national prophylaxis programme against blindness due to vitamin A deficiency was launched in India in 1970, the first country in the world to do so. It was initially started in seven states where the incidence was higher and was later extended to cover other states by 1995. Implementation of the programme has been described as extremely tardy, patchy, and inefficient, and the coverage very poor (Gopalan 1993). The national survey on blindness (1986–9), too, found low coverage of beneficiaries targeted by the programme, as well as poor awareness and knowledge about it and about vitamin A rich foods in the diet. The report stated that the majority of the PHCs surveyed indicated erratic and irregular supplies of vitamin A doses, thus affecting its distribution (Mohan 1989). A subsequent evaluation in 1990–1 in four states (Maharashtra, Orissa, Tamil Nadu, and Uttar Pradesh) reported inadequate doses, poor storage and inventory control, loss of about 20 per cent of vitamin A due to spilling or rejection, poor monitoring and supervisory visits, non-availability of IEC (information, education, and communication) material, and absence of training (Kapil, Saxena and Nayar 1996). The National Family Health Survey 1998–9 reported that poor coverage has continued to be a problem area. Only 30 per cent children 12-35 months had received at least one dose of vitamin A; only 17 per cent received a dose within the past six months. Children in urban areas were better covered (39 per cent) than children in rural areas (27 per cent).

For a long term solution of the problem of vitamin A deficiency, consumption of foods rich in vitamin A and carotene has to be promoted on a large-scale and mothers educated about its critical importance, so that such foods get included in the diets of women and children as a matter of course. Although such promotion and education is a component of the national programme as its long term strategy, in actual practice the efforts have been too weak to produce any impact. The emphasis has continued to be on the short term strategy of administering mega doses of vitamin A. What started, therefore, as a prophylaxis programme and an interim measure has acquired a virtually permanent status. The implementation of the vitamin A prophylaxis programme needs to be considerably strengthened and improved with special attention on removal of deficiencies in the delivery system.

IRON DEFICIENCY

Nutritional anaemia due to iron and folate deficiency is common, especially among children aged 6–36 months. Iron deficiency lowers the child's capacity to fight infection, and also affects its learning ability and stamina. Severe anaemia of pregnant women affects pregnancy outcome and could also result in maternal mortality and various ailments following childbirth. The prevalence rate of anaemia is higher among the disadvantaged segments of the population. It has also been found to be fairly high in adolescent girls from middle and upper middle class segments of society.

An ICMR Task Force study at six centres in 1971–4 on pre-school children reported 63 per cent children aged 1–3 years and 44 per cent aged 3–5 years to be suffering from anaemia. Severe and moderate anaemia was present in about 12 per cent children. Its prevalence was higher in children below 3 years of age (ICMR 1984). Micro-studies in different parts of the country in later years have indicated that anaemia continues to be a major nutritional disorder (Malin and Stones 1988; Raman et al. 1992; Vasanthi et al. 1994)). Even in a prosperous state like Punjab, nearly half of 2000 urban schoolchildren 5–15 years of age were found to be anaemic in a study conducted in Ludhiana district. A striking finding was that in upper and upper middle class children 38 per cent were found to have anaemia. Girls had a significantly higher prevalence of anaemia (Verma et al. 1998).

The National Family Health Survey 1998–9 found that 74.3 per cent children aged 6 to 35 months were having iron deficiency anaemia—22.9 per cent mildly anaemic (10.0–10.9 g/dl), 45.9 per cent moderately anaemic (7.0–9.9 g/dl) and 5.4 per cent severely anaemic (less than 7.0 g/dl). Among rural children under three years of age, 75.3 per cent were having anaemia and among urban children the percentage was 70.8. In four of the 16 bigger states 80 to 84 per cent children 6–35 months were found to have iron deficiency anaemia.

The main causative factors of nutritional anaemia have been identified as poor iron and folate stores at birth, delayed introduction of food supplements as the infant was being breastfed, intake of foods deficient in iron and other essential nutrients, worm infestation, and repeated episodes of diarrhoeal, respiratory, and other infections due to unsafe drinking water and poor environmental sanitation and hygiene.

The national programme of control of anaemia, which had its beginnings in 1970, covers children as well. Under the programme, a child gets one tablet containing iron and folic acid daily for 100 days in a year. The poor implementation of the programme was brought out by the ICMR Task Force study conducted in 11 states in 1984–5. It concluded that the programme had not made a significant impact on the prevalence of anaemia; there was little difference with regard to prevalence of anaemia between the supplemented and the non-supplemented group; 88 per cent of the pregnant women were still anaemic at the time of study; the quality of tablets distributed was poor; the number of beneficiaries who actually received the supplements was far less than the numbers shown in the records; many beneficiaries dropped out because of non-supply of supplements; knowledge of beneficiaries and of the functionaries about anaemia was unsatisfactory; and the educational component of the programme had not received adequate attention (ICMR 1989b). A subsequent evaluation on the implementation of the programme in four states indicated that it continued to suffer from low priority and weak implementation (Kapil, Saxena and Nayar 1996).

A long term and stable solution of the problem would involve an improvement in the health and nutrition status of the mother, introduction of food supplements in time, intake of foods rich in iron and folic acid, improvements in environmental sanitation and hygiene, control of morbidity, and education of the mother on the importance of diets rich in iron and folic acid.

Nutrition Policies and Programmes

Programmes specifically aimed at the problem of malnutrition and funded by the central and state governments have been under implementation for more than four decades. In the earlier phase these covered mainly supplementary feeding programmes. The Fourth Plan (1969–74) provided an outlay of Rs 45 crores for 38 schemes in the public sector, mainly in the central plan. These could be classified into four groups: (a) supplementary feeding; (b) production, processing, and supply of nutritious food; (c) production of nutritious food and its consumption through nutrition education and extension activities; (d) nutritional prophylaxis. The programmes were implemented by different departments at the Centre and in the states, mainly social welfare, education, community development, health, and food.

Supplementary nutrition feeding of pre-school children has been a prime thrust area of intervention to tackle energy malnutrition among children. It made a modest beginning in the Second and Third Five Year Plans as a component of the balwadi programme of the Central Social Welfare Board and of the State Social Welfare Departments. A large coverage was provided in states like Tamil Nadu, which had in place a mid-day meal scheme for schoolchildren, which covered the pre-primary sections as well. Substantial central government funding began from 1970–1 when the Prime Minister in her 1970 budget speech announced the launching of a supplementary nutrition feeding scheme for pre-school children, funded by the central government. It initially covered children aged up to 3 years from disadvantaged groups living in tribal and backward areas and urban slums. The next year it was modified to cover children up to 6 years of age, and pregnant and lactating women. In the Fifth Plan, the programme was shifted to the state sector under the Minimum Needs Programme head, for which outlays were earmarked by the Planning Commission.

The programme was reviewed by the Task Force constituted by the Planning Commission to advise on nutrition policies and programmes in the Sixth Plan. The Task Force took into consideration the report of Study Teams which visited different states and also considered the evaluation reports. It was of the view that supplementary nutrition feeding as an isolated scheme for tackling malnutrition of pre-school children and mothers was conceptually flawed and felt that an integrated package of services targeted at pre-school children and mothers was necessary for making an impact. The Task Force also took note of several weaknesses in the implementation of the scheme. These related to wrong selection of feeding centres and of beneficiaries, due to which nutrition was not reaching sections in dire need. There were interruptions in feeding resulting in reduction in the number of feeding days. Other problem areas were supplies not reaching in time, unsatisfactory storage of food commodities, malpractices in procurement and distribution, and misuse of food aid received from international agencies. The number of beneficiaries shown on record was found to be higher than the number which actually got the benefit; the children were also at times different. At some places, children did not consume the food at the centre, but carried it home where it became a part of the family food basket. Sometimes, sliced bread or other ready to eat food was served, the storage of which was at places not hygienically done. At the field level, the programme was implemented as a relief measure, and was perceived as such by the parents, the community, and field level functionaries. Participation of the village community in the implementation of the programme was perfunctory in nature. Supervision and monitoring were poor, and the health and nutrition education component was weak. The programme had little impact on the health and nutrition status of children.

Following the report of the Task Force, supplementary feeding as a separate single service programme was discontinued. It became a component of the new centrally sponsored scheme of Integrated Child Development Services (ICDS), which was launched in 1975 and now covers all rural and tribal development blocks in the country and major slum areas in cities. The cost of supplementary nutrition is borne by the state governments from their plan and non-plan budgets. Some states receive food assistance from international agencies for supplementary feeding. The programme of ICDS has been generously supported by the central government despite adverse comments on its perfornance. The Comptroller and Auditor General (CAG) in its 1983–4 report pointed out several weaknesses in the implementation of supplementary nutrition in ICDS project areas. The 1989–90 report is detailed and rather severe in its indictment. The weaknesses and malpractices, even though not present in all the anganwadis, are, none the less, characteristic of many centres. In some states the problem is quite deep-rooted. The main drawbacks and malpractices relating to supplementary nutrition in the ICDS programme pointed out by various studies and the CAG are: (a) children do not get supplementary feeding for the prescribed number of 300 days. In some projects the actual number of feeding days is half, or less. Interruptions are frequent and at times for very long periods. This happens due to inadequate budgetary provision or diversion of funds to other programmes. Interruptions are also due to administrative delays in procurement and supply, siphoning of funds and food supplies, pilferage, corruption, and absence of worker; (b) the food given at some places does not have the required calories or protein; it is at times sub-standard and infested; (c) the food is not consumed at the spot; (d) ready to eat food given is not liked by the children; (e) selection of beneficiaries and supplementary feeding do not follow the criteria laid down for the programme; some records show inflated figures and a discrepancy between children actually given food and children listed on the register; (f) equipment like weighing scales, medicine kits, teaching aids, play material, etc., have either not been supplied or supplied very late; (g) location of anganwadis was at times in unhygienic surroundings; (h) there were deficiencies in arrangements for supply of drinking water; (i) the programme is still largely run as a relief programme; the growth monitoring card is often not filled nor used for interacting with the mother; (j) nutrition and health education of mothers is unsatisfactory; and (k) community participation is rather perfunctory. Some state reports of the Comptroller and Auditor General

BOX 2.1. SUPPLEMENTARY NUTRITION IN ICDS

'Under supplementary nutrition, shortfalls up to 80 per cent occurred in coverage of women and children and in some cases supplementary nutrition was not at all provided. Feeding suffered from frequent interruptions for periods exceeding two years in some cases, and was provided for 28 days only against the norm of 300 days in some of the states test checked. The quality of supplementary nutrition was below the prescribed norm; therapeutic food, rich in calories and proteins, required to be supplied to severely malnourished children, has not been supplied in several states. In nine states, cases of supply of sub-standard and infested food were noticed. Although the necessity for development of a system of cheap and hygienically prepared ready to eat food has been recognized, no action in the matter had been taken.

As a result of inadequate, interrupted and sub-standard quality of supplementary nutrition, the desired effect of raising the health status of beneficiaries could not be achieved'.

Report of the Comptroller and Auditor General of India for the year ended 31 March, 1989, Union Government Civil, Integrated Child Development Services.

on the performance of ICDS have also made adverse comments (CAG, 1990, 1998, 2000 a, b and c). Media reports, too, have highlighted malpractices in procurement of food, in feeding, and in implementation (India Today 1996; Mohammad 1999; Narayan 1997).

A decade later the CAG, in its report ending March 1999, found that the deficiencies persisted in the implementation of the scheme. It reported:

> . . . Twenty-five years of operation of the scheme has done little in improving the health status of the children. . . .
>
> . . . The supplementary nutrition component had failed to improve the health status of beneficiaries due to various reasons like non-identification of beneficiaries, insufficient coverage of beneficiaries, significant interruptions in feeding, deficiencies in nutritive value of food, sub-standard food etc. Many state governments did not provide adequate budget for supplementary nutrition. . . . (CAG 2000e)

Another programme of supplementary nutrition which has a long history of implementation is the mid-day meal for schoolchildren. It began in 1956 in Tamil Nadu, and was subsequently implemented in several other states to increase enrolment and attendance of children from poor sections of society and improve their nutritional status. The Committee on Pre-school Children Feeding Programmes reported that in 1971–2, the school meals programme was in implementation in 14 states and union territories and covered about 12 million children (Planning Commission 1972). Apart from government funding, the scheme received assistance by way of food commodities from external agencies. Evaluation of the programme has shown mixed results. In some areas it improved school enrolment, attendance, and academic performance. In some, however, no significant difference was noticed (Planning Commission Task Force 1980). The programme received a big boost with the announcement by the Prime Minister in 1995 of supply of food grains free of cost to the states for implementing the scheme and reimbursement of some local costs. The scheme is now under implementation in all states and union territories. In some states, cooked food is served, while in others food grains are distributed. Deficiencies and malpractices in the implementation of the scheme have been brought out by some reports indicating that lessons from the past have not been learnt (CAG 1999, 2000 a, b, c and d; PROBE 1999).

A nutrition intervention of a different kind was the production and consumption of nutritious food by rural households. Prominent among the schemes in operation was the Applied Nutrition Programme (ANP) launched in 1963 as a centrally sponsored scheme and implemented by the departments of community development in the states. Its objectives were to improve local diets through extension services, give support for production and consumption of nutritious food such as eggs, fruits, and vegetables, and create awareness of nutritional needs of children and adults through demonstration feeding in Balwadis, Mahila Mandals, Health Centres, etc., and through educational messages using informal and formal channels. In 1977–8, the programme was under implementation in 1765 community development blocks. In 1978–9 it was transferred to the states. Evaluation of the programme showed that it was conceptually flawed and was based more on wishful thinking than on ground realities. Acceptance of the programme by the community was poor. Inadequate funding, poor coordination, and inertia of extension staff made matters worse. The production schemes at community or household level had limited impact by way of enlarging food supply for the household or increase in consumption of nutritious food. Nutrition education component of ANP was poorly implemented. Community involvement and participation was perfunctory. The programme, despite a decade and half of implementation, did not take roots, and withered away as soon as the prop of central funds was removed. Another centrally sponsored scheme of a similar nature launched in the Fourth Plan in rural areas not covered by ANP was the composite nutrition programme. This, too, was implemented by the Departments of Community Development in the states. It main objectives were nutrition education of mothers and demonstration feeding with the active support of Mahila Mandals. The programme suffered from poor implementation and had the same weaknesses as ANP. It did not take roots and withered on its transfer to the states. Currently, nutrition education of mothers is a component of ICDS programme and of programmes of Health and Family Welfare, Education, and other Departments which are targeted at children and women.

Another area of nutrition intervention has been the production of affordable nutritious ready to eat food for children and fortification of foods with nutrients. Some of the projects have received external assistance. Processed food has not found good acceptance by children in the supplementary feeding programmes. The Food and Nutrition Board, transferred in 1993 from the Department of Food to the Department of Women and Child Development, has under implementation programmes of development and promotion of nutritious foods, fortification of foods, and education and training.

In the area of public health, prophylaxis programmes for tackling nutritional iron deficiency anaemia, iodine deficiency and vitamin A deficiency, have been under implementation since 1970. These have been discussed earlier. Unfortunately, the implementation of these programmes has been unsatisfactory.

Though the government policy on nutrition was reflected in successive plan documents and programmes, a formal nutrition policy statement was prepared only in 1993, laying down the goals, strategies, long and short term policy instruments, and the programme areas. The policy envisages multi-sectoral intervention, involving both economic and social sectors, and participation of several departments/ministries. In 1995, a National Plan of Action on Nutrition (NPAN) was prepared, stating the national nutrition goals to be reached by the near 2000. These are:

- Reduction in moderate and severe malnutrition among pre-school children by half;
- Reduction in chronic undernutrition and stunted growth in children;
- Reduction in incidence of low birth weight to less than 10 per cent;
- Elimination of blindness due to vitamin A deficiency;
- Reduction in iron deficiency anaemia among pregnant women to 25 per cent;
- Universal iodization of salt for reduction of iodine deficiency disorders to 10 per cent;
- Production of 250 million tonnes of food grains;
- Improving household food security through poverty alleviation programmes;
- Promoting appropriate diets and healthy lifestyles.

On the whole, the targets set are rather an exercise in ambiguity and are speculative in nature. In the case of some of the objectives, the current levels from which reduction will be affected are not stated, for some the extent of reduction is not given, for some the objective is rather vague, and for some overambitious.The national nutrition policy statement has little to celebrate by way of progress in the attainment of its goals. For instance, the percentage of underweight children under 3 years of age, which was 51.5 per cent in 1992–3, came down to 46.7 per cent in 1998–9, a decline of only

9 per cent in six years, far less than the target of a 50 per cent decline. Similarly, the percentage of ever married women aged 15–49 years with anaemia has been reported by the National Family Health Survey 1998–9 to be 52 per cent, as against the target of 25 per cent laid down by NPAN for the year 2000. The target for food grains production set by NPAN for the year 2000 is 250 million tonnes. The production of food grains was 191.5 million tonnes in 1994–5 when NPAN was prepared. In 1999–2000, the estimated food grains production was 210 million tonnes, and in 2000–1 about 196 million tonnes.

SUMMING UP

India has achieved some success in addressing child health issues, more in some areas and less in others. A lot more needs to be done. Infant deaths in India in 1998 constituted 21 per cent of the total deaths, an unacceptably high figure. In some states like Rajasthan, Madhya Pradesh, and Uttar Pradesh, the percentage is higher. Infant mortality rate has shown a decline. During the period 1951–61, the average IMR is estimated to have been 146. Data compiled and published by the Sample Registration System from 1970 indicate a decline in IMR from 129 in 1970 to 68 in 2000, a fall of 47 per cent. A target of less than 60 IMR in 2000 was set by the National Health Policy 1983. This has not been reached.

The perinatal mortality rate which is an indicator of the extent of pregnancy wastage has shown little change since 1970, when it was 45. In 1998 it was marginally lower at 42. The National Health Policy target of 30–5 in 2000 will, therefore, not be reached. The first week of the infant's life continues to be an area of considerable concern. In 1998, early neonatal deaths constituted 47 per cent of infant deaths. Neonatal mortality and stillbirths have to be specifically addressed through improved antenatal and post-natal services to bring down PMR in any significant measure.

Neonatal mortality rate (NNMR) has fallen from 68 in 1970 to 45 in 1998, a decline of 34 per cent. The decline in post neonatal mortality rate (PNMR) is sharper, from 61 in 1970 to 27 in 1998, a fall of 56 per cent. Thus, the decline in PNMR is far greater than that of NNMR. This indicates that there has been greater success in reducing post neonatal mortality than neonatal mortality.

The rural-urban difference in IMR is very marked. In 2000, urban

India had an IMR of 43, but in rural areas it was 74, that is 72 per cent higher. The survival scenario is thus far more fragile in rural India where three-fourths of the population lives.

Interstate variations in IMR are very marked. In 1998, Orissa and Madhya Pradesh had the highest IMR. Close behind is Uttar Pradesh with an IMR of 83 and Rajasthan with an IMR of 79, as compared to only an IMR of 14 in Kerala. Ten out of the 16 bigger states had an IMR of more than 60 in 2000.

Female IMR (74 in 1998) is higher than male IMR (70 in 1998). A closer look, however, shows that at the neonatal stage (first four weeks), male mortality is higher (neonatal mortality rate of 52.2 in 1990–3 for males, as compared to 47.9 for females) because the female infant is biologically stronger. The position is reversed at the post neonatal stage, when female mortality is higher (post neonatal mortality rate of 30.7 for females in 1990–3 as compared to 25.2 for males). The difference is high in the states of Punjab, Haryana, Uttar Pradesh, Rajasthan, Orissa, and Madhya Pradesh. This shows gender bias, as a result of which the female infant receives less health and nutrition care and medical attention, and is, therefore, at higher risk of not surviving, more so in the rural areas. Two other practices which are morbid manifestations of gender bias are female foeticide and female infanticide, whose presence is indicated by research studies and media reports.

The 0–4 age specific mortality rate has declined from 53.0 in 1970 to 22.5 in 1998, a fall of 57 per cent. In the 5–9 year age group, the age specific death rate has declined from 4.8 in 1970 to 2.2 in 1998, a fall of 54 per cent. Here, too, rural age specific death rates are far above the urban rates. There is also considerable inter-state variation. Madhya Pradesh and Uttar Pradesh had 0–4 year age specific death rates of more than 29 in 1998, while in Kerala the rate was only 3.6.

The poor health and nutrition status of pregnant women is a major contributory factor to child mortality. Maternal malnutrition continues to be an area of concern. Low birthweight is a major problem area, with a prevalence rate estimated to be 20 to 35 per cent.

Health care facilities do not function satisfactorily. The reach of maternal health services is feeble. The population segments worst affected are the rural and urban poor who suffer the most when the public health care system malfunctions. The National Family Health

Survey 1998–9 found, for instance, that 40 per cent of rural pregnant women and 14 per cent of urban pregnant women (combined figure 34 per cent) had, during the three years preceding the survey, not made any antenatal visits. In the states of Rajasthan, Bihar, Uttar Pradesh, Madhya Pradesh, and Assam, the percentage was far higher. The Child Survival and Safe Motherhood Programme had aimed at a minimum of three antenatal check-ups of pregnant women. The National Family Health Survey, 1998–9 thus showed that in the case of 56 per cent of pregnancies this had not been achieved. The National Health Policy had laid the target of 100 per cent coverage of pregnant women by tetanus toxoid (TT) vaccine in 1990. The actual achievement of TT2 (two or more doses of tetanus toxoid vaccine) coverage, as reported by the National Family Health Survey 1998–9, was only 67 per cent.

The National Family Health Survey 1998–9 found that in the case of only 48 per cent live births during the three years preceding the survey, pregnant women had received iron folic tablets for three or more months. In Bihar the percentage was only 20, in Uttar Pradesh 21 per cent, and in Rajasthan 31 per cent.

Proper medical attention at delivery is a critical factor for safe motherhood and child survival. In 1998 only 54 per cent of the deliveries were by trained functionaries. In other words, even towards the close of the twentieth century, 46 per cent babies were ushered into the world by untrained hands. The National Health Policy, 1983 had laid down a target of 80 per cent deliveries in 1990 by trained functionary and 100 per cent by the year 2000. The target was not reached.

There has been some success in bringing down morbidity and mortality due to the vaccine preventable diseases, particularly tetanus and polio, and case fatality due to diarrhoeal diseases and acute respiratory infections.

The Universal Immunization Programme which limped initially has now gathered some momentum and is one of the biggest preventive public child health programmes in the world. Much, however, still remains to be done. The coverage brought out by the National Family Health Survey 1992–3 for different vaccines is far below the 1990 target set by the Universal Immunization Programme. Here, again, deficiencies in the delivery system have been the major impediment. The National Family Health Survey 1998–9 reported vaccine coverage of children aged 12–23 months to be

72 per cent for BCG, 55 per cent for DPT-3, 63 per cent for Polio-3, and 51 per cent for measles vaccine. Only 42 per cent children aged 12–23 months received all the vaccines, as against the UIP target of 85 per cent. There is considerable interstate variation in vaccine coverage. For instance, in Bihar the percentage of fully immunized children in 1998–9 was only 11.0, in Assam 17.0, in Rajasthan 17.3 per cent, Uttar Pradesh 21.2 per cent, and in Madhya Pradesh 22.4 per cent. The highest percentage of fully vaccinated children among the bigger states was in Tamil Nadu (88.8 per cent), followed by Himachal Pradesh (83.4 per cent), and Kerala (79.7 per cent).

The government has visualized an elaborate primary health infrastructure in rural areas for providing preventive, promotive, and curative services. The functioning of the primary health infrastructure has drawn flak, and its deficiencies brought out, in the evaluations by the ICMR and other bodies. The poor delivery system, which includes inadequate supplies, poor equipment, poor services, and malpractices have been mainly responsible for slippages in national health targets. Community Health Centres which were intended to function as first referrals for PHCs are ill-equipped in terms of manpower, physical facilities, and equipment, and are not providing the specialist services expected of them. The national child survival and safe motherhood programme, launched in 1992–3 has not made a visible impact on reduction in infant mortality. The newly conceived reproductive and child health programme seeks to ensure child survival, safe motherhood, and reproductive health care through upgradation of services at different levels. Its impact will depend upon the extent to which the health care infrastructure puts up an improved performance.

Malnutrition has been a major public health problem in the country. It has escaped public visibility despite its harmful potential. In India, about half the children less than 3 years of age were found by the National Family Health Survey 1998–9 to be undernourished. The worst affected are the children of the rural and urban poor. The prevalence of severe undernourishment has declined, but this should not lead to any complacency. Diets of children continue to be inadequate, not only in calories, but also in essential nutrients. Poor purchasing power, ignorance arising primarily from illiteracy, frequent episodes of illness, and poor access and utilization of public health services aggravate the problem. The unsatisfactory health and nutrition status of pregnant and lactating women adversely affects foetal outcome and the nutrition and health status of the infant. Malnutrition is often categorized as only a medical problem. It is, however, also the outcome of the operation of socio-cultural and economic factors as well and public policies relating to household food security. Malnutrition has important behavioural dimensions and, therefore, needs to be tackled through coordinated inter-sectoral intervention strategies that are properly executed.

For almost three decades, India has been implementing nutrition intervention programmes relating to supplementary feeding, nutritional prophylaxis, nutrition education, and production and consumption of nutritious foods. These have, unfortunately, suffered due to poor implementation. Some, like the Applied Nutrition Programme and the Composite Nutrition Programme were conceptually flawed and withered away. Supplementary feeding and nutritional prophylaxis programmes continue to be run as relief programmes, missing out their developmental long term objectives. The public distribution system has left uncovered large segments of the rural and urban poor who need to be reached till their purchasing power improves and they are ensured of better household food security. Malpractices in the public distribution system need to be eradicated.

The Government of India, as a signatory of the Alma Ata Declaration of 1978, committed itself to the goal of Health for All by AD 2000, and adopted in 1983 the National Health Policy which specified the targets to be achieved. There have been major slippages on almost all the targets, particularly in the bigger backward states, as is evident from Box 2.2, which gives in tabular form the child health goals and achievements. Health insecurity stares in the face of large segments of the population, even nearly five and a half decades after independence. While higher budgetary support, better physical infrastructure, more manpower, better equipment, and more supplies help, much will depend on the extent to which the delivery system can weed out the malpractices and show substantial improvement in functioning through firmness both at administrative and political level. The ugly features of health administration need to be wiped out. This will imply radical reforms to inject work ethics, accountability, fairness in appointments, promotions, postings and transfers, political non-interference in administration, and commitment at all levels, particularly at the higher echelons of decision making. Sadly, this has been missing in the past which has hurt the rural and urban poor the most. Reports of the Comptroller and Auditor General, the Indian Council of Medical Research, and the Programme Evaluation Organisation, which have with monotonous regularity pointed out at the malfunctioning of the system, have been ignored in the past. The standard alibi of the administration for poor performance has been to demand more allocations and more staff, when the crying need is reforms in the health care system and far better governance in the public health sector with emphasis on performance and accountability. It would be vital for public health strategists, policy makers, and administrators to act collectively to redeem the promises made to the children of India, so that they get a far better deal and the goal of 'Health for All' does not continue to be elusive and a distant dream.

BOX 2.2. CHILD HEALTH AND NUTRITION GOALS AND ACHIEVEMENTS

Indicator	Goals		Achievement		
	Year	Target set	Year	Target reached	Comment
Infant Mortality Rate	2000	Below 60 (National Health Policy 1983)	2000	68 (SRS)	The target set has not been reached mainly because of the poor performance in the populous backward states
Perinatal Mortality Rate (PMR)	2000	30–5 (National Health Policy 1983)	1998	42 (SRS)	The target set will not be reached. The decline in PMR has been very slow.
Mortality Rate (1–5 yrs)	2000	10 (National Health Policy 1983)	1997	7.6 (1–4 yrs) (SRS)	The age specific mortality rate 1–4 years has come down from 15.6 in 1982–4 to 7.7 in 1998.
Maternal Mortality Rate (no. of maternal deaths per 1000 live births)	2000	< 2 maternal deaths per 1000 live births (National Health Policy 1983)	1998	4.07 (SRS)	The target set will not be reached
Percentage of low birthweight babies (below 2500 g.)	2000	10 (National Health Policy 1983)	1990s	20 to 35 (estimated)	No attempt was made to collect data on the percentage of low birth weight babies in the country covering both institutional and non-institutional deliveries. The National Family Health Survey, 1998–9 found that 70 per cent of the infants were not weighed at birth. Of the babies whose birthweight was known, 23 per cent were found to be of low birthweight.

(Contd.)

Box 2.2 (Contd.)

Indicator	Goals		Achievement		
	Year	Target set	Year	Target reached	Comment
Percentage of pregnant women receiving antenatal care	2000	100 per cent (National Health Policy 1983)	1998–9 NFHS-2	44 per cent	Achievement far below target
Percentage of deliveries by trained birth attendant	2000	100 per cent (National Health Policy 1983)	1998	54 per cent (SRS)	The National Health Policy 1983 had set a target of 80 per cent deliveries by trained birth attendant in 1990. This was far from being reached in 1998.
Tetanus toxoid coverage of pregnant women with two or more doses	1990	100 per cent (National Health Policy 1983)	1992–3 (NFHS-1)	54 per cent	Achievement far below target
			1998–9 (NFHS-2)	67 per cent	Achievement still far below target
BCG	1990	80 per cent (National Health Policy 1983)	1992–3 (NFHS-1)	62 per cent	Achievement far below target
			1998–9 (NFHS-2)	72 per cent	Achievement still far below target
DPT (3 doses)	2000	85 per cent (National Health Policy 1983)	1992–3 (NFHS-1)	52 per cent	Achievement far below target
			1998–9 (NFHS-2)	55 per cent	Achievement till far below target
Polio (3 doses)	1990	85 per cent (Universal Immunization Programme)	1992–3 (NFHS-1)	54 per cent	Achievement far below target
			1998–9 (NFHS-2)	63 per cent	Achievement still far below target

Box 2.2 (Contd.)

Indicator	Goals		Achievement		
	Year	Target set	Year	Target reached	Comment
Measles	1990	85 per cent (Universal Immunization Programme)	1992–3 (NFHS-1)	42 per cent	Achievement far below target
			1998–9 (NFHS-2)	51 per cent	Achievement far below target
All vaccines	1990	85 per cent (Universal Immunization Programme)	1992–3 (NFHS-1)	36 per cent	Achievement far below target
			1998–9 (NFHS-2)	42 per cent	Achievement still far below target
Percentage of undernourished children	2000	Reduction in moderate and severe malnutrition by half (NPAN)	1992–3 (NFHS-1)	52 per cent children under 3 yrs underweight and 47 per cent stunted.	Achievement far below target
			1998–9 (NFHS-2)	47 per cent children under 3 yrs. underweight and 45 per cent stunted	Achievement far below target. Only a modest decline in underwight and stunted children
Anaemia among pregnant women	2000	Reduction to 25 per cent (NPAN)	1998–9 (NFHS-2)	52 per cent ever married women 15–49 yrs.	Micro studies from different parts of the country, too, point to continued presence of milder forms of iron deficiency anaemia

(Contd.)

Box 2.2 (Contd.)

Indicator	Goals		Achievement		
	Year	Target set	Year	Target reached	Comment
Vitamin A deficiency	2000	Elimination of blindness due to vitamin A deficiency	Not available	Not available	Micro studies from different parts of the country point to continued presence of milder forms of vitamin A deficiency
Iodine deficiency disorders	2000	Reduction to 10 per cent		Not available	No survey done. Empirical studies from different parts of the country point to its decline after the step up in the salt iodization programme.

Notes: NFHS-1 = National Family Health Survey, 1992–3
NFHS-2 = National Family Health Survey, 1998–9
NPAN = National Plan of Action on Nutrition
SRS = Sample Registration System
UIP = Universal Immunization Programme

3 In School, Out of School

The role of education in national development and in individual and social well-being has been well recognized. Its importance in capacity building and in improving the quality of life has generated a demand by planners throughout the world for a high priority to education, larger public sector allocations, and the strengthening of elementary education. Outlays on education are considered 'investments in human capital' as they help to build the human resource so vital for economic growth, reduction of poverty, equalization of opportunities, and social empowerment. The level of education has shown a high degree of correspondence with earnings, upward social and economic mobility, a wider range of choices in economic and social spheres, greater adaptability in adjusting to changing labour markets, enhanced ability to acquire new skills and competencies, greater social awareness and a better quality of life.

In the measurement of development, literacy and level of education are invariably listed among the key indicators. Female education, in particular, is recognized as a means to both a better quality of life for the child and the family, and the woman's own quest for self-fulfilment. A higher level of education of a woman considerably enhances the child's chances of survival and of entry and continuance in schooling. Elementary education is considered crucial because it lays the foundation for secondary and higher education and training, which is critically important in today's fast changing technology propelled growth.

It is in recognition of the vital role of elementary education that the Constitution of India directed the State to provide free and compulsory education within a period of 10 years, that is, by 1960 (Article 45). This is the only Directive Principle to set a time frame. The words 'within the limits of its economic capacity and development' in Article 41, which speaks of right to education, do not find a place in Article 45, thus indicating that the Constitution gave a clear mandate to the State on elementary education. Any doubt in this regard has been sealed by the Supreme Court, which has ruled that every child has the right to free education until he completes the age of 14 years. The Lok Sabha passed in November 2001 the Constitution Amendment Bill which makes the right to education a fundamental right. According to the Bill, Article 21A, which reads as follows, shall be inserted in the Constitution: 'The State shall provide free and compulsory education to all children of the age six to fourteen years in such manner as the State may, by law, decide.' For the existing Article 45, a new article shall be substituted as follows: 'The State shall endeavour to provide early childhood care and education for all children until they complete the age of six years.' Through an amendment of Article 51A, which lists the fundamental duties, the Bill provides for the addition of a clause whereby it shall become the fundamental duty of a parent or guardian to provide opportunities for education to his child or, as the case may be, ward between the age of six and fourteen years.

The pages that follow indicate the current state, the achievements and the failures.

LITERACY RATE

Literacy rate is the most widely used indicator of spread of education in a country, and even though it is a rudimentary one, it has acquired this status because of the ready availability of data on it. The Census has defined a literate person as one who can 'both read and write with understanding in any language'. Literacy rate in the 10–14 year and 15–19 year age groups is a better indicator of the state of literacy among children than the literacy rate in the 5–9 year age group, because children are expected to begin schooling at age 6 years. Table 3.1 gives the literacy rate in the age group 10–14 years and 15–19 years in rural and urban areas by gender for the period 1961 to 1991. The 2001 Census figures are not yet available. The data show that there has been an improvement in the extent of literacy in the 10–14 year age group from 42.3 per cent in 1961 to 68.8 per cent in 1991, and in the 15–19 year age group from 38.4 per cent in 1961 to 65.7 per cent in 1991. However, nearly one-third children aged 10–14 years and about the same percentage in the 15–19 years age group were still illiterate in 1991.

There is a marked difference in literacy rates between rural and urban areas, as the data in Table 3.1 show. Figure 3.1 presents the data in graphic form. The 1991 literacy rate of the 10–14 year age

TABLE 3.1: LITERACY RATE OF AGE GROUP 10–14 YEARS AND 15–19 YEARS BY SEX IN RURAL AND URBAN AREAS, INDIA, 1961 TO 1991

Age (yrs)	Year	Rural				Urban				Total			
		Male	Female	Total	M–F	Male	Female	Total	M–F	Male	Female	Total	M–F
10–14	1991	73.4	52.3	63.4	21.1	87.8	81.3	84.7	6.5	77.0	59.7	68.8	17.3
	1981	62.2	36.5	50.1	25.7	82.3	73.2	78.0	9.1	66.7	44.8	56.4	21.9
	1971	54.6	30.0	43.1	24.7	80.9	71.1	76.2	9.8	59.8	38.2	49.6	21.6
	1961	49.1	20.7	35.9	28.4	78.0	62.7	70.8	15.3	54.4	28.4	42.3	26.0
15–19	1991	71.0	45.8	59.3	25.2	86.4	78.3	82.6	8.1	75.3	54.9	65.7	20.4
	1981	60.4	33.6	47.8	26.8	82.1	71.1	77.0	11.0	66.2	43.3	55.4	22.8
	1971	57.4	28.5	43.7	28.9	82.8	69.6	76.7	13.2	63.4	37.7	51.3	25.7
	1961	45.2	16.3	31.1	28.9	77.7	56.7	68.3	21.0	52.0	23.8	38.4	28.2

Source: *Census of India.*

group in rural areas in 1991 (63.4 per cent) is lower than the literacy rate in urban areas three decades earlier (70.8 per cent). The gender difference is also very marked, particularly in rural areas where it is more than 20 per cent. A redeeming feature is the declining trend of the gender gap in literacy rates in both rural and urban areas, the decline being sharper in urban areas. However, the female literacy rate of the 10–14 year age group in 1991 (59.7 per cent) is almost 20 years behind the male literacy rate (59.8 per cent in 1971). In the 15–19 year age group, the broad trends are similar in nature but the gender gap in 1991 is moderately higher.

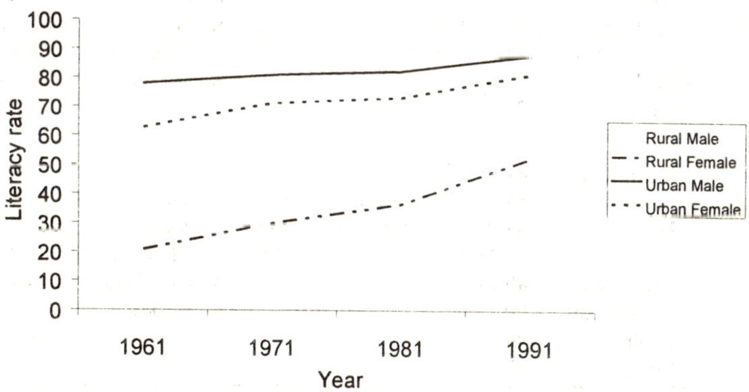

FIG. 3.1: LITERACY RATE OF AGE GROUP 10–14 YEARS BY SEX IN RURAL AND URBAN AREAS, INDIA, 1961 TO 1991.

There is considerable interstate variation in literacy rates in the 10–14 year group, as is evident from Table 3.2. If the combined rural and urban figures are considered, seven states have over 80 per cent literacy rates in the 10–14 year age group. However, Bihar, Rajasthan, and Uttar Pradesh have just over half the children in the 10–14 year age group literate. In these educationally backward states, less than 42 per cent girls aged 10–14 years are literate; also, the gender difference in literacy rate in the 10–14 year age group is more than 25 per cent, touching a high of 38 per cent in Rajasthan.

TABLE 3.2: PERCENTAGE LITERATE IN 10–14 YEAR AGE GROUP IN STATES, 1991

Literacy rate	Literacy rate		
	Boys	Girls	Persons
< 40		Rajasthan (34.0)	
		Bihar (39.9)	
40–59		Uttar Pradesh (42.0)	Bihar (53.7)
		Madhya Pradesh (52.5)	Rajasthan (54.3)
		Andhra Pradesh (55.0)	Uttar Pradesh (56.2)
		Orissa (56.9)	
		INDIA (59.7)	
60–79	Bihar (65.1)	Assam (63.3)	Madhya Pradesh (64.1)
	Uttar Pradesh (68.1)	West Bengal (63.5)	Andhra Pradesh (64.5)
	Rajasthan (72.1)	Karnataka (67.7)	Orissa (66.2)
	Assam (73.0)	Haryana (71.4)	Assam (68.3)
	A. Pradesh (73.4)	Gujarat (73.6)	INDIA (68.8)
	West Bengal (73.9)	Punjab (77.3)	West Bengal (68.8)
	M. Pradesh (74.5)		Karnataka (74.8)
	Orissa (75.5)		
	INDIA (77.0)		
80+	Karnataka (81.7)	Maharashtra (80.5)	Haryana (80.4)
	Punjab (84.1)	Tamil Nadu (80.6)	Punjab (80.9)
	Haryana (88.0)	Himachal Pradesh (85.7)	Gujarat (81.2)
	Gujarat (88.1)	Kerala (98.5)	Tamil Nadu (85.2)
	Tamil Nadu (89.7)		Maharashtra (85.4)
	Maharasthra (90.0)		H. Pradesh (90.2)
	H. Pradesh (94.5)		Kerala (98.6)
	Kerala (98.7)		

Source: *Census of India*, 1991.

Note: Data for 16 bigger states given here. States have been arranged in ascending order.

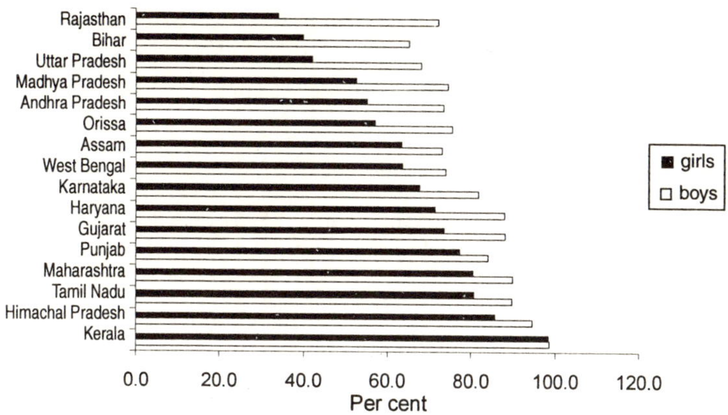

FIG. 3.2: PERCENTAGE OF LITERATE BOYS AND GIRLS AGED 10–14 YEARS IN STATES, 1991.

Figure 3.2 gives the comparative literacy rates for boys and girls aged 10–14 years in the 16 bigger states.

The unsatisfactory situation becomes more evident from a consideration of the percentage of illiterate children in rural areas where three-fourths of the population live. Two states (Bihar and Rajasthan) have more than half the rural children aged 10–14 years illiterate (see Table 3.3). Five states, viz., Rajasthan, Bihar, Uttar Pradesh, Madhya Pradesh, and Andhra Pradesh, have more than 50 per cent rural girls aged 10–14 years illiterate. Rajasthan has the highest percentage of illiterate rural girls with three-fourths of the 10–14 years old girls illiterate. The gender disparity is also the highest in Rajasthan—a difference of 44 per cent in the 10–14 year age group.

The magnitude of the unfinished task becomes evident by looking at the absolute figures (see Table 3.4). In 1991, 31 million children aged 10–14 years were illiterate, mostly in rural areas (88 per cent), and predominantly girls (61 per cent).

The distribution of illiterate children aged 10–14 years in different states in 1991 is given in Table 3.5. The data shows that there were more than two and a half million illiterate children in each of the six states of Uttar Pradesh, Bihar, Madhya Pradesh, Andhra Pradesh, Rajasthan, and West Bengal, with Uttar Pradesh having a staggering figure of nearly seven and a half million, which is almost the same as the total number of illiterate children in the ten states listed after

TABLE 3.3: PERCENTAGE OF ILLITERATE CHILDREN AGED 10–14 YEARS IN RURAL AREAS IN STATES, 1991

Range	Percentage illiterate					
	Males		Females		Total	
40+			Rajasthan	(75.8)	Rajasthan	(52.2)
			Bihar	(65.7)	Bihar	(50.5)
			Uttar Pradesh	(64.1)	Uttar Pradesh	(42.4)
			Madhya Pradesh	(56.5)	Madhaya Pradesh	(42.6)
			Andhra Pradesh	(54.2)	Andhra Pradesh	(42.3)
			INDIA	(47.4)		
			Orissa	(46.6)		
			West Bengal	(42.3)		
20–39	Bihar	(38.0)	Karnataka	(39.5)	INDIA	(36.6)
	Uttar Pradesh	(33.7)	Assam	(39.1)	Orissa	(36.6)
	Rajasthan	(31.6)	Haryana	(33.3)	West Bengal	(36.3)
	A. Pradesh	(31.4)	Gujarat	(32.8)	Assam	(33.9)
	West Bengal	(30.6)	Punjab	(26.2)	Karnataka	(30.4)
	M. Pradesh	(30.2)	Maharashtra	(25.6)	Gujarat	(22.9)
	Assam	(28.9)	Tamil Nadu	(24.3)	Haryana	(22.4)
	INDIA	(26.6)			Punjab	(21.5)
	Orissa	(26.5)				
	Karnataka	(21.6)				
< 20	Punjab	(17.4)	Himachal Pradesh	(15.1)	Maharashtra	(18.7)
	Gujarat	(13.9)	Kerala	(1.6)	Tamil Nadu	(18.0)
	Haryana	(13.2)			H. Pradesh	(10.3)
	Maharashtra	(12.3)			Kerala	(1.5)
	Tamil Nadu	(12.0)				
	H. Pradesh	(5.7)				
	Kerala	(1.4)				

Source: *Census of India*, 1991.
Note: Data for 16 bigger states given here. States have been arranged in descending order. Figures for India do not include Jammu & Kashmir.

TABLE 3.4: NUMBER OF ILLITERATE CHILDREN AGED 10–14 YEARS, INDIA, 1991

	Rural			Urban			Total		
	Males	Females	Total	Males	Females	Total	Males	Females	Total
Illiterate children 10–14 years (in million)	10.381	16.638	27.019	1.574	2.213	3.787	11.955	18.851	30.806

Source: *Census of India*, 1991.
Note: Figures exclude Jammu & Kashmir.

TABLE 3.5: DISTRIBUTION OF ILLITERATE CHILDREN AGED 10–14 YEARS IN STATES, 1991

States	No. of illiterate children (in '000)
Uttar Pradesh	7418
Bihar	4901
Madhya Pradesh	2756
Andhra Pradesh	2739
Rajasthan	2540
West Bengal	2515
Karnataka	1359
Maharashtra	1303
Orissa	1206
Gujarat	910
Tamil Nadu	888
Assam	862
Punjab	447
Haryana	410
Himachal Pradesh	62
Kerala	43
INDIA	30,806

Source: *Census of India*, 1991.
Note: Data relate to 16 bigger states arranged in descending order. Figures for India do not include Jammu & Kashmir.

West Bengal. Uttar Pradesh and Bihar together had 40 per cent of the illiterate children aged 10–14 years in the country in 1991.

ENROLMENT

Official school enrolment figures indicate a phenomenal growth in the number of both boys and girls at primary and middle/upper primary stages. In a time span of 49 years, enrolment at primary stage has increased from 19 million in 1950–1 to 114 million in 1999–2000, and at middle/upper primary stage from 3 million to 42 million (see Table 3.6). The decadal growth rate in enrolment was higher in the initial years, when school facilities increased at a fast pace. A welcome feature is the consistently higher decadal growth rate of girls at both primary and middle/upper primary stage, indicating greater acceptance of the need to educate girls. However, the enrolment of girls is still far behind that of boys, and it will take some more time before parity is reached. Another feature is the higher decadal growth rate in enrolment at the middle/upper primary

TABLE 3.6: GROWTH IN ENROLMENT AT PRIMARY AND MIDDLE/UPPER PRIMARY STAGE, INDIA, 1950–1 TO 1999–2000

Year		Primary (Classes I to V)			Middle (Classes VI to VIII)		
		Boys	Girls	Total	Boys	Girls	Total
1950–1	No. (mill.)	13.770	5.385	19.155	2.586	0.534	3.120
1955–6	No. (mill.)	17.530	7.640	25.170	3.420	0.870	4.290
	% increase	27.3	41.9	31.4	32.3	62.9	37.5
1960–1	No. (mill.)	23.593	11.401	34.994	5.074	1.630	6.705
	% increase	34.6	49.2	39.1	48.4	87.4	56.3
1965–6	No. (mill.)	32.178	18.293	50.471	7.686	2.846	10.532
	% increase	30.4	60.5	44.2	51.5	74.6	57.1
1970–1	No. (mill.)	35.729	21.306	57.035	9.426	3.889	13.315
	% increase	11.0	16.5	13.0	22.6	36.7	26.4
1975–6	No. (mill.)	40.649	25.011	65.660	10.990	5.034	16.024
	% increase	13.8	17.4	15.1	16.6	29.4	29.3
1980–1	No. (mill.)	45.286	28.488	73.774	13.934	6.790	20.724
	% increase	11.4	13.9	12.4	26.8	34.9	29.3
1985–6	No. (mill.)	51.732	34.733	86.465	18.132	9.992	28.124
	% increase	14.2	21.9	17.2	30.1	47.2	35.7
1990–1	No. (mill.)	58.095	41.024	99.119	20.844	12.439	33.283
	% increase	12.3	18.1	14.6	15.0	24.5	18.3
1995–6	No. (mill.)	62.361	47.373	109.734	24.971	16.043	41.014
	% increase	7.3	15.5	10.7	19.8	29.0	23.2
1999–	No. (mill.)	64.103	49.509	113.612	25.082	16.983	42.065
2000	% increase	2.8	4.5	3.5	0.4	5.9	2.6

Source: Department of Education.

stage in the case of both boys and girls as compared to the primary stage. Figure 3.3 presents the data in graphic form. The growth rate in enrolment has fallen from the mid-nineties.

The gross enrolment ratio (number of children enrolled in classes I to V and VI to VIII as a percentage of children of the corresponding age group, that is, 6–10 years and 11–13 years, respectively) has shown a rise for both boys and girls from 1960–1 to 1995–6. In the subsequent years, there has been a fluctuating trend in the case of both boys and girls at the primary and middle/upper primary stage (see Table 3.7). The situation needs to be monitored to assess whether this decline is due to a flaw in the reporting system in a particular year, or it reflects the ground reality. At the primary stage (classes I to V), the gross enrolment ratio in some years for boys exceeded 100 per cent because of boys of older age studying in these classes due to late entry in school or due to repetition of class. Enrolment figures also get inflated by the special drive to net more

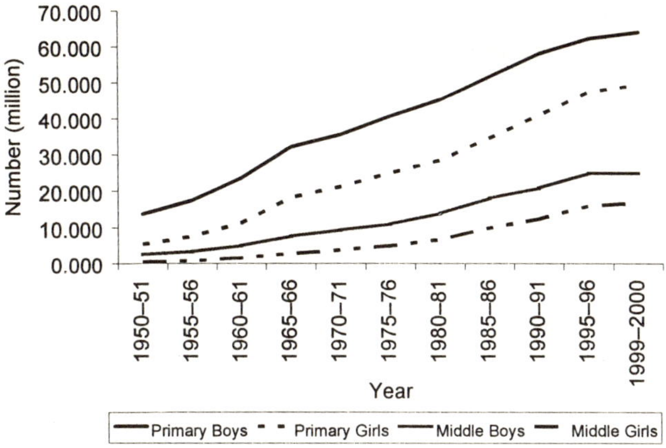

FIG. 3.3: GROWTH IN ENROLMENT OF BOYS AND GIRLS AT PRIMARY AND MIDDLE/UPPER PRIMARY STAGE, INDIA, 1950–1 TO 1999–2000

TABLE 3.7: ENROLMENT RATIO AT PRIMARY AND MIDDLE LEVEL, INDIA, 1960–1 TO 1999–2000

Year	Primary (Classes I to V)				Middle/Upper Primary (Classes VI to VIII)			
	Boys	Girls	Total	B–G	Boys	Girls	Total	B–G
1960–1	82.6	41.4	62.4	41.2	33.2	11.3	22.5	21.9
1970–1	92.6	59.1	76.4	33.5	46.5	20.8	34.2	25.7
1980–1	95.8	64.1	80.5	31.7	54.3	28.6	41.9	25.7
1990–1	115.3	86.0	101.0	29.3	73.4	46.1	60.1	27.3
1995–6	114.5	93.3	104.3	21.2	79.5	54.9	67.6	24.6
1999–2000	104.1	85.2	94.9	18.9	67.2	49.7	58.8	17.5

Source: Department of Education.

children in order to get additional posts sanctioned, which results in even under age children being shown as enrolled. Sometimes fake entries are made. Gross enrolment ratio continues to be low for girls at the middle/upper primary stage; even in 1999–2000, it was still only about 50 per cent for girls. This is undoubtedly a vast improvement over the situation in 1960–1, when 89 per cent of the girls in the relative age group had not enrolled at middle/upper primary stage. However, the current position is still a long way off from the goal, which seeks to ensure that all children 11–13 years attend middle/upper primary school. A welcome feature is that the gender gap in enrolment ratio has shown a declining trend at both primary and middle/upper primary stage.

The relative situation in the matter of enrolment of boys and girls become clearer if the gender parity in enrolment, that is, number of girls per 1,000 boys enrolled, is considered at primary and middle/upper primary stages (Table 3.8). The data, presented in graphical form in Fig. 3.4, show that there is considerable improvement in gender parity since 1950–1. Until 1980–1, at the middle/upper primary stage, the number of girls enrolled was less than half the number of boys. At the primary stage, the halfway mark was crossed in 1961–2. There is, however, still a very wide gap. Even after five decades of independence, girls enrolled at primary stage constituted only about three-fourths of the number of boys, while at the middle/

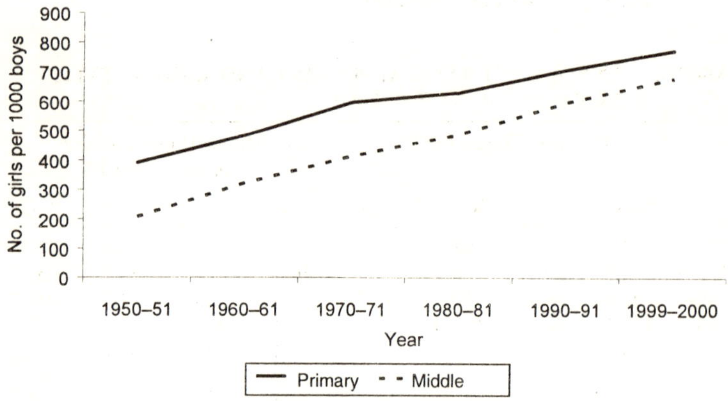

FIG. 3.4: GENDER PARITY IN ENROLMENT AT PRIMARY AND MIDDLE/UPPER PRIMARY STAGE, INDIA, 1950–1 TO 1999–2000

TABLE 3.8: GENDER PARITY IN ENROLMENT AT PRIMARY AND MIDDLE/UPPER PRIMARY STAGE, INDIA, 1950–1 TO 1999–2000

Stage	1999–2000	1990–1	1980–1	1970–1	1960–1	1950–1
Primary (Classes I – V)	772	706	629	596	483	391
Middle (Classes VI – VIII)	677	597	487	413	321	207

Source: Department of Education.

TABLE 3.9: GENDER PARITY IN SCHOOL ENROLMENT IN STATES, 1998–9

Gender parity (No. of girls per 1,000 boys)	Primary (Classes I – V)	Middle/Upper Primary (Classes VI – VIII)
< 500		Rajasthan (375) Uttar Pradesh (458) Bihar (465)
500 – 749	Rajasthan (547) Uttar Pradesh (584) Bihar (607) Orissa (706)	Orissa (561) Madhya Pradesh (579) Assam (720) West Bengal (720) Gujarat (728)
750 – 899	Gujarat (761) Madhya Pradesh (762) Assam (816) West Bengal (837) Haryana (891)	Andhra Pradesh (760) Haryana (778) Karnataka (833) Punjab (851) Tamil Nadu (862) Maharashtra (864)
900 & above	Punjab (912) Karnataka (915) Andhra Pradesh (923) Maharashtra (923) Tamil Nadu (937) Kerala (945) Himachal Pradesh (974)	Himachal Pradesh (909) Kerala (933)

Source: Department of Education.

upper primary stage they constituted about two-thirds the number of boys.

The gender parity situation in states, given in Table 3.9, shows considerable variation. It shows a very adverse gender parity at the middle/upper primary stage (classes VI to VIII) in the educationally backward states of Rajasthan, Bihar, and Uttar Pradesh, where girls enrolled are less than half the number of boys enrolled. The best gender parity in enrolment at the primary and middle stages is in Kerala and Himachal Pradesh, followed by Tamil Nadu and Maharashtra Fig. 3.5.

ATTENDING SCHOOL

Not all enrolled children are in school. Enrolment figures at the primary school stage give an exaggerated picture and partly reflect the outcome of periodic enrolment drives. The 1991 Census figures,

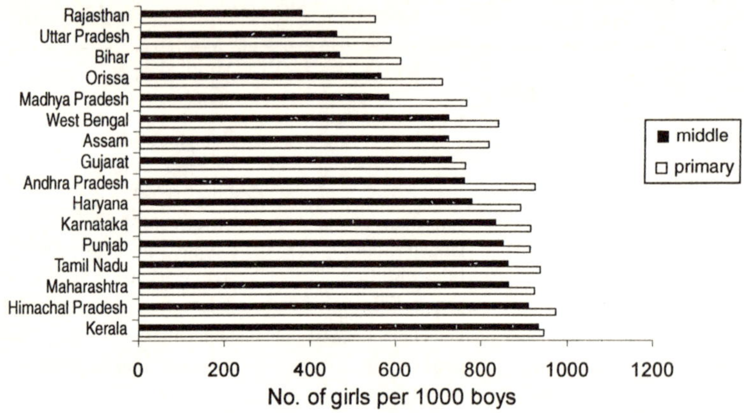

FIG. 3.5: GENDER PARITY IN ENROLMENT AT PRIMARY AND MIDDLE/ UPPER PRIMARY STAGE IN STATES, 1998–9.

given in Table 3.10, indicate that in the 6–10 year age group (primary school stage, classes I to V) 59.181 million children were attending school. In the 11–13 year age group (middle school stage, classes VI to VIII), the number attending school was 33.510 million. Thus, in

TABLE 3.10: NUMBER OF CHILDREN ATTENDING SCHOOL, INDIA, 1991

(in million)

	Primary stage (Class I to V) 6–10 years	Middle stage (Class VI to VIII) 11–13 years	Elementary stage (Class I to VIII) 6–13 years
Children enrolled (1990–1)	99.119	33.283	132.402
Children attending school (1991)	59.181	33.510	92.691
Children not attending school (1991)	56.464	19.011	75.475

Sources: *Census of India*, 1991.
Department of Education.

Note: Children 6–10 years are expected to be in primary school and 11–13 years in middle school/upper primary school. The enrolment figures refer to children enrolled at primary or middle/upper primary stage and may include older or younger children. The figures of children attending school refer to children of 6–10 years or 11–13 years who are attending school without reference to the stage. Children may be attending classes different from that expected of their age. The 1991 census figures exclude Jammu & Kashmir. The enrolment figures, too, exclude the state.

the age group 6–13 years (primary and middle school stage), the number of children attending school was 92.691 million.

At the primary stage, the number of children attending school as reported by the 1991 Census is 40 million short of the 1990–1 enrolment figure reported by the Department of Education, partly because many children shown as enrolled do not attend school and partly because of later than normal age of entry of children in school. At the middle/upper primary stage, however, the number of children attending school is slightly higher because older children are attending school in classes lower than expected at their age, that is children who have crossed the middle/upper primary school age are still in middle/upper primary school. The same phenomenon spills over to the 14–15 year age group. In view of this, combined figures for the 6–13 year age group (primary and middle/upper primary stage, which constitute the elementary education stage) give a better picture of the situation.

The percentage of children of primary and middle/upper primary school going age attending school in 1991 is given in Table 3.11. The data show that in urban areas 72 per cent children aged 6–13 years attended school; however, in rural areas only 50 per cent children did so. Putting it differently, nearly half the children 6–13 years in rural areas, and 28 per cent in urban areas, were not attending school. In the 6–10 year age group, 49 per cent children were not attending school. Thus, the resolve of the National Policy on Education (NPE) that all children who attain the age of about 11 years by 1990 will have had five years of schooling, or its equivalent through the non-formal stream, was far from being reached. This shows that considerable ground is yet to be covered to universalize education of children of elementary school going age, particularly in rural areas where three-fourths of the population lives. There is also marked gender disparity in attending school, which is far greater in rural areas.

The National Family Health Survey (1992–3) indicated a higher percentage of children aged 6–14 years attending school, 63 per cent in rural areas and 82 per cent in urban areas, giving a combined figure of 68 per cent. This survey, too, showed greater gender disparity in rural areas—a difference of 20 per cent in rural areas as compared to 6 per cent in urban areas (IIPS 1995). The National Family Health Survey 1998–9 has shown a further rise in percentage of children aged 6–14 years attending school, 76 per cent in rural areas and 88 per cent in urban areas, giving a combined figure of

TABLE 3.11: PERCENTAGE OF CHILDREN ATTENDING SCHOOL, INDIA, 1991

	Children 6–10 years			Children 11–13 years			Children 6–13 years		
	Boys	Girls	Total	Boys	Girls	Total	Boys	Girls	Total
Rural	52.3	39.3	46.0	69.1	46.6	58.5	57.5	41.5	49.8
Urban	70.7	65.8	68.3	82.3	75.3	79.0	74.7	69.0	71.9
Total	56.6	45.4	51.2	72.5	54.2	63.8	61.6	48.1	55.1

Source: *Census of India*, 1991.
Note: Figures for India do not include Jammu & Kashmir.

79 per cent (IIPS 2000). Most micro-studies, too, have shown a higher percentage of children, both boys and girls, attending school as compared to the census figures. The District Primary Education Programme, launched in 1994, reported, in its assessment after 3 years of operation, increases in enrolment and retention and reduction of inequities arising from gender and caste in the matter of access to education.

Data on children attending school has also been provided by the National Sample Survey Organisation from its Fifty-second Round (July 1995 to June 1996). Three indicators have been used—Gross Attendance Ratio (GAR), Age Specific Attendance Ratio (ASAR), and Net Attendance Ratio (NAR). The last indicator is both age and stage specific, and gives a far more realistic picture of the extent to which schooling among children conforms to the norm. ASAR follows the same method as the Census while reporting on children of specific age groups attending school. Table 3.12 shows that ASAR is higher in 1995–6 than the 1991 Census figure which is a welcome feature. The Net Attendance Ratio shows that two-thirds of children aged 6–10 years were in classes I to V. The Net Attendance Ratio in classes VI to VIII was, however, low, particularly in rural areas. Only 43 per cent children aged 11–13 years were in classes VI to VIII after nearly five decades of independence whereas in a successfully implemented education system the percentage should have been over 90, signifying thereby attainment of the Constitutional Directive in letter and in spirit. There is a big gap between ASAR and NAR in the 11–13 year age group. National Sample Survey data for 1995–6 clearly show that the Resolve of even the National Policy on Education of 1986, which had laid down a fresh target date of 1995 for providing free and compulsory education to all children up to 14 years of age, was not fulfilled.

TABLE 3.12: SCHOOL ATTENDANCE RATIO, INDIA, 1995–6

Class / Age group	Attendance Ratio	Rural			Urban			Total		
		Boys	Girls	Total	Boys	Girls	Total	Boys	Girls	Total
Primary (Classes I–V) / 6–10 years	GAR	90	72	81	102	98	100	92	77	85
	ASAR	71	58	65	84	82	83	73	63	69
	NAR	68	56	63	80	77	78	71	61	66
Middle/ Upper Primary (Classes VI–VIII) / 11–13 years	GAR	70	47	59	87	80	83	74	56	65
	ASAR	75	57	67	87	83	85	78	64	72
	NAR	44	32	39	60	57	58	48	38	43

Source: National Sample Survey Organisation, Fifty-second Round, July 1995 to June 1996.

Notes: Gross Attendance Ratio (GAR) (Classes I to V)

$$= \frac{\text{No. of children attending classes I–V}}{\text{Estimated population 6–10 years}} \times 100$$

Age Specific Attendance Ratio (ASAR) (age group 6–10 yrs)

$$= \frac{\text{No. of children 6–10 yrs attending classes}}{\text{Estimated population 6–10 years}} \times 100$$

Net Attendance Ratio (NAR) (Classes I to V / Age 6–10 yrs)

$$= \frac{\text{No. of children 6–10 years attending classes I–V}}{\text{Estimated population 6–10 years}} \times 100$$

Similar method followed for computing GAR, ASAR, and NAR for classes VI to VIII / children 11–13 years.

The extent of gender disparity in schooling is more realistically evident from data on the number of girls per 1,000 boys attending school, rather than from enrolment figures. The data in Table 3.13 show that in 1991, 666 girls per 1,000 boys aged 6–13 years in rural areas were attending school. In urban areas the gender parity improved to 860 girls per 1,000 boys. Gender parity is far higher in the 6–10 year age group as compared to the 11–13 year age group. In urban areas, gender disparity is far less, and has improved greatly since the situation in 1981. The 2001 Census data are likely to show a further improvement in gender parity.

A better picture of the magnitude of unfinished task in the universalization of education emerges if the number of children of

TABLE 3.13: NUMBER OF GIRLS PER 1,000 BOYS OF PRIMARY SCHOOL AGE (6–10 YEARS) AND MIDDLE SCHOOL AGE (11–13 YEARS) ATTENDING SCHOOL, 1991 AND 1981

Year	Rural			Urban			All areas		
	6–10 years	11–13 years	6–13 years	6–10 years	11–13 years	6–13 years	6–10 years	11–13 years	6–13 years
1991	703	604	666	871	842	860	751	674	722
1981	581	452	534	837	773	814	652	543	612

Source: *Census of India*.
Note: Figures for 1981 do not include Assam and those for 1991 do not include Jammu & Kashmir.

elementary school going age not attending school is seen. The 2001 Census figures are not yet available. The 1991 Census figures indicate that in the age group 6–10 years, 56.464 million children (48.8 per cent) were not attending school, while in the age group 11–13 years the number was 19.011 million (36.2 per cent). Thus, in the age group 6–13 years (age group for class I to VIII, that is elementary school stage), 75.475 million children (44.9 per cent) were out of school (see Table 3.14). Of these, a disproportionately higher percentage (85 per cent) were in rural areas, though only 75 per cent of the population lives there. Also, the number of girls not attending school far outnumbered the boys, there being 1,248 girls for every 1,000 boys aged 6–13 years not attending school.

The percentage of children aged 6–13 years not attending school varied in different states. The highest percentage was found by the 1991 Census to be in Bihar (61.1 per cent), followed by Uttar Pradesh

TABLE 3.14: NUMBER OF CHILDREN OF SCHOOL GOING AGE NOT ATTENDING SCHOOL, INDIA, 1991

(in million)

Area	6–10 years			11–13 years			6–13 years		
	Boys	Girls	Total	Boys	Girls	Total	Boys	Girls	Total
Rural	21.916	26.072	47.988	6.341	9.795	16.136	28.257	35.867	64.124
Urban	4.050	4.426	8.476	1.258	1.616	2.874	5.308	6.042	11.351
Total	25.966	30.498	56.464	7.599	11.411	19.011	33.565	41.909	75.475

Source: *Census of India*, 1991.
Note: Figures for 1981 do not include Assam and those for 1991 do not include Jammu & Kashmir.

(58.6 per cent), Rajasthan (56.9 per cent), Madhya Pradesh (49.1 per cent), West Bengal (48.8 per cent), Assam (48.4 per cent), Andhra Pradesh (45.6 per cent), and Orissa (44.1 per cent). Kerala had the lowest percentage of children not attending school. While there has been some improvement since the situation in 1991, the Census of 2001 will indicate the magnitude of the unfinished agenda.

The National Sample Survey in 1995–6 found that 26 per cent of the children aged 6–10 years (primary school going age) and 19 per cent of the children aged 11–13 years (middle/upper primary school going age) had never attended school (NSSO 1998). This is a high percentage of children not covered by the formal elementary school system even five decades after independence. In the 6–10 year age group, 5 per cent of the children, and in the 11–13 year age group 9 per cent, had in the past attended school but were not attending school now. The percentages currently attending school were 69 and 72 in the respective age groups.

INTERSTATE VARIATION

The National Sample Survey conducted in 1995–6 gives data on percentage of children aged 6–10 years and 11–13 years attending school corresponding to the expected stage. The findings given in Table 3.15, show that the worst placed state on the indicators of Age Specific Attendance Ratio and Net Attendance Ratio at both the levels is Bihar, closely followed by Rajasthan, Uttar Padesh, Madhya Pradesh, and Orissa. A disturbing feature is that the NAR for the 11–13 years/classes VI–VIII group is less than 50 in 8 out of the 16 bigger states. Figure 3.6 gives the comparative position in different states on NAR for the 6–10 years/classes I–V and 11–13 years/classes VI–VIII groups.

INTER-DISTRICT VARIATION

The percentage of children of school going age attending school shows variation not only between states, but also between districts within a state. Breakdown by district of the percentage of children attending school from the 1991 Census is presented here as the 2001 Census figures are not yet available. In the 16 bigger states, in 22 districts (5.5 per cent) the percentage of children aged 6–13 years attending school is less than 30 (see Table 3.16). All the 22 districts

TABLE 3.15: AGE SPECIFIC ATTENDANCE RATIO AND NET ATTENDANCE RATIO IN AGE GROUP 6–10 YEARS/CLASSES I–V AND 11–13 YEARS/CLASSES VI–VIII IN STATES, 1995–6

State	6–10 years/classes I–V		11–13 years/classes VI–VIII	
	ASAR	NAR	ASAR	NAR
Andhra Pradesh	75	70	60	41
Assam	73	72	80	43
Bihar	43	41	58	33
Gujarat	80	78	77	52
Haryana	83	78	87	52
Himachal Pradesh	91	85	94	54
Karnataka	75	73	70	50
Kerala	97	91	97	76
Madhya Pradesh	64	63	67	35
Maharashtra	88	85	85	55
Orissa	63	61	66	45
Punjab	85	81	86	59
Rajasthan	58	55	64	35
Tamil Nadu	91	84	74	61
Uttar Pradesh	61	59	66	33
West Bengal	67	66	74	33
INDIA	69	66	72	43

Source: National Sample Survey Organisation, Fifty-second Round, July 1995 to June 1996.

Notes: Age Specific Attendance Ratio (ASAR) (age group 6–10 yrs)

$$= \frac{\text{No. of children 6–10 yrs attending school}}{\text{Estimated population 6–10 years}} \times 100$$

Net Attendance Ratio (NAR) (Classes I to V/Age 6–10 yrs)

$$= \frac{\text{No. of children 6–10 years attending classes I to V}}{\text{Estimated population 6–10 years}} \times 100$$

Similar method followed for computing ASAR and NAR for children 11–13 years.

are in the four educationally backward states (10 in Bihar, 9 in Uttar Pradesh, 2 in Rajasthan, and 1 in Madhya Pradesh). If the primary school going age 6–10 years is considered, in 33 districts (8.3 per cent) the percentage of children attending school is less than 30. Of these 14 are in Uttar Pradesh, 12 in Bihar, 3 in Rajasthan, 3 in West Bengal and 1 in Madhya Pradesh. In Bihar, in Kishanganj district, less than 20 per cent children aged 6–10 years were attending school in 1991, the only district in the bigger states with such a poor record. The figures of 2001 Census will reflect the extent of improvement

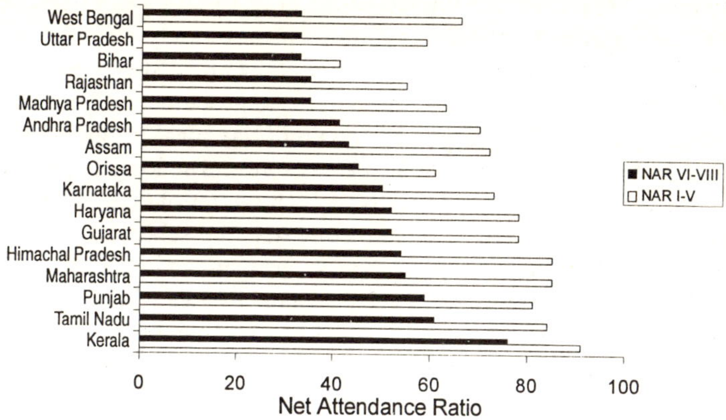

FIG. 3.6: NET ATTENDANCE RATIO 6–10 YEARS/CLASSES I–V AND 11–13 YEARS/CLASSES VI–VIII IN STATES, 1995–6.

TABLE 3.16: DISTRIBUTION OF DISTRICTS IN 16 BIGGER STATES BY PERCENTAGE OF CHILDREN OF SCHOOL GOING AGE ATTENDING SCHOOL, 1991

Age (in years)		Distribution of districts by percentage of children attending school									
		< 20	20–9	30–9	40–9	50–9	60–9	70–9	80–9	90+	Total
6–10	No. of districts	1	32	82	71	78	64	42	17	10	397
	%	0.3	8.1	20.6	17.9	19.7	16.1	10.6	4.3	2.5	100.0
6–13	No. of districts		22	55	88	79	67	51	23	12	397
	%		5.5	13.9	22.2	19.9	16.9	12.8	5.8	3.0	100.0

Source: *Census of India*.

from the District Primary Education Programme, Operation Blackboard and other schemes.

INCENTIVES

Various incentive schemes in addition to free tuition have been tried from time to time to encourage enrolment of children and continuance in school. These have taken the form of stipends, monetary payments to parents linked to days of school attendance, free textbooks and uniforms, and mid-day meals. Not all schools are covered. Moreover, the implementation of these schemes has been fitful and tardy. Textbooks and uniforms are rarely received at the beginning of the school session. Often, they are in short supply and of poor quality. Various malpractices in procurement and distribution have also been reported. The mid-day meal programme has been under implementation in several states. The longest period of its operation has been in Tamil Nadu. The states of Gujarat, Kerala, and Orissa, too, have been implementing the scheme for a fairly long period. In August 1995, the Government of India announced the launching of the mid-day meal scheme to give a boost to school enrolment and attendance, while at the same time providing nutritional support. The intention was to provide, in the interim period, food grains (dry ration) at the rate of 3 kg per student per month, subject to a minimum attendance of 80 per cent, till such time (within two years) that cooked or processed food could be given. The scheme now covers all children studying in primary classes in government, local body, and government aided schools in 5,440 blocks in 507 districts (Department of Education 1998a). While the objective of such a scheme is laudable, it adds to the non-teaching duties of the teacher. In most areas, it is difficult for teachers to impose the 80 per cent attendance rule. Attendance shoots up on the day the ration is distributed. In some areas, under age children are also registered for the sole purpose of getting the ration. Thus the scheme seems to reward, in some areas at least, enrolment rather than attendance. Even otherwise, when ration is given rather than a mid-day meal, it provides food support to the household. The PROBE team found that in many areas in the four states (Bihar, Madhya Pradesh, Rajasthan, and Uttar Pradesh) covered by it monthly rations had been replaced by quarterly rations. Also, there was bureaucratic apathy, delays and corruption (PROBE 1999). Reports of the Comptroller and Auditor General on the implementation of the scheme have brought out major weakness in the implementation of the scheme (CAG 1999, 2000a, b, c, d). Malpractices in the school feeding programme has been reported by the media in several states.

DROP-OUT

The school drop-out rate in India is very high, which partly explains why despite the official statistics showing high enrolment, the number of children actually attending school is far less as brought out by the 1991 census. The data in Table 3.17, presented in graphical form in Fig. 3.7, show that there has been a decline in drop-out rate from 64 per cent in 1976–7 to 40 per cent in 1998–9 at the primary stage (classes I to V), and from 77 per cent in 1976–7 to 57 per cent in 1998–9 at the elementary stage. The decline in the drop-out rate has been 'faster' at the primary stage than at the elementary stage. It has taken more than two decades to achieve this

TABLE 3.17: DROP-OUT RATE AT PRIMARY STAGE (CLASSES I TO V) AND ELEMENTARY STAGE (CLASSES I TO VIII), INDIA, 1976–7 TO 1998–9

Year	Classes I to V				Classes I to VIII			
	Boys	Girls	Total	G–B	Boys	Girls	Total	G–B
1976–7	61.8	67.8	64.2	6.0	74.0	82.2	77.1	8.2
1981–2	51.1	57.3	53.5	6.2	68.5	77.7	72.1	9.2
1991–2	41.0	45.2	42.8	4.2	54.3	62.0	57.5	7.7
1998–9	38.6	41.2	39.7	2.6	54.4	60.1	56.8	5.7

Source: Department of Education.
Note: Drop-out rate has been calculated from Classes I to V by the following method : (Enrolment in Class I preceding 4 years minus enrolment in Class V during the year) ÷ (Enrolment in Class I preceding 4 years) × 100. A similar method is followed for computing drop-out rate from Classes I to VIII.

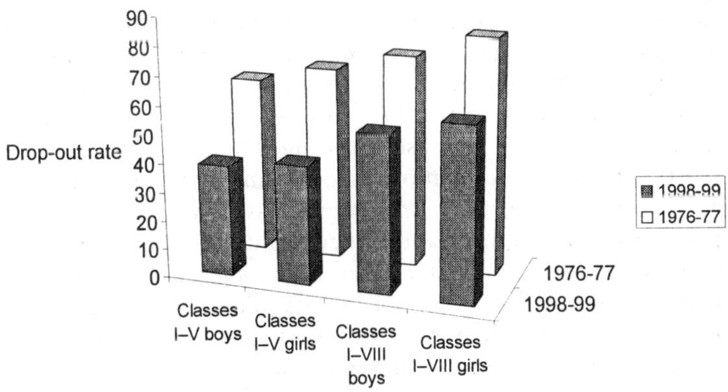

FIG. 3.7: DROP-OUT RATE AMONG BOYS AND GIRLS, CLASSES I–V AND CLASSES I–VIII, INDIA, 1976–7 AND 1998–9.

level, which is still unacceptably high with more than half the children dropping out between classes I to VIII. The 1998–9 drop-out rate is much higher than the Eighth Plan (1992–7) target of the 20 per cent drop-out rate between classes I to V and 40 per cent between classes I to VIII (Department of Education 1997a). However, a welcome trend is that the gender difference in drop-out rate has narrowed.

The drop-out rate is higher in the educationally backward states. Bihar heads the list with a drop-out rate of 59 per cent in classes I to V, and 77 per cent in classes I to VIII, in 1998–9. Andhra Pradesh, Assam, Orissa, Rajasthan, Uttar Pradesh, and West Bengal, too, had very high drop-out rates.

Empirical studies on the problem of drop-out, the magnitude of which has declined but is nowhere near a tolerable level, indicate that drop-out is usually preceded by irregular attendance. The factors contributing to drop-out can be divided into three broad categories:

(i) Family and home related factors;
(ii) School related factors;
(iii) Pupil related factors.

Among the family and home related factors are: (a) low and uncertain household income; (b) source of livelihood which leads to temporary (or continuous) change of place of work, as in the case of agricultural labourers or construction workers; (c) inability to spare the child for schooling, as help is needed for economic as well as household activities, the latter particularly in the case of girls; (d) illness in the family; (e) parental illiteracy due to which a first generation learner gets no academic support in learning, nor is the home environment supportive of learning; (f) poor parental motivation due to the perception that the type of education available and its quality will be of little use in getting jobs or improving earnings due to very limited occupational choices; and (g) parental perception that the education of girls is not very necessary and may even lead to problems of adjustment and difficulty in finding a groom. These factors operate with greater intensity among the poor and among lower castes, tribal communities, landless labourers, migrant workers, and some religious groups. Fortunately, negative attitudinal factors are undergoing a change and education is increasingly being viewed as necessary for both boys and girls, even among the poor and backward classes.

Among the school related factors brought out by various empirical studies are: (a) inconvenient location and distance specially in the case of girls; (b) unsuitable school timings; (c) poor physical facilities and teaching aids; (d) absence of toilets and drinking water; (e) irregular and delayed supply of books to students; (f) uninteresting school curriculum; (g) delay in drawing up the timetable and a schedule, and in following it; (h) irregular classes; (i) teaching of multiple classes; (j) poor teacher motivation; (k) absence of teachers for long periods due to vacant posts, and absenteeism; (l) coming late and wasting time in non-teaching activities; (m) unsatisfactory teaching material; (n) poor teaching methods coupled with absence of communication between teacher and student in regard to learning problems faced; (o) generally unsupportive and indifferent attitude towards students; (p) use of harsh language, even physical punishment, when students are not up to the mark; (q) biased perception that children of the urban and rural poor have inferior learning abilities; (r) absence of in-service training of teachers at regular intervals; (s) little supervision of teaching and guidance from headmaster; and (t) few school inspection visits. The presence of these factors in varying degrees reflects poor school administration and management of primary and middle schools by the state government and local authorities. They also reflect the outcome of malpractices in recruitment and postings, highlighted of and on by the media.

Among the pupil related factors are: (a) absence of learning experience in pre-school and, hence, greater problems of adjustment to school; (b) emotional problems resulting in lack of interest; (c) behavioural and adjustment problems; (d) physical or mental handicap; (e) language deficiencies; (f) inability to do homework and cope with studies, due to difficulty in following lessons, for which no help comes from family members due to their illiteracy or low level of education; and (g) illness for short or long periods.

Since drop-out is often preceded by absence for short or long periods, the teacher's role becomes important. Unfortunately, the teacher does little to try and sort out the child's learning problems and motivate the child and the family. The manner in which schools operate and teachers function show little sensitivity to the fact that when the child is a first generation learner and comes from a poor illiterate family the learning environment should aim at neutralizing this handicap. In most cases, the opposite is true. Schools run by state governments and local authorities in rural backward areas and slums are found to be far more deficient in physical infrastructure, as well as in teaching environment, resulting in higher drop-out rates in such institutions.

LEVEL OF EDUCATION

A child is expected to enter school at 6 years of age, complete primary school (classes I to V) at 11 years and middle/upper primary school (classes VI to VIII) at 14 years. In other words, a child is expected to complete elementary schooling by the time he completes the age of 14 years. Since the age of entry in school in the case of rural and urban children from poor families is often delayed, a good indicator of the extent to which the goal of universal elementary education has been achieved is the percentage of children aged

TABLE 3.18: PERCENTAGE OF PERSONS AGED 15–19 YEARS WHO HAVE COMPLETED PRIMARY AND MIDDLE LEVEL OF EDUCATION, INDIA, 1981, 1991 AND 1998–9

Year	Level of education	Rural				Urban				Total			
		M	F	T	M–F	M	F	T	M–F	M	F	T	M–F
1981	Primary and above	51.2	27.4	40.0	23.8	75.7	58.1	70.8	17.5	57.7	37.2	48.1	20.5
	Middle and above	32.2	14.4	23.8	17.8	58.1	48.8	53.8	9.3	39.1	23.3	31.7	7.4
1991	Primary and above	64.2	40.3	53.1	23.9	81.9	74.1	78.2	7.8	69.1	49.7	60.1	19.4
	Mddle and above	47.0	26.8	37.6	20.2	67.6	60.4	64.2	7.2	52.8	36.2	45.0	16.6
1998–9 (NFHS)	Primary and above	73.9	53.1	63.6	20.8	85.8	81.3	83.6	4.3	77.4	60.8	69.2	16.6
	Middle and above	51.2	34.5	42.9	16.7	67.7	64.0	65.9	3.7	56.0	42.6	49.4	13.4

Sources: *Census of India*, 1981 and 1991; *National Family Health Survey 1998–9*.

Note: Primary and above includes those who have completed levels above primary. Middle and above includes those who have completed levels higher than middle.

15–19 years who have attained primary/upper primary level of education. The 1991 Census data show an improvement over 1981 but even then less than half the children aged 15–19 years had completed middle level, and only about 60 per cent the primary level. The National Family Health Survey 1998–9 shows a further rise. In rural areas, where three-fourths of the population lives, the position is very unsatisfactory, especially among girls (Table 3.18).

TABLE 3.19: PERCENTAGE OF PERSONS AGED 15–19 YEARS WHO HAVE COMPLETED PRIMARY AND MIDDLE LEVEL OF EDUCATION IN STATES, 1991

Percentage of children	Primary and above	Middle and above
< 40		Madhya Pradesh (31.5) Rajasthan (31.9) Andhra Pradesh (38.1) Uttar Pradesh (39.1) West Bengal (39.4) Bihar (39.9)
40–9	Bihar (47.8) Rajasthan (48.1)	Orissa (41.1) INDIA (45.0) Gujarat (45.4) Haryana (46.1) Tamil Nadu (48.5) Assam (48.5) Karnataka (48.7)
50–9	Uttar Pradesh (50.7) Madhya Pradesh (50.8) Orissa (51.3) Andhra Pradesh (52.2)	Himachal Pradesh (50.5) Punjab (53.2)
60–9	West Bengal (60.0) INDIA (60.1) Assam (60.7) Karnataka (61.0) Haryana (67.7) Tamil Nadu (68.8) Gujarat (69.0)	Maharashtra (63.2)
70+	Punjab (70.7) Maharashtra (76.4) Himachal Pradesh (80.7) Kerala (95.7)	Kerala (83.1)

Source: *Census of India*, 1991.
Note: Data for 16 bigger states given here arranged in ascending order. Figures for India do not include Jammu & Kashmir.

These figures have to be viewed in the context that, in most states, promotions to the next class are made on a liberal basis; there is no formal external examination by a Board in many states which students have to pass to be eligible for a middle/upper primary school certificate. As such, the figures could be on the higher side, based as they are on the respondent's unverified statement.

There is considerable interstate variation in the attainment of primary and middle level of education, as the 1991 Census data for the 16 bigger states, given in Table 3.19, indicates. In six educationally backward states, the percentage of children aged 15–19 years who have attained the primary level of education varies between 48 and 52. In the case of middle level of education, the percentage of children who have attended this level is less than 50 in 12 out of the 16 bigger states. In fact in six states, the percentage is less than 40.

Extent of Learning

The learning achievements of students are at unsatisfactory levels, reflecting the poor quality of schooling for the mass of the population. Several studies conducted during the last three and a half decades have indicated not only low levels of learning, but also a worsening of the situation as children moved to higher classes (NCERT 1994). The survey in 1965–6 by the National Council of Educational Research and Training (NCERT) of achievement in Mathematics at the end of primary school, end of middle school, and end of secondary school found high variation between states, the averages at the primary level varying from 26 per cent to 48 per cent. This declined at the middle and secondary level. Boys generally were found to do better than girls. The direction of difference between rural and urban groups did not show a consistent pattern. The study also commented that the most important variables operated within the school, while variables like socio-economic condition or type of school (government or private) served only to improve teaching-learning situation (Kulkarni 1970). Several subsequent surveys also found little reason to be happy about the situation of learning achievements in school (Dave 1988; Shukla 1974).

The study by NCERT in 1991 to assess the levels of achievement of children at the end of primary school in the mother tongue and in numeracy at the end of class IV covered 23 states. The national average of the pupils of class IV on the battery of tests used was 45 per cent, which the researchers felt could be on the high side due to the possibility of some outside help, and factors such as absenteeism and elimination of data from largely unattempted scripts. Contrary to the general impression, the average score on Reading Comprehension was poorer than in Arithmetic, with considerable variation between states. On the whole, there was no difference in the achievement of children from urban or rural areas, but there was state-wise variation of the direction. Boys tended to achieve better in tests in Arithmetic and Word Knowledge. The differences did not have the same direction in all the states. Children in the capital cities tended to achieve at a higher level. Differences between the aggregate achievement of boys and girls did not move in the same direction in all the states—in some states it was in favour of boys, in some states in favour of girls, and in some the difference was not significant. The study found evidence of deterioration in achievement in class V, and observed that the findings were in conformity with other studies (NCERT 1994).

A baseline study in eight states in 1993–4, too, found low levels of learning achievement of students approaching the end of the primary school cycle. Though the study covered 46 educationally backward districts in eight states having low levels of female literacy (except Kerala), the findings are indicative of the unsatisfactory state of affairs. The study reported low achievement in Reading Comprehension Test and Word Meaning test. The achievement in Mathematics was still lower. The level of learning of class II students in reading of letters and words, and in numeracy was dismal, and in some districts alarming. The achievement in class II in recognition of numbers, addition, and subtraction was also very disappointing. The study observed:

> Poor performance of class II students on literacy and numeracy is the forerunner of poor performance in class V or IV. Regular teachers and relatively better infrastructure in Tamil Nadu and Kerala did not result in better performance. It implies poor quality of instruction. In other states, the schools are featured by both poorer infrastructure, poor management and poor quality of instruction.
>
> The low achievement of students is not prevalent only in school children. The drop-outs also achieved low. (Jangira 1994)

In the case of poor learning, students are required to repeat the class, but the policy in this regard shows a wide variation between states. Generally, a liberal policy is followed for promotion in classes I and II and, sometimes, even in class III. The absence of continuous assessment by the teachers compounds the problem. The survey of learning achievement in 1993–4 in educationally backward districts in eight states, referred to earlier, found that nearly one-third of the students reported repeating class at least once, with some districts reporting a higher percentage. In five states, repetition in class III varied from 14 to 24 per cent.

Achievement levels of learning have been investigated in several other studies as well. Though the results are not strictly comparable, they help to indicate firmly that the quality of primary education leaves much to be desired.

A study in West Bengal in 1991 in 882 sample schools in 17 districts showed that the mean minimum scores in Language and Mathematics were far below the minimum expected score. Only 28 per cent students obtained the minimum expected score (MES) in Language, while 36 per cent obtained it in Mathematics. There was hardly any difference in achievement between boys and girls or between rural and urban students (Guha Roy, Mitra and Roy 1995).

Similar results were reported from achievement tests in 59 sample schools in Madhya Pradesh. The level of achievement in the two core subjects of Language and Mathematics was found to be low. There was considerable inter-school variation and variation by region. Schools in backward areas performed poorly. Learners in private schools were found to fare better than learners in government schools though teachers in the former were paid less. Teachers in private schools adhered to a pre-planned calendar of activities; their work was supervised much better. There was greater stress on teacher performance. There was little difference in achievement between boys and girls. School infrastructure, number of teachers, teacher training, regular homework, possession of textbooks, and teaching methods influenced the achievement score. Learners in government schools moved to higher grades without proper evaluation at grades I and II. There was little internal monitoring. Several family related factors were also found to affect level of learning such as the educational level of parents and socio-economic background (Govinda and Verghese 1991). A study in Malwa Region of Madhya Pradesh reported low levels of learning achievement in Language and Mathematics (Yadav 1994). Very unsatisfactory levels of achievements in Language and Mathematics were also reported from Chattisgarh Region (Gupta 1995). In single teacher schools in tribal areas in

Andhra Pradesh, learning achievements were found to be very poor (Sujatha 1995).

A study in 1997 of progress in students' achievements in the learning of Language and Mathematics in classes III/IV in some of the districts covered by Phase I of the District Primary Education Programme indicated mixed results. Comparison of achievements in 1997 with that of 1994, when the programme was launched, indicated that in two states there was an improvement, while in three states there was a decline in some districts and an improvement in some. There was a large degree of variation between districts in mean percentage of students' performance in both Language and Mathematics within a state as well as between states (Department of Education 1998b).

Another study on learning of Mathematics, covering five government primary schools in Haryana and four municipal schools in Delhi, found a 'precarious learning environment' and poor level of learning in all the ten competencies tested (Maheshwari and Gupta 1998).

Learning achievement is affected mainly by school and teacher related factors and family and home environment related factors. In some cases, pupil related factors also play a role. Various studies have analysed the role of school related factors and family and home related factors. The relative importance of these do not indicate a consistent trend. The NCERT survey on achievement in Mathematics stated that the most important variables operated within the school, while variables like socio-economic condition or type of school (government or private) served to improve the teaching-learning situations (Kulkarni 1970). A subsequent survey also found school (and teacher) related variables very important in learning achievements (Shukla 1974). The 1991 survey found that school related variables appeared to be more significant for Arithmetic, and seemed nearly equally important for language learning. The role of school (and teacher) related variables and family and home environment related factors in learning achievement have also been discussed in several other studies (Guha Roy, Mitra and Roy 1995; Govinda and Verghese 1991; Jangira 1994). In the case of the first generation learners from poor families, the school is expected to offset the disadvantage of the family background. Unfortunately, this rarely happens.

The low levels of learning at the primary and subsequent stages get reflected in the external evaluations systems at the end of the middle and high school/higher secondary stage. The results of examinations conducted by the State Boards show a large incidence of failures (almost half) in several states. In some states, less than 40 per cent pass the high school examination conducted by the State Board. The overall pass percentage of students in high school examinations conducted by 26 Boards across the country in 1996 was 45 per cent. The pass percentage of girls was 48, as compared to 41 in the case of boys, indicating that girls who are in school take their studies more seriously (Department of Education 1999). The pass percentage in private schools in a number of states is far better than in government schools. School Board examination results of different states are not comparable for assessing the standard of the school system because of varying standards of evaluation in different states. An additional factor is the extent of examination related malpractices, sometimes as an individual endeavour, but lately assuming the dimensions of a collective organized activity. At several places, networks operate at different points for leakage of question papers, mass copying at examination centres, help to students in answering questions inside the examination halls, and tampering with answer books and marks. Teachers who do not cooperate in these matters are required to keep quiet, or feign ignorance, as muscle power and money are liberally used to prevent any interference. Complicity of officials, teachers, and politicians has been reported. In some states, unfair practices have reached serious proportions, but only half-hearted attempts, if at all, have been made to check a menace which calls for stringent measures. Uttar Pradesh enacted a special law in 1992 to prevent the use of unfair means in public examinations. The Act imposed heavy punishment to deter copying, but it was repealed in 1993 by an ordinance as soon as the government changed, only to be enacted once again when the previous government came back into power, indicating how politics dominates decisions on academic matters.

Poor standards of teaching, particularly in government and local authority schools, has led to a flourishing practice of private tuition at the residence of the teacher or in coaching classes. The teachers themselves, at many places, advise the students to take tuition. The State Directorates of Education have a record of poor performance in developing and sustaining a satisfactory education system in which students can achieve satisfactory levels of learning. There is a lack of accountability for failure to uphold minimum standards.

The poor suffer the most, as a substandard education is most unjust to their children. They cannot afford private schools, which in any case are not available in most rural areas. The children are totally dependent on the schools run by local authorities and the state government. Yet, political parties which aggressively seek votes on the plank of social uplift and social justice do little to have a good educational system, as the record of their governance in different states shows. Universalization of education of good quality, in actual practice, figures at the bottom of the list of priorities of politicians despite occasional declarations of the need to provide education to the masses. A good indicator of this is the low literacy level even in the constituencies of high profile politicians and education ministers of successive governments, irrespective of the political party in power.

Growth of Schools

Existence of a school is the first prerequisite for ensuring universalization of education. There has been considerable increase in the number of schools in the country, as Table 3.20 shows. The number of primary schools increased from 209,671 in 1950–1 to 641,695 in 1999–2000, more than three times the number in 1950–1. The increase in number of middle/upper primary schools has been much greater, from 13,596 in 1950–1 to 198,004 in 1999–2000, that is more than 14 times the number in 1950–1. The 1950s witnessed the maximum growth followed by the 1960s and 1970s. However, the number of schools in 1960–1 was nowhere near the number required to fulfil the constitutional directive in 1950 of

TABLE 3.20: GROWTH OF PRIMARY AND MIDDLE SCHOOLS, INDIA, 1950–1 TO 1999–2000

Year	Primary		Middle/ Upper primary		No. of middle/upper primary schools per 1,000 primary schools
	No.	% increase	No.	% increase	
1950–1	209,671		13,596		65
1960–1	330,399	57.58	49,663	256.28	150
1970–1	408,378	23.60	90,621	82.47	222
1980–1	494,503	21.09	118,555	30.82	240
1990–1	560,935	13.43	151,456	27.75	270
1995–6	590,421	5.26	171,216	13.05	290
1999–2000	641,695	8.68	198,004	15.64	309

Source: Department of Education.

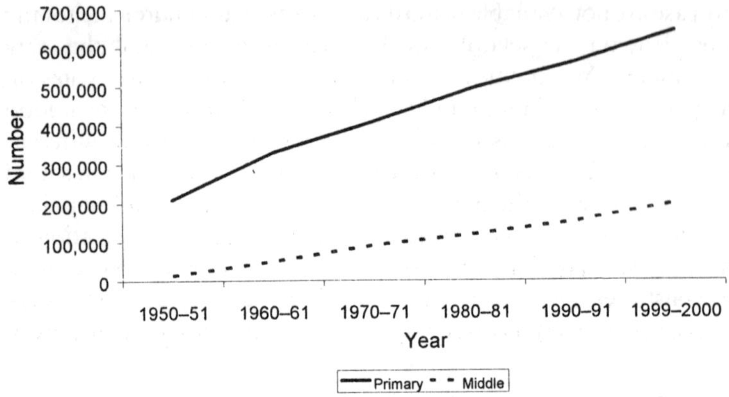

FIG. 3.8: GROWTH OF PRIMARY AND MIDDLE SCHOOLS, INDIA, 1950–1 TO 1999–2000.

providing, within a period of ten years, free and compulsory education to children until the age of 14 years.

Despite the growth in the number of middle/upper primary schools the ratio of middle to primary schools was three primary schools for every middle school in 1999–2000 which is far short of the Eighth Plan (1992–7) target of two primary schools for every middle school. Figure 3.8 gives the growth of primary and middle/upper primary schools in India.

Distance of primary or middle school/section is important, particularly in the case of girls and children in the lower age groups. The Sixth All India Educational Survey reported that in 1993 more than three-fourths of the rural population was served by a primary school/ section within the habitation, and 94 per cent with a primary school/ section within 1 km (see Table 3.21). The position in this regard is almost the same as reported by the Fourth and Fifth All India Educational Surveys (1978 and 1986 respectively).

As regards middle/upper primary schools/sections in rural areas, the Sixth All India Educational Survey reported 57 per cent of the population in 1993 having the facility within 1 km of the habitation (37 per cent within the habitation). The situation represents a moderate improvement over 1986 (see Table 3.22). In 1993, 28 per cent of rural children were expected to travel 1–3 km to attend middle/upper primary school, as compared to 32 per cent in 1986, and 15 per cent were expected to travel more than 3 km to reach school. For most

TABLE 3.21: PERCENTAGE DISTRIBUTION OF RURAL HABITATIONS ACCORDING TO DISTANCE OF PRIMARY SCHOOL/SECTION, INDIA

Survey		Rural habitations with primary school/section at a distance of								
		Within habitation	Up to 0.5 km	0.6 to 1.0 km.	Up to 1 km	1.1 to 1.5 km	1.6 to 2.0 km.	Up to 2.0 km	More than 2 km	Total
Fourth (1978)	No. of habitations'	451,457 (46.8)	141,519 (14.7)	181,022 (18.8)	773,998 (80.2)	52,633 (5.5)	72,046 (7.5)	898,677 (93.2)	65,987 (6.8)	964,664 (100.0)
	% of population covered	78.5	6.6	7.7	92.8	2.2	2.8	7.8	2.2	100.0
Fifth (1986)	No. of habitations	502,343 (51.2)	145,491 (14.8)	175,343 (17.9)	823,177 (83.8)	43,926 (4.5)	62,218 (6.3)	929,321 (94.6)	52,543 (5.4)	981,864 (100.0)
	% of population covered	80.4	6.7	3	94.4	.8	2.3	98.5	1.5	100.0
Sixth (1993)	No. of habitations	528,051 (49.8)	159,187 (15.0)	196,851 (18.6)	884,089 (83.4)	113,747 (10.7)		997,836 (94.1)	62,776 (5.9)	1,060,612 (100.0)
	% of population covered	77.8	7.7	8.3	93.8	4.2		98.0	2.0	100.0

Source: *All India Educational Surveys*, NCERT.

Note: Figures in brackets give the percentage distribution of habitations by distance of school.

TABLE 3.22: PERCENTAGE DISTRIBUTION OF RURAL HABITATIONS ACCORDING TO DISTANCE OF MIDDLE/UPPER PRIMARY SCHOOL/SECTION, INDIA

Survey		Within habitation	Up to 1 km	1.1 to 2.0 km	2.1 to 3.0 km	Upto 3.0 km	3.1 to 4.0 km	4.1 to 5.0 km	More than 5 km	Total
Fourth (1978)	No. of habitations	103,604 (10.7)	157,705 (16.35)	237,714 (21.5)	175,948 (18.2)	644,971 (66.9)	105,563 (10.9)	74,488 (7.7)	139,642 (14.5)	964,664 (100.0)
	% of population covered	33.5	13.1	17.8	14.5	78.8	7.9	5.4	7.9	100.0
Fifth (1986)	No. of habitations	128,951 (13.1)	187,105 (19.1)	229,138 (23.3)	181,400 (18.5)	726,594 (74.0)	93,423 (9.5)	62,077 (6.3)	99,770 (10.2)	981,864 (100.0)
	% of population covered	6.9	14.9	18.4	13.8	84.0	6.5	4.2	5.3	100.0
Sixth (1993)	No. of habitations	147,140 (13.9)	270,003 (25.5)	226,809 (21.4)	163,704 (15.4)	807,656 (76.2)	85,269 (8.0)	64,552 (6.1)	103,135 (9.7)	1,060,612 (100.0)
	% of population covered	37.0	19.9	16.4	11.7	85.0	5.5	4.2	5.3	100.0

Source: *All India Educational Surveys*, NCERT.
Note: Figures in brackets give the percentage distribution of habitations by distance of school.

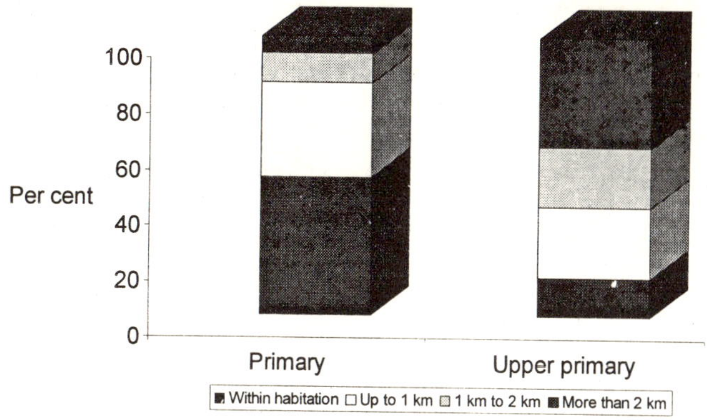

FIG. 3.9: PERCENTAGE DISTRIBUTION OF RURAL HABITATIONS ACCORDING TO DISTANCE OF SCHOOL/SECTION, INDIA, 1993.

girls, the long distance of a middle/upper primary school acts as a strong dissuading factor. Figure 3.9 presents the data on distance of primary schools and middle/upper primary schools from the habitation in graphical form.

STRUCTURE OF SCHOOL BUILDINGS

The school building plays an important role in determining the physical environment in which learning takes place. Even in 1993, there were 21,858 primary schools which had only an open space to function from, as is evident from Table 3.23. Classes naturally get disrupted when there is rain. Interruptions take place at other times of the year, too, due to inclement weather. Almost two-thirds of rural primary schools had pucca buildings, while 19 per cent had partly pucca and partly kutcha buildings. In urban areas, the situation is a little better. The situation varies from state to state, and within a state, between developed and backward regions.

A study based on a sample of 491 single teacher schools in the tribal areas of East Godavari and Khammam of Andhra Pradesh found a dismal situation. Almost all the single teacher schools did not have a school building. A majority of them were functioning in dilapidated thatched houses and in verandahs of houses of villagers. Some were conducted in the open space (Sujatha 1995).

TABLE 3.23: TYPE OF BUILDING OF PRIMARY SCHOOLS, INDIA

Area	Survey	Type of buildings						
		Open Space	Tents	Thatched huts	Katcha buildings	Partly pucca buildings	Pucca buildings	Total
Rural	Fourth	39,606	360	46,457	97,744	55,291	192,144	431,602
	(1978)	(9.2)	(0.1)	(10.8)	(22.6)	(12.8)	(44.5)	(100.0)
	Fifth	38,094	2,509	28,299	70,351	77,288	259,282	475,823
	(1986)	(8.0)	(0.5)	(6.0)	(14.8)	(16.2)	(54.5)	(100.00)
	Sixth	20,418	1,947	16,292	48,253	94,807	325,864	507,581
	(1993)	(4.0)	(0.4)	(3.2)	(9.5)	(18.7)	(64.2)	(100.0)
Urban	Fourth	1,124	196	1,262	3,608	6,127	30,717	43,034
	(1978)	(2.6)	(0.5)	(2.9)	(8.4)	(14.2)	(71.4)	(100.0)
	Fifth	1,677	63	924	3,264	8,778	38,201	52,907
	(1986)	(3.2)	(0.1)	(1.7)	(6.2)	(16.6)	(72.2)	(100.0)
	Sixth	1,440	143	958	3,350	11,661	45,322	62,874
	(1993)	(2.3)	(0.2)	(1.5)	(5.3)	(18.6)	(72.1)	(100.0)
Total	Fourth	40,730	556	47,719	101,352	61,418	222,861	474,636
	(1978)	(8.6)	(0.1)	(10.1)	(21.4)	(12.9)	(46.9)	100.00)
	Fifth	39,771	2,572	29,223	73,615	86,066	297,483	528,730
	(1986)	(7.5)	(0.5)	(5.5)	(13.9)	(16.3)	(56.3)	(100.0)
	Sixth	21,858	2,090	17,250	51,603	106,468	371,186	570,455
	(1993)	(3.8)	(0.4)	(3.0)	(9.0)	(18.7)	(65.1)	(100.0)

Source: *All India Educational Surveys*, NCERT.
Note: Figures in brackets give the percentage distribution.

Two-thirds of the middle/upper primary schools in 1993 in rural areas had pucca buildings (see Table 3.24). The percentage has remained the same as in 1978. About 22 per cent had partly pucca structures. In urban areas, about four-fifths of the buildings in 1993 had pucca structures and 14 per cent had partly pucca structures.

The structures, particularly in rural backward areas, are, in many cases, in a bad shape, due to the poor standard of construction and bad maintenance. Most of the state education budget is spent on paying salaries, leaving very little for upgradation, maintenance, or expansion. Maintenance of school buildings is given an extraordinarily low priority by the State Directorates of Education. The PROBE team, which covered Bihar, Madhya Pradesh, Rajasthan, and Uttar Pradesh in its survey, found that out of 162 government primary schools in its sample, 60 per cent had a leaking roof, which caused a major disruption during the rainy season. It further found that among all school buildings constructed after 1986, 46 per cent need a repair of the roof, 58 per cent repair of floor and 73 per cent

TABLE 3.24: TYPE OF BUILDING OF MIDDLE/UPPER PRIMARY SCHOOLS, INDIA

Area	Survey	Type of buildings						
		Open space	Tents	Thatched huts	Kutcha building	Partly pucca building	Pucca building	Total
Rural	Fourth	1,757	22	2,025	11,062	15,969	63,345	94,180
	(1978)	(1.9)	(0.0)	(2.1)	(11.7)	(17.0)	(67.3)	(100.0)
	Fifth	2,773	258	2,301	10,459	22,224	75,072	113,087
	(1986)	(2.4)	(0.2)	(2.0)	(9.3)	(19.7)	(66.4)	(100.0)
	Sixth	2,701	103	2,253	10,261	29,053	84,875	129,246
	(1993)	(2.1)	(0.1)	(1.7)	(7.9)	(22.5)	(65.7)	(100.0)
Urban	Fourth	53	44	202	769	2,030	15,126	18,224
	(1978)	(0.3)	(0.2)	(1.1)	(4.2)	(11.1)	(83.0)	(100.0)
	Fifth	178	57	159	851	3337	21,347	25,929
	(1986)	(0.7)	(0.2)	(0.6)	(3.3)	(12.9)	(82.3)	(100.0)
	Sixth	265	52	264	1514	4768	26,696	33,559
	(1993)	(0.8)	(0.1)	(0.8)	(4.5)	(14.2)	(79.6)	(100.0)
Total	Fourth	1,810	66	2,227	11,831	17,999	78,471	112,404
	(1978)	(1.6)	(0.1)	(2.0)	(10.5)	(16.0)	(69.8)	(100.0)
	Fifth	2,951	315	2,460	11,310	25,561	96,419	139,016
	(1986)	(2.1)	(0.2)	(1.8)	(8.1)	(18.4)	(69.4)	(100.0)
	Sixth	2,966	155	2,517	11,775	33,821	111,571	162,805
	(1993)	(1.8)	(0.1)	(1.6)	(7.2)	(20.8)	(68.5)	(100.0)

Source: *All India Educational Surveys*, NCERT.
Note: Figures in brackets give the percentage distribution.

major repair of some kind. Furthermore, the school premises often present a dismal and unattractive appearance, with dirty and unhygienic surroundings, an environment which could hardly be expected to stimulate the child (PROBE 1999). Media and other reports have also from time to time brought out the poor condition of school buildings and the state of disrepair of many of them.

NUMBER OF ROOMS

In normal circumstances, a school should have a separate room for each class. In actual practice, as reported by the Sixth Educational Survey, 29 per cent of rural primary schools in 1993 had either no room or only one room, 32 per cent had two rooms, and 39 per cent had three or more rooms (see Table 3.25). In other words, 61 per cent of rural primary schools had only up to two rooms. The situation in 1993 shows an improvement over 1978, when 50 per

TABLE 3.25: PERCENTAGE DISTRIBUTION OF PRIMARY SCHOOLS ACCORDING TO NUMBER OF ROOMS AVAILABLE, INDIA

Area	Survey	No. of rooms per school									
		Nil	1	2	3	4	5	6–7	8–9	10 +	Total
Rural	Fourth (1978)	35,325	178,968	107,324	54,173	28,518	15,164	7,136	2,702	2,292	431,602
		(8.2)	(41.5)	(24.9)	(12.6)	(6.6)	(3.5)	(1.6)	(0.6)	(0.5)	(100.0)
	Fifth (1986)	38,152	177,207	119,313	67,816	36,144	18,796	11,332	3,800	3,263	475,823
		(8.0)	(37.2)	(25.1)	(14.3)	(7.6)	(3.9)	(2.4)	(0.8)	(0.7)	(100.0)
	Sixth (1993)	26,927	121,197	159,786	102,325	45,327	24,297	16,849	5,851	5,022	507,581
		(5.3)	(23.9)	(31.5)	(20.2)	(8.9)	(4.8)	(3.3)	(1.1)	(1.0)	(100.0)
Urban	Fourth (1978)	1,114	5,214	6,375	5,856	6,641	5,879	5,127	2,824	4,004	43,034
		(2.6)	(12.1)	(14.8)	(13.6)	(15.4)	(13.7)	(11.9)	(6.6)	(9.3)	(100.0)
	Fifth (1986)	1,805	6495	7,339	6,765	8,184	6,184	6,292	3,592	6,251	52,907
		(3.4)	(12.3)	(13.9)	(12.8)	(15.5)	(11.7)	(11.9)	(6.8)	(11.8)	(100.0)
	Sixth (1993)	1,980	5,902	8,824	7,562	7,394	7,622	10,188	4,970	8,432	62,874
		(3.2)	(9.4)	(14.0)	(12.0)	(11.8)	(12.1)	(16.2)	(7.9)	(13.4)	(100.0)
Total	Fourth (1978)	36,439	184,182	113,699	60,029	35,159	21,043	12,263	5,526	6,296	474,636
		(7.7)	(38.8)	(23.9)	(12.6)	(7.4)	(4.4)	(2.6)	(1.2)	(1.4)	(100.0)
	Fifth (1986)	39,957	183,702	126,652	74,581	44,328	24,980	17,624	7,392	9,514	528,730
		(7.6)	(34.7)	(24.0)	(14.1)	(8.4)	(4.7)	(3.3)	(1.4)	(1.8)	(100.0)
	Sixth (1993)	28,907	127,099	168,610	109,887	52,721	31,919	27,037	10,821	13,454	570,455
		(5.1)	(22.3)	(29.5)	(19.3)	(9.2)	(5.6)	(4.7)	(1.9)	(2.4)	(100.0)

Source: *All India Educational Surveys*, NCERT.
Note: Figures in brackets give the percentage distribution.

cent rural primary schools had either no room or only one room, 25 per cent had two rooms, and only 25 per cent had three or more rooms. In urban areas, the situation is better than in rural areas. In 1993, in urban areas 27 per cent primary schools had up to two rooms, while 73 per cent had three or more rooms. If we take the norm of a minimum of five rooms in a primary school, then in rural areas only 10 per cent primary schools and in urban areas 50 per cent fulfil this criterion.

The National Policy on Education, 1986 had stated that every primary school would be provided at least two reasonably large rooms that were usable in all weather conditions. The centrally sponsored scheme of Operation Blackboard, launched in 1987–8 set this as the target. In 1993, that is 46 years after independence, 27 per cent primary schools were yet to reach even this modest minimum. The scope of Operation Blackboard was expanded in 1994 to provide a third room to primary schools where enrolment exceeded 100 students. Priority has been given to rural areas. Hopefully, this will result in some improvement in the physical capacity of schools. The current practice is to hold more than one class in the same room by dividing/partitioning the room to provide teaching space to two teachers, which is not quite learner friendly.

In the case of middle/upper primary schools, 41 per cent schools in rural areas have more than five rooms, 29 per cent have up to 3 rooms only, while 30 per cent have 4–5 rooms (see Table 3.26). In urban areas, 75 per cent middle/upper primary schools have more than five rooms, 9 per cent have up to 3 rooms only, while 16 per cent have 4–5 rooms. Thus, in a large number of middle/upper primary schools, too, accommodation is far short of the requirement. The situation is particularly deficient in rural areas.

Drinking Water and Toilet Facilities

Drinking water and toilet facilities are, apparently, not considered essential parts of a school structure and are often classified as ancillary facilities. The situation in regard to toilet facilities is dismal particularly in rural areas. Even in urban areas, primary schools are poorly served. Separate facilities are virtually non-existent for girls in rural primary schools, as the data in Table 3.27 show. It is evident that Operation Blackboard launched in 1987 had not even remotely met the stipulated goal of separate toilet facilities for boys and girls by 1993. The PROBE team, in its survey of primary education covering

TABLE 3.26: PERCENTAGE DISTRIBUTION OF MIDDLE/UPPER PRIMARY SCHOOLS ACCORDING TO NUMBER OF ROOMS AVAILABLE, INDIA, 1993

Area		No. of rooms per school										
		0	1	2	3	4	5	6–7	8–9	10 & above	Total	Average no. per school
Rural	No.	3,465	2,707	11,804	18,865	21,154	17,849	24,596	14,526	14,280	129,246	
	%	2.7	2.1	9.1	14.6	16.4	13.8	19.0	11.2	11.1	100.0	5.64
Urban	No.	454	302	774	1,514	2,569	2,801	5,746	5,830	13,569	33,559	
	%	1.3	0.9	2.3	4.5	7.7	8.4	17.1	17.4	40.4	100.0	9.72
Total	No.	3,919	3,009	12,578	20,379	23,723	20,650	30,342	20,356	27,849	162,805	
	%	2.4	1.9	7.7	12.5	14.6	12.7	18.6	12.5	17.1	100.0	6.48

Source: *Sixth All India Educational Survey*, NCERT.

TABLE 3.27: NUMBER OF PRIMARY AND MIDDLE/UPPER PRIMARY SCHOOLS WITH DRINKING WATER AND TOILET FACILITIES, INDIA, 1993

Stage	Area	Total no. of schools	No. and percentage of schools having facilities for				
			Drinking water	Urinal	Separate urinal for girls	Lavatory	Separate lavatory for girls
Primary school	Rural	507,581	210,034 (41.4)	71,188 (14.0)	28,138 (5.5)	32,463 (6.4)	12,186 (2.4)
	Urban	62,874	42,279 (67.2)	36,798 (58.5)	21,282 (33.9)	29,463 (48.9)	16,998 (27.0)
	Total	570,455	252,313 (44.2)	107,986 (18.9)	49,420 (8.7)	61,926 (10.9)	29,184 (5.1)
Middle/ Upper Primary school	Rural	129,246	75,404 (58.3)	52,444 (40.6)	31,673 (24.5)	25,812 (20.0)	11,965 (9.3)
	Urban	33,559	27,930 (83.2)	26,421 (78.7)	19,681 (58.7)	22,836 (68.1)	15,982 (47.6)
	Total	162,805	103,334 (63.5)	78,865 (48.4)	51,354 (31.5)	48,648 (29.9)	27,947 (17.2)

Source: *Sixth All India Educational Survey*, NCERT.
Note: Percentage calculated from total number of schools.

188 sample villages in Bihar, Madhya Pradesh, Rajasthan, and Orissa in 1996, found that 89 per cent of the primary schools did not have a functioning toilet (PROBE 1999). Urban primary schools, also, are very poorly served. The situation, though moderately better in middle/upper primary schools, is still very unsatisfactory. Even in urban areas, less than half the middle/upper primary schools in 1993 had a separate lavatory for girls; only 59 per cent had a separate urinal. Fig. 3.10 graphically illustrates the extent of availability of these basic facilities in schools.

The situation in regard to toilet facilities is far worse in government schools. According to the Sixth All India Educational Survey in 1993, in upper primary schools in urban areas only 23 per cent government schools had a separate lavatory for girls, while 39 per cent local body schools, 56 per cent private aided schools, and 72 per cent private unaided schools had this facility. The same wide difference is found between government and private schools in the matter of other facilities, including separate urinals for girls. Maintenance of the facilities is extremely poor, and they are, at most times, unusable.

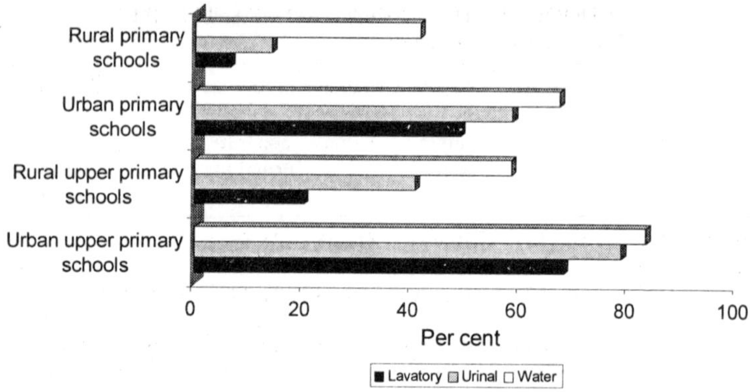

FIG. 3.10: PERCENTAGE OF PRIMARY AND UPPER PRIMARY SCHOOLS IN RURAL AND URBAN AREAS HAVING DRINKING WATER AND TOILET FACILITIES, INDIA, 1993.

TEACHING AIDS

Among the basic needs of a classroom or section are a usable blackboard and furniture for teachers and students. The Sixth All India Educational Survey reported that in 1993 only 62 per cent of rural primary sections had usable blackboards (see Table 3.28). Worse off were government schools, where only 53 per cent sections had usable blackboards. While this is an improvement over 1986, when 52 per cent rural primary sections were so placed, it does reflect the sad state of affairs four and a half decades after independence, despite the launch of the centrally sponsored scheme of Operation Blackboard in 1987–8, which had as its objective the provision of blackboards and other learning material. Only half the rural primary school sections had furniture for teachers. Of rural primary school sections, 38 per cent had no mats or furniture. Urban primary school sections were somewhat better placed, but here, too, 15 per cent did not have blackboards in 1993, 25 per cent did not have furniture for teachers, and 18 per cent did not have mats or furniture for students. The situation in primary schools located in tribal and backward rural areas is far worse. For instance, a study of nearly 500 single teacher schools in tribal areas in East Godavari and Khammam districts

TABLE 3.28: AVAILABILITY OF BLACKBOARD AND FURNITURE FOR TEACHERS AND STUDENTS, INDIA, 1993

Stage	Rural/ Urban		Total no. of sections	No. of usable black-boards	No. of sections having furniture for teachers	No. of sections having mats/ furniture for students		
						Adequate	Inade-quate	No mats/ furniture
Primary schools	Rural	No.	2,339,412	1,458,658	1,158,636	1,010,319	444,886	884,207
		%		62.4	49.5•	43.2	19.0	37.8
	Urban	No.	361,896	307,785	272,589	252,050	43,860	65,986
		%		85.1	75.3	69.7	12.1	18.2
	Total	No.	2,701,308	1,766,443	1,431,225	1,262,369	488,746	950,193
		%		65.4	53.0	46.7	18.1	35.2
Middle/ Upper primary schools	Rural	No.	850,094	674,892	574,939	382,517	139,222	328,355
		%		79.4	67.6	45.0	16.4	38.6
	Urban	No.	291,859	272,819	241,512	213,935	28,394	49,530
		%		93.5	82.7	73.3	9.7	17.0
	Total	No.	1,141,953	947,711	816,451	596,452	167,616	377,885
		%		83.0	71.5	52.2	14.7	33.1

Source: *Sixth All India Educational Survey*, NCERT.
Note: Percentages have been calculated with reference to the total number of sections.

showed that though 73 per cent had a blackboard, in the majority they were not in usable condition (Sujatha 1995). The deprivation of primary schools of basic teaching aids has to be seen in the context that 87 per cent of primary school sections are in rural areas. Teaching aids and furniture received are often of poor quality. Teaching aids are not put to regular use in many places and are kept locked by teachers due to fear of being blamed for their loss or damage (PROBE 1999).

In middle/upper primary schools/sections in rural areas, the situation is better than in primary schools. Even then, 21 per cent did not have usable blackboards, 32 per cent had no furniture for teachers, and 39 per cent had no mats/furniture for students. Urban middle/ upper primary school sections are somewhat better placed, but here, too, 7 per cent did not have usable blackboards, 17 per cent did not have furniture for teachers, and 17 per cent did not have mats/ furniture for students. Fig. 3.11 gives a comparative picture of extent of availability of teaching aids in rural and urban primary and upper primary schools.

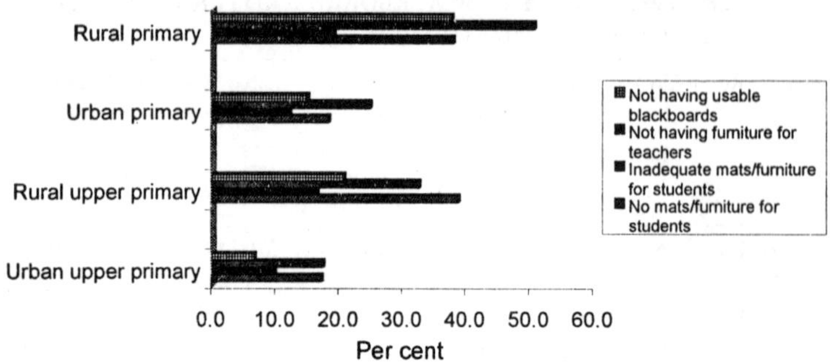

FIG. 3.11: PERCENTAGE OF SECTIONS IN PRIMARY AND UPPER PRIMARY SCHOOLS IN RURAL AND URBAN AREAS HAVING NO TEACHING AIDS, INDIA, 1993.

School Management

The Sixth All India Educational Survey (1993) found that the management of 95 per cent rural primary schools was with the government or local bodies (see Table 3.29). Less than 5 per cent rural primary schools were private schools, the number of aided private schools being larger than the number of unaided private schools. The Fourth (1978) and Fifth (1986) All India Educational Surveys had reported a similar pattern. However, while in 1978 the number of private aided rural primary schools was more than three times the unaided ones, in 1993 they were a little over one and half times the number of unaided schools. Thus, the growth of private unaided schools was much faster between 1978 and 1993 (153 per cent growth) as compared to private aided schools (28 per cent). In general, the growth of private schools (aided plus unaided) in rural areas was 59 per cent between 1978 and 1993, as compared to 16 per cent growth in the case of government and local body schools. This is a reflection of the developing market for private schools, even in rural areas, and a demand for better schools. The public perception of government and local body schools is that even though no fees have to be paid, the education provided in them is not of a good standard, while private schools are better run, teachers are regular and more committed, and the learning environment far better. The PROBE team, which covered Bihar, Madhya Pradesh, Rajasthan, and Orissa, found that parents from even low income groups and backward

TABLE 3.29: MANAGEMENT OF PRIMARY SCHOOLS, INDIA

Area	Survey		Management				
			Government	Local body	Private aided	Private unaided	Total
Rural	Fourth	No.	172,861	243,842	11,280	3,619	431,602
	(1978)	%	40.1	56.5	2.6	0.8	100.0
	Fifth	No.	203,656	255,331	12,038	4,798	475,823
	(1986)	%	42.8	53.7	2.5	1.0	100.0
	Sixth	No.	235,958	247,974	14,478	9,171	507,581
	(1993)	%	46.5	48.8	2.9	1.8	100.0
Urban	Fourth	No.	12,039	17,354	9702	3,939	43,034
	(1978)	%	28.0	40.3	22.5	9.2	100.0
	Fifth	No.	15,101	18,101	10,911	8,794	52,907
	(1986)	%	28.5	34.2	20.6	16.6	100.0
	Sixth	No.	18,648	22,832	7079	14,315	62,874
	(1993)	%	29.6	36.3	11.3	22.8	100.0
Total	Fourth	No.	184,900	261,196	20,982	7,558	474,636
	(1978)	%	39.0	55.0	4.4	1.6	100.0
	Fifth	No.	218,757	273,432	22,949	13,592	528,730
	(1986)	%	41.4	51.7	4.3	2.6	100.0
	Sixth	No.	254,606	270,806	21,557	23,486	570,455
	(1993)	%	44.6	47.5	3.8	4.1	100.0

Source: *All India Educational Surveys*, NCERT.

communities are now sending their children to private schools when the fees are affordable, reflecting the value that they now attach to education, particularly of boys (PROBE 1999).

In the case of urban primary schools, the management of two-thirds of these institutions in 1993 was under government or local bodies, and the rest under private management. Here, too, their proportion is almost the same as in 1978. However, in the case of private schools the ratio of aided and unaided institutions has undergone a change. The Fourth All India Educational Survey had found that private aided schools were almost two and a half times the number of private unaided schools. However, in 1993, as reported by the Sixth All India Educational Survey, the situation reversed and unaided private primary schools were twice the number of private unaided primary schools. The number of urban private aided schools declined between 1978 and 1993, but the number of unaided schools increased by 263 per cent. As a general category, private schools grew at a higher rate than government and local body schools.

In rural middle/upper primary schools, an overwhelming majority continue to be under the management of government or local bodies, as in the case of rural primary schools. The Sixth All India Educational Survey reported that the management of 87 per cent rural middle/upper primary schols was with government or local bodies, as compared to 81 per cent in 1978 (see Table 3.30). The percentage of private aided middle/upper primary schools has declined in rural areas, while that of private unaided schools has increased. In urban areas, 51 per cent of middle/upper primary schools were found by the Sixth All India Educational Survey (1993) to be under the management of government or local bodies. This is lower than the percentage reported by the Fourth All India Educational Survey (64 per cent). Private unaided schools increased considerably in number from 2169 in 1978 to 10,592 in 1993, an increase of 388 per cent. They constituted the single largest category. The number of urban private aided schools also increased, but in lesser number (growth 32 per cent); their percentage, however, declined from 24 in

TABLE 3.30: MANAGEMENT OF MIDDLE/UPPER PRIMARY SCHOOLS, INDIA

Area	Survey		Management				
			Government	Local body	Private aided	Private unaided	Total
Rural	Fourth	No.	39,137	37,344	14,625	3,074	94,180
	(1978)	%	41.6	39.6	15.5	3.3	100.0
	Fifth	No.	51,561	38,560	17,361	5,605	113,087
	(1986)	%	45.6	34.1	15.3	5.0	100.0
	Sixth	No.	65,332	46,830	9,743	7,341	129,246
	(1993)	%	50.6	36.2	7.5	5.7	100.0
Urban	Fourth	No.	6,169	5,514	4,372	2,169	18,224
	(1978)	%	33.8	30.3	24.0	11.9	100.0
	Fifth	No.	7,926	6,386	5,297	6,320	25,929
	(1986)	%	30.6	24.6	20.4	24.4	100.0
	Sixth	No.	9,464	7,726	5,777	10,592	33,559
	(1993)	%	28.2	23.02	17.2	31.6	100.0
Total	Fourth	No.	45,306	42,858	18,997	5,243	112,404
	(1978)	%	40.3	38.1	16.9	4.7	100.0
	Fifth	No.	59,487	44,946	22,658	11,925	139,016
	(1986)	%	42.8	32.3	16.3	8.6	100.0
	Sixth	No.	74,796	54,556	15,520	17,933	162,805
	(1993)	%	45.9	33.5	9.5	11.0	100.0

Source: *All India Educational Surveys*, NCERT.

1978 to 17 in 1993. The increase in private educational institutions is a reflection of what parents think of the quality of education in government or local body schools. These institutions have a poor image. No tuition fees are charged in these schools, yet many parents prefer to pay fees in private schools which are perceived as offering a better quality of education. The growth in number of private schools is in response to the expanding market. Unfortunately, a growing number of private schools are run as commercial ventures, rather than as not-for-profit institutions for the development of good quality education at an affordable price.

Teachers and their Qualifications

The teacher occupies the centre stage in the classroom where the learning process takes place. The role of teachers is critically important in the learning achievement of students, especially when the child comes from a family where parents are poor, illiterate, or have low levels of learning and can, therefore, provide little learning support at home. Teachers and the school hold the key to the success of any elementary education programme.

Primary schools in India suffer not only from poor physical infrastructure; they also do not have enough teachers. The number of sanctioned posts for teachers in a school and the number in position are determined not only by availability of funds which in any case have been far short of the requirements. Another factor is the number of students who are on the rolls. In view of the time lag in appointment of teachers which is based on number of students, a teacher has to teach children of different classes, which adversely affects teaching and learning.

In 1993, 22 per cent rural primary schools had a single teacher. In numbers this meant 112,026 rural primary schools (see Table 3.31). Such schools become non-functional when the teacher is absent. Absence of teachers is a chronic problem in tribal and backward rural areas. Even otherwise, learning is affected when children studying in different classes are attended to by a single teacher. Multi-grade teaching is a compromise, and a reflection of expediency at the cost of the learning process. The situation in 1993 does represent an improvement over the position in 1978, when 38 per cent of rural primary schools had a single teacher, and 1986 when the percentage of single teacher schools was 31. However, in some states, even in 1993, the percentage of single teachers in rural schools is higher than

TABLE 3.31: DISTRIBUTION OF PRIMARY SCHOOLS ACCORDING TO NUMBER OF TEACHERS PER SCHOOL, INDIA

Area	Survey		No. of schools according to number of teachers per school							
			None	1	2	3	4	5	6 & above	Total
Rural	Fourth	No.	2,825	162,203	125,190	66,562	32,598	18,567	23,657	431,602
	(1978)	%	0.7	37.6	29.0	15.4	7.5	4.3	5.5	100.00
	Fifth	No.	2,221	149,548	162,116	73,103	38,903	22,724	27,208	475,823
	(1986)	%	0.5	31.4	34.1	15.4	8.2	4.8	5.7	100.0
	Sixth	No.	4105	112,026	228,946	76,437	36,751	21,944	27,372	507,581
	(1993)	%	0.8	22.1	45.1	15.1	7.2	4.3	5.4	100.0
Urban	Fourth	No.	112	2,728	4,261	5,096	6,128	6,341	18,368	43,034
	(1978)	%	0.3	6.3	9.9	11.8	14.2	14.8	42.7	100.0
	Fifth	No.	29	3,300	6,307	6,783	8,030	7,260	21,198	52,907
	(1986)	%	0.1	6.2	11.9	12.8	15.2	13.7	40.1	100.0
	Sixth	No.	268	2,724	10,193	8,504	9,196	9,575	22,414	62,874
	(1993)	%	0.4	4.3	16.2	13.5	14.6	15.2	35.7	100.0
Total	Fourth	No.	2,937	164,931	129,451	71,658	38,726	24,908	42,025	474,636
	(1978)	%	0.6	34.7	27.3	15.1	8.2	5.2	8.9	100.0
	Fifth	No.	2,250	152,848	168,423	79,886	46,933	29,984	48,406	528,730
	(1986)	%	0.4	28.9	31.8	15.1	8.9	5.7	9.2	100.0
	Sixth	No.	4,373	114,750	239,139	84,941	45,947	31,519	49,786	570,455
	(1993)	%	0.8	20.1	41.9	14.9	8.1	5.5	8.7	100.0

Source: All India Educational Surveys, NCERT.

the national aggregate of 22 per cent as, for instance, in Rajasthan (32 per cent), Madhya Pradesh (34 per cent), and Andhra Pradesh (36 per cent).

Two-thirds of rural primary schools in 1993 had up to only two teachers per school (22 per cent one teacher and 45 per cent two teachers). The relative position has not altered in 15 years in terms of three or more teachers per school. The only noticeable change has been the increase of two teacher schools and decrease of single teacher schools. This took place mainly after 1986 as a result of the centrally sponsored scheme of Operation Blackboard, launched in 1987–8 with the objective of having at least two teachers in a primary school and providing full central assistance for the additional teacher in single teacher schools. However, even in 1993, 23 per cent rural primary schools were below the two teacher norm laid down by Operation Blackboard. In 1993–4, the scheme was modified to provide at least three teachers. This would, hopefully, result in some improvement in the provision of an additional teacher in two teacher schools in the coming years.

It is clear, therefore, that even in 1993, that is 43 years after the Constitutional Directive contained in Article 45 which required the State to provide, by 1960, for free and compulsory education for all children until 14 years of age, the country was still very far from having the minimum infrastructure of learning even for the primary stage.

The presence of female teachers in primary and middle schools promotes enrolment and retention of girls in school. In rural areas, only one-fourth of the teachers, both at primary and middle school, are females. However, there has been a steady increase in the percentage of female teachers between 1978 and 1993, as is evident from Table 3.32. In urban areas, six-tenths of the teachers in 1993, both in primary and middle schools, were females.

The minimum educational qualifications of primary school teachers vary in different states. Some have prescribed a minimum of ten years of schooling; some require 12 years. A two year diploma in elementary education is also required. However, in many states, initial recruitments were made of teachers with lower educational qualifications because of the difficulty in getting teachers to work in backward rural and tribal areas and remote places.

Data on the educational qualifications of school teachers is collected in All India Educational Surveys. Table 3.33 which gives the educational qualifications of primary school teachers shows that the percentage of teachers who are graduate and above has been rising. In 1993, in rural areas, 22 per cent of the rural primary school teachers, and in urban areas 38 per cent, were graduate and above, according to the Sixth All India Educational Survey. The percentage of teachers with lower than higher secondary education has been going down, even in rural areas.

The educational qualifications of middle/upper primary school teachers, given in Table 3.34, show that the percentage of teachers with level of education graduate and above has been increasing in both rural and urban areas, but the latter have a higher percentage of such teachers. The percentage of teachers with educational qualifications up to secondary level has been declining in both rural and urban areas, due to greater availability of teachers with higher educational qualifications.

Most teachers in rural and urban primary and middle/upper primary schools are trained. Even the Fourth All India Educational Survey (1978) had reported more than 85 per cent trained teachers. Only a small percentage of teachers have, however, undergone in-

TABLE 3.32: NUMBER OF FEMALE TEACHERS IN PRIMARY AND MIDDLE/UPPER PRIMARY SCHOOLS, INDIA

Stage	Survey		Rural			Urban			Total		
			Male	Female	Total	Male	Female	Total	Male	Female	Total
Primary schools	Fourth (1978)	No.	1,002,494	233,593	1,236,087	158,982	204,113	363,095	1,161,476	437,706	1,599,182
		%	81.1	18.9	100.0	43.8	56.2	100.0	72.6	27.4	100.0
	Fifth (1986)	No.	932,896	247,024	1,179,920	138,821	173,980	312,801	1,071,717	421,004	1,492,721
		%	79.1	20.9	100.0	44.4	55.6	100.0	71.8	28.2	100.0
	Sixth (1993)	No.	975,481	299,737	1,275,218	134,774	213,387	348,161	1,110,255	513,124	1,623,379
		%	76.5	23.5	100.0	38.7	61.3	100.0	68.4	31.6	100.0
Middle/Upper primary schools	Fourth (1978)	No.	411,364	96,932	508,296	126,737	109,885	236,622	538,101	206,817	744,918
		%	80.9	19.1	100.0	53.6	46.4	100.0	72.2	27.8	100.0
	Fifth (1986)	No.	551,050	169,037	720,087	122,365	159,684	282,049	673,415	328,721	1,002,136
		%	76.5	23.5	100.0	43.4	56.6	100.0	67.2	32.8	100.0
	Sixth (1993)	No.	589,573	200,698	790,271	133,766	205,710	339,476	723,339	406,408	1,129,747
		%	74.6	25.4	100.0	39.4	60.6	100.0	64.0	36.0	100.0

Source: *All India Educational Surveys*, NCERT.

TABLE 3.33: EDUCATIONAL QUALIFICATIONS OF TEACHERS AT PRIMARY STAGE, INDIA

Area	Survey		Educational qualifications				
			Up to secondary	Higher secondary	Graduate & above	Other	Total
Rural	Fourth	No.	980,330	176,987	71,712	7,058	1,236,087
	(1978)	%	79.3	14.3	5.8	0.6	100.0
	Fifth	No.	972,563	265,185	131,509	7,757	1,377,014
	(1986)	%	70.6	19.3	9.5	0.6	100.0
	Sixth	No.	785,624	371,291	337,100	7,830	1,501,845
	(1993)	%	52.3	24.7	22.5	0.5	100.0
Urban	Fourth	No.	253,489	51,502	52,392	5,712	363,095
	(1978)	%	69.8	14.2	14.4	1.6	100.0
	Fifth	No.	274,014	80,367	78,762	5,288	438,431
	(1986)	%	62.5	18.3	18.0	1.2	100.0
	Sixth	No.	200,269	110,878	196,703	3,817	511,667
	(1993)	%	39.1	21.7	38.4	0.8	100.0
Total	Fourth	No.	1,233,819	228,489	124,104	12,770	1,599,182
	(1978)	%	77.1	14.3	7.8	0.8	100.0
	Fifth	No.	1,246,577	345,552	210,271	13,045	1,815,445
	(1986)	%	68.7	19.0	11.6	0.7	100.0
	Sixth	No.	985,893	482,169	533,803	11,647	2,013,512
	(1993)	%	49.0	23.9	26.5	0.6	100.0

Source: *All India Educational Surveys*, NCERT.

service training. The Fifth All India Educational Survey (1986) found that only 5.6 per cent primary school teachers and 7.3 per cent middle/upper primary school teachers had undergone in-service training. The situation found by the Sixth All India Educational Survey was not very different. A study on primary school teachers, covering 49 districts in 9 states, observed that no state could provide a policy on in-service training or staff structure of elementary teacher training institutions. The duration of the current in-service training programmes usually ranged between 1 and 2 weeks, and these were mainly one time affairs, with little follow-up. The study also found that the training content followed a top-down approach, rather than being developed from an assessment of training needs at the field level. Few teachers received training in multi-grade teaching, development of teaching aids and their use, and on the role these can play in improving enrolment, retention, and learning. The study concluded that the impact of training on classroom practice is doubtful (Jangira, Singh and Yadav 1994).

TABLE 3.34: EDUCATIONAL QUALIFICATIONS OF TEACHERS AT MIDDLE/UPPER PRIMARY STAGE, INDIA

Area	Survey		Educational qualifications				
			Up to Secondary	Higher Secondary	Graduate & above	Other	Total
Rural	Fourth	No.	257,344	70,562	143,875	36,515	508,296
	(1978)	%	50.6	13.9	28.3	7.2	100.0
	Fifth	No.	280,138	108,833	229,065	25,163	643,199
	(1986)	%	43.6	16.9	35.6	3.9	100.0
	Sixth	No.	236,117	140,532	322,973	6,036	705,658
	(1993)	%	33.5	19.9	45.8	0.9	100.0
Urban	Fourth	No.	108,825	26,109	84,113	17,575	236,622
	(1978)	%	46.0	11.0	35.6	7.4	100.0
	Fifth	No.	83,814	43,169	132,793	11,897	271,673
	(1986)	%	30.8	15.9	48.9	4.4	100.0
	Sixth	No.	94,008	50,543	182,655	3252	330,458
	(1993)	%	28.4	15.3	55.3	1.0	100.0
Total	Fourth	No.	366,169	96,671	227,988	54,090	744,918
	(1978)	%	49.2	13.0	30.6	7.3	100.0
	Fifth	No.	363,952	152,002	361,858	37,060	914,872
	(1986)	%	39.8	16.6	39.5	4.1	100.0
	Sixth	No.	330,125	191,075	505,628	9,288	1,036,116
	(1993)	%	31.9	18.4	48.8	0.9	100.0

Source: *All India Educational Surveys*, NCERT.

PERFORMANCE OF TEACHERS

Teacher competence is at times not of the expected level, thus adversely affecting the achievement level of students. A study done in a development block under the District Primary Education Programme to assess the competence of teachers in Mathematics and Language by administering a test meant for class V students gave disquieting results. The study found that the percentage of teachers achieving a score of more than 80 per cent was 40. LCM was not completed successfully by 83 per cent teachers, place value in sums was not successfully completed by 62 per cent teachers, and multiplication by zero could not be solved by 45 per cent teachers. More than 25 per cent teachers were unable to successfully complete the problems based on addition, subtraction, multiplication, and division. Performance test in language, too, was not satisfactory. Sixty-four per cent could not provide a title to a paragraph, 48 per cent could not provide the meaning of a phrase, and 38 per cent the meaning of a sentence (Gupta 1996). It is difficult to say to what extent the study, based on a small sample, reflects the general picture. The study underscores, however, the need for a much larger study covering different states so that the true magnitude of teacher inadequacy is fully comprehended.

The learning process in a school is adversely affected if the teaching environment is not friendly and the teaching methods are unsatisfactory. A calendar of activities for school work is not usually prepared in government or local body schools or, even if notionally prepared, is not followed. The practice of not detaining a student in the earlier classes results in a rather casual approach of the teacher in the matter of progress in learning. Assessments and tests are not done on a continuing basis with the result that children move to higher grades without proper evaluation and without learning even the basic minimum.

There is hardly any supervision of teaching. The system of inspection has been devalued to a considerable extent due to shortage of staff, long distances to be covered, shortage of funds, delayed payment of travel expenses, and low priority. Inspections, even when they take place, are done in a perfunctory manner. Hardly any importance is attached to the inspection reports. Most teachers get little help from the head teacher or the Education Officer. A study of learning achievements of primary school children commented that 'supervision seemed to be the weakest link in the primary school system' (Jangira 1994).

Teacher motivation is low, as there are few opportunities for career advancement. Discipline and punctuality are rarely enforced. Teachers coming late, leaving early, or absenting themselves unauthorizedly are no longer rare occurrences. Accountability is poor. Political contacts, trade unionism, and other considerations provide protection to non-performing teachers and negate attempts to enforce discipline in the system. The Education Commission, Government of West Bengal came across irregular attendance of teachers and cases of habitual absenteeism. Its attention was drawn to malpractices of some teachers drawing full-time salary but actively engaged in other pursuits. Cases of subcontracting of teaching functions were also reported (Government of West Bengal 1992). Malfunctioning of school education has been reported from other states as well. The PROBE team, which surveyed primary education in 188 sample villages in Bihar, Madhya Pradesh, Rajasthan, and Uttar Pradesh in 1996, found an unsatisfactory state of teaching learning environment. There was limited teaching activity and that, too, for a short while only. In half the sample schools there was no teaching activity going on when the investigator visited the place. The limited number of teaching days due to vacations and holidays gets further reduced due to various non-teaching duties, absenteeism, late coming, and early departure. Sometimes teachers take turns in attending school. In one-third of the schools covered by the PROBE survey, the headmaster was absent when the investigator visited the school (PROBE 1999). The teachers on their side complain that the management is unsupportive and unappreciative of the problems of working in difficult areas with little or no support or recognition.

Reports of the dismal state of primary education in large parts of the country appear with amazing regularity in both the electronic and print media, but such accounts fail to move the authorities (Goswami and Narula 1998; Ramamoorthy 1998; Vinod Kumar 1998; Wadhwa 2000). This is very unfortunate because even the poor and the illiterate now want their children to have the benefit of good schooling but are deprived of it because of the disappointing state of school education. In an instance highlighted by the media, 23 tribal children of ages 10–13 years of a government ashram school, took a trek of 70 km to bring to the notice of the authorities the rampant malpractices in the school and the poor learning environment (Menezes 1998). The PROBE survey on primary education in Bihar, Madhya Pradesh, Rajasthan, and Uttar Pradesh showed an overwhelming majority of parents wanting to educate their children (PROBE 1999). The National Family Health Survey, 1998–9 reported similar findings. Media reports and feedback from non-governmental organizations (NGOs) indicate a similar trend (Wadhwa 2000). Families marshall their meagre resources to put at least the male child in a private school, due to their poor opinion of the education provided by government or local body run schools.

BOX 3.1. OBSERVATIONS ON THE STATE OF PRIMARY EDUCATION IN WEST BENGAL BY THE EDUCATION COMMISSION, GOVERNMENT OF WEST BENGAL, 1992

3.8 '. . . We cannot get away from the fact that as much as 95 per cent of this outlay (Rs. 1000 crores nearly) is for the payment of remuneration and other benefits to the staff. . . .'

3.9 '. . . The promise of an extensive school building programme notwithstanding, not much has been achieved in this direction in the past fifteen years; a vast majority of the schools continue to be overcrowded; children are huddled in worn out, ramshackle

(Contd.)

Box 3.1 (Contd.)

structures or kutcha sheds exceedingly vulnerable to the elements. The supply of equipment such as blackboards, maps, globes etc. is either minimal or non-existent. The attendance on the part of teachers is irregular and fitful. Members of the Commission during their tour of the districts had some evidence of habitual absenteeism on the part of the teachers . . . .'

3.10 '. . . the practice of no detention has encouraged greater slipshodness in teaching and learning. Economically hard up parents soon discover that attendance in schools for one year—and even two years—has not meant any substantial improvement in the general level of awareness of their children or in the content of their learning. Such a realization has sometimes led to the decision it would make better sense to withdraw the children from school and to put them to work in fields or workshops, thereby adding immediately to the household income.

3.11 '. . . The number of teachers has increased substantially in the course of the past fifteen years, and emoluments made quite attractive. But the quality of teaching has marked time. The appointed teachers may on paper possess the minimum academic qualifications to teach at a primary school; their interest in teaching may, however, be only marginal. This could be for several reasons. The individual appointed as teacher may combine the profession of teaching with a number of other activities. He may be a full-fledged political functionary or an elected member of a panchayat body. He may even devote the time he should spend on teaching in the school for actual cultivation. The Commission's attention has been drawn to instances where the teachers drawing full-time salary from the primary school are actively engaged in money-lending or in dealerships. Cases are not altogether rare either where a teacher has subcontracted his teaching function to a number of cronies whose qualifications and flair for teaching are altogether suspect.

3.12 'Many of these deficiencies have arisen because the system of school inspection has, in practice, become defunct and no real accountability exists anywhere. . . .'

3.15 '. . . With no tests and no system of detentions, teachers wanting in a sense of responsibility have taken lightly their assigned duties. The suggestion to organise an internal evaluation in each class on a monthly, or even a weekly basis has fallen by the wayside. Teachers are often away, official inspection is nominal or non-existent, the school attendance committees are either complacent or ineffective.'

Many villagers have a poor opinion of the commitment of teachers and feel demotivated. They feel their children do not get a fair deal due to the poor learning environment, caused to a large extent by the indifference of the teacher. On their side, the teachers feel that there is little understanding on the part of the government of the environment in which they have to teach, the poor physical state of schools, shortage of teaching aids, and the problems of teaching multiple classes. Recruitment of teachers, posting, and transfers have come to be associated with malpractices, rather than being guided by academic considerations. The policy pursued in the matter of postings and transfers lacks transparency and consistency. Some commentators allege that transfers and postings are a flourishing industry. There are also allegations of bureaucratic and political interference for securing desired postings, and payments for getting or stalling transfers. Vacancies in remote and backward areas remain unfilled for long periods. Many teachers consider frequent transfers or postings in distant places as a punishment. An NCERT study on primary school teachers reported that about 30 per cent teachers were transferred up to three times in one state within five years. Transfers often follow soon after a new government is elected (Jangira, Singh and Yadav 1994).

The deficiencies in teaching in public sector primary and middle/ upper primary schools has led to the growth in urban areas of a flourishing private sector where a growing number of schools are run as commercial ventures. Once they acquire a reputation, they begin to charge hefty sums as capitation fee, donations, and security money, and demand payments for various other heads, even when the tuition fee is high and land has been obtained from government at a subsidized cost. Political contacts and other considerations enable the management to get the schools recognized by the State Directorate of Education.

A vibrant secondary market in tuitions and coaching classes has come into existence, which children from disadvantaged families can ill afford. For school teachers this has become an important secondary source of income. At some places, teachers encourage students to take private tuitions at the home of the teacher or attend private coaching classes in which they have an interest.

NON-FORMAL EDUCATION

The National Policy on Education, 1986 recommended a programme of non-formal education (NFE) for children not attending formal school. It gave NFE considerable importance, by making it an essential constituent of its policy to universalize education. It considered NFE a vital sector of elementary education and desired that measures should be taken to ensure that the quality of non-formal education is comparable with formal education to facilitate the entry of children in NFE into the formal stream in cases where they had achieved the expected standard of learning.

The programme of non-formal education was launched as a centrally sponsored scheme in 1980 to cover those children who were out of school. The programme is targeted at children aged 9–14 years and is specially focused on nine educationally backward states and areas with a concentration of working children, urban slums, and hilly, tribal, and desert tracts. The non-formal education programme provides an abridged primary level course of about two years through part-time instructors in small groups at a convenient time and place. Some NFE centres also organize upper primary level courses.

As an instrument of universalization of elementary education, the concept of non-formal education has a strong appeal as it helps to fill the void in the reach of the formal system. If properly developed and delivered it can be a potent instrument of reaching children who would otherwise be bereft of the benefits of education. However, the implementation of the scheme has suffered from weaknesses, and it is increasingly being perceived as a weakly developed, poorly implemented alternative to formal education. A large number of NFE centres, particularly those run by the government, suffer from inadequate accommodation, poor instructor motivation, indifferent teaching, large incidence of drop-outs, and a big turnover of instructors. Training of instructors and supervisors has been unsatisfactory. Only some children are able to reach a level which can help them to make a lateral entry into the formal stream. There are also complaints of poor performance of instructors, who are in any case paid a paltry sum of Rs. 200 a month as honorarium and are yet expected to motivate a difficult target group.

The Programme Evaluation Organisation of the Planning Commission made an evaluation of the non-formal education programme. The study covered 18 districts in six states, namely, Andhra Pradesh, Bihar, Madhya Pradesh, Orissa, Rajasthan, and Uttar Pradesh. In all these states, state run NFE centres far outnumbered NGO-run centres. The study reported that about one-fifth to one-third of those enrolled dropped out within the same year. The percentage of NFE learners who completed the primary level of the NFE course was as low as 12 per cent in Rajasthan, while in Uttar Pradesh it was 44 per cent.

In Orissa and Rajasthan, more than two-thirds of the successful NFE learners were admitted to the formal system. The percentages were, however, very low in Andhra Pradesh (13.5 per cent), Madhya Pradesh (12.8 per cent), and Uttar Pradesh (7.6 per cent). At the macro level, NFE appeared to have enabled a little over 1 per cent out-of-school children to complete primary level of education and get admission in the formal school system. The non-formal education programme has, thus, contributed only marginally towards addressing the problem of non-enrolment among elementary school age children. The study found inadequacies in the supply of teaching learning material. Even the meagre honorarium of Rs. 200 per month was not paid regularly to the instructors of state run NFE centres. The flow of funds to NFE centres in the state sector was erratic and much less than that required to implement the scheme. A large percentage of instructors varying from 22 per cent in Bihar to 83 per cent in Orissa had not passed the matriculation examination, and yet they were expected to teach primary and middle level courses. Bureaucratic delays, weak administrative machinery and inertia impeded the progress of the scheme. Two-thirds to three-fourths of the parents reported that the centres remained closed for more than ten days. Absenteeism among learners was also fairly high.

The PROBE survey in 1996, which covered 188 sample villages in four states (Bihar, Madhya Pradesh, Rajasthan, and Uttar Pradesh), found less than 10 functional NFE centres. One village had nine NFE centres, all non-functional. Even in functional centres teaching activity was minimal. In 122 sample households, only two children were actually enrolled. No child was found to have joined the formal school after completing the course at an NFE centre (PROBE 1999). Questions have also been raised about the adequacy of the funding pattern. There have been delays in the release of funds and supply of instruction material. Some good NGOs which have a strong base of development and are not solely dependent on the government's pattern of funding are able to achieve satisfactory outcomes, as the evaluation of the non-formal education programme in the Lok Jumbish project of Rajasthan has shown (ORG 1996).

FINANCING OF ELEMENTARY EDUCATION

Financing of elementary education from public funds has been recognized as being absolutely necessary to provide disadvantaged children access to schooling. The Constitution of India, the National

Policy in Education, the five year plans, and official pronouncements from time to time have reiterated the responsibility of the State in the matter of providing facilities for elementary education.

The Department of Education, Government of India, made a study of budgetary resources for education from 1951–2 to 1993–4 (Department of Education 1995). The main findings as reported in this study and other official sources are given below:

- Public expenditure on education in India as a percentage of the Gross National Product has varied between 3 and 4 per cent between 1981–2 and 1994–5. It is still less than the 6 per cent target set by the National Policy on Education, 1986.
- Most of the bigger states spent less than 5 per cent of the state net domestic product on education in 1993–4. However, Kerala spent about 6 per cent and Himachal Pradesh 7 per cent.
- Education was, and continues to be, overwhelmingly dependent on government funds and local body funds, which are mostly grants and transfers from the central and state governments. In 1988–9, for instance, 83.1 per cent of the expenditure was from government, 6.7 per cent from local bodies, 6.1 per cent from fees, and 4.1 per cent from endowments and other private sources. Funding by local bodies is almost always for elementary education. The role of local bodies is brought out by the Sixth All India Educational Survey, which has indicated that 45 per cent of the primary schools and 46 per cent of the middle/upper primary schools were under government management, while 47 per cent of the primary schools and 34 per cent of the middle/upper primary schools were under the management of local bodies (NCERT 1998).
- The bulk of the expenditure on elementary education has been borne by the states. For instance, in 1993–4, out of Rs. 110,398 million expenditure on elementary education, Rs. 105,922 million (96 per cent) was spent by states/union territories and Rs. 4,476 million by the Centre (4 per cent). Of the total expenditure by states/union territories, 88 per cent was under non-plan expenditure, and only 12 per cent under plan expenditure. Almost the entire expenditure by the Centre was on plan schemes. The non-plan expenditure by the states and the Centre was incurred on salaries and maintenance,

while the plan expenditure was for new schemes and for expansion.

- At constant prices, public expenditure on education has increased at an annual compound rate of 8.3 per cent during the period 1951–2 to 1991–2. The growth rate, however, varied considerably during different plan periods.
- Of the total expenditure on education by the state Departments of Education, elementary education got an allocation of 44 to 50 per cent during the period 1951–2 to 1993–4. At the Centre, the share of elementary education was rather small in the earlier plans. It increased from 1987–8, following the National Policy on Education (1986) and the subsequent launching of centrally sponsored schemes of Operation Blackboard and non-formal education. In the Sixth Plan, the expenditure by the central government on elementary education was Rs. 7,241 million. In the Seventh Plan (1985–90), this increased to Rs. 6585 million, and in the Eighth Plan to Rs. 42,150 million. It touched 21 per cent of the central plan budget for education in 1993–4. In subsequent years, the central budgetary allocation for elementary education has increased considerably. In 2000–1, Rs. 38,020 million was provided for elementary education in the central budget.
- The role of the private sector in elementary education is increasing, particularly in urban areas, to cater to the demand by all socio-economic categories for a better quality of education, which in general perception many government or local body schools are unable to provide. It also reflects greater willingness of parents to pay if the quality of the service is good, or because the government or local body run institution is so poor that there is no other alternative but to send the child to a private school. The Sixth All India Educational Survey (1993) reported nearly 5 per cent primary schools and 13 per cent upper primary schools in rural areas under private management. In urban areas, the percentages were 34 and 49, respectively.

Compulsory Elementary Education

The issue of compulsory elementary education is once again high on the agenda after the Supreme Court judgement in 1993 that citizens have a fundamental right to free education up to the age of 14 years.

A brief review of previous attempts in this regard is given in the paragraphs that follow.

The desirability and feasibility of compulsory primary education in India has been advocated, debated, attempted, given up, and revived. The move for compulsory education was initiated more than a century and a half back when proposals were made to the government by a British educationist and a senior revenue official for a law requiring every village to have a primary school. The levy of a local cess for meeting the expenses was also proposed. The proposals, however, did not find acceptance as the idea was at that point far ahead of the times and could, therefore, muster only limited support. Among the arguments given against compulsory education were that the idea was impractical and would unnecessarily alienate the population, especially since no such demand had been made. People would, therefore, use all possible means to evade the application of the law. It was argued that a much better alternative would be to spread education without the use of force and to let the people be motivated through appointment of literate persons in government service.

The enactment of compulsory primary education legislation in Britain in 1870, exposure to developments in European countries in the matter of spreading primary education, strong advocacy by eminent Indians, and national awakening renewed the demand for compulsory schooling as a means to enlighten the masses and free them from ignorance. The official response, however, continued to be un-supportive. The Indian Education Commission, 1882 ignored the issue (Saiyidain et al. 1966).

The beginning of the twentieth century witnessed renewed attempts, and with greater vigour, to have legislation for compulsory education. Considerable support for the movement came from the State of Baroda, where its progressive ruler first introduced compulsory education in a Division of the State in 1893 as an experimental measure. Enthused by the response, a law was enacted for the State in 1906. The path shown by Baroda greatly encouraged advocates of compulsory education throughout the country who argued that the measure was not only desirable, but also feasible. The first moves were initiated in Bombay, the most prominent among the attempts being that of Gopal Krishna Gokhale who moved a Resolution in the Legislature to demand the appointment of a Commission to consider the proposal of compulsory education and submit its report. In 1911, he introduced a private Bill to provide for the introduction of compulsory education. The Bill, however, suffered a defeat despite strong support from national leaders and other eminent persons (Saiyidain et al. 1966).

The battle for compulsory education was reopened in 1917, when a Bill was moved in the Bombay Legislative Council by Vithalbhai Patel for the introduction of compulsory education in the municipal areas of the state. His Bill took note of the main points on which Gokhale's Bill had been criticized. It is the first legislation in British India which accepted the principle of compulsory education. The Government of India Act, 1919 which led to the transfer of power on matters relating to education to elected Indian representatives, facilitated the passing of similar legislation in other provinces.

With eminent public figures prodding the governments of the provinces, legislation for compulsory education was enacted between 1918 and 1930 by the provinces under British rule. Several progressive Indian States made similar enactments. These legislations assigned to local bodies the initiative to introduce compulsory education. Areas were to be notified, schools were to be set up within a specified distance, lists of all eligible children drawn up, and attendance officers appointed. Procedures were laid down to ensure that children did attend school in the notified areas. Penal provisions for non-compliance were to be enforced by launching prosecutions and imposing penalties. Exemption to certain categories of children was allowed on specified grounds.

Progress in the implementation of the legislation was slow. While there was a reasonable degree of success in Baroda due to the keen interest of His Highness, elsewhere the results were not satisfactory because it was not taken seriously by the official machinery. The Departments/Directorates of Education showed little seriousness of purpose and made rather half-hearted attempts. Areas notified under the Act were few, these were mostly urban and covered a small population. Census of eligible children was poorly done, and implementation badly monitored. Progress was reviewed at irregular and infrequent intervals. There were considerable delays in initiating action for non-attendance, and reluctance in applying penalty measures such as fines. Even when these were imposed, the fines realized were small in amount. The officials seemed to view the measure as unwarranted, causing uncalled for problems for the parents as well as the administration until the educational system was put on a sound footing, funds mobilized, and the community prepared for the schooling of their children. They also believed that children of the poor and the lower castes did not attend school because of economic compulsions, and in the case of girls, inhibiting socio-cultural factors, which, too, need to be addressed if the measure was to find ready acceptance. Without such simultaneous measures, the poorer classes would consider compulsory attendance in school as an imposition from outside and do everything possible to thwart the objective. The officials cited in justification the unenthusiastic response of the masses for whose benefit the existing Acts were passed. The examples of Travancore and Cochin states were cited where education progressed very well without the use of compulsion because of the generally favourable public attitude towards education of both boys and girls, the existence of a vibrant primary education system, the efforts of missionaries, and the initiative of the Christian community.

The Report on Post War Educational Development in India, 1944 (Sargent Report) which was approved by the Central Advisory Board of Education in 1944, however, visualized a national education system in which there would be free and compulsory basic education of five years for all children aged 6–11 years and three years senior basic education for four-fifths of the children aged 11–14 years. The Committee on Ways and Means of Financing Educational Development in India, 1950 (Kher Committee) recommended that the State should undertake the responsibility of providing at least Junior Basic Education and the Provinces should aim at introducing universal compulsory education for children aged 6–11 years within a period of ten years.

When the Constitution of India was being framed, the nation's leaders recognized the critical role of education for a vibrant democratic system of government in independent India. The Constitution of India, accordingly, laid down under Article 45 as a Directive Principle of State Policy that 'the State shall endeavor to provide, within a period of ten years from the commencement of the Constitution for free and compulsory children until they complete the age of fourteen years'. Under Article 41, another Directive Principle of State Policy, the Constitution gave the right to education and laid down that the State shall within the limits of economic capacity and development, make effective provisions for securing this right. It is evident, therefore, that the framers of the Constitution were convinced that education had to be free and compulsory, and that the child has a right to education. These provisions were expected to pave the way for universalization of education within ten years.

Despite the Constitutional directives in 1950 there was little progress in the direction of putting in place compulsory education in the decade that followed. The administration continued to emphasize expansion of elementary education facilities, free tuition and incentives by way of free textbooks, school uniforms, and in some states, school meals and school health services. The official machinery was in favour of voluntariness, generation of awareness, creation of demand, and persuasion rather than use of compulsion. This was considered a smooth hassle-free non-conflicting alternative which would provide for gradual spread of education and would not make excessive demands on financial resources and manpower. Thus, even in the 1950s, the official line of thinking, as expressed in action, did not differ very much from that four decades earlier. An added reason against the use of compulsion was the feared political fallout of coercing parents and penalizing them. Progress in education in the 1950s was poor. Only 42 per cent of the children aged 10–14 years (54 per cent boys and 28 per cent girls) were reported by the 1961 Census to be literate.

Official statistics do indicate an increase in the number of areas notified by different states between 1951–2 and 1961–2 and the number of children covered under compulsory education, which is approximately one-fourth of the children enrolled. Figures on the extent of use of coercive measures available for the years 1951–2 and 1960–1 are given in Table 3.35. Figures for later years are not available. The data show a decline not because all children were in school, but because of slowdown in invoking penal provisions.

The desirability of compulsory education came into public focus again when, in 1960, Parliament passed The Delhi Primary Education Act, 1960 to 'provide for free and compulsory primary education for children in the Union Territory of Delhi'. This was intended to serve

TABLE 3.35: ENFORCEMENT OF COMPULSORY EDUCATION IN INDIA

Year	No. of notices	No. of orders passed	Prosecutions for non-attendance	Prosecutions for non-enrolment	Fines realized (in Rs.)
1951–2	591,793	239,474	80,536	41,834	42,110
1956–7	781,924	268,671	56,971	39,755	20,785
1960–1	573,921	202,026	33,648	20,795	26,534

Source: Saiyidain, Naik et al., Compulsory Education; Progress of Compulsory Education in India, 1951–66.

as a model for other states. The need for a fresh law was felt as the existing primary education Acts were drafted several decades earlier, and there was a need to benefit from the experience of implementing the same. Within a few years, compulsory primary education Acts were passed in 16 states and 3 Union Territories. In Himachal Pradesh, the Act covered the elementary stage. While action to enact legislations was being taken, the views of those involved in educational administration were reflected in the deliberations of the Second National Seminar on Compulsory Education in 1962, which concluded that 'penal measures of compulsory education should not be over-emphasized and special measures should be adopted to attract children to schools. These would include school meals, school health services, free supply of books and writing material, supply of uniforms and educating public opinion' (Saiyidain et al. 1966). The compulsory primary education Acts of states continued to be poorly implemented, with the officials pursuing the line of achieving universal coverage through better access, persuasion, and incentives, rather than compulsion. Several administrative and financial problems continued to be cited. The political fallout of using compulsion on unwilling parents and penalizing them was feared, and was ground enough not to invoke the Act.

The necessity of free and compulsory education was reiterated by the National Education Policy, 1968. The redrawn National Policy on Education announced in 1986 reasserted that 'by 1995 all children will be provided free and compulsory education up to 14 years of age'. The Committee to Review the National Policy on Education recommended that the right to education should be examined for inclusion amongst the Fundamental Rights guaranteed by the Constitution of India. The UN Convention on the Rights of the Child, 1989 ratified by India requires countries to recognize the child's right to education, and hence make primary education compulsory and available free for all (Article 28).

The issue of compulsory education received judicial endorsement with the Supreme Court's judgement in 1993 in the Unnikrishnan JP vs. Andhra Pradesh case that citizens have a fundamental right to free education up to the age of 14 years. Thereafter, his right to education is subject to the limits of economic capacity and development of the State. The Committee of State Education Ministers constituted by the Government of India recommended in 1997 that the Constitution should be amended to make the right to free elementary education until the age of 14 years a Fundamental Right.

It also recommended that it should be the fundamental duty of every parent to provide to the child opportunities of elementary education. Further, each state should have legislation in this regard, by either amending the existing Act or passing a new one. No central legislation was considered necessary. However, certain guidelines could be provided by the central government, giving the broad framework as worked out in consultation with the states.

Given the poor state of educational administration in the country, it is difficult to visualize how the law on compulsory education will be implemented as enforcement usually requires the following steps: (i) notification of areas under compulsion in a phased manner; (ii) census of all children of elementary school age in each area; (iii) having schools with the required teaching infrastructure where free and compulsory education will be provided at a reasonable distance; (iv) assigning children to respective schools; (v) sanctioning and appointing teachers and administrative staff, including attendance officers; (vi) notice to parents in case of non-attendance; (vii) drawing up the grounds on which exemption from school attendance can be given and deciding on applications for exemption; (viii) issuing summons to the defaulting parent to appear before the School Board/Committee/Officer concerned and issuing an Attendance Order in case the reasons given for non-attendance are not accepted; and (ix) launching prosecution and imposing penalty as laid down by law.

The task is indeed formidable. The 1991 Census reported that 74.5 million children aged 6–13 years (excluding Jammu & Kashmir), constituting 45 per cent were not attending school. The National Sample Survey found in 1995–6 that 31 per cent children aged 6–10 years and 28 per cent aged 11–13 years were not attending school. Implementation of the law, thus, involves a massive endeavour and a mission so that children not only attend school but also achieve a minimum level of learning. Most of these children are in states which are economically and educationally backward, give low priority to education, have poor political will to universalize education, and are saddled with poorly run schools and a rather ineffective school administrative structure. Apart from the bureaucratic hassles and inertia, and the political indifference, the extent to which corruption free enforcement of the law will be possible is indeed a big question. Simultaneously, measures to prevent child labour by tackling the socio-economic causes will be necessary so that children attend school rather than become workers. The government has to give high priority to elementary education so that a properly functioning school system is in place to provide a conducive learning environment. Accountability has to be enforced at different levels. Incentives like mid-day meals will have an important place. The schools, both in infrastructure and in teaching, need considerable improvement in standards for which funds have to be provided. Teacher training and motivation must receive importance. The reasons for poor levels of learning have to be identified and addressed. Parents need to be convinced that children do learn when they go to school and can hope to improve their prospects in adult life, and not join the ranks of casual workers like their parents. The reasons for drop-out, too, need to be seriously addressed. School administration and supervision is ridden with problems and malpractices. The entire system needs overhauling. This is a frightfully long list of 'things to be done', but the steps are unavoidable if universalization has to take place and children benefit from attending school.

SUMMING UP

The Constitution of India, recognizing the vital role of elementary education, directed the State to provide free and compulsory education within a period of ten years, that is by 1960. The National Policy on Education (1968 and 1986) and the UN Convention on Rights of the Child (1989), which India has ratified, reiterated the importance of fulfilment of this basic need.

Some progress towards universalization of elementary education has been achieved since independence, but the attainment of this goal even after nearly five decades of independence is still a long way off. Nearly one-third children aged 10–14 years were illiterate in 1991 (40 per cent girls as compared to 23 per cent boys). In numbers, this meant 31 million illiterate children aged 10–14 years, 88 per cent in rural areas and predominantly girls (61 per cent). Uttar Pradesh and Bihar together had 40 per cent of the total number of illiterate children aged 10–14 years in India.

Official enrolment figures show a massive increase in numbers at primary as well as middle stages in the case of both boys and girls. In a time span of 49 years, enrolment at the primary stage has increased from 19 million in 1950–1 to 114 million in 1999–2000, and at the middle/upper primary stage from 3 million to 42 million. A positive development is the consistently higher rate of decadal growth rate of enrolment of girls, both at the primary and middle stages. The gender gap in enrolment is also declining.

Not all children who figure in the enrolment statistics attend school. In 1991, the number of children aged 6–13 years attending school as per the Census was 40 million lower than the enrolment figure in that year. Only 55 per cent children aged 6–13 years (62 per cent boys and 48 per cent girls) were found by the 1991 Census to be attending school. The National Family Health Survey conducted in 1992–3 reported a higher figure of 68 per cent. The National Family Health Survey 1998–9 reported a further rise to 79 per cent. The National Sample Survey in 1995–6 found 69 per cent children aged 6–10 years and 72 per cent children aged 11–13 years attending school. The Net Attendance Ratio, a more refined indicator which measures percentage of children aged 6–10 years and 11–13 years attending classes in the corresponding primary or middle/upper primary stage, was 66 per cent for classes I to V (primary) and only 43 per cent for classes VI to VIII (middle/upper primary).

The 1991 Census reported 75 million children aged 6–13 years (33 million boys and 42 million girls) as not attending school (excluding Jammu & Kashmir). The percentage of such children was more than half in Bihar, Uttar Pradesh, and Rajasthan, while it was nearly half in Assam, Madhya Pradesh, and West Bengal. In the 16 bigger states, in 22 districts the percentage of children aged 6–13 years attending school was less than 30. All these districts are located in the four educationally backward states (10 in Bihar, 9 in Uttar Pradesh, 2 in Rajasthan, and 1 in Madhya Pradesh). The National Sample Survey found in 1995–6 that one-fourth of the children aged 6–10 years and one-fifth of the children aged 11–13 years had never attended school (NSSO, 1998). This is a very high percentage of children not covered by the formal education system even after nearly five decades of independence.

The school drop-out rate continues to be very high. In 1998–9, it was 40 per cent between classes I to V and 57 per cent between Classes I to VIII. It was considerably higher than the Eighth Plan (1992–7) target which had the objective of reducing the drop-out rate to 20 per cent between classes I to V and 40 per cent between classes I to VIII. The main causes of drop-out are school related, and family and home related factors.

A child is expected to complete class VIII (middle/upper primary) before the age of 15 years. The 1991 Census figures indicate that among children 15–19 years, 60 per cent had completed primary education and only 45 per cent has completed middle level of education. A matter of deep concern is the generally unsatisfactory learning achievement of students reflecting the poor quality of schooling for the mass of the students. Studies by NCERT as well as others on learning achievement found them to be unsatisfactory in mathematics, language, and other subjects.

There has been phenomenal growth in the number of primary and middle/upper primary schools since independence. The Sixth All India Educational Survey (1993) reported that more than three-fourths of the rural population (78 per cent) was being served by a primary school/section within the habitation and 94 per cent with a primary school/section within 1 km. In the case of middle/upper primary schools/sections, 57 per cent of the population had the facility within 1 km of the habitation (37 per cent within the habitation). However, the norm of one middle/upper primary school for two primary schools is yet to be reached, the ratio in 1999 being 1:3.

The physical infrastructure of schools has shown some improvement but is still deficient, particularly in rural areas where poor construction and bad maintenance causes fast deterioration of the structure. The Sixth All India Educational Survey (1993) reported 29 per cent rural primary schools having either no room or only one room, 31 per cent having two rooms, and 40 per cent having three or more rooms. The National Policy on Education (1986) had stipulated that every primary school must have at least two reasonably large rooms usable in all weather conditions. Shortage of space leads to several classes being held in the same room by dividing the space which is not quite a learner friendly situation. Drinking water and toilet facilities, particularly for girls, are poor. Teaching aids in school are still lagging behind. The Sixth All India Educational Survey (1993) reported only 62 per rural primary sections having usable blackboards reflecting the sad state of affairs four and a half decades after independence. Only half of the rural primary school sections had furniture for teachers.

Primary schools suffer not only from poor physical infrastructure, but also because they do not have enough teachers. According to the Sixth All India Educational Survey (1993), 22 per cent rural primary schools had a single teacher, while 45 per cent had two teachers. Only one-third rural primary schools had three or more teachers.

Thus, even in 1993, that is four and half decades after independence, the minimum learning infrastructure was not available in a large percentage of rural primary schools.

The teaching learning environment in a large percentage of schools is poor and the teaching methods unsatisfactory. Assessments are not done on a continuing basis. Teacher motivation is low. There is hardly any supervision of teaching. Several malpractices have cropped up. Many villagers have a negative opinion of the commitment of teachers and feel that their children do not get a fair deal due to the indifference of teachers, absenteeism, and poor functioning of schools. This is very unfortunate, as even the poor and the illiterate now want their children to have the benefit of good schooling but are deprived of it because of the disappointing state of school education.

The programme of non-formal education, which was intended to be a vital sector of elementary education targeted to cover out of school children aged 9–14 years in the educationally backward states, urban slums, and hard to reach areas, has generally suffered from lack of conviction and weak implementation.

Expenditure on elementary education in the initial years suffered from low priority and inadequate allocations by the states on whom the primary responsibility for elementary education lay. Inclusion of unversalization of elementary education in the Twenty Point Programme, or in the Minimum Needs Programme in the Fifth Plan with earmarked outlays in the state plans, did not make a significant difference. Inclusion of education in the Concurrent List facilitated larger central allocations for elementary education, which increased considerably following the National Policy on Education (1986) and launching of the centrally sponsored schemes of Operation Blackboard and non-formal education. Some important initiatives were taken by the central government in selected areas in educationally backward states, in many cases with the help of external funding. Important among these are the Shiksha Karmi Project, launched in Rajasthan in 1987 as a non-formal education programme with assistance from the Swedish International Development Agency (SIDA). In 1992, the Lok Jumbish Project was launched in the same state with assistance from SIDA. UNICEF assisted the Bihar Education Project and the Overseas Development Agency (ODA) of the UK assisted the Andhra Pradesh Primary Education Project, aimed at improving significantly primary education. Currently, the most comprehensive programme for improvement of primary education is the centrally sponsored scheme of the District

Primary Education Programme (DPEP), launched in 1994, for which 85 per cent of the project cost is borne by the central government, which in turn gets external funding from the World Bank, the European Community, and several other aid agencies. The DPEP aims to revitalize and strengthen the existing system, tackle problem areas, develop innovative approaches with the district as the unit of planning, adopt a holistic approach with emphasis on convergence of existing programmes and services, and encourage community participation. In 1999–2000, the programme covered 219 districts in 15 states. Initial reports indicate improvements in access and retention, lower rates of repetition of classes, and greater gender and social equity in enrolment. The sustainability of the gains remains to be seen. Several initiatives have also been taken by state governments. Madhya Pradesh has recently launched an education guarantee scheme whereby the government comes up with assistance if a local community demands a school, agrees to provide a place, and undertakes to identify a local resident capable of teaching and willing to teach on a modest salary (Aiyar 1998).

Elementary education has suffered from insufficient funds, poor functioning of schools, and a weak school administration. The political will and administrative commitment have been weak as evident from poor levels of literacy even in constituencies/districts from which successive Prime Ministers and Education Ministers have been elected. The situation has not materially altered, irrespective of the political party in power at the Centre, or in the states, and its ideological leanings. There has, however, been no dearth of declarations of firm resolve at national and international forums. Even poor communities now understand the value of education and want a good school for their children so that they can find better employment in adulthood. Their aspirations have, however, been belied by political and bureaucratic shortcomings. There is urgent need to shed inertia and in order to substantially improve the performance of the system, remove malpractices, and inject accountability at all levels. Until this happens, the efficiency of the system will continue its downslide, adversely affecting the chances for a better life of the underprivileged in rural and urban areas.

There has, unfortunately, come into existence a big class divide and a rural-urban divide in education in terms of facilities and quality, which has serious social consequences and could lead to social upheaval. Schools in backward rural and tribal areas are the most neglected, and the standard of teaching very poor. Even in other areas, schools to which children of the underprivileged have access are run by the state or local authorities and have a poor record of performance. The low quality of education in schools meant for the masses adversely affects their employment prospects in a modernizing economy, thus adding to the number of unemployable youth. Children from the middle and upper classes attend private schools, which charge high fees not affordable by the poor, but which are far ahead in offering a much better quality of education. It is the children of the poor who need most a good public sector school as their families cannot muster financial support for private schools, compensatory teaching, and coaching, and have, further, the disadvantage of little or no academic support at home due to the generally low levels of education of their family members. Thus, though theoretically the State seeks to provide equal opportunities through heavily subsidized education, its poor quality adversely affects the chances in life of the socially and economically disadvantaged and is likely to accentuate the divide between the haves and the have-nots. Access and quality are, therefore, issues which need to be seriously addressed. Statistics on expansion of physical facilities, manpower, or increase in expenditure are necessary but not sufficient indicators of educational progress. The setting up of a few schools in different parts of the country as showpieces with the help of central funds do not fulfil the mandatory responsibility of the State in the matter of elementary education as long as the mass of the students continue to suffer from its poor quality.

Box 3.2 gives in summary form the achievements in universalizing elementary education and the unfinished agenda.

BOX 3.2. ELEMENTARY EDUCATION GOALS AND ACHIEVEMENTS

Indicator	Goals		Achievement		
	Year	Target	Year	Target reached	Comment
Free and compulsory education up to the age of 14 years	1960 (Constitution of India)	Universal coverage	1991 (Census)	Only 55 per cent children aged 6–13 years were in school (62 per cent boys and 48 per cent girls). In numbers it meant 75.5 million children (excluding J & K) out of school. Census figures for 2001 not yet available. NFHS 1998–9 reported that in rural areas 76 per cent of children in the age group 6–14 years were attending school while in urban areas the percentage was 88.	In Bihar 61 per cent children 6–13 years were not attending school, followed by Uttar Pradesh 59 per cent, Rajasthan 57 per cent, Madhya Pradesh 49 per cent and Assam 48 per cent. (1991)
	1990 (NPE 1986)	All children who attain the age of 11 years will have had five years of schooling	1995–6 (NSS)	69 per cent children 6–10 years and 72 per cent 11–13 years were attending school. The Net Attendance Ratio 6–10 years classes I–V was 66 and 11–13 years classes VI–VIII only 43.	Bihar, Uttar Pradesh, Rajasthan, Madhya Pradesh and West Bengal had the poorest NAR
	1995 (NPE 1986)	All children up to the age of 14 years	1998–9	NSS 1995–6 indicated that 26 per cent children aged 6–14 years and 19 per cent aged 11–13 years had not attended school. Drop out rate was 40 in classes I–V and 57 in classes I–VIII,	Drop-out rate in 1986–7 was 49 in classes I–V and 65 in classes I–VIII. There has been some reduction in drop-out rate but the inci-

(Contd.)

Box 3.2 (Contd.)

Indicator	Goals		Achievement		
	Year	Target	Year	Target reached	Comment
		will be provided free and compulsory education		which is much higher than the Eighth Plan target of 20 in classes I–V and 40 in classes I–VIII for 1996–7.	dence is still very high. There can be little hope of achieving universalization unless this problem is seriously addressed.
Non-formal education	Not set	Children not covered by the formal stream	1999–2000	2,97,000 NFE centres set up to cover 7.42 million children	The Scheme of NFE was launched in 1979–80. It was strongly recommended by NPE, 1986. Its implementation has been marred by poor performance.
Infrastructure	Not set	At least two reasonably large rooms (NPE 1986)	1993	Sixth All India Educational survey reported 24 per cent rural primary schools had only one room and 32 per cent had two rooms; 59 per cent rural primary schools did not have drinking water facilities, 38 per cent sections in rural primary schools did not have blackboard and 50 per cent did not have furniture for teachers.	Some progress has been made in improving physical infrastructure, particularly after the launching of Operation Blackboard in 1986–7 by the Government of India to improve school infrastructure. Considerable ground, however remains to be covered.

(Contd.)

Box 3.2 (Contd.)

Indicator	Goals			Achievement	
		At least two teachers (NPE 1986)	1993 1990 and later	Sixth Educational survey reported 22 per cent rural schools had a single teacher and 45 per cent only two teachers National Council of Educational Re-	Considerable ground is yet to be covered. The revised scheme of Operation Black-board provides for assistance from the Government of India for the appointment of a third teacher in a primary school when the enrolment exceeds 100.
Substantial improvement in quality of education	Not set	Minimum level of	years	search and Training's study in 1991 and subsequent studies by researchers have indicated unsatisfactory progress in learning.	The teaching-learning environment is poor in a large number of schools. Teacher motivation is low. The school educational system needs considerable improvement. To ensure that children benefit from attending school the Government of India launched the scheme of Minimum Level of Learning to be attained at the primary stage.

Notes: NPE: National Policy on Education.
NSS: National Sample Survey.

4 Little Toiling Hands

Child labour has now moved up the agenda of social concerns. For a long time, assistance by children on family farms or family based occupations was accepted as a normal process of growing up. It took place within the family setting, and involved sharing and learning of adult economic roles under a protected paternalistic umbrella. Also, going to school was not considered a necessity for children of the lower social and economic classes. There existed, undoubtedly, several abusive situations. Sometimes children were forcibly sent by poor parents to work in the homes of the well-to-do in repayment of loans or advances, or they became an active member of a bonded family. There were also instances of abuse of orphan or destitute children by making them work for long hours in harsh conditions. The importance of childhood for its own sake in the case of children of the poor does not appear to have had social recognition. Expression of social abhorrence of child labour was rare. Consequently, the early crusaders against child labour had to face an uphill task. Recent years have, however, witnessed a significant change in social perception of the problem and wide acceptance of the undesirability of child labour. Global advocacy against child labour and internal pressures have forced governments to initiate a range of measures to tackle the problem.

A distinction is often drawn between children engaged in work and child labour. The rationale given for the distinction is that all work is not necessarily exploitative. Help by children is perceived as a necessity by families in certain sectors of economic activity and, if it is not at the cost of schooling, play, recreation, or growth of the child, it is not to be considered undesirable as it does not risk the child's future. In much of the developing world and in rural areas of the developed world, children are engaged in different kinds of activity at home, workshed, or farm, and also share with parents various types of domestic work and non-market activities. This is a part of the process of growing up, learning skills, and preparing for adult roles. However, when work is exploitative in nature and the child is made to work too early in life for long hours for a pittance in harsh intimidating conditions without any opportunities for schooling, recreation, play, and development, it becomes a fit case for being categorized as child labour and needs to be prevented. In other words, when the child is denied his childhood, deprived of opportunities to develop, cannot go to school, and has to work in conditions which endanger his physical and mental health, it becomes a clear case where the child's future is being abused by adults to fulfil their needs at the cost of the child's needs. Child labour is undesirable and needs to be eradicated, but prohibiting all forms of child work is not practicable in much of the developing world. While making the distinction, it is none the less important to bear in mind that increasing landlessness has led to dependence on wage and contractual employment, which is neither protective nor does it safeguard the well-being of the workers. Increasingly, therefore, children are forced to move from work in a protected home environment to a harsh exploitative work situation. And since almost all of this is in the unorganized sector, which is unregulated and outside the orbit of labour legislation, the abuses are far greater.

MAGNITUDE

Estimates of the number of working children in India vary. Census figures are often commented upon as being underestimates. Such comments follow largely from the contentious problem of the definition of a worker. The Census includes in the category of workers only those children who are engaged in an economic activity. Thus, even though children may be spending several hours in various activities within the household (bringing water, for instance), they are not classified as workers. Not included, too, are children engaged in activities, particularly in rural areas, the output of which is for domestic use rather than for sale, as, for instance, collecting wood, cowdung or crop residues for use as fuel, making cowdung cakes, tending animals, cutting fodder, or milking cattle, which saves expenditure for the household. Children engaged in part-time seasonal economic activity or engaged in paid work intermittently, too, tend to be left out, partly because of lack of thoroughness of the enumerator, and partly because parents consider such part-time activity which does not bring a cash income, or brings only a very small income, as not falling in the category of economic activity. Unpaid family work, even though it generates income, also tends to be left out both by the enumerator and the household head.

The 1981 Census reported 11.196 million main workers less than 15 years of age (those who worked for the major part of the reference year). In addition, there were 2.445 million marginal workers (those who did some work during the reference period), making a total of 13.641 million child workers in the country, excluding Assam. This figure is less than one-third of the estimate of 44 million working children made by the Operations Research Group (ORG) based on a survey in 1980. The difference is primarily due to the wider age range (less than 16 years as compared to less than 15 years in the Census) adopted by ORG, and the inclusion of children engaged in activities which occupied a child's time even though they are not conventionally defined as economic activities. Such, for instance, are washing, cleaning, cooking, child care, and other types of household work. The same report estimated only 2.3 million to be earning children, who received remuneration either in cash or kind or both (Khatu, Tamang and Rao 1983). The National Sample Survey (NSS) in its thirty-eighth round in 1983, estimated 21.344 million child workers (aged 5–14 years) as per usual status (16.644 million as per principal status and 4.700 million as per subsidiary status). The NSS estimate was, thus, less than half the ORG estimate, but more than one and a half times the 1981 Census estimate.

The 1991 Census reported 9.082 million main workers and 2.203 million marginal workers less than 15 years of age in India (excluding Jammu & Kashmir), indicating a decline of more than 2 million child workers since 1981 (see Table 4.1). The National Sample Survey Organization's forty-third round survey (1987–8), too, reported a lower figure of 17.107 million child workers (11.778 million as per principal status and 5.329 million as per subsidiary

TABLE 4.1: NUMBER OF WORKERS LESS THAN 15 YEARS OF AGE, INDIA, 1981 AND 1991

	1981			1991		
	Main workers	Marginal workers	Total	Main workers	Marginal workers	Total
No.	11,195,544	2,445,328	13,640,872	9,082,141	2,203,208	11,285,349
%	82.07	17.93	100.00	80.47	19.53	100.00

Source: *Census of India*. Figures for 1991 do not include Jammu & Kashmir, and for 1981 do not include Assam.

status), as compared to its 1983 survey figure of 21.344 million child workers. In both the Censuses, about four-fifths child workers are main workers and one-fifth are marginal workers.

Estimates of child labour given by child labour activists and non-governmental organizations (NGOs) do not hesitate to mention figures of up to 50 million working children. Some international agencies, too, quote very high figures, relying on estimates which are of the nature of guesses, based as they are on small surveys in some selected areas. Even if one proceeds on the basis of Census figures, bearing in mind that it is much lower than the actual figure, the number is still very large. The decline in the proportion of child workers (main) to total workers (main) from 5.03 per cent in 1981 to 3.18 per cent in 1991 cannot be a cause of complacency. Even this is an unacceptably high figure.

There is a larger concentration of child workers in rural areas. Of the 9.082 million main workers less than 15 years of age in 1991, 8.127 million, or 89.49 per cent, were in rural areas, though only 74.29 per cent of the population is rural.

AGE DISTRIBUTION

Nearly one million, or 9 per cent, child workers enumerated in the 1991 Census were less than 10 years of age (see Table 4.2). This was higher than the 1981 figure of 5.7 per cent. Thus, though the number of child workers aged less than 15 years declined in 1991 as

TABLE 4.2: AGE DISTRIBUTION OF CHILD WORKERS, INDIA, 1981 AND 1991

Age (in years)	Year	Main workers		Marginal workers		Total		No. of marginal workers per 1000 main workers
		No.	%	No.	%	No.	%	
5–9	1991	705,562	7.8	293,603	13.3	999,165	8.9	416
	1981	564,334	5.0	212,856	8.7	777,190	5.7	377
10–14	1991	8,376,579	92.2	1,909,605	86.7	10,286,184	91.1	228
	1981	10,627,918	95.0	2,232,257	91.3	12,860,175	94.3	210
5–14	1991	9,082,141	100.0	2,203,208	100.0	11,285,349	100.0	243
	1981	11,192,252	100.0	2,445,113	100.0	13,637,365	100.0	218

Source: *Census of India*.

compared to 1981, the number as well as the proportion of the very young increased in the case of both main workers and marginal workers. The number of marginal workers per 1,000 main workers in 1991 in the 5–9 year age group is 416, as compared to 228 in the 10–14 year age group, indicating that older children tend to be engaged more as main workers. The comparative figure in 1981 in the 5–9 year age group was 377, and in the 10–14 year age group 210. In other words, the proportion of marginal workers to main workers has increased in both the age groups.

The NSSO's thirty-eighth round (1983) and forty-third round (1987–8) indicated similar trends. However, unlike the Census findings, it reported a decline in the percentage of child workers in the age group 5–9 years from 9.42 in the thirty-eighth round to 5.40 in the forty-third round.

Age specific work participation rates (number of working children per 100 children in the age group), presented in Table 4.3, give a better indication of the extent of involvement of children in the world of work. A redeeming feature is the very low work participation rate of children aged less than 10 years (less than 1 per cent). In the age group 10–14 years, however, the rate continues to be uncomfortably high, even though there is a decline in 1991 (10.4 per cent) as compared to 1981 (15.0 per cent). The overall work participation rate in the 5–14 year age group is 5.4 per cent. The Fifth Quinquennial Survey by the NSSO in 1993–4 reported similar results (NSSO 1997).

Census figures give only an aggregate picture. In several sectors of economic activity, very young children continue to be employed. The abusive practice was first brought to official notice in the 1870s,

TABLE 4.3: AGE SPECIFIC WORK PARTICIPATION RATE, INDIA, 1981 AND 1991

Year	5–9 years			10–14 years			5–14 years		
	Main workers	Marginal workers	Main + Marginal workers	Main workers	Marginal workers	Main + Marginal workers	Main workers	Marginal workers	Main + Marginal workers
1981	0.60	0.23	0.83	12.37	2.60	14.97	6.23	1.36	7.59
1991	0.63	0.26	0.89	8.49	1.93	10.42	4.32	1.05	5.37

Source: *Census of India*.
Note: Figures for 1991 do not include Jammu & Kashmir and for 1981 do not include Assam.

highlighting that children of even six years of age were being employed in textile mills, thus paving the demand for the passing of the Factories Act of 1881, prescribing a minimum age of employment in factories (Clow 1926). Subsequently, other legislations were passed, but these cover the organized sector and a few other industrial categories only. Most types of economic activities in which children are engaged do not have the benefit of protective legislation. The unfortunate reality is that even in the 1980s and 1990s in some production and servicing units, both new and traditional, very small children continue to be employed as has been brought out by several empirical studies.

The match industry at Sivakasi, a drought prone backward area of Tamil Nadu, has drawn the maximum flak for employing very young children. Even since the first unit was set up in 1923, the area has seen a phenomenal growth of the match industry, mainly in the unorganized sector, in the form of cottage and small scale units employing child workers to produce matches for them. Sivakasi has, thus, more than a seven and a half decade history of exploiting tender children, which has been extensively documented and highlighted in official reports and research studies. Kothari's investigation of the problem of child labour in Sivakasi reported 45,000 child workers in match and fireworks industries in the unregulated sector comprising cottage or small factory units. Some of the children employed were less than 6 years of age. In many units, some production processes were fully undertaken by children below 7 years of age. The youngest child found working was of age three and a half years. In one unit employing 250 children, most were below 10 years of age, some barely 5 years, working at a feverish pace as the payment was on piece rate basis. In other units visited, too, very young children were found (Kothari 1983). Sekar's study of girls employed in the match industry at Sivakasi reported 7 per cent in the age group 4–7 years, 33 per cent in the age group 8–11 years and 60 per cent 12–14 years. The study also found children of even three years of age helping their mothers inside match factories. The units usually employed girls below the age of 10 years (Sekar 1993). Children working in match industry were transported in factory buses from their homes every day at dawn and brought back later in the day. To evade laws, larger units have resorted to the device of subcontracting work to smaller units located in interior rural areas or to households which employ both family labour and hired labour. Since payment is on piece rate basis, the children work for very long hours, even much beyond sunset, in congested unhygienic conditions in badly illuminated rooms, and are exposed to various health hazards and risk of accidents at a very tender age. Large numbers of children continue to be employed in the industry; only the system of engaging children has undergone a change, thereby reducing the visibility of child labour because of the dispersed character and the household production arrangements (Krishnakumar 2000).

The hand woven carpet industry, too, has a long history of employing very young children, which has drawn considerable public attention and strong criticism. The Royal Commission on Labour had reported children beginning to work in Amritsar carpet factories at 9 years of age, but in some cases as low as 6 years (Government of India 1931). The Labour Investigation Committee, reporting a decade and a half later, found children 5 or 6 years of age working in carpet weaving in Kashmir (Government of India 1946). Almost three and a half decades later, the Committee on Child Labour found employment of children 8 to 10 years of age engaged in carpet weaving in Jammu and Kashmir (Ministry of Labour 1979). A more recent study on child workers in the carpet weaving industry of Jammu & Kashmir reported that a majority of children belonged to the 8–12 year age group (NLI 1993). Juyal's study of child labour in the carpet industry in two clusters of villages in the Mirzapur Bhadoli belt in 1991 reported the presence of very young child workers—23 per cent below the age of 9 years and 69 per cent in the age group 9–13 years. Inquiries on the age at which children began work indicated that more than three-fourths had started to work before they crossed 10 years of age (Juyal 1993). The study by the National Council of Applied Economic Research (NCAER) of child labour in the handloom carpet industry in the same area in 1992 indicated 24.4 per cent children below the age of 9 years in the family labour segment and 5.7 per cent in the hired labour segment. In the age group 9–11 years, 32.0 per cent were in the family labour segment and 21.6 per cent in the hired labour segment. In the age group 12–14 years, 43.6 per cent were in the family labour segment and nearly three-fourths of the children were in the hired labour segment (Vijayagopalan 1993). A follow-up study by NCAER in 1994 reported a substantial decline in the employment of very young children in the hired labour segment. The decline was reported to reflect the cautious attitude of the employers in view of the mounting pressure from NGOs and importing countries, and media publicity (NCAER 1994).

The slate pencil industry in Andhra Pradesh has also been found to employ very young children. A study on the industry in Markapur (Andhra Pradesh) showed that one-third of the child workers were below 11 years of age (Naidu and Parthasarathy 1992). Another study in Mandsaur indicated the same trend. It further reported that the age of entry was less than 8 years for more than half the child workers. The employment of their parents in the same industry facilitated the process of entry (ORG 1993).

BOX 4.1. NEVER TOO YOUNG TO WORK: DECADES OF BRUTALITY

'He (Marquis of Salisbury, then Secretary of State for India) said he was informed that children were taken to work at six years of age and had frequently to walk a distance of 2 or 3 miles to the factory, that they worked from sunrise to sunset with only half an hour's interval including most Sundays and not uncommonly dropped down from exhaustion between alleys and passages of the machines.'

Note: This describes the situation in the 1870s before the passage of the Factories Act, 1881.

Source: A.G. Clow, 1926, *Indian Factory Legislation: A Historical Survey*, Bulletins of Indian Industries and Labour, No. 37, December.

'In many cities, large numbers of young boys are employed for long hours and discipline is strict. Indeed there is reason to believe that corporal punishments and other disciplinary measures of a reprehensible kind are sometimes resorted to in the case of smaller children. Workers as young as five years of age may be found in some of these places working without adequate meal intervals or weekly rest holidays, and often for 10 to 12 hours daily, for sums as low as 2 annas in the case of those of tenderest years.'

Source: *Report of the Royal Commission on Labour in India, 1931.*

'The entire production of matches in this area is non-mechanised. . . . The children, mostly belonging to the neighbouring villages, either work in small cottage units in their own villages or are brought by organised transport to the small scale factories scattered in the neighbouring villages or in Sivakasi town. Between 3 and 5 a.m. every morning, children in these villages, some as far as 30 kilometres away, are woken up and loaded on to buses or vans belonging to the industries in Sivakasi town. . . . The transport drops them back to their respective villages between 6 and 9 p.m. The children, who put in a nearly 12 hour working day are, therefore, away from their

(Contd.)

Box 4.1 (Contd.)

homes for over fifteen hours. . . . The age of the youngest child whom we found working was 3.5 years. Legally, children employed at these industries have to acquire a doctor's certificate clearing them for employment. At the large villages and in Sivakasi town, we found that a racket flourished where doctors, some on the grounds of compassion, issued certificates, without ensuring the age and health of the child.

In many factories, some activities were fully undertaken by children below 7 years of age. Girls outnumber boys three to one. In the match industries, they work in filling frames, making boxes, counting, pasting labels, etc., while in the fireworks industry, children are employed to dye outer paper, make small crackers, roll gunpowder and pack the final product.

The working conditions in the industries are unsafe and detrimental to the mental and physical health of the child. Staying a total of fifteen hours away from home, twelve at work, they work in cramped environments with hazardous chemicals and inadequate ventilation. Dust from the chemical powders and strong vapours in both the store room and the boiler room were obvious at practically every site we visited. Minimum safety standards were not maintained in most of these units.

'In spite of an over twelve-hour work day and this feverish activity, the younger children between four and ten years earn an average of Rs. 2 a day. The older children earn a maximum of Rs. 6–7 per day.'

Source: S. Kothari, 1983, 'There's Blood on Those Matchsticks: Child Labour in Sivakasi', *Economic and Political Weekly*, vol. 18, 2 July.

'Girls are introduced to beedi making when they are as young as four years old. . . . About half the beedi assistants were introduced to the work when they were between five and ten years old, and the other half were introduced between 11 and 15 years of age.'

Source: A. Dharmalingam, 1993, 'Female Beedi Workers in a South Indian Village', *Economic and Political Weekly*, 3–10 July.

Mishra's study of working children in the saree industry in Varanasi in 1995 reported the presence in significant numbers of very young children, as a long period of apprenticeship is believed to be necessary if the child is to become a master weaver. The study reported 47 per cent child workers below the age of 10 years. A large number join the industry as soon as they are 6 to 7 years of age, about two-thirds in their own household and one-third in units owned by others (Misra 1995).

The presence of very young child workers has also been reported in the glass factories of Firozabad (Burra 1986; Kapoor 1993), gem polishing industry in Jaipur (Burra 1991; Batra 1990), brassware industry of Moradabad (NLI 1992a), lock industry of Aligarh (Burra 1987; Laskar 2000), beedi industry (Dharmalingam 1993), power loom industry in Bhiwandi (Ghosh 1997), garment export industry of Tirupur (Peace Trust and SAVE 1997), and sports goods industry in Meerut and Jallandhar (Sachdev 1999). Some of these are home based, while in others children often accompany older siblings or parents for work in small, often ill-ventilated and congested work-sheds.

EXTENT OF CHILD LABOUR IN STATES

Andhra Pradesh has the largest number of main child workers (1.537 million), as per the 1991 Census (see Table 4.4). Other states with a very large number of child workers (main) are Uttar Pradesh (1.145 million), Madhya Pradesh (0.998 million), Karnataka (0.818 million), Maharashtra (0.806 million), and Bihar (0.795 million). Together, these six states have two-thirds of the child workers in the country. Figure 4.1 gives the relative situation of the 16 bigger states. The 5–14 year age specific work participation rate (main workers) is the highest in Andhra Pradesh (9.23 per cent), followed by Karnataka (7.38 per cent) and Madhya Pradesh (5.96 per cent). In

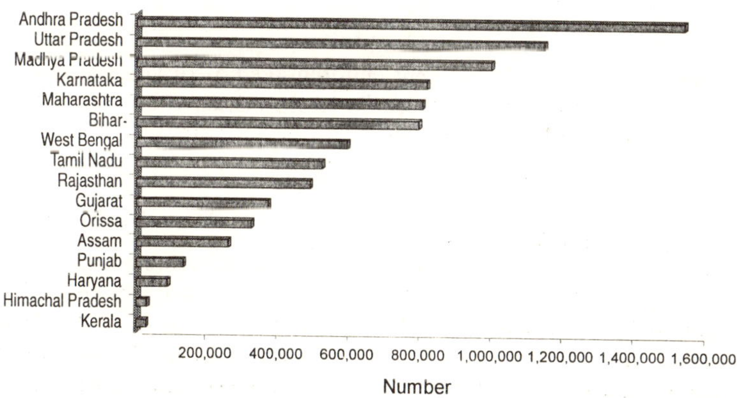

FIG. 4.1: NUMBER OF MAIN WORKERS AGED LESS THAN 15 YEARS IN STATES, 1991.

TABLE 4.4: NUMBER OF MAIN AND MARGINAL WORKERS AGED 5–14 YEARS AND THE AGE SPECIFIC WORK PARTICIPATION RATE, INDIA AND STATES, 1991

State	Main workers	Marginal workers	Total workers	No. of marginal workers per 1000 main workers	Age specific work participation rate		
					Main workers	Marginal workers	Total workers
INDIA	9,082,141	2,203,208	11,285,349	243	4.33	1.05	5.37
Andhra Pradesh	1,537,293	124,647	1,661,940	81	9.23	0.75	9.98
Uttar Pradesh	1,145,087	264,999	1,410,086	231	3.09	0.72	3.81
Madhya Pradesh	997,940	354,623	1,352,563	355	5.96	2.12	8.08
Karnataka	818,159	158,088	976,247	193	7.38	1.43	8.81
Maharashtra	805,847	262,571	1,068,418	326	4.32	1.41	5.73
Bihar	795,444	146,801	942,245	185	3.37	0.62	3.99
West Bengal	593,387	118,304	711,691	199	3.47	0.69	4.16
Tamil Nadu	523,125	55,764	578,889	107	4.37	0.47	4.83
Rajasthan	490,522	283,677	774,199	578	4.09	2.37	6.46
Gujarat	373,027	150,558	523,585	404	3.75	1.51	5.26
Orissa	325,250	127,144	452,394	391	4.22	1.65	5.87
Assam	259,953	67,645	327,598	260	4.33	1.13	5.46
Punjab	132,414	10,454	142,868	79	2.82	0.22	3.04
Haryana	89,030	20,661	109,691	232	2.07	0.48	2.55
Himachal Pradesh	30,771	25,667	56,438	834	2.48	2.07	4.55
Kerala	28,590	6,210	34,800	217	0.48	0.10	0.58

Source: *Census of India*.
Note: States have been arranged in descending order of number of main workers. Data for bigger states given here.

Kerala, which has 85 per cent children aged 5–14 years attending school, the 5–14 year age specific work participation rate is only 0.48 per cent.

FEMALE CHILD WORKERS

Of the 9.082 million main workers less than 15 years of age, 3.149 million (37.64 per cent) are females (see Table 4.5). Of the 2.203 million marginal workers less than 15 years of age, 1.677 million (77 per cent) are females. Thus, in the main worker category, males exceed females (62 per cent males), while in the marginal workers category females far exceed males (77 per cent females). Putting it differently, among males there are only 93 marginal workers per

TABLE 4.5: DISTRIBUTION OF WORKERS AGED LESS THAN 15 YEARS AND WORK PARTICIPATION RATE BY SEX, INDIA, 1991

Sex	No. and percentage of workers			Work participation rate					
	Main workers No. (%)	Marginal workers No. (%)	Total workers No. (%)	5–9 years			10–14 years		
				Main workers	Marginal workers	Total workers	Main workers	Marginal workers	Total workers
Males	5,663,226	526,608	6,189,834						
	(62.36)	(23.00)	(54.85)	0.77	0.26	0.94	10.05	0.82	10.87
Females	3,418,915	1,676,600	5,095,515						
	(37.64)	(77.00)	(45.15)	0.49	0.36	0.85	6.75	3.17	9.92
Total	9,082,141	2,203,208	11,285,349						
	(100.00)	(100.00)	(100.00)	0.63	0.26	0.89	8.49	1.93	10.42

Source: *Census of India*. Figures do not include Jammu & Kashmir.

1,000 main workers, but among females there are 490 marginal workers per 1,000 main workers.

The age specific work participation rate by sex shows that in the 5–9 year age group it is less than 1 per cent in the case of both males and females. In the 10–14 year age group, it is higher for males in the main worker category but lower in the marginal worker category. Combined figures for main and marginal workers indicate 11 per cent work participation rate for males and 10 per cent for females in the 10–14 year age group. The thirty-eighth round of the National Sample Survey (1983) and the forty-third round (1987–8) reported about the same percentage of male child workers as reported by the Census in the main child worker category. A study of the urban poor by the National Institute of Urban Affairs covering 20 urban centres, indicated a similar pattern (NIUA 1989).

The distribution of child workers by sex and industrial category, given in Table 4.6, indicates that in 1991 more than four-fifths of child workers were engaged in agriculture and allied activities (82.4 per cent males and 86.1 per cent females) and about 9 per cent in manufacturing, processing, servicing, and repairs. A larger percentage of female child workers were agricultural labourers or were engaged in household industry, while a larger percentage of male child workers were cultivators or were engaged in manufacturing, processing, services, and repairs in other than household industry, or in trade and commerce.

TABLE 4.6: PERCENTAGE DISTRIBUTION OF MAIN WORKERS AGED 5–14 YEARS BY SEX IN DIFFERENT INDUSTRIAL CATEGORIES, INDIA, 1991

Sex	Industrial Category										
	I	II	III	IV	V(a)	V(b)	VI	VII	VIII	IX	Total
Male	38.14	39.73	4.55	0.28	2.18	6.19	0.98	3.91	0.52	3.52	100.00
Female	31.10	52.27	2.72	0.31	4.68	4.65	0.44	0.59	0.05	3.19	100.00
Total	35.49	44.45	3.86	0.29	3.12	5.61	0.78	2.66	0.34	3.40	100.00

Source: *Census of India*, 1991. Figures do not include Jammu & Kashmir.
Category: I Cultivator
II Agricultural Labourer
III Livestock, Forestry, Fishing and Allied Activities
IV Mining and Quarrying
V Manufacturing, Processing, Servicing and Repairs in
(a) Household Industry
(b) Other than Household Industry
VI Construction
VII Trade and Commerce
VIII Transport, Storage and Communications
IX Other Services

Census figures give the aggregate picture. There are some types of industries in which girls tend to be employed in very large numbers. A typical case in the unorganized sector is the match industry in Sivakasi where an overwhelming majority are girls (Kothari 1983; Krishnakumar 2000; Sekar 1993). In the rolling of beedis, too, girls are employed in large numbers. In the household domestic worker segment, girls are predominantly employed as they are preferred by housewives on grounds of safety, easier handling and control, and better suitability for household tasks, including looking after small children and work in the kitchen.

The hand knotted carpet weaving industry shows an interesting variation. In the Mirzapur Bhadohi belt in Uttar Pradesh, some girls are found working in family looms, but the hired labour segment comprises almost entirely of boys (Juyal 1993; Vijayagopalan 1993). In the Jammu & Kashmir region, however, where hand knotted carpet making is mainly a household industry, the number of female child workers is quite high, but female participation is lower in the Ladakh region as compared to male participation (NLI, 1993). Similar variation exists in the case of saree weaving. Misra's study of child labour in the saree industry in Varanasi reported only 18 per cent female workers (Misra 1995). However, a study in the Sivakasi area reported that 70 per cent of the child workers engaged in weaving were girls, indicating how local factors and pattern of organization of production units play an important role (Vijayalakshmi 1984).

In some types of establishments like food shops/tea stalls, battery recycling, lock making, and stitching of footballs, only boys are employed. In several other types of establishments where the hired labour segment predominates, most of the children employed are boys. Typical examples are gem polishing (Surat), lock making (Aligarh), glass industry (Firozabad), and brassware industry (Moradabad).

Girls usually work in or near their homes in the company of other female members from the village or neighbourhood, or with members of their family in home based production or wage labour segment. Traditional patterns of employment and availability of production units which can employ girl child workers also play an important role. Even when boys and girls are engaged in the same production units, the processes in which girls are engaged often differ from that of the boys. The type of work girls do usually offer no scope for upward mobility, which is generally not true in the case of boys. In the matter of working and employment conditions no special consideration is given to girl child workers. On the contrary they are paid less.

EDUCATION

Work interferes with schooling, and usually means withdrawal from school in case a child has been enrolled. Census data indicate that only one-fourth child workers were literate in 1991 (see Table 4.7). The literacy rate is lower in rural areas and among female child workers. The literacy situation of child workers in 1991 is only moderately better than in 1981, when only 18.5 per cent child workers were literate. The high incidence of illiteracy casts a shadow on their potential earning capacity in a modernizing economy in which workers without education will have few occupational choices and hardly any opportunities for upward mobility. Several microstudies on child labour point in the same direction. The incidence of illiteracy among child workers is higher in the hired labour segment than in the family labour segment (Misra 1995; Vijayagopalan 1993; Juyal 1993, ORG 1993).

TABLE 4.7: LEVEL OF EDUCATION OF MAIN WORKERS AGED LESS THAN 15 YEARS, INDIA, 1991

(percentage)

Level of education	Rural			Urban			Total		
	Males	Females	Total	Males	Females	Total	Males	Females	Total
Illiterate	72.38	82.64	76.38	56.10	68.38	59.34	70.36	81.59	74.59
Literate without education level	11.38	7.90	10.03	15.20	13.25	14.69	11.86	8.29	10.52
Primary & above	16.23	9.46	13.59	28.69	18.37	25.97	17.77	10.12	14.89
Total	100.00	100.00	100.00	100.00	100.00	100.00	100.00	100.00	100.00

Source: *Census of India*, 1991.

Very few children are able to combine work with attending school. The 1991 Census data, given in Table 4.8, shows that among main workers in the primary school going age group of 6–10 years, less than 3 per cent were attending school, while in the middle/upper primary school going age group of 11–13 years, less than 2 per cent were attending school. The rural urban difference and the gender

TABLE 4.8: PERCENTAGE OF MAIN AND MARGINAL WORKERS AGED LESS THAN 15 YEARS ATTENDING SCHOOL, INDIA, 1991

	Age (in years)	Rural			Urban			Total		
		Male	Female	Total	Male	Female	Total	Male	Female	Total
Main workers	6–10	2.91	2.10	2.59	5.85	7.36	6.28	3.24	2.47	2.94
	11–13	1.81	1.30	1.60	2.62	2.99	2.72	1.91	1.42	1.72
	6–13	2.13	1.53	1.89	3.50	4.19	3.69	2.29	1.72	2.07
Marginal workers	6–10	32.93	9.26	15.98	35.82	31.02	33.01	33.09	9.94	16.62
	11–13	40.37	6.73	14.21	38.30	18.52	25.99	40.26	7.03	14.58
	6–13	37.31	7.58	14.84	37.26	23.26	28.76	37.31	8.01	15.31

Source: *Census of India*, 1991. Figures do not include Jammu & Kashmir.

Note: The percentages are specific to each category. Thus, of the male main workers aged 6–10 years in rural areas, only 2.91 per cent are attending school; of the female main workers aged 6–10 years in rural areas only 2.10 per cent are attending school; of the male main workers aged 6–10 years in urban areas, only 5.85 per cent are attending school; of the female main workers aged 6–10 years in urban areas only 7.36 per cent are attending school.

difference in the age specific school going rates of main workers is modest. Among marginal workers, however, there is a sharp increase in the percentage of children attending school. There is also a marked gender difference in the case of marginal workers of both age groups attending school. Far more males than females were attending school particularly in rural areas where the difference is very large.

CAUSES OF CHILD LABOUR

Child labour is the outcome of several factors. Poverty of families is cited as the most important cause by committees which have examined the problem (Report of the Committee for the Preparation of a Programme for Children, 1968; Report of the National Commission on Labour, 1969; Report of the Committee on Child Labour, 1979; Report of the National Commission on Rural Labour, 1991). The National Policy on Child Labour, 1987 observed that the origins and compulsions of child labour are too often rooted in poverty. Several national surveys and micro-studies, too, cite economic necessity as the primary cause of child labour (George 1975; Ghosh 1997; Juyal 1993; Laskar 2000; NSSO 1997; Sekar 1993; Singh, et al. 1980).

There is overwhelming empirical evidence that working children come from very low income families with uncertain incomes and a large number of dependants. Some are from single parent families and are the sole or main earner. The families hardly own any assets of production. In rural areas, they fall in the category of landless and marginal farmers, and casual workers. In a labour surplus market, they get paid very low wages, usually below the minimum wage. Some crisis in the family (death, desertion, ill-health, loss of source of livelihood), alcoholism, or a heavy loan liability pushes the children into the labour market.

Some commentators are of the view that the economic contribution of children is exaggerated. They argue that the entry of children in the labour market depresses wage levels of adults and reduces adult employment, thus affecting the income of families. If children do not work, more adults will get employment; also, due to the non-availability of cheap child labour, adults would get better wages resulting in higher family income. Thus, child labour in a labour surplus economy is dispensable. Such macro reasoning, however, provides little comfort to families which benefit from the earning of their children to meet their immediate survival needs.

Demand for child labour comes from employers who find child labour cheap, docile, non-unionized, and easy to discipline and extract work. Children require less space to work and can more easily be huddled in a small area. They are less troublesome, complain less, and can easily be thrown out. They produce virtually the same output as an adult in certain types of production processes and work for as many hours. Some employers express the view that children work better in certain types of operations as, for instance, filling match frames, making matchboxes and tying carpet knots, an opinion disputed by child labour activists who argue that the real reason is that they come cheap and can fit easily into the existing production systems of certain categories of units. These units largely follow labour intensive non-mechanized operations, use outdated technology, have low capital investment, provide a low cost working environment, and engage unskilled or semi-skilled manpower at the first point of entry. Employers save money on labour and capital, and defer the introduction of new technology or production systems. Child labour, thus, contributes to the perpetuation of outdated methods of producing goods.

The reality is that children are employed because employers find it profitable. Employers like to express unhappiness that their benevolence is not appreciated. They state that they are wrongly accused when in fact they are helping a family in dire economic straits and also helping the child in becoming a disciplined worker, rather than loitering about or getting involved in delinquent acts. They argue that in some industries (carpet weaving and saree weaving, for instance), early initiation is necessary to acquire skills by the use of nimble fingers and to acquire the capacity to work for long hours on the looms. Employers view the criticism of child labour as not based on an understanding of socio-economic realities of families and the operation of market forces. They do not consider employing children as morally wrong. The views expressed by contemporary employers of child labour are hardly different from the views of employers in the latter half of the nineteenth century when the first attempts were made to statutorily lay down the minimum age of employment of children in factories (Clow 1926). The Labour Investigation Committee (1946), the National Commission on Labour (1969), and the Committee on Child Labour (1979), too, reported similar claims made before them by employers.

Parents of children are no less responsible for engaging them full-time in home based employment or sending them to work on wages, even taking the initiative in this regard by contacting potential employers and taking an advance or a loan to be repaid by the child through his labour. Even when no loan or advance has been taken, wages due to the child are collected by the parent. Parents of child workers do not perceive entry into the workforce at an early age as abnormal since they, too, had entered the labour force as a child and not gone to school. In many areas, early entry into the workforce, whether as family worker, wage employed, or apprentice, has been traditional. At times the motivation, apart from the income, is the opportunity of a child to acquire skills which will improve his earning capacity later in life. Cases have been reported of parents even using force on their children and punishing them when the employers complained of lack of interest and poor work output (Dharmalingam 1993). In the case of children who are sent out by parents to work away from their homes for which an advance has been taken, hardly any visits are made to the workplaces, leaving the child isolated and lonely and at the mercy of the employer. Thus, parental role in the perpetuation of child labour and its pledging, rather than sending the child to school, is a social reality.

The poor functioning of schools run by government or local bodies, which cater to children from lower income groups, is also a contributory factor. Such schools have not been able to establish their role as a better alternative for usefully utilizing the time of a child. Many children drop out early after being enrolled as teaching is irregular, school infrastructure poor, and learning environment unfriendly. Teachers take little interest in stimulating the interest of a first generation learner from a poor illiterate or semi-literate family. Parental perception of the utility of schooling flounders when children are seen to make little progress. Whatever children learn is not perceived by parents as being helpful in securing employment or earning more money. Parents, therefore, feel that it is better for children to be withdrawn from school, or if they have dropped out, to engage them in economic activities, wherever such an opportunity exists.

Child labour is, thus, the outcome of economic, social, and school related factors which determine its demand and supply. Their relative importance varies in different situations. Intervention strategies, therefore, need to be area specific, based on an understanding of the relative role of different factors. The point to note, however, is that the child has no say in the matter of his employment. All decisions are taken by adults acting supposedly for his well-being.

BOX 4.2. PUSHED BY PARENTS: CASE OF A GIRL BEEDI WORKER

'A 12 year old girl who was a main beedi worker had been borrowing from professional beedi lenders for some time. She had to do that because it was her parents (particularly mother's) order to submit a fixed amount of beedis every week, failing which she would be beaten. Whenever there was a shortfall she borrowed from a professional beedi lender; her debt along with the interest gradually increased to about 100 bundles of beedis. Realizing that the girl would not pay the beedis back, the lender informed the girl's parents. Fearing that her mother would beat her, the girl went to the forest and committed suicide by eating the seeds of a wild plant. The victim's parents were not driven by poverty to enforce rigid rules on their daughter. . . . To earn economic and social status all available resources including children are put to use. . . . In the child suicide case mentioned above while the girl's brother (two years elder) was in school, she had to earn money not only to give profit to the beedi company and beedi lender, but also to give prestige and status (primarily a function of wealth) to her parents. Of course, her own future depended on how much she could contribute toward her future dowry and jewellery.'

Source: A. Dharmalingam, 1993, 'Female Beedi Workers in a South Indian Village', *Economic and Political Weekly*, 3–10 July 1993.

EMPLOYMENT STATUS

The most common employment status of children is as family worker in family based economic activities. In agriculture and allied sectors, when the family owns the assets of production children are engaged in work which is seasonal and light in character, depending on the extent of availability of family labour. Children assist in ploughing, sowing, weeding, harvesting, grazing cattle and feeding and tending them, storing grains and various sundry activities. There are, however, other family based economic activities, where the family obtains work on contract from small and medium enterprises through intermediaries and the children get involved as family workers. The arrangement works to the advantage of the owners of the enterprises who are able to reduce costs as they are free from all obligations in respect of labour laws, do not have to keep workers on their rolls, and do not have any responsibility towards them. In view of surplus labour and keen competition to get work, the contract amounts to toiling for long hours for a meagre income, a pursuit which engages children apart from adults. Among the small-scale industries which resort to contracting out work in varying degrees are glass, gem polishing, brassware, lock making, embroidery, beedi rolling and many others. Misra and Pande's study of child labour in the glass industry in Firozabad reported that three and a half times the number of children were engaged in the household sector as compared to the factory sector (Misra and Pande 1992). In beedi making, too, the piece rate contractual arrangement is resorted to fairly extensively.

The next most common employment status is as wage earner. In production units which employ child workers along with other adult workers, children are given independent tasks which they can perform on their own. Several industries have, over the years, identified the tasks children can do. For instance, in the match making units in Sivakasi, children, particularly girls, are extensively engaged in filling frames, making boxes, counting and pasting labels, and related activities, while in the fireworks industry they are engaged in dyeing paper, making small crackers, rolling gun powder, and packing the final product (Kothari 1983). In the glass industry in Firozabad, in the factory premises, children work along with adults, performing mainly complementary functions. They are predominantly engaged in bangle factories in *jurai* (joining the ends), *chhatai* (sorting), *katai* (engraving), *pakai* (heating), packing, etc. In other categories of glass industries, children are engaged in the making of electric bulbs (blowing), cleaning the glass apparatus, putting shine on the manufactured products, sorting defective pieces, carrying molten glass, and helping adult workers. Approximately 35 to 40 per cent workers in the glass industry in Firozabad are estimated to be children (Misra and Pande 1992). Not all wage employment, however, is for long periods. Children are sometimes recruited for wage employment for only a few days by agents of the glass factory from the *mandis* (informal labour markets). Kapoor found, in her visit to these markets, children between 7 and 14 years of age arriving in the early morning cold from far-off villages, hoping to get work. They were waiting along with adults for the *jagaiyas* (contractors) from the factories who would select some workers for a day or two (Kapoor 1993). A similar pattern is evident in the brassware industry in Moradabad. The transition from the cottage system of production to the small-scale factory system in response to market forces has to led more and more children of artisans, who were earlier in the family labour segment, to move to the wage labour segment (NLI 1992a). The hand carpet weaving industry in the Mirzapur-Bhadoli belt, too, has faced this transition resulting in an increase in hired child labour with the expansion of looms in response to the market forces and the phenomenon of child workers outnumbering adults (Juyal 1993). Here, family child labour and hired child labour are often found working together in the same premises under a master craftsman. A similar pattern of hired child labour and family child labour working together has been found in the saree industry of Varanasi (Misra 1995). The export industry, too, has in some areas contributed to the growing employment of children, as has been reported in the case of the hosiery knitwear export industry of Tirupur where production systems have developed in a manner which facilitate the employment of children (Peace Trust and SAVE 1997).

Another type of wage employment which is exploitative, because of the very long working hours, is work in small eating places and tea stalls. Children get some food and a place to sleep but are paid very poorly. Some even get physically punished for non-performance of tasks specifically allotted to them.

The worst employment status of children is often in situations where the labour of children is pledged by their parents (almost always the father) against an advance taken either directly from the employer or an intermediary, to be repaid through work done by the child over a period of time which may extend to two or more years. If the work is to be done in some other district or state, the cost of travel is added to the advance paid. The child is under obligation to work for the same employer. No change is possible, unless the advance has been repaid in cash or through work done. The employer has, thus, with him an assured workforce. The practice has been in vogue for decades and has been virtually institutionalized. Children are exploited not only by having to put in long hours of work in deplorable working conditions; payments due to them are cut by adopting dubious ways of computing wages and making deductions on account of wastage or lower than required daily work output. If accommodation is provided, additional deductions are made, even though the children may be sleeping in sheds or in the work premises.

The Royal Commission on Labour (1931) had strongly recommended the abolition of the practice of pledging of labour and the abuses it gave rise to. The government accordingly passed the Children (Pledging of Labour) Act in 1933. The Constitution of

India prohibits forced labour (Article 23). The Bonded Labour System (Abolition) Act, 1976 prohibits children being held in bondage for work. Despite the legislations, the pledging of labour continues unabated and parents continue to mortgage the labour of their children against an advance or loan. Among the industries where the practice of pledging of labour of children has been reported are carpet weaving, saree weaving, brick kilns, match making, and beedi rolling, to name some. Many other industries, too, resort to this practice, as it facilitates procurement and retention of child workers at cheap rates. The expansion of enterprises of varying sizes in the cottage and small-scale sector in response to the expanding market, and their transformation from production units based entirely on family labour to enterprises based on both family labour and hired labour or only hired labour, have contributed to the phenomenon of hiring children whose labour has been pledged (Juyal 1993; Mehta 1983; Dharmalingam 1993; Ghosh 1997; Krishnakumar 1995; Patil 1985). Another segment where pledging of child labour is to be found is the domestic sector. Middle and upper class families in need of domestic help pay an advance to poor parents and bring the child away from his village and family for doing household work for which live-in facilities and meals are provided and the advance is adjusted against the monthly wage. In several instances, the child has to put up with abusive treatment at the hands of the family members of the employer.

Sometimes whole families are bonded. The national survey on bonded labour in 1978 in ten states reported that bonded obligations covered children of the bonded family (Marla 1981). The passage of the Bonded Labour System (Abolition) Act, 1976 does not seem to have deterred employers. In the brick kiln industry, stone quarries, and match industry, for instance, the practice continues. Employers as well as official agencies deny its existence. Denial of the ground reality suits the employers very well, and worsens the situation.

There are fewer working children in the self-employed category. The more common categories are rag pickers, shoeshine boys, vendors of articles of daily use, and load carriers at market places, railway stations, and road terminals.

The most vulnerable among self-employed children are the rag pickers, who are called as such though they pick up anything but rags. They collect scrap from streets, market places, garbage bins, and waste dumps, picking up material such as paper, cardboard, plastic, iron scrap, tin containers, and broken glass, in fact anything thrown away by households, shops, workshops, or other establishments which can be sold to dealers who buy these for the recycling industry. Children, both boys and girls, begin their rounds early in the morning slinging huge sacks on their slender shoulders as they scrounge places for scrap, travelling 8 to 10 kilometres, even more, in a day. Very young children usually move in groups, as also the girls who are sometimes accompanied by an adult female who, too, is a scrap picker.

Some of the child rag pickers are very young, hardly 6 years of age, moving along with older children and learning to identify scrap items to be collected. The children come from a very poor socio-economic background. Not all have families. Some have come to the city alone and sleep on pavements or shacks along with other street children, while many others have rather weak links with their families and are, by and large, on their own. Most have never gone to school. Some who did, dropped out early. Rag picking is an extremely hazardous occupation. The children constantly expose themselves to the danger of accidents, injuries, and disease through contacts with sharp material and poisonous substances as they scrounge with bare hands and sometimes even bare feet. It is not only their working environment which is very unhygienic and disease prone, their living environment is hardly better. Rag picker children, thus, rank among the most vulnerable category of working children. A matter of great concern is that with urbanization, and the increased volume of throw away packing and waste material, the number of such children is growing.

Children also work as apprentices, particularly in production processes which require skills that can be acquired through learning under the supervision of a master craftsman, as, for instance, in the hand knotted carpet weaving, silk saree weaving, embroidery, gem polishing, and repair workshops. The initiative for placing the child as an apprentice is often taken by his parents. Sometimes, intermediaries are engaged for procuring apprentices. During the early period of apprenticeship, no wages are earned but small amounts may be given for out of pocket expenses. After a few months, payments are made, which increase as the child acquires more skills, his productivity increases, and he is able to work without much guidance. Often, the period of apprenticeship is prolonged, as it is a source of cheap labour and it is advantageous to the master craftsman to have a skilled hand on modest payment. Although the child learns a craft, he is subject to rigorous discipline and has to spend long hours in a cramped place with no opportunities of play or recreation. Formal education becomes the biggest casualty.

HAZARDS

Physical abuse of child workers by employers, and even by parents who pledge the labour of their children or forcibly send them to work, makes the child labour scene still more unsavoury. The Royal Commission on Labour had reported about corporal punishments and other disciplining measures of a reprehensible kind (Government of India 1931). The practice seems to have continued unabated, taking on occasion sadistic manifestations. Cases of 8 to 10 year old child workers being severely beaten by their employers and virtually held captive have been reported in the media (*Times of India* 1993; *Sunday Observer* 1997). Instances of domestic child workers being physically tortured and subjected to inhuman treatment have also been reported from time to time (Dubey 2000; *Hindustan Times* 2000; Iyer 1999; *Times of India* 2000). Live-in domestic child workers are totally unprotected and are soft targets of violence. Information about their real state of living is scarce as domestic workers function within the confines of four walls. The invisibility of their real state is the primary cause of their vulnerability. They are under the control of their employer round the clock and have little freedom to make contacts or complain about their ill treatment.

Physical punishments meted out to children in other segments of employment have also been reported (Ghosh 1997). Vijayagopalan's study of child labour in the carpet industry in the Mirzapur–Bhadohi area reported punishments of children working in the hired labour segment, ranging from physical assault to refusal of permission to take even food (Vijayagopalan 1993). There are also instances of sexual harassment and sexual abuse of girl child workers (Dharmalingam 1993; Sekar 1993).

Working children face several health hazards, especially when they have to work for long hours in poor light and ventilation in cramped spaces at worksites surrounded by filth, overflowing drains, and insanitary conditions. The nature of the industry and the work processes in which they are engaged expose them to additional health hazards, especially when their health and nutrition status are often at unsatisfactory levels.

Based on field observations, a graphic description of the extremely adverse conditions in which children work was reported by the

Royal Commission on Labour (Government of India 1931). Five decades later, the Committee on Child Labour (1979) described in detail the adverse working conditions in different industries in which children were employed making it evident that little change had taken place over the years (Ministry of Labour 1979). The conditions have, in fact, deteriorated, and the number of children subjected to health hazards has increased as the market for products which engage children has expanded and the cost of hiring space has gone up. A large number of empirical studies have in recent years highlighted the problem. The media, both print and television, have portrayed vividly the miserable working conditions and the health hazards to which even very young children are exposed due to the callous attitude of employers who are keen to cut costs, taking full advantage of the docile nature, anxiety, fear of loss of work, and helplessness of children. Parents of child workers are fully aware of the adverse and hazardous working conditions, but do little to protest against the same.

The NCAER study of child labour in the carpet industry in the Mirzapur-Bhadohi belt in Uttar Pradesh reported a very high incidence of cuts and injuries from sharp knives used in carpet weaving. It also found swellings in the lower limbs, pain, skin problems, respiratory diseases, and eyesight problems. These ailments were compounded by the utter lack of concern of the employer about the seriousness of the health problem (Vijayagopalan 1993). Juyal's study of child labour in the carpet industry, too, reported the occurrence of fever, frequent cough and cold, tuberculosis, and eyesight problems (Juyal 1993). Some studies based on medical examination of children engaged in carpet weaving have confirmed the occurrence of headache, backache, lower limb pains, acute respiratory infections, and blurring of vision (Joshi et al. 1994).

Studies on child labour in the brassware industry of Moradabad have brought out that children are constantly exposed to very high temperatures, molten metal, dangerous chemicals, fumes, and dust, causing a variety of health problems, burns, and injuries. Moulding, polishing, electroplating, and welding are particularly hazardous (NLI 1992a). A study of occupational morbidity among children employed in the brassware industry reported a high prevalence of respiratory ailments, which could be attributed to chronic exposure to fumes and the dust of metals. High incidence of musculoskeletal disorders was also found, which could be due to continuous faulty posture during work and physical stress (Bihari et al. 1992).

Health hazards of children working in the glass industry of Firozabad are similar in nature, as they are continuously exposed to very high temperatures, molten glass, dangerous chemicals, fumes, and dust and are in constant risk of burns and injuries (Burra 1986; Kapoor 1993). The Committee on Child Labour (1979), in the course of its investigations, found a large incidence of asthma, bronchitis, eye diseases, and tuberculosis among child workers in the glass bangle industry of Firozabad (Ministry of Labour 1979).

Health hazards of children working in the match industry are no less, due to constant exposure to heat, chemicals, dust, and bad working conditions, causing health problems such as respiratory diseases, tuberculosis, eye diseases, skin disorders, digestive disorders, and burn injuries (Kothari 1983; Sekar 1993).

Beedi rolling, which engages a large number of children, causes constant exposure to tobacco fumes for long working hours, resulting in a high incidence of tuberculosis, asthma, allergy, skin diseases, and constant cold. Faulty sitting posture for hours in a cramped room having poor light and ventilation, without taking the eyes off the beedi being rolled, takes its toll by way of defective eyesight, backache, legache, headache, piles, and rheumatism. When beedi rolling is done at home, other children and adults, too, inhale tobacco fumes and risk their health (Dharmalingam 1993; Mohandas 1980).

Children working in the lock industry, in processes involving polishing on buffing machines, electroplating, and spray painting, are exposed to health hazards of a different but no less serious kind which cause respiratory disorders, tuberculosis, bronchitis, asthma, pneumoconiosis, skin diseases, and possibly even lung cancer. They also stand the risk of injuries from accidents due to unsafe working conditions (Laskar 2000; NLI 1992b). In the pottery industry in Khurja which employs a large number of children, common health problems are frequent cough and cold, asthmatic bronchitis, tuberculosis, and silicosis. Some of the processes affect the eyes (NLI 1992c).

In the slate pencil industry of Mandsaur (Madhya Pradesh) and Markapur (Andhra Pradesh) which engages a large number of children, inhaling of silica dust causes silicosis, a dangerous lung disease. Other health problems are tuberculosis, respiratory disease, allergy, skin diseases, and eye problems. Cuts and sores also cause suffering to the children (Naidu and Parthasarathy 1992; ORG 1993).

In a number of other industries in which children are engaged, the situation is equally bad (Bansal and Banerjee 1991; Ghosh 1997; NLI 1991; ORG 1993; Venkatramani 1983). The Committee on Child Labour (1979) brought out the adverse effect on the eyes of the children in gem polishing work, zari making, and embroidery work. It found the physical condition of children working in foundries of Howrah 'most pathetic and gruesome'. The health hazards of children who engage in picking scrap and waste from garbage are all too evident.

Unsafe working conditions due to violation of safety norms cause accidents which may lead to permanent disability, and even death. No compensation is paid, as names of child workers are not entered when they are engaged in prohibited operations. Explosions in factories manufacturing firecrackers leading to deaths of child workers, reported from time to time in the media, indicate how blatantly the law is violated (*Statesman* 1995; Vidyasagar 1991). In one such instance, the National Human Rights Commission took suo moto cognizance of press reports about an explosion in a firecracker factory in Rohtak in May 1995 in which 23 persons, including six children, were killed. It found that the unlicensed factory was operating in violation of the law and ordered compensation to be paid to the next of kin (NHRC 1996).

It is unfortunate that the health hazards that are so evident, and which, apart from causing suffering to working children, curtail the working span of their lives (as also of adults), continue unabated. The Constitution of India has, under Article 24, prohibited the employment of children below the age of 14 years in hazardous employment, granting this protection to children as a Fundamental Right. The Committee on Child Labour (1979) underlined the need for more systematic efforts to identify hazardous occupations, detect occupational diseases, and treat them.

The Child Labour (Prohibition and Regulation) Act, 1986 prohibits the employment of children in certain occupations and processes listed in the Schedule to the Act. The CLPR Act under Section 5 has provided for the constitution of a Technical Advisory Committee to advise the government on the addition of occupations and processes in the Schedule of the Act. Though the word 'hazardous' does not find mention in the Act, and, hence, no definition or explanation is given in the legislation, the assumption is that the occupations and processes listed in the Schedule to the Act are of a hazardous nature. A March 1994 notification, which made additions to the Schedule to the Act, included in Part B 'hazardous processes' as defined in Section 2 (cb) of the Factories Act, 1948. The CLPR Act separately provides for the regulation of conditions of work in non-prohibited occupations and processes. These relate to hours and period of work, health and safety, and related matters. It does not consider long hours of work or extremely adverse working conditions, whatever be the occupation or process, as hazardous. The poor enforcement of the legislation makes matters worse. If to the hazards of the worksite are added the hazards of an unhealthy living environment, overcrowding, poor sanitation and hygiene, and malnutrition the toll taken on the health of the working children becomes all too evident. The steps taken in this regard since independence have in reality given little protection to the lives of millions of children working and living in conditions hazardous to their health, which will definitely curtail their working life and earnings, not to speak of their sufferings from ailments. Official agencies have been reluctant to take stern measures to eliminate the problem and to prosecute the offenders for blatant violation of the legislative provisions.

Legislative Action

The first legislation in the direction of prohibiting child labour was enacted in 1881 when the Factories Act was passed in the face of stiff opposition from mill owners. It fixed the minimum age of employment at 7 years in textile factories employing 100 or more persons, restricted the hours of work of children between 7 and 12 years of age to nine in a day, entitled them to four holidays in a month, and allowed them to be employed in only one factory on any one day. The Act is a benchmark in the matter of acceptance by the State of the principle that child labour is entitled to legal protection and the State has a fundamental duty in this regard. Successive amendments of the Act since 1891 have increased the scope, added provisions for improving working conditions, raised the minimum age of employment, restricted the hours of work, and brought more factories within the purview of the Act.

The beginning of the twentieth century witnessed new areas of industrial activity being brought under legislation that contained protective provisions pertaining to children. The Mines Act, 1901 was followed by legislation covering ports, plantations, merchant shipping, motor transport, shops and commercial establishments, and some other areas of industrial activity. Simultaneously, amendments were made in the existing legislations to provide better protection to workers.

The 1930s witnessed for the first time two specific legislations relating to child labour. The first had a limited, but very important, objective of eradicating the practice of pledging of labour of children, while the second sought to prohibit employment of children in some specified occupations.

The Children (Pledging of Labour) Act, 1933 was enacted following the Report of the Royal Commission on Labour, which pointed out the abusive presence of pledging of labour of children in several parts of the country and urged strong measures to curb the evil. The Act declared void any agreement to pledge the labour of a child under 15 years of age for any employment. It laid down a penalty (fine) for violation of the Act. The parent or guardian making the agreement to pledge the labour of a child, the person making the agreement with a parent or guardian, and the person employing a child whose labour had been pledged were liable for prosecution. The Act has, however, till date remained a mere piece of social legislation, a mute witness to the continuing abusive practice of pledging of labour of a growing number of children, as, evident from a number of empirical studies on child labour and media reports.

The second legislation exclusively for working children was the Employment of Children Act, 1938. It was enacted to implement the ILO Convention, adopted in 1937 by the International Labour Conference, which prohibited employment of children aged below 15 years in occupations connected with the transport of goods, passengers, or mails on railways and raised the minimum age for handling goods in docks to 15 years. The Act was amended in 1939 to include a subsection prohibiting the employment of children aged below 12 years (raised to 14 years in 1948 through an amendment) in any workshop wherein any of the processes listed in the Schedule to the Act were carried out. It, however, exempted a workshop wherein any process is carried out by the occupier with the aid of his family only and without employing hired labour, or any school established by or receiving assistance or recognition from a Provincial Government. It, thus, opened the door for employers to bypass the protection given by the law. Very weak enforcement made matters worse.

After independence, the protective role of the State was best expressed by the Constitution of India. Recognizing the right against exploitation as a Fundamental Right, Article 24 prohibits the employment of any child below the age of 14 years in any factory or mine or engaged in any other hazardous employment. As a Directive Principle of State Policy, the Constitution has provided that the State shall, in particular, direct its policy towards securing that the health and strength of workers, men and women, and the tender age of children are not abused, and that citizens are not forced by economic necessity to enter vocations unsuited to their age or strength [Article 39(e)]. Another Directive Principle of State Policy which has direct relevance to child labour requires that children are given opportunities to develop and to be protected against exploitation [Article 39(f)]. The Lok Sabha has passed the Constitution Amendment Bill to make the right to education a fundamental right, requiring the State to provide free and compulsory education to all children aged six to fourteen years.

An interesting legislative development having a direct bearing on child labour is the passage of the Compulsory Education Acts by several states in the 1960s. For instance, the Delhi Primary Education Act, 1960, under Section 14, prohibited persons from employing children in a manner which prevented them from attending school. It also laid down, under Section 19, a penalty for contravention of the provision. Almost similar provisions were made in the Compulsory Primary Education Acts enacted by other states (Andhra Pradesh, 1961; Assam, 1962; Gujarat 1961; Punjab, 1960; Rajasthan, 1964; West Bengal, 1963, to mention some). The provision has not been enforced.

The Children Act, 1960 had provided protection against exploitation of child employees, making the offence punishable with fine (Section 44). The Juvenile Justice Act, 1986, which repealed the Children Act, made the penal provision more stringent by providing for imposition of fine and imprisonment (Section 44). Apparently, the provision was not enforced either in the Children Act or the Juvenile Justice Act which took its place. The Juvenile Justice (Care and Protection of Children) Act, 2000 which replaced the Juvenile Justice Act, 1986 retained the provision but diluted it by limiting it to cases of hazardous employment.

The Bonded Labour System (Abolition) Act, 1976 prohibited forced labour, including that of children. The Act rendered void any current bonded obligation and freed every bonded labour from any obligation in this regard. The Act, like other legislations, is very poorly enforced. Bonded labour continues despite official claims to the contrary.

The Committee on Child Labour, commenting in 1979 on the state of enforcement of legislations to protect child labour, observed: 'There were practically no prosecutions in most parts of the country of any violation of existing laws pertaining to child labour. In one of the states it was pointed out with pride that the first prosecution ever launched by them was only in the International Year of the Child' (Ministry of Labour 1979).

In 1986, the Child Labour (Prohibition and Regulation) Act (CLPR) was passed, repealing the Employment of Children Act, 1938. The Act prohibits the employment of children aged less than 14 years in occupations and processes listed in the Schedule of the Act, and prescribes penalties (fine and/or imprisonment) for violation, which are more stringent than those of the 1938 Act. It regulates the conditions of work of children in employments in which they are not prohibited from working through provisions relating to hours and period of work, weekly holidays, health and safety, and some other matters. The provisions relating to prohibition of employment of children came into force with immediate effect, while those relating to the regulation of child labour were to come into effect from the date to be notified in this regard. Three processes were notified in August 1987 for the regulation of child labour in the two states listed against each process. A general notification on regulation of child labour throughout the country as per the provisions contained in Part III of the CLPR Act was made in May 1993. In occupations and processes that were not prohibited, permissible hours of work by children were not to exceed six hours between 8 a.m. and 6 p.m., with a day's weekly rest. Thus, it took more than six years since the passage of the Act to bring Part III into force to cover establishments in which none of the occupations and processes referred to in the Schedule listed under Section 3 of the Act were carried on. The ground reality is that even now different establishments remain as unregulated as before, bringing little relief or protection to the children employed therein.

The CLPR Act was criticized by NGOs and child labour activists as soon as it was passed in 1986. It was branded as a toothless piece of legislation as it fell far short of the demand for radical changes in the 1938 Act. The Act was viewed as a continuation of the policy to tolerate, and thus perpetuate, the practice of child labour, which amounted virtually to a negation of the provisions in the Constitution and the philosophy underlying them. One commentator described it as the most farcical piece of social legislation (*Economic and Political Weekly* 1986). The Act has been flawed for exempting, as in the Employment of Children Act, 1938, workshops wherein any process is carried on by the occupier with the aid of his family, thus continuing to provide a major loophole. The Act virtually limits itself to wage employment and makes the fallacious assumption that home based work in the prohibited occupations and processes listed in the schedule is not hazardous for children. The exemption paved the way to shift the site of production activities to the home from a workshop premise.

Another major criticism is that in employments not prohibited, no minimum age of employment has been prescribed. The view of the Committee on Child Labour that minimum age of 15 years should be prescribed for children for entering any employment was, thus, not accepted (Ministry of Labour 1979). On the contrary, the Act lowered the minimum age of employment in some of the existing legislations for conformity with the CLPR Act.

When passed in 1986, the Act contained virtually the same list of prohibited occupations and processes as the 1938 Act, indicating that in almost 50 years hardly any progress was made in adding to the list. The Committee on Child Labour (1979) had in fact earlier commented that 'a lot more was being ignored compared to what was being regulated so far by law'. However, after 1986, some additions were made, and in March 1994, through a notification, the employment of children was prohibited in hazardous processes as defined in Section 2 (cb) of the Factories Act and dangerous operations as notified in the rules made under Section 87 of the Factories Act. Apparently, no distinction was made between an adult and a child when deciding to add to the Schedule of occupations and processes. The Act, even at this stage, continued to leave out a number of occupations and processes in the unorganized manufacturing sector that were of a hazardous nature. Agricultural operations and processes such as, for instance, those involving use of pesticides and fertilizers or work on choppers and threshers were left out even though the Committee on Child Labour had drawn attention to the occupational health hazards and risks of injury arising therefrom. State governments do not have the power to add occupations or processes which should be prohibited in the state. The identification of additional hazardous occupations and processes has been slow, reflecting a rather casual approach though the

Committee on Child Labour had stressed the need for a more systematic effort for identification of hazardous occupations, detection of occupational diseases, and their treatment. Between 1986 and 1998, only nine occupations and processes were added in the Schedule. In a sudden burst of enthusiasm, a decision was taken to expand the list of prohibited occupations and processes, and through a notification in January 1999, the existing list was substantially expanded from the existing 25 to 64 (13 occupations and 51 processes), a belated action prompted partly to exhibit earnestness by responding to rising public opinion within the country and outside against child labour, and partly to deny a ground for the imposition of trade restrictions on India by developed countries on the plea of the use of child labour in the manufacture of products. In May 2001, six processes were added to the schedule to make a total of 13 prohibited occupations and 57 prohibited processes.

Some commentators are of the view that the penal provisions, even though more stringent than in the Employment of Children Act, do not go far enough to exercise a deterrent effect. They suggest that violations of the CLPR Act should be made a cognizable offence; there should be a specific penal provision against use of false age certificate, and burden of proof in regard to the age of the employed child should be put on the employer. Also, culpability of the parent or guardian who often plays a prominent role in the employment of children should not be ignored.

The CLPR Act, even if some teeth are missing, would have provided some relief if it was enforced with a reasonable degree of commitment. Like its predecessor, the Employment of Children Act, 1938, the current Act has been largely ineffective due to poor enforcement by the states for whom child labour and its eradication has low priority. This is evident from the inadequate staff sanctioned for inspection and the manner of their deployment. Prosecutions under the Act for violation of provisions prohibiting employment are few; prosecutions for violation of the provisions relating to regulation of employment are rare. This clearly indicates the poor functioning of the enforcement machinery despite rampant violation of the provisions of the Act throughout the country, highlighted by empirical studies as well as the media. Even when inspections are made, advance information gets leaked so that child workers are either asked not to come on that day, are made to disappear at the time the inspecting staff arrive, or are passed off as children who have brought food for adult workers. Sometimes, the employers explain the presence of children by claiming them as their own or that of relatives, who have come to play in the premises. Concealment of the actual age of the child worker is common. They are tutored in advance to state on inquiry by the inspecting staff that they are over 14 years of age. Such explanations find ready acceptance for a consideration, as employers like to keep the inspecting staff happy. Informal understandings between the inspectors and the employers result in non-interference in the way the unit is run (Sekar 1993; Ghosh 1997; Gupta 1994).

Parents of the children who are employed cooperate with the employer to evade the law rather than help the inspecting staff. Independent witnesses to help the prosecution case are not readily available due to the general tendency to keep away from such matters. In fact, people tend to sympathize with child workers and the situation of their families. Trade unions have shown little interest in tackling the problem. The state machinery has not tried to seek the help and cooperation of NGOs to make enforcement a joint endeavour.

The low priority which enforcement occupies is evident from the fact that data on violation of the CLPR Act are not published, probably also not compiled. Partial information available indicates that the conviction rate is very poor (Varma 1994). Inspectors do not have proper knowledge or training on matters relating to various sections of the Act, the legal requirements that have to be met, and the procedures that have necessarily to be followed for launching prosecution. Cases are lost because of procedural lapses and weak presentations. Even when convictions take place, the penalties imposed are not high enough to act as a deterrent. The attitude of the officials entrusted with the responsibility of enforcement of the Act determines how seriously they apply themselves to the job. Quite a number among them lack the strength of conviction about their role, and feel that children from poor families have to work to supplement the meagre family income. They, therefore, do not see anything abnormal about child labour. On the contrary, they view directives from the top as not being based on an understanding of the ground realities.

The lethargic performance of the executive organ of the State has to some extent been compensated by relief from the judiciary. The Supreme Court has responded to writ petitions of public interest to protect the interests of child workers in the match and fireworks industry and beedi industry. In a comprehensive judgement delivered on 12 December 1996 in response to a writ petition, the Supreme Court gave specific directions to the government for the protection, welfare, and rehabilitation of child workers. These include:

- Survey for identification of working children within six months;
- Withdrawal of child workers in hazardous employment and ensuring their education;
- Regulating hours of work of children in non-hazardous occupations, so that their working hours do not exceed six per day and education for at least two hours is ensured, the entire expenditure on which is to be borne by the employer;
- Contribution at Rs. 20,000 per child by the offending employer to a Welfare Fund;
- Employment to one adult member of the family of a child withdrawn from work, failing which the appropriate government would make a contribution of Rs. 5,000 to the Welfare Fund in each case;
- Financial assistance to families of children withdrawn from work to be paid as long as the child is actually sent to school.

The Supreme Court judgement does not alter the dual policy of the State in the matter of employment of children, viz., prohibiting it in hazardous employments and regulating it in others. It does not direct the State to lay down a minimum age of employment in occupations and processes not prohibited, not even in the case of wage employment, but does give direction to the State in the matter of education of working children in employments not prohibited but regulated, requiring the employer to bear the expenditure. It also directs the undertaking of welfare measures for working children and their families.

The attempt by the central government to get the survey done for identification of working children through the state Labour Directorates yielded poor figures as these agencies are ill-equipped for this function. Even the administration which normally tries to play down the seriousness of the problem found it difficult to accept them. Fresh attempts have, therefore, been initiated. The extent to which court directives get implemented and relief provided to the children will only be known in the coming years when independent observers give a feedback.

OTHER AREAS OF STATE ACTION

For almost a hundred years, beginning in 1875 when a Commission was appointed in Bombay to consider various aspects relating to labour in factories, including the employment of children, to the 1970s, the primary role of the State has been legislative cum administrative. In the performance of these functions, the government has been assisted by Commissions and Committees constituted from time to time. Among the more important of them after independence are the Committee for the Preparation of Programme for Children (1968), National Commission on Labour (1969), the Committee on Child Labour (1979), and the National Commission on Rural Labour (1991). While making important recommendations for tackling the problem of child labour, these Commissions/ Committees brought out the interrelationship between child labour, poverty, education facilities, and support services.

The 1980s witnessed several administrative actions in response to internal demands, global efforts spearheaded by the International Labour Organisation, and strong advocacy by UN agencies and NGOs for determined action. A number of standing bodies were constituted by the Government of India. Among these are the Central Advisory Board on Child Labour, the Child Labour Technical Advisory Committee set up under Section 5 of the Child Labour (Prohibition and Regulation) Act 1986, and the National Authority for the Elimination of Child Labour.

In 1987, the Government of India came out with a National Policy on Child Labour (NPCL) which accepted, even though it did not explicitly state so, that in the context of the current socio-economic realities, child labour cannot be prohibited in every sector of the economy. It advocated protection and regulation. It called for focusing attention on sectors or establishments where children are deployed on wage or quasi-wage employment outside the family, as it felt it was more likely that exploitation of children took place in such situations. It announced the commitment of the State to implement specially targeted development programmes to tackle the problem of child labour, thus indicating a shift from an almost exclusively protective cum regulatory role to a protective, regulatory cum developmental role. The Policy has three components:

- Legislative plan of action.
- Welfare and development programmes for the benefit of child labour and their families.

- Project based plan of action.

The legislative plan of action stresses enforcement of the CLPR Act, 1986 and the addition, from time to time, to the list of occupations and processes given in its Schedule. It also proposes amendment to the Minimum Wages Act, so that children are paid the same as adults, removing thereby the economic incentive for employing child labour. However, even though almost 15 years have passed, the amendment is yet to be carried out.

The second component of the NPCL stresses focusing of programmes of education, health and nutrition, and poverty alleviation so that benefits accrue to child labour and their families, and improve their socio-economic status. However, little has been achieved in actual practice in this direction and different sectoral schemes continue to be implemented following their own trajectory.

The project based plan of action is focused on specific sectors in which the incidence of child labour is very high. It envisages an integrated programme package, covering enforcement of legislation; poverty alleviation to benefit the families of working children; education of children (formal and non-formal); adult education programmes for parents of working children; increase of public awareness about child labour; and opening of special schools which will provide education and vocational training, supplementary nutrition, stipends, and health care. National Child Labour Projects (NCLP) are funded by the Ministry of Labour, Government of India. In 1988, eight NCLPs were sanctioned in different parts of the country, one for each type of production activity in which a large number of children are employed such as, for instance, match making in Sivakasi, slate pencil making in Mandsaur, lock making in Aligarh, hand woven carpets in Bhadohi, and brassware in Moradabad. The number of projects sanctioned has increased substantially in subsequent years, totalling 96 projects in December 2000 in 13 states. In each project area, NCLP schools have been opened for children weaned away from employment. The schools provide general education and vocational training. Each child is given a stipend of Rs. 100 per month, supplementary nutrition, and health care. By December 2000, NCLPs had set up 3,090 special schools with 181,004 children. The projects follow a schematic pattern in regard to items for which funds are given.

In addition to the NCLPs, 54 voluntary agencies were given grants-in-aid in 2000–1 for programmes of non-formal education, supplementary nutrition, health care and vocational training. A Child Labour Action and Support Programme (CLASP), aided by the Government of Germany, was also implemented for four years from 1992 for supporting on-going activities under the NPCL.

The International Programme on the Elimination of Child Labour (IPECL) was launched in India in 1992. It covered, apart from direct support programmes for rehabilitation of child labour, activities relating to research and training, advocacy, institution building, mobilization of support of trade unions and employers, and information, education, and communication activities. During the period 1992–2000, 156 programmes were taken up to benefit 90,574 children.

National Child Labour projects of the Ministry of Labour, even though they cover only about 1 per cent of child workers in the country, have provided some relief. However, the concept is flawed. A project approach usually implies a life cycle of 3 to 5 years and assumes that within this period the factors which push children into employment will have been neutralized, a very naïve assumption. The strategy of starting a parallel school system at almost three times the cost per pupil of the normal school system is unsustainable and is an expensive alternative. Attempts to mainstream children at the end of their schooling in the special school have met with limited success. Even when, with the District Collector's intervention, children have been admitted in the normal school after finishing at the special school, the drop-out rate has been very high because of the inability to cope with the syllabus and the non-availability of stipends. The concept of special schools does not tackle the demand side of child labour. The supply side is also imperfectly tackled because the place of the child weaned from employment to bring him to school is taken up by another child. Juyal's study of child labour in the carpet industry in Mirzapur-Bhadohi belt which also covered NCLPs reported, for instance, family child labour being replaced by hired child labour (Juyal 1993).

Role of International Agencies and Non-governmental Institutions

The State alone cannot solve a complex and massive socio-economic problem like child labour, but it has to be the major player in several critical areas. Legislation and its enforcement are essentially State functions. Alleviation of mass poverty, universalization of education, and programmes for the removal of child labour throughout the country require funds which primarily have to come from the government. Eradication of child labour, however, requires co-ordinated effort of the State and other agencies. The campaign has been facilitated and strengthened by the role played by international agencies, particularly the International Labour Organisation (ILO), and institutions of civil society such as voluntary organizations, academic institutions, trade unions, employers' associations, corporate bodies, and the media.

The International Labour Organisation has been at the forefront of global endeavours to eliminate child labour in different countries. As early as 1919, it adopted a Convention laying down the minimum age of employment in industry (Convention no. 5). In 1973, the ILO adopted Convention no. 138 on minimum ages for admission to employment, which required countries to undertake measures for the abolition of child labour. The ILO also adopted Recommendation no. 146 to supplement the Convention and apply its provisions in conjunction with it. In between, the ILO adopted several Conventions covering employment of children and young persons in specific areas of activity. The close of the twentieth century witnessed the adoption in 1999 by the ILO of Convention no. 182 on the prohibition of, and immediate action for, the elimination of the worst forms of child labour. It simultaneously adopted Recommendation no. 190 to supplement the Convention and act in conjunction with it. Recommendation no. 190 indicates the programmes, identifies types of child labour at risk, defines hazardous work, and gives suggestions on implementation.

India has participated in the activities of the ILO and in the conferences and seminars organized by it on child labour. It has ratified ILO Convention nos. 6, 15, 16, 90, and 123 pertaining to employment of children, which are specific in regard to coverage and sector of activity. It has been, however, slow to ratify the major Conventions pertaining to minimum age of employment, though it has endorsed the spirit behind them and has progressively undertaken some legislative, administrative, and developmental measures to prohibit and regulate child labour. The Minimum Age (Industry) Convention no. 5 of 1919 was ratified only in 1955 after three and a half decades. Convention no. 138 of 1973 on minimum ages for admission to employment is comprehensive in nature, and is yet to be ratified. Convention no. 182 is likely to face stiffer resistance in ratification since it, too, is very comprehensive and, additionally, covers persons below 18 years of age, and not just below 14 years of age laid down in Indian laws when defining child workers.

In recent years, UNICEF has been taking considerable interest in the fight against child labour. Both ILO and UNICEF are providing funding support for research, advocacy, training, workshops, sensitization, and project activities to help build a favourable climate in the fight against child labour.

The last two decades have witnessed the growth of voluntary organizations working in the field of child labour, a development facilitated by the promotive role played by international agencies active in the prevention of child labour and the support they have provided for research, seminars/workshops, documentation, dissemination of information, and child labour projects. Funding support from agencies within the country and outside have enabled voluntary organizations to strengthen their work in the area of child labour. The government, as a matter of policy, has sought the participation of voluntary organizations and given grants for the implementation of child labour projects. The bulk of the assistance was for National Child Labour Projects, in which the services provided are predetermined and to that extent, the voluntary organizations performed an agency function. In the case of programmes assisted under the general scheme of grant-in-aid, assistance was given for projects formulated within the broad framework of the general scheme of grant-in-aid.

The core areas of interest and activities of voluntary organizations show a wide variation. Some voluntary organizations are primarily advocacy groups agitating against child labour, particularly its exploitative forms. They have pursued a multi-pronged approach through a range of strategies which include organizing marches and other forms of agitation in full public view; negotiations in which child workers have also participated; mobilization of public opinion and support of eminent persons; networking; forging alliances; and interacting with political parties and other groups, so that eradication of child labour figures high on the agenda. For some non-governmental organizations, the main areas of interest are research, documentation, holding of seminars and workshops for discussion and debate, and dissemination of information. A large number of organizations are involved in the direct delivery of services targeted at child workers and their families to wean children away from employment and put them in school; they also interact with working children and their parents, and try to convince them of how important it is for the child to attend school.

Non-governmental organizations in developed countries active on issues of child labour have been pressing their governments to impose a ban on import of goods in the manufacturing of which child labour has been used. Visits have been made by officials and non-officials from the developed countries to check the ground reality and to interact with local organizations and the official agencies. The apprehensions have led to the evolving of acceptable methods of certification by organizations of exporters that no child labour has been used. A welcome fallout has been the realization of the urgent need for more action to contain the problem.

The involvement of NGOs in combating child labour has provided some relief and rehabilitation to children. Their innovativeness, commitment, flexibility, and ability to respond to local needs and deliver services more effectively at a lower cost have been their strength. However, the uneven spread, localized areas of influence, limited scale of operations, and difficulties in recruiting and retaining trained manpower have not enabled them to achieve their full potential. The expansion and sustainability of services and other activities by NGOs have to a large extent depended upon the extent to which they could mobilize funds from the government and donor agencies in India and abroad, and their own ability to raise funds. Unfortunately, some organizations, with influence in the corridors of power and contacts with donor agencies abroad, have received grants but have shown an unsatisfactory record of service and utilization of funds, which has hurt the image of the voluntary sector, emphasizing the importance of much greater transparency in funding, delivery of services, accountability and participation of the community. These are, however, aberrations and NGOs have been playing a vital complementary role in addressing the problem. A large number of them have innovative achievements to their credit.

Universities and research institutions have developed an interest on child labour issues and conducted research studies, mainly from the mid-1980s onwards, when funds started becoming available from national and international sources. The research output has strengthened the database. Findings of studies sponsored by government agencies, particularly evaluation studies, rarely get disseminated. A large number are not even available for consultation on the plea that these are for internal use, thus effectively blocking useful feedback on programme implementation which would be of use to planners, research scholars, and development agencies.

A welcome development in recent years is the interest shown by trade unions on issues concerning child workers and the launching of some programmes in this area. This has been facilitated by the organization of workshops for trade union leaders, and their participation in conferences and seminars. Employers' associations have also shown interest in tackling the problem. Some industrial houses and corporate bodies have not only supported the cause against child labour, but have also provided funds for projects. Endorsements by eminent persons of the campaign against child labour have helped to raise funds and draw public attention to the sufferings caused to child workers.

The media, both print and electronic, have contributed to the battle being waged against child labour by giving visibility to the problem. Television has brought the stark reality of their existence to the homes of large segments of the population, hitherto largely unaware of the sufferings of child workers at a tender age. Features on child labour now appear at fairly regular intervals. These have graphically shown how children continue to be employed in adverse working and employment conditions in poor physical environment, even in hazardous employments prohibited by the Child Labour (Prohibition and Regulation) Act of 1986. The coverage of child labour by the media has helped funding agencies both in India and abroad to include child labour as a priority area of concern.

SUMMING UP

Acceptance by the State of its protective role towards child labour dates back to 1881 when the first Factories Act was passed. Subsequent legislations and amendments to cover more industrial categories and specific legislations pertaining to child labour reflect the adoption of an approach of gradualness in expanding this protective role. The basic objective was to prohibit the employment of children below a prescribed age in specified industries and to regulate the employment of working children in matters such as maximum hours of work, time of the day when children could work, weekly rest, safety, and related matters, in order to soften the adverse impact of employment. The Constitution of India reaffirmed the protective role by giving a Fundamental Right to children against exploitation through Article 24 which prohibits the employment of a child below 14 years of age in any factory or mine or their engagement in any other hazardous employment. The protective role was expanded through the Directive Principles of State Policy laid down by Article 39 (e) and (f), while the developmental role found expression in Article 45 which stated that all children up to the age of 14 years should be provided free and compulsory education.

Child labour has virtually been eradicated from the organized sector of production, partly due to legislation, but also partly due to transformation of production systems and processes which require skilled adult manpower. However, with respect to production activities in the unorganized sector, the problem continues to be acute due to very poor enforcement of legislations and the inability to enrol and retain a large number of children in school. The labour of children continues to be pledged despite a specific Act passed in 1933 prohibiting it. The Employment of Children Act, 1938 was very poorly implemented till the date of its repeal in 1986. The Committee on Child Labour very aptly summed up the position till 1979 when it stated that the situation was characterized by continuing drift with little evidence of change since 1931 when the Royal Commission on Labour submitted its Report (Ministry of Labour 1979). Children continue to suffer in hazardous employments, even in occupations and processes prohibited by the Child Labour (Prohibition and Regulation) Act, 1986, which till 1998 was able to list only 25 of these. In January 1999, 39 occupations and processes were added. In May 2001, there was a further addition of 7 processes making a total of 70 prohibited occupations and processes (13 occupations and 57 processes). The employment of children in non-prohibited occupations continued to enjoy unregulated status, despite the provision in the 1986 Act, till the notification of May 1993. Even after this notification, there has hardly been any enforcement of the regulatory provisions or convictions for violation.

The importance of following a strategy not limited to prohibition and regulation of employment of children was suggested by the Royal Commission on Labour (1931). The National Commission on Labour (1969), the Committee for the Preparation of a Programme for Children (1968), the Committee on Child Labour (1979), and the National Commission on Rural Labour (1991) stressed the need for a broader strategy covering education and other development measures. This approach has also found reflection in the National

Policy on Child Labour (1987). The developmental dimensions have found expression in the launching of National Child Labour Projects, assistance to non-governmental organizations, and directives to different ministries for coordination and convergence of programmes in areas where the incidence of child labour is greater. These have, however, had rather limited impact, apart from the problem of covering only a small percentage of child workers and the exorbitant costs of a parallel system of education in the National Child Labour Projects. A project approach is indicative of the unrealistic assumption that a problem as complex as child labour can be eradicated within the short time frame of a project's life cycle. The state governments have depended on central funding and initiatives, and have not come up with their own programmes of action reflecting the very low priority they accord to the tackling of child labour.

The failure of the public sector elementary education system in enrolling and retaining the child in school, and helping the child to acquire some level of learning which will be useful, has been a major contributory factor in the perpetuation of the problem. The poor physical infrastructure of schools and their dismal functioning in large parts of the country contribute towards keeping the child away from school. Any long-term solution to the problem of child labour will be possible only when children are inside the school and not outside it. Whether compulsory education will be a practicable proposition as is the current view of policy makers, remains to be seen particularly in the context of extremely poor enforcement of social legislations. Unfortunately, in this area as in other social sectors, rhetoric has not been matched by performance.

Even after five decades of independence, the Government of India has not prescribed a minimum age for entry into any type of employment. It has done so only in the case of certain categories of economic activity listed in the Schedule to the Child Labour (Prohibition and Regulation) Act of 1986 and in other labour legislations. For the overwhelming majority of working children, there is no minimum age for wage employment in the sectors not covered by labour legislation. In other words, the State has tacitly recognized employment of children, whatever the age, as a current socio-economic reality. This is clearly reflected in the National Policy on Child Labour (1987). The Government has not accepted the recommendation of the Committee on Child Labour (1979) and the National Commission on Rural Labour (1991) in this regard, nor the recommendation of the United Nations Convention on the Rights of the Child. The Government of India has also not ratified the ILO Convention no. 138, adopted in 1973 on minimum ages for admission to employment. Convention no. 182, adopted by the ILO in 1999, is likely to meet the same fate.

The protective role pursued by the State has, thus, not extended to prohibiting all forms of child labour. The official approach has been to move ahead only gradually in the eradication of child labour through a mix of prohibition in some segments and regulation in others. Even if all forms of child labour were prohibited, the poor record of implementation of legislations shows that mere passing of Acts is not a solution. A wide range of developmental, rehabilitative, and protective measures are necessary, particularly a good functional elementary education system, if the coming generations of children are to escape from the hazards of toiling very early in life.

The third organ of the State, viz., the judiciary, has responded to public interest litigation and given elaborate directions to the executive for tackling the problem of child labour, a role which has been widely acclaimed. It remains to be seen to what extent success will be achieved in carrying them out. If the role of two organs of the State, the legislature and the executive is analysed, it becomes evident that while the legislative wing has enacted laws, which if properly enforced would have brought some relief, the executive wing has not achieved much in the last five decades. In fact, the first four decades after independence could be characterized as a prolonged period of dormancy, as the problem of child labour received little funding support for tackling the problem in a developmental perspective as recommended by the various Committees/Commissions, and the laws were hardly enforced. The fifth decade has seen a spate of announcements, declarations, and conferences, a sudden increase in funding, and a burst of activities, but has not produced a visible impact on the problem. The demand and supply factors which give rise to the problem of child labour, and sustain it, have not been satisfactorily tackled. The five and a half decades since independence have, thus, seen millions of children of successive generations toil in workplaces, instead of studying in school and realizing their potential for growth and development.

On 15 August 1994, in his address to the nation from the Red Fort, the Prime Minister declared the resolve of the government to free two million children in hazardous employment by the year

2000. This was described by the Secretary to the Ministry of Labour as a display of 'rare political will and commitment', 'a splendid initiative', and a 'truly momentous and historic event'. The year came and passed like any other year. There has not been much achievement on the ground so far. Pronouncements, declarations need to be backed by effective implementation of policies and programmes.

5 Other Disadvantaged Children in Need of Care and Protection

A large number of disadvantaged children in especially difficult circumstances need protection, care, and rehabilitative services for their growth and development. Unfortunately, statistics are not available on the magnitude of the problem in different areas, the nature of difficult circumstances, causative factors, and the extent of deprivation of such children. However, the enormity of the problems faced cannot be doubted in a country where more than one-fourth of the population lives below the poverty line, natural calamities take their toll, unemployment exists on a large-scale, the incidence of illiteracy, malnutrition, unsatisfactory housing, and poor health is large, the state of public social services is very unsatisfactory, and there is little social security coverage for the masses. It cannot be denied that large numbers of children are deprived of opportunities for growth and development. Furthermore, erosion of values relating to the acceptance of obligations by the extended family when the child becomes vulnerable due to the death of a parent, abandonment, long illness of parent, maltreatment, acute poverty, or pathogenic home environment, has made the present state and future of children placed in circumstances such as these very difficult. In recent years, terrorism, insurgency, and communal conflicts have devastated families and traumatized the children. Only a small number of children in especially difficult circumstances are currently covered by welfare services. The rest lead a very marginalized existence.

The categories of children in need of care and protection dealt with in this chapter are:

- Street children
- Children in conflict with law
- Sexually abused children
- Other vulnerable children such as beggars, destitutes, children of prostitutes, children affected by AIDS, drugs, and armed conflicts.

CHILDREN ON THE STREET, OF THE STREET

The presence of street children in urban areas is not a new phenomenon. They have been a part of the urban scene mainly due to unabated migration from villages to cities in search of a livelihood. Acute poverty of their families has denied them a proper shelter, forcing them to squat on public land on pavements, below flyovers, at or near railway stations, bus stations, and other public places. A non-supportive social, economic, and administrative structure does not provide the children with opportunities for growth and development and a normal childhood, and has pushed the children to street life. Family breakdown and weakening support within the family, an increasing phenomenon in urban slums, has also been a contributing factor. The family tends to wilt under the stress of poverty, while problems of alcoholism, drug addiction, unemployment, chronic illness, desertion, and disharmony often act to weaken the emotional and economic support which the child receives within the family resulting in the family's dysfunctioning and weakening of a caring relationship. Street children are, thus, a living and sordid symbol of urban malaise, their growing numbers giving the problem a high degree of visibility in cities where squatter settlements as well as the numbers of such children are mushrooming.

The term street children is of recent origin and derives its name because of the place the street occupies in the lives of some children and the special relationships that develop around it. The word street has acquired a wider connotation to include public places other than streets, such as pavements, markets, commercial centres, road flyovers, street crossings, car parking areas, railway stations, bus stations, public parks, places of tourist interest, entertainment centres, and the like. Street children received a distinct identity globally when UNICEF categorized them as a separate category under the broad classification of Children in Especially Difficult Circumstances (CEDC) and the UNICEF Executive Board approved a resolution in 1986 directing UNICEF to play a major role in this sphere. In the same year, CHILD HOPE was founded to serve as a new inter-NGO partnership on behalf of the world's street children. These international initiatives provided the base for considerable advocacy work to draw the attention of governments, NGOs, and society at large to the problem of street children and the need for separate programmes for their protection, care, and development.

CATEGORIES

Street children comprise three subcategories:

- Children on the street. These are children who make a living on the street, spend time there aimlessly, or hang around lazily, usually in the company of peers. They live with their families. The children return to their families at the end of the day. They lead a marginal existence in the city's slums and squatter settlements.
- Children who seek the street as their place of shelter, source of livelihood, and place of companionship. They have only occasional contacts with their families for a variety of reasons—poverty, broken home, maltreatment, neglect, and abuse. Such children are victims of the failure of the family to provide protection and care, and meet the child's development needs.
- Children who are on their own and for whom the street is their place of shelter, place for earning a livelihood for meeting survival needs, and place of companionship. These children have little contact with their families. Some have run away from home because of abject poverty and intolerable home situation due to ill-treatment, rejection, neglect, and physical and emotional abuse, or because of death of parents, family breakdown, or destitution. A small number in this subcategory (almost always boys) come to the city to support their impoverished families at home; they retain links with their families in the village. The situation of single migrant children is more difficult due to the unfamiliar environment in which they find themselves, virtually no contacts, no experience of city life, and little support from peer group or others.

All the above categories have inadequate protection, guidance, nurturing care of adults, and help to meet their developmental needs, the last subcategory being the most deprived. They share certain common problems arising from acute poverty, adverse physical and social environment, and a constant struggle to meet survival needs. Their distinct categorization helps in the designing of programmes, because it suggests intervention starting from a place of congregation loosely referred to as street where the children spend a considerable period of time.

SOCIO-ECONOMIC CHARACTERISTICS

Figures of the number of street children in India are not available. The magnitude is, however, large enough to have high visibility. Their growing number is becoming an important social concern. A study of working and street children of Delhi estimated 100,000 street children (Panicker and Nangia 1992). A Bangalore study estimated 45,000 street children in the city while a study carried out in Madras estimated 25,000 street children (Reddy 1992; Arimpoor 1992). According to NGOs working in these cities, the figures are underestimates and actual numbers are much higher.

Towards the late 1980s, studies on street children were conducted in Delhi, Bombay, Calcutta, Bangalore, Madras, Kanpur, Indore, and a few other cities (Arimpoor 1992; Ghosh 1992; Pandey 1991; Panicker and Nangia 1992; Panicker and Desai 1993; Phillips 1992; Reddy 1992). Although the studies had common sponsorship, the absence of a common methodology, framework, and tabulation plan makes comparison of findings difficult, specially in regard to the statistical dimensions. Some broad features, however, emerge which are not very dissimilar from the situation in other countries, though the statistical dimensions show variation.

Most street children of the first subcategory are with their families after the day's activities which are usually carried out with the knowledge and support of their families. Sometime, the child and the family together pursue their livelihood on the street. The Delhi and Bombay studies reported about three-fourths children staying with their families, while the Kanpur study reported 84 per cent such children. Less than 10 per cent children were found living alone (D'Lima and Gosalia 1989; Pandey 1991; Panicker and Nangia 1992). However, a higher percentage of such children are found in certain specific locations of cities. For instance, a survey in 1989 in Calcutta covering 200 street children found that 44 per cent were living in and around Sealdah station and were without families (CINI 1996).

Most street children do not fall in the category of fresh migrants. They have been in the city for a number of years. Most of them came with their families and are still coping with poverty. The Bombay study, for instance, reported only 29.6 per cent children as having migrated within three years (D'Lima and Gosalia 1989). While most migrants are from districts within the state, a sizeable number is also from neighbouring states, and some are even from across the border, mainly Bangladesh. Most street children are above 6 years of age, the majority above 8 years of age. The Kanpur study showed that only 5 per cent were less than 6 years of age (Pandey 1991). The Bangalore study found 20 per cent in the age group 6–10 years, and 79 per cent in the age group 11–15 years (Reddy 1992). The Indore study reported three-fourths children in the age group 10 years and above (Phillips 1992). The younger the child, the more likely was he to be in the company of a older sibling, relation, or parent.

An overwhelming majority of street children are boys. For instance, the Kanpur study reported only 8.6 per cent girls (Pandey 1991). An important socio-cultural factor explaining the sex differential is that boys move about freely while girls live in a protected environment; also, their movements are restricted. They do only some types of work. Girls rarely work alone and are usually in the company of an adult relative, sibling, or friend, and that, too, near the place where they live.

More than half the street children have had no schooling. Most of those who went to school dropped out and have not even completed the primary stage. Few are currently in school. Girls have a much lower literacy rate than boys. The Bombay study on street children, for instance, reported 54.5 per cent as having never enrolled and only 11.4 per cent as continuing their education (D'Lima and Gosalia 1989). The Indore study reported two-thirds as illiterate, the incidence being much higher in the case of girls (Phillips 1992).

The majority of street children work for a living to supplement the family income and are a part of the city's economy. Their work is irregular and is in the informal sector. The jobs they do show a wide range depending on their availability—collecting scrap, carrying load, vending, shoe-shining, cleaning cars, and doing other sundry jobs that require hardly any skills. Sometimes, they combine more than one kind of work during the same day. The work also changes to suit seasonal variations. Their working hours show a wide fluctuation, some jobs being possible only in the early morning or evening. As a class, street children are not prone to crime, though a small number may engage on some occasions in deviant activities. A small percentage of children, particularly the very young, make a living through begging, often at the behest of their families, at street crossings, markets, and other public places. Some are vagrants moving aimlessly. Street children have very limited occupational mobility, because of lack of education, skills, training, and guidance, and have no occupational choice. The future holds no promises for them. They are thus children without the joys of childhood, a favourable living environment, or opportunities for preparing for a promising and stable adult life.

The earnings of street children vary from Rs. 25 to Rs. 75 per day, but this is uncertain. There are too many children chasing too few jobs, some in competition with adults or older children, in which the younger children are at a disadvantage due to poorer physical strength. Those who are on their own tend to spend what they earn. Those who live alone do not like to keep money on their person as they are in constant fear of the money being stolen or forcibly taken away by the older boys or the police.

Street children are engaged in a survival battle, and that too, for a virtually subhuman existence. Since the environment surrounding their life does not have a human face, they develop the resourcefulness, self-reliance, and survival skills for coping with an unfriendly and unsupportive street existence, a function which should have been the responsibility of adults. The worst placed are those who do not have families or have very loose contacts with them and are, therefore, unprotected. However, they value considerably their independence, their earnings, and life without any set parameters. Those who have a shelter prefer not to be in institutions and follow a regimen. They welcome various support services.

The nutrition and health status of street children is poor due to a combination of individual and environmental factors. Important among the individual-centred factors are poverty, ignorance, illiteracy, dietary inadequacies, poor personal hygiene due to absence of bathing and washing facilities, and non-availability of medical care when illness strikes or in case of accidents and injuries. Prominent among the environmental factors are poor shelter, offering virtually no protection against rain or cold, bad environmental sanitation and hygiene which constantly exposes them to infections, pollution, and unsafe drinking water.

Street children are unprotected and exposed to hazards and risks such as physical abuse and extortion by older children, adults, and local *dadas* (bullies). Sometimes, there is violence over territorial rights, with local toughs demanding a share of their meagre earnings. Some children have perforce to seek the support and protection of local gangs. For carrying out vending or other activities at place not permissible, street children have to give a cut to the police and municipal staff. They are occasionally harassed by police, thrashed, put in the lock-up for several days, and robbed of their money when there is a theft in the area or a report of some illegal activity. Children practising their vocation on road crossings (selling flowers, newspapers, and sundry articles of daily use), or engaged in begging at traffic crossings when vehicles stop at signals, expose themselves to the risk of accidents.

Street children are exposed to the risk of sexual abuse. A study which specifically investigated the problem found some of the younger boys to be sexually abused by the older boys, either by cajoling or by coercion. Such children accept the relationship of being a passive partner because of the protection it provides and a caring relationship it promises. Sometimes there is no choice in the matter. Street children become aware of sex by virtue of close physical proximity while sleeping; curiosity which leads to exploring and fondling of private parts and sexual stimulation. Sooner or later the older street boys begin a heterosexual relationship with sex workers or with female children (Nayyar and Rajasekhar 1998).

Girls are the most unprotected among street children and are more vulnerable to physical and sexual abuse, especially those who have crossed puberty. They have no guidance on the changes that take place with puberty and on sexual matters, and also, virtually no privacy. They are afraid of molestation, and have to put up with dirty looks and suggestive gestures. Some girls get sexually abused by family members, relatives, and adults whom they trust. Quite a few are forcibly abused by local toughs, either for their own sexual gratification or that of others. Some studies have reported that the actual number of girls who made a mention of sexual abuse was small, may be because this was not specifically probed (CINI 1996; Pandey 1991; Panicker and Nangia 1992; Reddy 1992). Some have, however, reported a much wider incidence (Mehra 1996; Panicker 1998).

Parents of street children who have families are mainly in low paid unskilled jobs or in self-employment. Their earnings are uncertain, and the socio-economic status of the families is low. Parents exercise little control over their children's activities or mode of living. A fairly large number of families are female headed, due to death, or more frequently, desertion by the husband. Some families have to put up with alcoholism of the father and domestic violence. Most children are, however, emotionally attached to their mothers and siblings, particularly the sister.

While most street children are law abiding, the presence of a deviant role model, lure of easy money offered by adults engaged in criminal activities, and the sheer need for survival forces some of them into activities like pushing drugs and contraband. Some also get apprehended for delinquent acts (Panicker and Nangia 1992). Street children (boys) acquire the habit of smoking, drinking, and occasional gambling at a very young age. Some of the earlier studies on street children reported a low incidence of drug abuse. A later study covering Bombay, Calcutta, Delhi, and Hyderabad, which specially focused on drug abuse and risk behaviour related to HIV/AIDS and sexually transmitted diseases (STD) among street children, reported that drug abuse is widespread and increasing. Unsafe sex was also found to be common (Mehra 1996). A study in Delhi, too, reported a high incidence of drug abuse, mainly alcohol. About 50 per cent of the 100 sample children reported having experimented with *charas* (a drug prepared from the hemp plant cannabis sativa) and about 10 per cent having used heroin at least once (Panicker 1998).

Street children of a particular area tend to develop a group identity, a bond and a spirit of camaraderie which meets, even if imperfectly, their emotional and psychosocial needs. Sometimes, the bonding is provided by a physical relationship. However, this is rarely stable.

Street children hardly have a status in the larger society. Their existence is tolerated but not trusted as their abode and background are not known. Most city dwellers would prefer the children to be out of their sight, as they feel uncomfortable when the children are around and even consider their presence as undesirable for themselves as well as their children. Shopkeepers view them as a nuisance and potential pilferers, government officials consider them a headache, while the police look at them with suspicion. Street children have, thus, not only a deprived but also a marginalized existence, alienated from the mainstream of life. They are in dire need of caring relationships, opportunities, and support which will give them access to social services to help them acquire education, skills, and a positive approach to life.

POLICIES AND PROGRAMMES

In the first four decades of development planning, street children did not figure in the plan documents and the schemes of the central and state governments as a separate target group needing specific services. They were subsumed under the broad plan category of children in need of care and protection. In actual practice, however, few services reached them. Some non-governmental organizations (NGOs) did cater to small groups of such children as well as others from slums. There was, however, little cognizance among policy makers of the special problems of street children and of their needs arising from a precarious existence on the streets in an unprotective and unsupportive environment. If anything, there was ignorance about their real state. They were widely believed to be abandoned, homeless, and vagrant children. Some even viewed them with apprehension as a public safety concern and an avoidable nuisance, best put in an institution under strict discipline. The local authorities showed an indifferent and, at times, a negative attitude towards such children. A policy, planning, and programming void, therefore, existed at all levels in matters relating to their problems and social service needs.

The 1990s witnessed some attention by government and voluntary organizations largely as a result of strong advocacy by the UNICEF and international NGOs. They sponsored research studies, seminars, and workshops, and facilitated interaction between government, NGOs, media, researchers, and public figures.

The Government of India launched, for the first time in the Eighth Five Year Plan (1992–7), a grant-in-aid programme under which assistance is given to voluntary organizations for organizing services for street children. In 2000–1, assistance was given by the Ministry of Social Justice & Empowerment to 118 voluntary organizations for providing integrated services. A child helpline service, operated round the clock, has also been launched in 26 cities to respond to children in emergency situations, extend referral services, and provide a platform for networking to facilitate rehabilitation. Some state governments, too, have responded to the social service needs of street children. In some of the metropolitan cities, senior police officers are trying to develop institutional mechanisms through voluntary organizations, to help street children. The local authorities have, however, been largely indifferent, though they, too, have a very important role to play.

Largely as an outcome of strong advocacy by the UNICEF and international NGOs, and some funding assistance from them as well as the government, the voluntary sector has responded to the problem more actively. Some new NGOs have come into existence while a number of existing NGOs have expanded their activities to include street children. In some cities an inter-agency forum of NGOs has been formed for interaction among themselves and a dialogue with the government and local authorities on problems faced, and facilities and other support needed. However, the totality of the services provided by voluntary agencies is still very inadequate compared to the needs.

Services for street children, particularly those by voluntary organizations, have a wide range and indicate flexibility in responding to ground realities. Some of these services are street based, some centre based, and some community based, depending on the background of the children and their needs.

Among the services provided are the following:

- Drop-in centres with facilities for bathing, toilet, washing, recreation, non-formal education, subsidized meals, small savings and credit, and counselling and guidance in an informal friendly environment. The centres follow flexible timings, which suit such children, and are run at convenient locations in a friendly and understanding environment. Children are free to come and go;
- Halfway or transit homes where children who have no homes are given shelter, food, clothing, counselling, and non-formal education and training till a rehabilitation plan has been worked out;
- Night shelters which also provide some basic services;
- Street schools which adopt a non-formal approach, and follow a curriculum suited to the learners' needs and relevant for helping them to cope with their life situation;
- Vocational training and skill development of street children. Some examples are those run by Vatsalya, Salam Balak Trust, Prayas, and the Child in Need Institute (CINI), to name a few. A Rotary YMCA project provided training in 'business skills' in vocations which the children engage in as, for instance, retail selling and the making and supply of articles. The idea was to help the children to understand, in a non-formal learning process, the mechanics of business. Soft loans were also given to the children;
- Counselling which also addresses the coping problems of these children and seeks to strengthen them;
- Access to health services;
- Residential rehabilitation services covering food, clothing, shelter, education, vocational training, health care, and counselling in a caring environment;

- Foster care;
- Enlisting of volunteers and providing training. Organizing of social and cultural programmes by street children, sports events, festivals, get-togethers;
- Issue of identity cards to street children, liaising with the police and municipal authorities for their right to operate in a regulated manner thus protecting them from harassment by police, civic officials, and violence by local toughs;
- Organizing and supporting income earning opportunities for street children and their families. Examples are a restaurant run by street children outside the inter-state bus terminal of Delhi, sponsored by Butterfly, and a beautician centre run by street children, sponsored by Prayas. These are just two examples of NGO endeavours;
- Helpline services, operated round the clock, whereby children in a desperate situation needing immediate help can contact on phone the agency for rescue and relief, thereby saving some lives and initiating the process of their protection, rehabilitation, and development.

In addition to providing one or more of the above services, several voluntary organizations engage in advocacy, research, and documentation; networking with other organizations working for street children in India and abroad; interacting with the media, government agencies, and eminent persons for generating awareness and support; organizing marches of street children on specified days to draw public attention to their problems and developmental needs, remove suspicion and apprehension in the public mind about them, and promote better understanding of the phenomenon and the issues involved.

An important feature characterizing most NGO programmes is to make contacts with the child, build a relationship of trust, and meet the child's needs for affection, love, care, understanding, and security, and thus win his confidence. Quite often the services are offered as an integrated package, planned and designed as community based programmes after a careful assessment of needs. Also, the services are delivered right at or near the points where the children congregate or earn their living. The attempt is to create an organizational infrastructure which harnesses local initiative and leadership and integrates the children into the mainstream of society. Organizing the street children under the aegis of an agency is instrumental in giving them a sense of belonging, an identity, a legitimacy, and an access to various community facilities and services.

CHILDREN IN CONFLICT WITH LAW

Vagrancy, delinquency, and crime are emerging as serious social problems in India. Children who are abandoned, run away from home, or come from problem or broken families form a vulnerable group. Recent years have witnessed a growing incidence of delinquency and crime among children from middle and upper classes, indicating that adverse economic factors are clearly not sufficient to explain deviant behaviour.

Some criminologists are of the view that delinquency has early behavioural manifestations like, for instance, playing truant from school, gambling, taking part in gang fights, damaging property, bullying, carrying out errands for criminals, and the like. There is usually a period of transition when the child transgresses social norms, even though he does not engage in activities which are in conflict with law. This is because there is always a gap between social norms and legal codes. While there is rarely total behavioural conformity with social norms, there is always a threshold of tolerance of transgression, this itself being a product of the times.

Deviance is relative rather than absolute. Norms of the peer group or primary reference group may differ in different classes, communities, or regions. They may also differ by gender.

CAUSES

Delinquency and crime are the result of the interplay of a large number of predisposing factors which have a greater propensity to operate in urban areas, particularly in depressed urban slum neighbourhoods. Various theories of causation of crime exist. The divergence in explanations is indicative of the complexity of the phenomenon.

Factors often cited (direct or indirect) to be causative of juvenile delinquency are:

- A family environment which exercises a negative influence because of presence of alcoholism, drug addiction, or the illegal nature of activities of family members;
- A family environment where parents have no time for their

children, care little for what they do or where they go or over-indulge on their children by giving too much money without bothering to know how it is spent.
- Broken home, resulting in emotional deprivation and absence of a caring and loving relationship; neglect; physical; emotional and psychological abuse. A study of delinquent children in Agra, for instance, reported 41 per cent children from broken homes; another study reported 58 per cent (Dayal et al. 1986; Sharma and Qureshi 1997);
- Bad peer group influence;
- Impulsive response to a provocative situation;
- Poverty due to which even the basic needs cannot be met virtually forcing children to illegitimate ways of making money. Sharma and Qureshi's study, for instance, found that a large number of children apprehended for delinquency were supplementing family income (Sharma and Qureshi 1997);
- Property and family conflicts;
- Lure of making money at any cost to lead a life of luxury, spend on friends, and impress by life-style;
- Absence of constructive and legitimate ways of spending time. Most of these children either could not go to school, dropped out of school, or absented themselves from school,
- Sexual abuse;
- Bad habits such as gambling, smoking, drug abuse, and drinking for which money has to be found;
- Crisis situations in which deviant action appears to be the only solution to the child;
- Initiative of gang leaders who are on the look out for vulnerable children to use them for illegal activities.

EXTENT

The incidence of juvenile delinquency is not easy to measure. Statistics on juvenile delinquency follow a legal definition—violation of law by a juvenile, defined in the Juvenile Justice Act, 1986 as a boy below 16 years or a girl below 18 years. The reported cases reflect only a part of the incidence. A large number of violations of the law go unreported, depending on the strength of the enforcement machinery in different states, the extent to which it is active, and the unwritten policy in the matter of registration of cases. The analysis of trends is rendered still more difficult because of changes in laws that take place and the enactment of new laws (or their repeal) in a particular state (prohibition, for instance). There is also a distinct class bias. For the same behavioural deviance a child from an upper class family may not be apprehended due to the use of influence, money, or indulgence of the law enforcement machinery, whereas a child from a poor family may be taken into custody. The current status of the child is also a factor. The enforcement agencies, for instance, are more indulgent towards students.

Figures on the incidence of juvenile crime are compiled by the National Crime Records Bureau (NCRB). They indicate the involvement of juveniles in a wide range of crimes, from petty thieving to heinous crimes like murder. These are broadly divided by NCRB into two categories, namely, crimes registered under the Indian Penal Code (IPC), and crimes registered under Special and Local Laws (SLL). Data on juvenile crimes from 1988 are given in Table 5.1. Figures for earlier years have not been used here because of the change in definition of juvenile used from 1988. In the compilation of statistics earlier, a juvenile was defined as a person, male or female, below the age of 21 years. The Juvenile Justice Act, 1986, which came into force on 2 October 1987, defines a juvenile as a boy below 16 years and a girl below 18 years. Surprisingly, the number of cases of IPC crimes has shown a significant decline—form 24,827 in 1988 to 8,888 in 1999, which is only 36 per cent of

TABLE 5.1: COGNIZABLE CRIME BY JUVENILES UNDER IPC, INDIA, 1988 TO 1999

Year	No. of cases reported under IPC	Percentage of juvenile IPC crimes to total IPC crimes	Juvenile crime rate (IPC) per 100,000 population
1988	24,827	1.7	3.1
1989	18,457	1.2	2.3
1990	15,230	0.9	1.8
1991	12,588	0.8	1.5
1992	11,100	0.7	1.3
1993	9,465	0.6	1.1
1994	8,561	0.5	1.0
1995	9,766	0.6	1.1
1996	10,024	0.6	1.1
1997	7,909	0.5	0.8
1998	9,352	0.5	1.0
1999	8,888	0.5	0.9

Source: National Crime Records Bureau.

the figure in 1988. The decline has been reported even though the population of juveniles has increased by about 22 per cent during this period. To what extent this reflects ground reality and is indicative of increased under-registration, or the manner in which age is recorded so that fewer violators of law are categorized as juveniles, needs to be carefully investigated.

The type of IPC crime cases involving juveniles shows an interesting pattern (see Table 5.2). In 1998, 37 per cent of the juveniles apprehended were for burglary and theft and 16 per cent for causing hurt/grievous hurt. About 4 per cent were apprehended for serious crimes like murder and attempt to commit murder, and 3.5 per cent for rape, kidnapping and abduction, and dacoity.

There is a clear gender difference in certain types of IPC crimes by juveniles, as the data in Table 5.2 shows. Of the juvenile males apprehended in 1998 for IPC crimes, 47 per cent were apprehended for offences relating to burglary and theft, as compared to 11 per cent juvenile females apprehended for such crimes.

TABLE 5.2: NUMBER OF JUVENILES APPREHENDED FOR IPC CRIMES, INDIA, 1998

Crime head	Male		Female		Total	
	No.	%	No.	%	No.	%
Murder	226	2.6	78	2.5	304	2.5
Attempt to commit murder	155	1.8	29	0.9	184	1.5
Culpable homicide not amounting to murder	17	0.2	10	0.3	27	0.2
Rape	205	2.3	10	0.3	215	1.8
Kidnapping and abduction	39	0.4	126	4.0	165	1.4
Dacoity	35	0.4	3	0.1	38	0.3
Robbery	69	0.8	2	0.1	71	0.6
Burglary	1,674	18.9	38	1.2	1,712	14.3
Theft	2,466	27.9	297	9.5	2,763	23.1
Riots	469	5.3	415	13.3	884	7.4
Hurt/Grievous hurt	1,316	14.9	549	17.5	1,865	15.6
Cheating	29	0.3	11	0.4	40	0.3
Dowry death	24	0.3	85	2.7	109	0.9
Molestation	138	1.6	88	2.8	226	1.9
Others	1,987	22.5	1,392	44.4	3,379	28.2
Total	8,849	100.0	3,133	100.00	11,982	100.00

Source: National Crime Records Bureau.

TABLE 5.3: LEVEL OF EDUCATION OF JUVENILES APPREHENDED UNDER IPC AND SLL LAWS, 1998

	Illiterate	Primary	Above primary but below matric/higher secondary	Higher	Total
No.	7,230	7,460	3,500	774	18,964
%	38.1	39.3	18.5	4.1	100.0

Source: National Crime Records Bureau.
Notes: IPC: India Penal Code;
SLL: Special and Local Laws.

Among juveniles apprehended for violation of IPC and SLL laws, boys far outnumber girls. In 1998, among juveniles less than 16 years apprehended for IPC crimes, 92 per cent were boys. In the case of SLL crimes, the percentage of boys was 98.

Among juvenile delinquents (less than 16 years) apprehended for IPC crimes, 84 per cent were in the 12–15 year age group, and only 16 per cent in the 7–11 year age group. In the case of juveniles under 16 years of age apprehended for SLL crimes, the percentage in the age group 7–11 years was 34 per cent, while in the age group 12–15 years it was 66 per cent. Older children are more mobile and liable to delinquent acts when other predisposing factors act in conjunction. A matter of concern is that out of 1,326 boys aged 7–11 years apprehended in 1998 for IPC crimes, 26 were apprehended for murder, 15 for attempt to murder, and 9 for rape.

Of the juveniles (below 16 years in the case of boys and below 18 years in the case of girls) apprehended under IPC and SLL laws in 1998, 38 per cent were illiterate while 39 per cent had studied up to different classes of the primary stage (see Table 5.3). Various studies have pointed in the same direction—a large percentage not going to school or dropping out early because of poverty, or poor learning environment in the school, or both (Dayal et al. 1986, Sharma and Qureshi 1997).

The position in regard to disposal of juveniles arrested under IPC and SLL crimes and sent to courts in 1998, given in Table 5.4, shows that 36 per cent were pending disposal. The situation varies in different states. In some states, the case of more than 50 per cent of the arrested juveniles was pending.

TABLE 5.4: DISPOSAL OF JUVENILES ARRESTED UNDER IPC AND SLL CRIMES AND SENT TO COURTS, INDIA, 1998

	Arrested and sent to court	Sent home after advice or admonition	Released on probation and placed under care of		Sent to Special Home	Dealt with fine	Acquitted or otherwise disposed of	Pending disposal
			Parent/ Guardian	Fit institution				
No.	18,964	2,620	3,889	829	1,751	908	2,107	6,860
%	100.0	13.8	20.5	4.4	9.2	4.8	11.1	36.2

Source: National Crime Records Bureau.

LEGISLATION

Children (boys below age 16 years and girls below 18 years) who have committed an offence punishable by law were dealt with under the Juvenile Justice Act, 1986, which repealed the Children Acts of the Centre and the states. The 1986 Act adopted a welfare cum rehabilitation approach so that the child could be helped to lead a normal life. The Act provided for the 'care, protection, treatment, development and rehabilitation of neglected or delinquent juveniles and for the adjudication of certain matters relating to, and disposition of delinquent juveniles'. It shunned a punitive approach and forbade the lodging of a juvenile in a penal institution, confinement in a police station, or sentence of death or imprisonment (with some exceptions). Before the passage of the Act, many juveniles were languishing in jails. The Act prescribed several ways of deciding a case against delinquent juveniles, which include allowing the juvenile to go home after advice or admonition; releasing the juvenile on probation of good conduct under the care of any parent, guardian, other fit person or institution; sending the juvenile to special home; and ordering the payment of a fine if he was over 14 years of age and earned money. The basic idea, thus, was to choose an alternative which is in the best interest of the child. The Act envisaged the constitution of Juvenile Welfare Boards, Juvenile Courts, and the setting up of special homes, or the certifying of an institution as a special home, where services specified had to be provided. The Act provided for the creation of a Fund by a state government for the welfare and rehabilitation of juveniles dealt with under the Act. It established norms and standards for the administration of juvenile justice and the procedures to be followed for investigation, prosecution, adjudication, disposal, care, and rehabilitation. The Act also gave protection to children against cruelty, exploitation, and other offences against juveniles by parents, guardians, or others, and lists the offences and penal provisions which cover fine and imprisonment.

The implementation of the Juvenile Justice Act has not been satisfactory. Though special legislation to deal with juvenile delinquency came into existence in the 1920s, progress to date in providing services or developing programmes indicate drift and a lack of commitment. States give low priority to it. Services, both institutional and non-institutional, are grossly inadequate. Some provisions of the Act did not receive proper attention because of funding problems, administrative deficiencies, poor training of personnel, and the way they interacted with the children. In 1996, there were only 189 juvenile courts, 280 observation homes, 251 juvenile homes, 36 special homes, and 46 aftercare institutions in the whole country. These are very unevenly distributed both between and within states. The central government's scheme of strengthening services through expansion and upgradation on a cost sharing basis with states has not evoked satisfactory response from a large number of states. Non-governmental organizations (NGOs) are also relatively inactive in the area of juvenile delinquency in most of the states. The way some police apprehend children, and even thrash them on mere suspicion if they happen to be near the place of occurrence of a crime, especially if they are homeless, or come from poor disadvantaged families living in neighbourhoods with a bad reputation, show a lack of training, orientation, and sensitivity. Probation services are limited both in number and the quality of services they provide. Aftercare, too, is a weak link in the chain. The institutions functioning under the Act of 1986 provide food, clothing, shelter, and rehabilitative services, but are often overcrowded, impersonal, and lack a caring environment. Several malpractices have been reported from time to time in the functioning of these institutions which are left to be run by the subordinate staff with little supervision. Cases of children running away from homes have been reported in the media as the children find the environment stifling, authoritarian, and unfriendly. Inquiry committees are set up but their reports are rarely acted upon. In several cases, the courts, responding to public interest litigations, have hauled up the government and made adverse comments on the services provided. The machinery becomes activated for a brief period but relapses into inertia thereafter.

Attitudinal and behavioural changes in the staff engaged in running institutions are necessary. Only professionally qualified staff should be recruited and given sensitivity and orientation training at regular intervals. The objective is to build a caring environment in the institutions. The police need to be sensitized to the needs of juveniles through proper training. Special cells for dealing with juvenile delinquents need to be established in police departments. The interest of NGOs in juvenile delinquency has been rather limited, and that, too, in only a few states. The NGOs should be assisted to develop and run programmes for children and adolescents in delinquency prone areas, so that children get proper counselling and direction about their future.

On 30 December 2000, the Juvenile Justice Act, 1986 stood repealed and the Juvenile Justice (Care and Protection of Children) Act took its place. The new Act covers both boys and girls under 18 years of age, unlike the previous Act which covered boys under 16 years and girls under 18 years. Like its predecessor, it makes separate provision for juveniles in conflict with law, and children in need of care and protection. For the former there is provision for Juvenile Justice Boards, observation homes and special homes while for the latter there is provision for Child Welfare Committees, children's homes and shelter homes. For both the categories of children, there is provision for adoption, foster care, sponsorship, after care, establishment of Fund and setting up of central, state, district, and city advisory boards. Provision has also been made for setting up special juvenile police units or having a designated police officer in each district. The new legislation has drawn considerable flak from voluntary organizations working in the field of social defence and from child development experts. The law was drafted without a detailed examination of the problems faced by the states in the implementation of the 1986 Act and the case law. It gives an exaggerated role to the police and does not give the child the right to be heard through a counsel. It makes no mention of the borstal institutions set up for adolescents under specific state legislations. Several sections display clumsy drafting. Little consideration has been given to the cost of the machinery that will be needed to handle the wide net cast for children in need of care and protection, the large increase in case load due to the inclusion of boys 16–17 years of age, and the manpower and resources needed which the state governments are ill-equipped to provide.

SEXUALLY ABUSED CHILDREN

Sexual abuse of children, both boys and girls, is now drawing considerable public and media attention, and is gradually being recognized as a major child abuse problem. There has been much greater public outcry and anger against rape and incest, though other forms of sexual abuse, too, leave deep scars on the mind of a child whose innocence, trust, and vulnerability have been mercilessly exploited. More common among these are: hugging or kissing a child on the face or on different parts of the body with sexual undertones, fondling or caressing of the child's private parts by an adult or vice versa, using the child for masturbation, penetration by the adult or attempted penetration (anal or vaginal) for intercourse, penetration with finger or some object, and oral sex. Sexual abuse can and does take place without body contact through pornography or exposing sexual organs to the child. The overriding factor is that it is engaged in by an adult for his or her sexual gratification. Most sexual abuse is often not a one-time episode. It may and does at times continue for a fairly long period.

Research evidence on sexual abuse in India is scarce. In the developed countries, too, the problem began receiving the serious attention of researchers from the 1970s when medical practitioners found evidence of sexual abuse of very young boys as well as girls. Since then a number of empirical studies have been carried out on the nature and dimensions of the problem (Baker and Duncan 1985; Finkelhor 1994; Gelles and Edfeldt 1986; Goldman and Padayachi 1997; Hobbs and Wynne 1986; Kempe 1978; Russell 1983). There are several broad findings of these studies which have relevance for India as evident from information that becomes available from time to time.

NATURE AND MAGNITUDE

The prevalence of sexual abuse of both boys and girls is certainly not as rare as is generally believed and is not confined to the lower classes. Only a very small fraction gets reported to the police or even to parents. Sexual abuse cuts across economic and social class and education levels. It is not confined to problem families or problem children. In most cases, the abusers are far older and are from all age groups (including middle aged and old persons). They take advantage of their proximity to the child by virtue of being a family member (either co-resident or visiting), a friend or acquaintance of the family, relation of a friend of the child, neighbour, relation of a school friend, an older student in the same school, or a school teacher or school employee. In the Indian context, domestic servants are also known to abuse the child. Child domestic workers are sometimes abused in their employer's houses. Sexual abuse by total strangers is uncommon. Intra-familial sexual abuse is far more prevalent than what people would like to believe. Abuse takes place usually within the residence of the child by an adult who has access there or at the residence of an adult, more often the former in the case of girls and the latter in the case of boys. There are also cases of sexual abuse which is incestuous, where the protector becomes the predator. In such cases, incestuous relationship of father with own or step-daughter is more common than of mother with son. The first reaction is to keep the incestuous relationship under wraps, even when this is known to the mother, to protect the name of the family or for fear of physical abuse, break-up of marriage, or being thrown out of the house. Even children of age less than 5 years become victims of sexual abuse. Some studies have found that female children are likely to be abused at an older age than male children. Also, girls are far more likely to be sexually abused than boys. The abusers are persons who carry out their social and family roles and responsibilities just like normal persons. It is not, therefore, easy to identify them as they do not manifest in public symptoms which stand out to reveal their misdemeanour. A study on reported rape cases in 1996 in Delhi found that in nearly 88 per cent of the cases, the victims were known to the perpetrator—6.4 per cent were relatives, 4.3 per cent family friends, 58.1 per cent neighbours, 3.6 per cent friends, 4.0 per cent employers, 11.5 per cent other known persons, and only 12.1 per cent were unknown persons (Sharma 1997).

Information on sexual abuse in childhood, collected from 348 girl students in the age group 15–21 years studying in and around Bangalore, showed that sexual abuse of girls are not stray, isolated, one-time incidents but the experience of a fairly large number of girls. The abusers were normally close relatives who abused the child's trust. Fifteen per cent girls reported serious form of sexual abuse (attempts at penetration, forced oral sex, using victim to masturbate, and rape); 38 per cent among them had repeated experience of abuse. About one-third of these girls were subjected to this before they were 11 years of age. Fifty-five per cent of the serious abusers were family members. The abuse invariably left the girls with a sense of shock, confusion, shame, humiliation, disgust, and helplessness (Ganesh 1995). Cases of sexual abuse by family members, including the father, have been reported by other investigators as well (MARG 1996).

Findings of some other studies, though not directly focused on child abuse, have data on the prevalence of the problem. A community based study of gynaecological and sexual diseases among rural women in two villages in a backward district of Maharashtra reported that 46.7 per cent of the unmarried girls were on examination, found to have had sexual intercourse (Bang et al. 1989). Another community based study of six villages in Gujarat reported 30 per cent girls 12–17 years having had premarital sex (Sridhar et al. 1991). Since in rural communities, most girls are married off early, the findings provide evidence of sexual abuse in childhood or adolescence.

A study on sexual abuse of male children, based on information collected from 146 college boys between the ages of 16 and 20 years, reported that 14.3 per cent were victims of homosexual abuse and 7.5 per cent to sexual advances from older women (Seshadri 1995). Male child abuse has been reported from inmates of juvenile institutions, domestic child workers, street children, rag pickers, runaway children, and abandoned children. Evidence of sexual abuse of children, boys and girls, has also been provided in some hospital based studies on sexually transmitted diseases (Handa et al. 1995; Mendiratta et al. 1996).

Cases of sexual abuse of both boys and girls in welfare institutions, hostels, and protective homes for the custody and care of children have also been reported. The abusers are often the staff in these institutions, officers, or outsiders with whom the staff colludes in return of monetary gains and other benefits or under pressure and fear of sanctions. Sexual abuse in welfare institutions is a morbid expression of sexual exploitation of children by those entrusted with the responsibility of protecting them, and needs to be put down with a heavy hand. The offenders are, however, rarely punished due to the position they enjoy and the protection they get from corrupt politicians and bureaucrats.

RAPE OF CHILDREN

Rape of a child is considered the most serious and abominable form of child abuse. Statistics on cases of rape of girls of age under 16 years are compiled by the National Crime Records Bureau. The data refer to reported cases which, in the case of such crimes, is far below the actual incidence of the problem. There is often great hesitation on the part of the family to report such cases since the girl's reputation and marriage prospects are involved. There is also apprehension about unhelpful police investigations and long-drawn embarrassing court trials which will revive the traumatic experience and prolong the agony and humiliation. The first reaction of the victim's family is often to hide the incident and to blame, even ostracize the girl if she is old enough, for walking into a situation in which rape becomes possible. Where the perpetrator is a relative, there is strong pressure from the side of the abuser and his family to keep the incident under wraps and not let anyone outside the family know about it on the ground that it will bring shame to the family. An attempt is made to treat the incident as an act of indiscretion by the perpetrator and express regrets for the incident, or offer some compensation if the victim comes from a poor family. Economic dependence on the perpetrator of the crime or his family and threat of physical harm or destruction of property, too, deter reporting of the case. The police, when they can, do not register such cases easily, particularly in rural areas, when the girl or the family comes from a lower social and economic class, in order to keep down the number of cases of heinous crime within the jurisdiction of the police station. Political and administrative pressure, when the perpetrator or his family has important connections, and lucre are other factors which play a role in reducing the number of reported cases of rape. Even when cases are registered and prosecution takes place, conviction rates are low reflecting the poor performance of the prosecution in bringing the guilty to book. Only 27 per cent of the accused in rape cases (all ages), the trials of whom were completed in 1998, were convicted. The trial of 84 per cent accused persons in rape cases numbering 72,707 was pending in 1998, indicating a huge backlog and an agonizing long period of waiting.

The number of reported cases of girls of age less than 16 years who are victims of rape in India is given in Table 5.5. The number shows an increase from 858 in 1977 to 4,059 in 1998. A disturbing feature is the increase in proportion of victims of rape who are

TABLE 5.5: VICTIMS OF RAPE AGED BELOW 16 YEARS, INDIA, 1977 TO 1998

	1977	1980	1983	1986	1989	1992	1995	1998
No. of victims of rape aged below 16 years	858	1,033	1,170	1,261	2,334	3,113	4,067	4,059
Percentage of girls aged below 16 years out of the total victims of rape	21.1	20.6	19.4	15.9	23.9	26.5	29.5	27.0

Source: National Crime Records Bureau.

below 16 years, the percentage rising from 21 per cent of the total number of cases in 1977 to 27 per cent in 1998.

The break-up of age of victims of rape who are below 16 years of age are being reported from 1988. The data given in Table 5.6 show that in 1998, 4.2 per cent of the victims of rape were of age below 10 years (2.6 per cent in 1988), 22.8 per cent aged between 10 and 16 years (20.5 per cent in 1988), and 73.0 per cent were of age 16 years and above (76.9 per cent in 1988). There is thus a lowering of the age of rape victims. This is also evident if the percentage of girl child victims of age below 10 years as a percentage of victims of age below 16 years in considered. In 1988, only 11.1 per cent of victims of rape of age below 16 years were less than 10 years of age. In 1998, this figure rose to 15.4 per cent.

TABLE 5.6: AGE DISTRIBUTION OF VICTIMS OF RAPE, INDIA, 1988 TO 1998

Year		Age (in years)				
		Below 10	10–15	16–29	30 & above	Total
1988	No.	233	1,869	5,832	1,165	9,099
	%	2.6	20.5	64.1	12.8	100.0
1992	No.	532	2,581	7,000	1,621	11,734
	%	4.5	22.0	59.7	13.8	100.0
1996	No.	608	3,475	8,281	2,485	14,849
	%	4.1	23.4	55.8	16.7	100.0
1998	No.	626	3,433	8,414	2,560	15,033
	%	4.2	22.8	56.0	17.0	100.0

Source: National Crime Records Bureau.
Note: Age is in complete years.

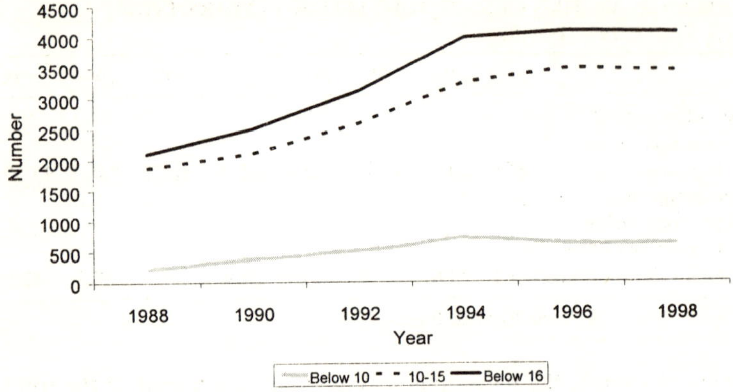

FIG. 5.1: VICTIMS OF RAPE AGED BELOW 16 YEARS, INDIA, 1988 TO 1998.

PROGRAMME NEEDS

The sexual abuse of children has received very little research attention in India. The reported cases of sexual abuse of children in India are a small fraction of the actual incidence. Research by medical and social scientists on sexual abuse in childhood is necessary for a proper understanding of the nature and magnitude of the problem, the situational factors, and the perpetrators to enable suitable intervention programmes to be designed.

Trial procedures of sexual abuse are cumbersome and drag on. The environment in which the trial takes place and the cross-examination by the prosecution is often felt by the victim to be intimidating. Pressures are put on the child's family to withdraw the case. Family members and witnesses are pressurized to withdraw or change their statement, for which, sometimes, threats, money power, and muscle power is used. In the absence of support services and help, the child and the family feel confused, insecure, and traumatized.

There are very few preventive intervention programmes which could make parents (specially mothers) aware of the existence of the problem, and help them to identify potential situations, the first symptoms, and ways in which such situations need to be handled, including the registration of cases to apprehend and prosecute the perpetrator. Where the abuser is the father of the child, the situation becomes far more complex and difficult for both the child and the mother, as the home becomes an unsafe place when the protector becomes the predator. Victims of sexual abuse and their families need counselling, psychiatric help, and support services to overcome the shock and trauma. Change in social attitudes is necessary to accept the existence of the problem. Unfortunately, very few services are currently available. In recent years, a few NGOs have come up in metropolitan cities to provide help and support services.

The handling of cases of rape of children by the police leaves much to be desired. It is very important that law enforcement agencies and court procedures do not traumatize the victim further. A close look at current procedures is urgently needed. Sensitization programmes for the personnel involved at different stages of apprehension, prosecution, and trial are very necessary.

CHILDREN IN PROSTITUTION

The worst form of sexual abuse of children is their use for prostitution. The problem has been known to exist for a long time, but seldom received the serious attention of policy makers because of the covert way in which it is carried out. In recent years, the plight of these children has drawn considerable public attention, with international agencies, NGOs, and the media highlighting the serious nature of the problem, its rising trend, lowering of the age of children being trafficked, and increasing trafficking in girls from Nepal and Bangladesh. There is growing pressure for concerted and co-ordinated action with and between countries to tackle child trafficking and prostitution. Stories filed by alert reporters have depicted graphically the exploitation of helpless children by procurers, traffickers, brothel owners, and clients who view the victims only as a tradable commodity to be used for profit and pleasure. The untold physical, mental, and emotional sufferings of these children have not moved them. Societal inertia, police complicity, and political patronage have provided protection to the operators, and ensured continuance of the abuse, with money and muscle power combining to exploit the hapless children to the hilt.

MAGNITUDE

Data on the magnitude of child prostitution is not only scanty, but also speculative. Estimates of numbers are difficult to make, given the nature of the problem, the unlawful and covert character of operations connected with the trade, and the resistance of those involved in running it. Inquiries are avoided and, when that fails, wrong or partially true information is given in response to questions asked about the background of the girls or the trade. Poor research interest of academicians who have the necessary skills, perseverance, resources, and motivation to investigate a complex problem like child prostitution has also been a problem. An added factor is the difficulty in getting information on the age of the girl, due to deliberate attempts to conceal it under strict instructions of the brothel owner. Also, in the absence of any standardization, the age groups vary from one survey to another. Some do not make a distinction between a child (less than 16 years of age according to the Immortal Traffic (Prevention) Act, 1956) and a minor (completed age 16 years but not completed 18 years). Moreover, disaggregation of data below age 18 years is normally not done. Inferences of the extent of child prostitution are often drawn from information on the current age distribution of sex workers or enquiring from them about the age when they began to serve clients.

The six city study of prostitution sponsored by the Central Social Welfare Board (CSWB) reported that in Calcutta the age of entry into prostitution of sex workers in the sample was less than 15 years for 10 per cent and 15–18 years for 16 per cent of sex workers. In the case of Delhi, the percentages were 19 and 33 respectively. For the other four cities, data were not available (Mukherjee and Das 1996). Rozario's sample survey indicated 35 per cent sex workers below the age of 18 years. Fifty-three per cent of the women reported that their age at the time of initial sexual exploitation was below 18 years. Age break-up below 18 years has not been given (Rozario 1988). A study in Paradip, Orissa reported that 15 per cent of the prostitutes covered by the sample survey were below the age of 18 years. Here, too, age break-up of girls aged below 18 years has not been given. Data on age of entry into prostitution was also not collected (Jeeevan Raksha Parishad 1997). The large variation in percentages is a reflection of the research methodology adopted, the way the sample was drawn, and locally operative factors. If information available from other surveys is also considered, it would appear that for about one-fifth of the sex workers, the age of entry into prostitution is less than 18 years, but this, again, is a guesstimate.

Problems arise when estimates of the number of children engaged in prostitution in the country are made from ad hoc studies, each following a different definition of child and based on small samples purposively selected by individual researchers from different parts of the country, especially when national or state level estimates were not intended. Some activist NGO groups give figures of half a million or more of such children, which appear to be speculative. The basis of arriving at these estimates is never given. Conservative estimates place the number between 100,000 and 200,000 but here, again, it has to be admitted that no scientific justification is available. Even though there is a difference of opinion in regard to numbers, it is generally agreed that the problem is growing in magnitude. What is particularly bothersome is the rise in trafficking of minor girls both within and between countries. Sex tourism, paedophilia, and pornography are also spreading their tentacles.

From the 1980s, research activity that is specially focused on child prostitution has increased largely as a result of global concern at the rising incidence of the problem, its inter-country ramifications, and advocacy for concerted action by governments and NGOs. Sponsorship and funding support of international and national agencies have resulted in a number of micro-studies in different parts of the country with the involvement of NGOs. The aim was to collect facts on what has been largely a covert operation, so that the problem could be diagnosed and follow-up discussion, dialogue, and debate based on the findings could help in designing strategies to combat the problem. The studies used different sampling designs, study procedures, and tools of data collection. The statistical dimensions are not, therefore, comparable. However, they shed some light on the problem and bring to public view the inhuman exploitation of hapless children and the organized manner in which the clandestine operations are carried out through meticulous planning and networking. The broad findings that emerge from these studies and others are given in the paragraphs that follow (Debabrata 1997; Jeevan Raksha Parishad 1997; Mukherjee 1997; National Commission for Women 1996; Patkar 1991; Prerana 1995; Rozario 1988; Sanlap 1996; Sinha 1997). Unfortunately, there are hardly any research studies on male child prostitution. The problem exists, though on a much smaller scale, and surfaces in the media from time to time.

CAUSES

Child prostitution exists because of the interplay of demand and supply factors. Since the child is viewed only as a commodity, her market value depends almost entirely on age, looks, figure, virginity status, and freshness. Some customers have a special fancy for children propelled by the belief that sex with a child is safe because she is unlikely to have a sexually transmitted disease (STD) or HIV/AIDS. Some believe that sex with a virgin would cure them of their own STD. Customers of child prostitutes cover a wide spectrum—young, middle aged, and old persons from all social classes, castes, and communities. They have varying educational levels and come from different occupational groups. They comprise unmarried, married, divorced, widowed, and separated men. Students, and the unemployed, as well as white-collar workers, truck drivers, labourers, peddlers, and businessmen, visit them. Customers want to get the most for the money they have paid to the brothel owner, the pimp, the girl's family, or the girl herself. The child has no alternative but to comply. In almost all cases, it is unprotected sex, unless the client himself chooses to use a condom.

There are several supply side factors. Girls get trapped into prostitution due to a variety of circumstances. Poverty is a big contributing factor. Girls usually come from very poor families with low and uncertain incomes, often from backward areas, which accounts for the disproportionately higher percentage of girls from backward communities, mainly the Scheduled Castes and Scheduled Tribes. Most have a rural background, though in recent years, slums in big cities have become a hunting ground of procurers (Debabrata 1997). Tribal communities adversely affected by development projects are becoming increasingly vulnerable to prostitution rings (Jeevan Raksha Parishad 1997). A very large percentage of girls and their families are illiterate or semi-literate. With this socio-economic background it is not difficult for some girls and their parents to be lured into fake marriages. A more frequent ploy is the promise of employment by a procurer (male as well as female), posing as a well-wisher or recruitment agent, who often makes an attractive advance payment to the girl's family which pledges her services ostensibly for employment till the debt is redeemed. Yet another device adopted by a procurer, usually a handsome young person with persuasive skills, is to befriend a girl, convince her of his undying love, impress her with gifts and stories of his social and economic standing, and make false promises to motivate her to run away from home. Deceit and betrayal of trust become apparent soon after the girl has left her home and village or town and finds herself totally helpless in a strange environment without money or help. Some are sexually abused by the person and his friends for a number of days and then deserted, making her a soft target for anti-social and criminal elements. Others are sold off to brothel owner or an agent. The breakdown of the family support system, and its dysfunctioning, is also a contributing factor. Girls who have an unbearable home environment (maltreatment, verbal, physical, and sexual abuse, rejection) or no help or resources to fall back upon during times of crisis become soft targets. They are befriended by procurers of their agents, usually women, and persuaded to leave home and accompany them or their acquaintance, assuring them of employment and a place of stay. In several cases, the family of the girl including the biological father, gives away the girl in return for money or in redemption of debt knowing that the girl will be sexually abused. This happens more often when it is a broken or problem family, dysfunctional because of alcoholism, loss of livelihood, or the presence of a cruel abusive step-parent or a guardian who has no compunction in giving away the girl for money. Cases of married young girls being given away by the husband for money, deserted, and forced into prostitution have also been reported.

Once the girl is trapped, she is sold and resold, landing finally in a brothel. Brute force is used (confinement, assault, torture, and rape) to break her resistance, control her, and make her follow ungrudgingly the commands of her captor, and later the owner. Escape is virtually impossible as the brothel owner having paid the money treats the girl as her/his property and a profit centre, and jealously guards her. The few who try to escape with the help of a customer are tracked down, brought back, and physically punished to break their will and subdue them. The girl is made to sign (or give thumb impression) on a deed that she is an adult, living in the premises of her own volition, and had taken a loan (a large sum is mentioned). The girl is, thus, held in virtual bondage by the brothel owner. Most of the earnings of the girl are kept by the brothel owner, ostensibly in payment to recover the amount spent to procure her.

A few years in prostitution, and the girls end up with sexually transmitted diseases of HIV/AIDS, due to unprotected sex. Tuberculosis, gynaecological diseases, and other ailments are common. One or more abortions also affect their health. There is little time for treatment, cure, and recuperation. The girls have no option; their body has to be offered whenever there is a customer, whatever the physical or mental state.

Not all children enter prostitution through deceit or force exercised on the girl. There are some castes and denotified communities (Bedias, Kanjars, Nats, Bachadas, Sansis, and Koltas, to mention some) where it has for decades been customary among some families for one of the girls to earn through prostitution with the full knowledge of the family and the caste Panchayat, indicating how customary practice becomes a ground for abuse of young daughters. The girls growing up in the community are exposed to this role and come to accept it. The male family members are either non-earners or have small uncertain incomes. They are lethargic and have little interest in trying to make a living and support a family. There is, thus, acceptance of prostitution at the individual, family, and community level. The girls get used to easy money and occasional gifts given by clients, apart from the negotiated cash sum. There is also the ceremonial offering of the virgin girl to a rich man who pays a handsome amount for the right to have a sexual relationship with her, followed by feasting by her family and community for which the man pays. These communities are poor, own no assets of production, possess no skills, and have no stable sources of income from other modes. They depend on the earnings of the daughter who becomes a provider for the family. The girl may continue to stay with her family, or move to a brothel or some other place (Debabrata 1997; Kulkarni 1997; Kumar 2000; Mukherjee 1997; Mukherjee, Daripa and Mukherjee 1997; Parashar 1998; UNICEF 1995).

There are pockets of the country which are poor, backward, and remote where touts operate and procure girls after paying a lump sum to the family. This has become evident from several studies which have been able to identify the places from where a large number of girls are regularly procured by agents with some vague assurances of employment in the city. Due to abject poverty and isolation of the area parents are unable to verify the statements (Mukherjee 1997; Rozario 1988). There is now a growing market for pre-pubescent girls. In a profession in which virgins and young girls are in great demand, agents are always on the look out for 'fresh supplies' to meet the expanding market as well as to replace the older ones who get fewer clients and are no longer profit centres.

Yet another source from which girls land up in prostitution is the tradition, commonly known as *devadasi*, the literal meaning of which is servant of God. The practice has a long history. While it has disappeared from other parts of the country, it is still found, though on a much reduced scale, in some parts of Andhra Pradesh, Karnataka, Maharashtra, and Tamil Nadu among some of the lower castes. A virgin girl is dedicated to the deity by the family in the belief that it will get protection and blessings. Originally, the girls so dedicated performed the duties of keeping the temple premises clean, scrubbing the temple lamps, putting oil in them and lighting them, assisting the temple priest in worship, and singing and dancing in praise of the deity. Over the years, the practice deviated from its original purpose and became a source of exploitation of girls from poor families of lower castes under the garb of religious tradition. Very few girls so dedicated now actually serve the deity on a daily basis or sing and dance at the time of *puja* (worship of the deity). The ritual of dedication is a community affair and has the sanction of the family, the community, and the priests, and is thus given the colour of a pious act. Expenses on the ritual and on the feast that follows is borne by a rich middle-aged or older person from an upper caste, usually married and belonging to the landowning and the business class. The girl, on attaining puberty, gives the first use of her body to the person who pays a lump sum to the family. This is often preceded by a ceremony. The girl has no choice in the matter. She becomes the mistress; the raising of children she bears are her responsibility. After some time, the girl gets detached when the master no longer has a fancy for her and stops giving financial support. She can then have sexual relationships with other men. The children she bears as a result of such liaison are again her responsibility. The men who dominate her life bear no responsibility for the children she bears, who thus have a marginalized existence. Many *devadasis* end up in brothels in one of the metropolitan cities (Aiyar 1997; Gilada 1990; Ravindran 2000; Shankar 1990).

Some states have enacted legislation to prohibit the *devadasi* custom. The earliest of these was the Bombay Devdasis Protection Act, 1934 which was adopted by some other states. Later, Andhra Pradesh, Karnataka, and Tamil Nadu enacted their own legislation.

Some girls are initiated into prostitution by their prostitute mothers who, as they grow older, are unable to attract customers or pay off their debts. They have little or no savings for the sustenance and have no other source of livelihood. These girls are constantly exposed to the trading of sex, and have no other alternative (Patkar, 1991). However, many prostitute mothers have been reported by several studies as not wanting their daughters to follow their mother's footsteps. They would like them to have education, get married, and lead a normal life. Sex workers who can afford it, send their children to some other place for upbringing and education to protect them from the degrading environment of the brothel. (Mukherjee and Das 1996; UNICEF 1995).

Increasingly children, both boys and girls, are becoming victims of tourist paedophiles. A child sex industry with an international network is developing. The beaches of Goa and Kerala have in recent years drawn media attention because of the presence of tourist paedophiles. Child pornography is an offshoot of this development. Some paedophiles operate on their own, befriending poor and homeless children with food and gifts. The magnitude of the problem is not known. Local police have information, but do not have the will or the resources to apprehend the culprits (Randall 1996).

TRAFFICKING

There is very well organized trafficking in girls by flesh trade syndicates with operations spread over large areas. Some have links with similar syndicates in other countries, particularly Bangladesh and Nepal. The press has from time to time come out with vivid details on regular trafficking in girls from Nepal landing up in Bombay's dens, and of poor inter-country coordination, and bureaucratic inertia in eradicating it (Wadhwa 1998). Trafficking routes are well laid and known to the operators. The movement of a girl, soon after she has been procured, is pre-planned, covering transit, business centres where transactions including bidding take place, and the destination (Sanlaap 1997; Rozario 1988). Money changes hands between procurers, intermediaries, and the brothel owner. Market forces governed by supply and demand factors and risks involved determine the price tag of a girl, with very young virgins and attractive, fair complexioned, shapely girls fetching the highest price. Brute force, including annihilation, is carried out if any person is found giving information to law enforcing agencies. The protection provided to trafficking and the strong nexus between corrupt policemen, politicians, and bureaucrats in return for sexual favours and regular payments have been brought out by the media and several studies. Some NGOs working in the field, as well as girls, have a very negative view about the police whom they perceive not as protectors, but as active exploiters who for personal gain go all out to abuse the law, help the brothel owner and the traffickers, and provide protection to them.

VENUE

The venue of child prostitution is not only a red-light area. Some girls operate on their own and offer themselves to clients in their homes or other pre-arranged places. Hotels, guest houses, and residential areas are also used for carrying out the trade. At or near railway and bus stations, touts operate. They are also active at centres which bustle with trade and commercial activity, have a regular stream of short or long duration visitors without their families, or have a floating population of males living alone. Selected spots on national highways where truck drivers halt for meals or night rest have on them improvised structures where girls are available for prostitution, many of them from nearby areas or roadside settlements (Kulkarni 1997; Kumar 2000; Parashar 1998; Rao et al. 1999; Saxena 1996).

LEGAL MEASURES

The Indian Penal Code penalizes procurement, kidnapping, trafficking, and sexual offences against children. The Immoral Traffic (Prevention) Act, 1956 (as amended up to 1986) (ITP Act) covers both boys and girls. The Act has made offences involving children and minors more stringent, put the onus of proving innocence in specified situations on the person accused, and provided for the appointment of trafficking police officers empowered to investigate offences having interstate ramifications. Enforcement of the laws, however, continues to be very poor as is evident from the low figures of registration of cases under the IPC and ITP Act, and the considerable interstate variation which is more a reflection on the enforcement machinery than on the intensity of the problem in the state. Table 5.7 gives the number of cases registered from 1994 to 1999. The figures are a small fraction of the incidence of the problem and are far removed from ground reality. They reflect gross underregistration of cases. Only a small number of persons are prosecuted because of complicity of the investigating agencies, use of money and muscle power, and the protection and patronage available to the offender if he or his family has influence in the corridors of power. Fewer still are convicted due to intimidation of the girls and other witnesses, lapses in procedures required to be followed, and poor preparation and presentation of cases when they come up for hearing. Prosecution weaknesses are exploited to the

TABLE 5.7: INCIDENCE OF PROCURATION OF MINOR GIRLS, SELLING OF GIRLS FOR PROSTITUTION AND BUYING OF GIRLS FOR PROSTITUTION, INDIA, 1994 TO 1999

	1994	1995	1996	1997	1998	1999
Procuration of minor girls	206	107	94	87	171	172
Selling of girls for prostitution	34	17	6	9	11	13
Buying of girls for prostitution	4	19	22	13	13	5

Source: National Crime Records Bureau.

hilt by defence lawyers. Bail is obtained without much difficulty. Fake relatives suddenly surface to take back the girl and give an undertaking to look after her. While the procedural wrangles and the cases drag on, the helpless victim has to ensure a long period of waiting and detention in a home till her case is decided. The business of trafficking continues by changing names and places or going underground for a while. A rescued girl has a bleak future for leading a normal life as she faces rejection in most cases in her family, community, and society at large. She is considered to be a fallen woman, even though she is a victim and it is the abuser who is fallen. Most girls are mentally broken and reconciled to the life of a sex worker due to years of abuse and use of force. They also get used to this kind of life and money, not involving hard work. Social workers face difficulty in motivating the girl and strengthening her will to wage the struggle for an alternate life.

POLICIES AND PROGRAMMES

The Constitution of India, under Article 39, a Directive Principle of State Policy, requires the State to ensure that children are not abused, and childhood is protected against exploitation and against moral and material abandonment. The United Nations Convention on the Rights of the Child, 1989, which India has ratified requires the State to protect the child from all forms of sexual exploitation and sexual abuse. Fulfilment of these duties requires the participation of the State as well as institutions of civil society.

Governmental response to the problem of child prostitution has in the past been primarily within the framework of existing legislations such as the Indian Penal Code, the Juvenile Justice Act, 1986, the Immoral Traffic (Prevention) Act, 1956, and some welfare services. These children were not separately identified as a target group and did not get focused attention to their special problems and situation. The position changed somewhat when in response to a public interest litigation the Supreme Court directed in 1990 that the central and state governments set up an Advisory Committee to examine the problem of child prostitution, and suggest measures for its eradication and for the welfare of these children. The Committee constituted by the Government of India met for the first time after four years in 1994. It constituted a Sub-Committee which prepared a report giving a comprehensive set of recommendations covering prevention, rehabilitation, welfare and enforcement. A series of seminars, conferences, and workshops have also been organized, some sponsored by the governmental and international agencies to deliberate on various issues and recommend areas of action. A National Plan of Action has also been prepared. The National Commission on Women sponsored a number of surveys and conferences/seminars/workshops with the participation of NGOs, and came up with recommendations. Some state governments have initiated administrative and welfare measures against the *devadasi* system, though the effort is still too weak to break the tradition and the patronage it has.

The emergence of NGOs whose activities are focused on child prostitution is a recent development. They are located in some cities only. Some NGOs have received assistance from state governments for welfare and rehabilitation work. Some have received assistance from international funding agencies for specific activities. NGOs also raise their own resources. Apart from providing services, they engage in advocacy work, documentation, organization of seminars and workshops, networking with other NGOs in India and abroad, and dialogue and discussion with government agencies.

State governments, on whom the primary responsibility of prevention, treatment, care, and rehabilitation lies, continue to perceive child prostitution as a low priority area, some even not recognizing that the problem exists. The National Human Rights Commission, for instance, when alerted by press reports to the alarming increase in child prostitution in Tamil Nadu and Goa wrote to these state governments. They responded by stating that 'there were no reported cases of child prostitution in their States' (NHRC 1996). A similar view has been expressed by some other state governments (Menon 2000).

Children rescued by the police, often at the behest of NGOs or because of media exposure or information received, are sent to welfare homes. A massive operation brings a sudden load on these institutions. As a result of poor coordination between social welfare departments and the police, problems arise during the period of remand due to physical incapacity and shortage of manpower to handle a sudden increase in numbers. This became apparent in Bombay, when immediate action was taken to rescue the girls after the Chief Justice of the Bombay High Court issued a suo moto order and directed the state government of Maharashtra to prepare a scheme to rehabilitate the girls (Agnes 1996). In any case, such one-time raids hardly serve as a deterrent. Even otherwise, the homes function like custodial institutions. The environment is sterile and impersonal. They do not provide an individualized approach, a caring environment, or effective counselling. The homes show little understanding of the differential family and social circumstances of the girls, their aspirations, attitude, mental state, behavioural problems, and distrust of motives. Lack of education and vocational skills and social prejudices about their past make the task of rehabilitation very difficult. Girls who want to rehabilitate themselves face an uphill task and need strong supportive services and a caring attitude, as soon after release the girls are haunted by their past, pursued by traffickers, pimps, and brothel owners, and threatened by them. In many cases, the girls have no option but to land once again in brothels, rendering the whole process infructuous.

There has hardly been any success in the prevention of child prostitution and its trafficking. The problem shows no signs of even having been contained. On the contrary, media and other reports seem to suggest that child prostitution is on the increase (Menon 2000). Rescue and rehabilitation efforts continue to be weak, a lot of discussion, assurances and declarations in seminars and conferences notwithstanding.

Child prostitution cannot be tackled by just legal and administrative measures. Strong political will, development of intelligence on trafficking, training of enforcement agency officials, accountability for deliberate lapses, and stringent measures by police to crack trafficking networks, apprehend and prosecute the criminals, and secure their conviction are necessary. The police departments have to be cleaned up, protection currently provided by corrupt politicians and officials made totally ineffective, and the situation closely monitored at the higher levels with the close involvement of NGOs. The trial procedures, too, need to be improved, especially in matters concerning deposition by the child. It is equally important to undertake preventive measures. Non-governmental organizations can play a very important role in identifying families and communities at risk, developing contacts for supplying information, setting up short stay homes, and keeping vigil at railway stations, bus stations, pilgrimage centres, tourist spots, and the like. It is also important for NGOs to expand their work in areas and communities from where a large number of such girls are procured, and where girls customarily enter into prostitution with full family and community support. The current programmes of some of the state governments do not attack the problem in a determined manner and are rather perfunctory in nature. Economic and social development programmes need to be implemented in these areas so that alternate sources of livelihood are found. Social awareness campaigns and close interaction with communities to change their perceptions and give them a sense of dignity are necessary. The case of a village in Kerala where the main source of livelihood was prostitution, and of some villages in Madhya Pradesh inhabited by Bedias who have traditionally depended on prostitution of girls, are two of several successful examples of how vision, commitment, perseverance, and actions of individuals and NGOs can have a sustained impact in tackling the problem and opening an entirely new chapter in their lives (Mukherjee 1998; Radhakrishnan 1997).

Other Children in Difficult Circumstances

There are some other categories of children who, too, need protection and rehabilitative services as, for instance, children engaged in begging, destitute and neglected children, and children of prostitutes. More recent additions to this category are children suffering from AIDS, children whose parents have AIDS, AIDS orphans, and children addicted to drugs.

CHILD BEGGARS

Begging by children is a common scene at public places. It takes place usually at the behest of adult family members. The causes of begging are multiple and not just poverty, incapacity to earn due to old age, distress, or physical handicap, though these are important causative factors. Several families have made begging their source of livelihood. Parents do not hesitate to use small children for begging in tattered clothes even in extremes of cold to draw attention and pity to their state. They teach them how to beg, planning sites and accompanying them, thus making it a joint endeavour. Women often carry severely malnourished infants in their arms to evoke sympathy. Some of these children do not belong to the women but are obtained on payment of a fixed sum. However, some children who engage in begging are unattached, abandoned or destitute, or have run away from home due to poverty, physical abuse, and an intolerable home environment. Not many cases are known of kidnapping and maiming of children for use for begging or of the existence of organized begging rackets. The Committee on Begging by Children: How many of Them are Kidnapped reported that it did not come across any case of maiming of a child for purposes of begging. It cautioned, however, that conclusive evidence would be possible only if the background of handicapped children found begging was investigated (CBCS 1971). No follow-up action was taken.

The Code of Criminal Procedure, the Indian Penal Code (Section 363A), the Indian Railway Act, Police Acts of states, and Municipal Acts have provisions to restrict begging. The Juvenile Justice Act, 1986 covered beggary and contained penal provisions (imprisonment and fine) for use of a juvenile for begging. So does the newly enacted Juvenile Justice (Care and Protection of Children) Act, 2000 which repealed the 1986 Act. Sixteen states and two union territories have specific anti-beggary legislations which are comprehensive in nature. However, the legislations are very poorly enforced. The number of beggar homes in the country is small—117 in 1992–3. The centrally sponsored scheme of beggary prevention through care and rehabilitative services has evoked a poor response from state governments. Out of a modest budget allocation of Rs. 3.4 crores in the five year period 1992–3 to 1996–7, only Rs. 2.2 crores could be utilized (Ministry of Social Justice and Empowerment 2000).

The approach to the problem of beggary has been largely legislative cum correctional—apprehending beggars and providing them correctional and rehabilitation services in beggars' homes. The basic factors which cause begging have not been tackled. Social tolerance of begging, and even encouraging it by giving alms, indifference of law enforcement agencies, and low priority to the problem in terms of funding, administrative action, and services has not helped in any way in tackling the problem. There is poor coordination between the police and the welfare departments in apprehending beggars. The services and the environment in beggar homes is very unsatisfactory. The political will and administrative action to tackle it is minimal, except when drives are conducted during the tourist season in areas frequented by tourists. Despite the juvenile justice and specific anti-beggary legislation, hundreds of child beggars can be seen at the public places reflecting administrative inaction.

DESTITUTE, ABANDONED, AND NEGLECTED CHILDREN

Statistics on destitution or near destitution among children are not available. The problem is far more visible in urban areas, but is present in rural areas as well when the family faces destitution or near destitution. Factors such as natural calamities (cyclone, drought, flood, or earthquake), terrorism, insurgency, or communal riots cause severe disruption in the lives of children, especially when it is accompanied by the death of parents. Some children run away from home because of unbearable treatment, which includes physical, emotional and sexual abuse and mental torture. Death of parents, family breakdown, desertion, alcoholism, drug abuse, or criminal activities of family members also contribute to the problem. Some children get lost or are deliberately abandoned by poor parents in a public place or near an orphanage in the hope that they will be picked up by a state agency or voluntary organization. Illegitimacy is another contributory factor (Bose 1980).

The Juvenile Justice Act, 1986 provided for services for the care of certain categories of neglected children, which include destitute and abandoned children. The Act defined a neglected juvenile (boy below 16 years or a girl below 18 years) as one '(i) who is found begging; or (ii) is found without having any home or settled place of abode and without any ostensible means of subsistence and is destitute; (iii) has a parent or guardian who is unfit or incapacitated to exercise control over the juvenile; or (iv) lives in a brothel or with a prostitute or frequently goes to any place used for the purpose of prostitution, or is found to associate with any prostitute or any other person who leads an immoral, drunken or depraved life; (v) who is being, or is likely to be, abused or exploited for immoral or illegal purposes or unconscionable gain'. The Act also covered victimized juveniles, and prescribed punishment for cruelty to juveniles, employment of juveniles for begging, giving intoxicating liquor or narcotic drug or psychotropic substance, procuring a juvenile for employment and withholding the earnings or using the same for own purpose. The Act laid down the procedure for production of neglected juveniles before the Juvenile Welfare Board, and for keeping the child in an observation home/juvenile home or under the care and supervision of a parent, guardian, or fit person. Responsibility for implementation of the provisions of the Juvenile Justice Act rested with the states. Very few services have, however, come into existence for neglected juveniles under the aegis of the Act. Most of the services for neglected children are provided by voluntary organizations outside the statutory framework. They raise their own resources. Some of these organizations get some grant-in-aid from the government. The services provided include children's homes and non-institutional services like foster care, sponsorship, and adoption. The newly enacted Juvenile Justice (Care and Protection of Children) Act, 2000 has repealed the 1986 Act. It, too, envisages a range of services for children below 18 years who are in need of care and protection. However, unless child friendly institutional and non-institutional structures, procedures and systems of functioning are put in place, trained personnel deployed and adequate funding assured, little benefit is likely to accrue.

Children's homes (or orphanages as they were earlier called) represent the earliest response through voluntary effort to cater to children in need of a home. They were sponsored and aided mainly through private initiative and show a great degree of heterogeneity in objectives, organization, structure, size, standard of service, and clientele. Their geographical distribution, both between states and within states, also shows considerable variation. Several states where there is much greater need for such services have few voluntary organizations. Good professionally run voluntary organizations with trained manpower and a committed management are not many in number. Evaluation studies of children's homes assisted by the central government indicated uneven standards, inadequate funding, release of grants without proper assessment of the capability of the organization due to political patronage or other considerations, untrained or inadequately trained staff, delays in releasing grants, and lapses on the part of voluntary organizations in the selection of beneficiaries. Abuse of grant-in-aid by some voluntary organizations has been reported from time to time, resulting in blacklisting of some organizations by the government and other grant giving bodies. The standard of services in several homes run by government as well as voluntary organizations has been found to be poor. Malpractices have also been reported in the media. There are several variants of children's homes, of which the SOS Children's Village is among the better known and better established. Under this form of residential care, individualized attention to the child is made possible by placing a small group of eight to ten children of different ages and sex under a house mother who looks after them as if they were her own children. Abandoned and orphaned children are thus enabled to have the love and attention of a foster mother whose role is crucial in creating and nurturing the children in a family like environment. A group of such family homes forms a children's village. The children draw on existing community services for meeting their diverse needs, as in the case of normal family, and function in close contact and interaction with the community. Funding for the programme is raised through donations and sponsorship of children. The number of SOS children's villages has increased in number and spread all over the country. These have also provided home-like care opportunities for growth and development to children orphaned by cyclones, earthquakes, drought, communal riots, and other mishaps.

Foster care is a non-institutional form of care of orphaned, abandoned, neglected, or other types of children deprived of home care. In foster care, a family agrees to provide a substitute home for a long or short period till the child can be restored to his family, given out in adoption, or some other alternative emerges which is in the best interest of the child. Foster care is considered to be conceptually superior to a children's home which tends to be impersonal, whereas foster care provides a family type of environment. Foster care has, however, not made much progress as the concept is conceived to be somewhat alien to the Indian social milieu; also, the professional back-up for locating families who would be in the best position to provide care is not available. Good casework services, orientation of families accepting children in foster care, and good supervision are lacking in the social welfare administrative structure.

Sponsorship programme for the care of children, both in their families as well as in other families or in an institution, is a relatively new arrival in India. Sponsorship services are organized and developed under the aegis of an NGO. Under the programme, a person sponsoring a child agrees to pay a monthly/yearly allowance for the child for subsistence and for meeting educational, health, and other requirements, thus enabling the child to meet his developmental needs while living in his family which would otherwise not have been possible because of poverty or low and uncertain incomes. Sponsorship enables the child to be in school and continue his education. He is, thus, saved from entering the employment market or wasting time in fruitless endeavours. Several sponsors give preference to girls because of the discrimination they suffer within the family in education and other matters. Some agencies make a more comprehensive approach to sponsorship by covering more than one child in the same family or helping the family to increase is income through income generating projects. Sponsorship is gaining in popularity because it helps the child while at the same time it strengthens the responsibilities of the family in meeting the educational and other needs of children. It also provides an interactive, supportive relationship between the sponsor and the recipient, and is something more than just making a monetary contribution. Initially, most sponsors were from developed countries abroad. However, now a large number of sponsors are from within the country. Fund-raising organizations now appeal regularly for sponsors through correspondence and advertisements for support of a child's education and care for a year or for a longer period.

Abandoned children (infants or a child of a very young age) sometimes find a home through adoption, which gives the same legal status to the child as would accrue if the child was born in that family. Adoption among Hindus is governed by the Hindu Adoptions and Maintenance Act of 1956. Since there are no laws of adoption among some communities, social workers have been urging for the enactment of a law applicable to all communities, giving primacy to the well-being of the child being adopted. Several memoranda have been presented to the Government of India in this regard. The Government of India introduced in the Rajya Sabha in 1972 the Adoption of Children Bill, but due to opposition from a minority community on the ground that adoption is not permitted in their religion and that such a law will be tantamount to interference in their personal law, the Bill was withdrawn even though it had been approved by a Joint Select Committee after six years in limbo. A new Bill was introduced in the Lok Sabha in 1980, but could not be passed. Representations by voluntary organizations for having even an enabling legislation drew a blank, showing how political considerations tend to supersede welfare.

Indian children are taken out by foreigners under the Guardians and Wards Act of 1890 with a view to adoption in their own countries after obtaining permission from the High Court for guardianship of the child. Detailed guidelines have been prepared by the Central Adoption Resource Agency (CARA) of the Ministry of Social Justice and Empowerment in regard to the procedure to be followed by foreign nationals. Indian parents, too, can get guardianship of a child under the Act and give a home to the child who does not, however, have the same rights as a legally adopted child.

The Ministry of Social Justice and Empowerment has tried to streamline the procedure relating to adoption by granting recognition to Indian and foreign agencies engaged in adoption work. In 2000–1, there were 80 agencies in the country which had been given recognition for undertaking work for inter-country adoption. In addition, 306 foreign agencies have been enlisted in more than 27 countries to sponsor inter-country adoption of Indian children. The official policy is to promote in-country adoption. Table 5.8 gives the number of children who have found adoptive homes inside the country and outside. The number of such children has varied between 1,970 and 3,152 in a eleven year period beginning in 1989.

The Ministry of Social Justice and Empowerment gives grants to voluntary agencies for preparation of communication and publicity material for promoting adoption within the country. It also gives grants for foundling homes where the infant is kept till adoption takes place. In 1999–2000, Rs. 1.62 crores were given to 38 NGOs for the purpose. Grants were also given to Voluntary Coordinating Agencies to promote in-country adoption. These agencies maintain a list of Indian parents who want to adopt, and match them with children available in various adoption agencies.

TABLE 5.8: NUMBER OF CHILDREN WHO HAVE BEEN FOUND ADOPTIVE HOME BY AGENCIES RECOGNIZED BY THE CENTRAL ADOPTION RESOURCE AGENCY, INDIA, 1989 TO 1999

Year	Inter-country adoption		In-country adoption		Total	
	No.	%	No.	%	No.	%
1989	1,213	61.6	757	38.4	1,970	100.0
1990	1,272	54.2	1,075	45.8	2,347	100.0
1991	936	44.0	1,190	56.0	2,126	100.0
1992	1,007	43.8	1,293	56.2	2,300	100.0
1993	1,134	45.1	1,382	54.9	2,516	100.0
1994	1,128	44.5	1,409	55.5	2,537	100.0
1995	1,236	46.5	1,424	53.5	2,660	100.0
1996	990	37.9	1,623	62.1	2,613	100.0
1997	1,026	43.5	1,330	56.5	2,356	100.0
1998	1,406	44.6	1,746	55.4	3,152	100.0
1999	1,293	45.4	1,558	54.6	2,851	100.0

Source: Ministry of Social Justice and Empowerment.

CHILDREN OF PROSTITUTES

Surveys have shown that most sex workers want to have children of their own. The study, sponsored by the CSWB, of six metropolitan cities reported that two-thirds of the sex workers had one to two children whom they treated with love and affection and whose well-being they felt concerned about (Mukherjee and Das 1996). There are, however, problems of looking after them, especially during the night when they are busy with their customers. The process of growing up of these children in unhealthy surroundings in an environment of pimps, brothel owners, alcoholics, customers of all description, characterized by drunken brawls, gambling, drug peddling, abuses, filthy language, and various forms of deviant behaviour is an unsavoury experience. Children are exposed to negotiations, payments, and actual sex by strangers with their mother. The stigma of illegitimacy, the occupation of the mother, and the humiliation of being abused as an offspring of a prostitute are not easy for the child to come to terms with. While the very young are put to sleep, even drugged during the night when the mother is looking for or entertaining customers, the older children roam the streets, sleep on the pavement, enter into fights, and learn to fend for themselves. Some run errands for customers. Girls over the age of ten years are subjected to lewd overtures and remarks by the customers who offer attractive sums to tempt the mother of the girl (Patkar 1991).

Studies have reported that many sex workers do not want their children to be a part of the prostitution racket. They would like their children to go to school and have a different and a better future. They want their daughters to get married and lead a normal life and the sons to get employment (Mukherjee and Das 1996). Those who can afford, that is, have enough savings and a strong motivation, send the children, both male and female, to live with their relatives and go to school or study in residential schools. Even when prostitutes do not want their daughters to follow their footsteps, this becomes inevitable in a number of cases, when there are no savings, there is no alternate source of sustenance, the girl has no education or training to make a living, or when there is a debt to redeem or other compulsions. In many cases, a good alternative that becomes available is when the girl is married off. While some marriages are successful, in several cases the marriage breaks up and the husband begins to use force to offer his wife to customers to support him and to find money for his drinking, gambling and drugs.

Non-governmental organizations working in red-light areas in the metropolitan cities have found good response from sex workers to the welfare services they provide to the children—day and/or night care centres, pre-school education, health and nutrition care, recreation, counselling, financial support for entering school and for stay in residential school, and rehabilitation programmes. These NGOs are optimistic about the outcome of their efforts on the lives of these children and their future. Some state governments have begun giving grants to support such programmes, but the coverage is a small fraction of the need.

The central government, under its scheme of grant-in-aid to voluntary organizations assisted 25 organizations in 1999–2000 to provide welfare services to children of sex workers. Large areas, however, remain uncovered, and there continues to be a very wide gap between the need for such services and the services available.

AIDS-AFFECTED CHILDREN

HIV, an illness which threatens life and causes untold suffering, is spreading in India. There is, unfortunately, very little data on the impact of AIDS on children of parents with AIDS, children who have AIDS themselves, and AIDS orphans. The current emphasis in AIDS control is on prevention and treatment. The nature of problems faced by children has not been researched upon, nor does the programme provide for services for such children. This is an area which needs immediate attention so that child, family, and community focused intervention strategies can be designed and services provided.

CHILDREN AFFECTED BY DRUGS

Not much is known about the extent of drug abuse among children (in school as well as out of school) or their involvement in drug trafficking or other drug related offences. Some of the earlier studies on street children sponsored by UNICEF in the 1980s reported a very low incidence of drug abuse, but the problem was not specifically investigated or probed. A later study covering Bombay, Calcutta, Delhi, and Hyderabad, however, reported that drug abuse is widespread and is increasing (Mehra 1996). The incidence of drug abuse is no longer confined to slums, the poor, and the criminals. Media reports and data from de-addiction centres, hospitals, counselling centres, and NGO groups indicate that drug abuse now cuts across various social and economic classes though, mercifully, the incidence among girls is very low. The problem of drug abuse among children needs to be scientifically investigated so that interventions can be designed and services provided. The family and the community need to be closely involved in prevention as well as in de-addiction endeavours.

OTHER VULNERABLE CHILDREN

There are other categories of vulnerable children who need not only care and protection but also services for their rehabilitation and development. Their special needs and circumstances have not been carefully investigated as, for instance, in the case of children affected by terrorism, insurgency, riots, natural calamities, and displacement due to major development projects. Girl child victims of sexual abuse is another category that needs attention. Children in broken families, or in families where adults are engaged in deviant behaviour or are unfit to provide a proper environment for the child's growth and development, are at risk and need protection, care, and opportunities for growth and development. The number of such categories of children is increasing, but because of their dispersed character, they have escaped the attention of policy makers. Response to their needs has been ad hoc and largely of the nature of relief. It is important that such categories of children are identified, their problems studied, and programmes developed.

SUMMING UP

A large number of children are in especially difficult circumstances and need carefully designed welfare services. Unfortunately, not much is known either of the nature of the problems faced by such children or of the numbers involved.

The problem of street children has acquired a high degree of visibility in urban areas. The problem needs to be given immediate attention failing which the social fallout could be serious. Current services for street children cover only a small fraction and are focused on relief and rehabilitation. The gap between the growing number of street children and those receiving services shows no signs of being narrowed. On the contrary, it is widening. The basic causes which give birth to the phenomenon will continue to be there in the coming years and, in all probability, operate with greater vigour. A matter of concern is the low priority given by state governments and local authorities who do not seem to appreciate the gravity of the problem, though its magnitude is increasing not only in the metropolitan cities but in other urban areas as well. Programmes currently under way face problems of uncertain funding, schematic rigidity, paucity if trained manpower, and poor interdepartmental coordination. A large number of cities have no NGOs working for street children, clearly indicating the need not only for strengthening NGO activity in existing cities, but covering new cities as well.

For the bulk of street children who live with their families, child focused community based projects rather than an institutional approach which separates the children from their families would be necessary, as a preventive strategy pays dividends in the long run. Programmes for street children need to identify families at risk of breakdown such as, for instance, poor single parent families engaged in a grim struggle or problem families having to cope with alcoholism, drug addiction, criminal activities, or chronic illness. The goal should be to provide a safety net for such children and strengthen the capacity of families to cope with such situations through support services. A local level situational analysis would result in better targeting, while the involvement of the families and children will lead to more pragmatic programming. Children who are on their own and who have little or no contacts with their families and are for all practical purposes without a home would need a different package of services which would include shelter, food and clothing, education, health care, and counselling.

Policy makers must recognize that the existence of street children cannot be swept away by clearing the streets through special drives under the Juvenile Justice (Care and Protection of Children) Act, anti-beggary Acts, and administrative measures. Street children need a humane, flexible, and a largely non-institutional strategy, and not a policing or custodial cum institutional approach. The children are resourceful with proven ability to survive in difficult situations. They need supportive services and a caring approach so that they can improve their self-image, aspire for a better future, start having hopes, and try to rebuild their lives. It is of outmost urgency that street children receive high priority and move up the agenda of child development concerns of not only central and state governments, but also local authorities and non-governmental organizations. Coordination of endeavours between administrative departments and NGOs is necessary for successful implementation of projects.

Juvenile delinquency is the outcome of a number of predisposing social and economic factors. Though juvenile delinquency is perceived by people to be increasing, official statistics of IPC crimes by juveniles collected by the National Crime Records Bureau indicates a decline from 24,827 cases in 1988 to 8,888 in 1999. To what extent this reflects ground reality or under-reporting by police, because it is administratively more convenient to deal with the violator and control crime if the apprehended person is not a juvenile, needs serious probing.

Implementation of the Juvenile Justice Act has not been satisfactory. States give very low priority to juvenile justice matters. Services, both institutional and non-institutional, are grossly inadequate and provide unsatisfactory quality of care. Police are not trained to show sensitivity when dealing with a juvenile. The establishment of special cells in police departments with properly trained personnel would be helpful in dealing with juvenile delinquents. Non-governmental organizations too, need to be promoted and assisted.

Sexual abuse of children is not as rare a phenomenon as is generally believed, nor is it confined to only the poorer classes. The abusers are usually adults who are known to the child and the family. Sexual abuse in institutions for the care and protection of children has also been reported. There is an urgent need for designing effective intervention strategies. A disturbing feature is the increase in cases of rape of children, which is the most abominable form of child abuse, and the increase in the percentage of very young children being raped. Intervention programmes for abused children and their families need to be promoted, supported, and developed. Perpetrators of the crime need to be prosecuted and given deterrent punishment.

Trafficking in children is on the rise. There has hardly been any success in the prevention of child prostitution and its trafficking. Rescue and rehabilitation efforts continue to be weak, a lot of discussion, assurances, and declarations in seminars and conferences, and plans of action notwithstanding.

Child prostitution cannot be tackled by just legal and administrative measures. Strong political will, development of intelligence on trafficking, training of enforcement agency officials, accountability for deliberate lapses, and stringent measures by police to crack trafficking networks, apprehend and prosecute the criminals, and secure their conviction are necessary. The police departments have to be cleaned up, protection currently provided by corrupt politicians and officials made totally ineffective, and the situation closely monitored at the higher levels with the close involvement of NGOs. The trial procedures, too, need to be improved, especially in matters concerning deposition by the child. It is equally important to undertake preventive measures. Non-governmental organizations can play a very important role in identifying families at risk, developing contacts for supplying information, setting up short stay homes, and keeping vigil at railway stations, bus stations, pilgrimage centres, tourist spots, and the like. It is also important for NGOs to expand their work in areas and communities from where a large number of such girls are procured. Economic and social development programmes need to be implemented in these areas, so that alternate sources of livelihood can be found. Social awareness campaigns and close interaction with communities to change their perceptions and give them a sense of dignity are necessary.

Some categories of disadvantaged children such as child beggars and destitute, abandoned, and neglected children were the earliest to draw a response from social workers and policy makers. The State responded by way of legislation and welfare services (mainly institutional) stipulated under the Act, as well as through grant-in-aid to voluntary organizations. A much larger number of welfare services came into being as a result of the efforts of voluntary organizations. However, there has been, and continues to be, a very wide gap between the need for such services and the children reached.

Despite the existence of specific anti-beggary legislation, clauses in other legislations, and the Juvenile Justice (Care and Protection of Children) Act, 2000 (which replaced the Juvenile Justice Act, 1986), hundreds of children can be seen begging in cities and towns, usually pushed into it by their families who collect the earnings. The political will to tackle the problem of begging has been missing, while administrative action for prevention and rehabilitation has been rather perfunctory. Services for destitute, abandoned, and neglected children, and for children of prostitutes, are scanty and fall far short of the need. The standards of service in most state run institutions and a fairly large number of institutions run by voluntary organizations are not satisfactory. Instances of maltreatment of children surface in the media from time to time. Children facing difficult circumstances in their families due to alcoholism, drug addiction, mental illness, imprisonment, or long term ailment or disability of earning members have received hardly any attention. Even a proper assessment of the nature and magnitude of the problems faced, and the interventions needed, has not been done. Sponsorship programmes have expanded considerably in recent years. These need to be strengthened. Adoption services have been streamlined. It is of utmost importance, however, that an adoption law, even an enabling one, applicable to all communities is passed, giving primacy to the well-being of the child.

Some other categories of children in need of care and protection are emerging on the social scene. Prominent among these are children of prostitutes, children suffering from AIDS, children whose parents have AIDS, AIDS orphans, children affected by drugs, terrorism, riots, and calamities, and children living in broken or problem families. Very few services are currently focused on such children due to low priority, paucity and funds, and inadequate awareness of policy makers. Since interventions and programmes should not be based on hunches, it is important that new and old problem areas are researched in depth so that long and short term strategies can be designed, and focused need based services can be organized.

Bibliography

Adithi, 1995, *Female Infanticide in Bihar*, Patna (cyclostyled).

Agarwal, D.K., A. Dutta, R.R. Arora and M.R.V. Nair, 1976, 'Natural History of Measles in Rural and Urban Community of Varanasi', *Journal of Communicable Diseases*, vol. 8, pp. 289–96.

Agarwal, D.K., K.N. Agarwal and A.M. Tripathi, 1987, 'Nutrition Status of Rural Pregnant Women of Bihar and Uttar Pradesh, *Indian Pediatrics*, vol. 24, February, pp. 119–25.

Agarwal, D.K., S.K. Kasana, A.M. Tripathi and K.N. Agarwal, 1986, 'Environmental Factors in Childhood Diarrhoea in Rural Areas', *Indian Pediatrics*, vol. 23, February, pp. 89–95.

Aggarwal, Arun Kumar, 1998, 'Low Birth Weight Prevalence and Antenatal Care Practices in a Rural Area of Haryana', *Indian Pediatrics*, vol. 35, October, p. 1031.

Agnes, Flavia, 1996, 'Rescuing Mumbai's Child Sex Workers', *Economic and Political Weekly*, 6 April, p. 873.

Aiyar, Shahnaz Anklesaria, 1997, 'Child Prostitution: A Symptom of Our Sick Society', *Times of India*, 16 April.

Aiyar, Swaminathan S.A., 1998, 'From Bimaru to a World Record', *Times of India*, 25 October.

Antonisamy, B., P.S.S. Rao, and M. Sivaram, 1994, 'Changing Scenario of Birth Weight in South India', *Indian Pediatrics*, vol. 31, August, pp. 931–7.

Aras, Radha Y., Nalini P. Pai and Anuja Purandare, 1990, 'Perinatal Mortality—A Retrospective Hospital Study', *Journal of Obstetrics and Gynaecology of India*, vol. 8, pp. 365–9.

Arimpoor, Joe, 1992, *Street Children of Madras: A Situational Analysis*, Noida: National Labour Institute.

Awasthi, Shally, Vinod K. Pande and Henry Glick, 1996, 'Under Fives Mortality in the Urban Slums of Lucknow, *Indian Journal of Pediatrics*, vol. 63, no. 3, pp. 363–8.

BAIF Development Research Foundation (BAIF DRF), 1997, *Factors Affecting Health Seeking Behaviour and Utilization of Curative Health Care*, Pune: BAIF-DRF.

Baker, A.W. and S.P. Duncan, 1985, 'Child Sexual Abuse: A Study of Prevalence in Great Britain, *Child Abuse and Neglect*, vol. 9, pp. 457–67.

Bandopadhyaya, Shibani, K. Banerjee, K.K. Khanna, R.S. Sharma and T. Verghese, 1992, 'Drinking Water Quality and Diarrhoea in Delhi', *Journal of Communicable Diseases*, vol. 24, no. 3, pp. 156–8.

Bandopadhyaya, Shibani, K. Banerjee and R.S. Sharma, 1993, 'Practices of Preparation of Oral Rehydration Solution among Mothers Reporting to the Drug Distribution Centres in Delhi, India, '*Journal of Diarrhoeal Disease Research,* vol. 11, no. 4, December, pp. 249–51.

Banerjee, K.B. and Jai P. Narain (eds.),1988, *Combined Surveys on ARI, Diarrhoea and EPI.* New Delhi: National Institute of Communicable Diseases.

Bang, R.A., M. Baitule, S. Sarmukaddam, A.T. Bang. Y. Choudhary, and O. Tale, 1989, 'High Prevalence of Gynaecological Diseases in Rural Indian Women', *Lancet,* 14 January, pp. 85–7.

Bansal, Raj Kumar and Sanjay Banerjee, 1991, 'Child Labour in Surat', *Indian Journal of Maternal and Child Health*, vol. 2, no. 4, pp. 121–4.

Basu, R.N. and J. Sokhey, 1984, 'Prevalence of Poliomyelitis in India', *Indian Journal of Pediatrics,* vol. 51, September–October, pp. 515–19.

Batra, Meenakshi, 1990, *Child Labour in Gem Polishing Industry of Jaipur: Some Observations.* Noida: National Labour Institute.

Bavdekar, S.B., M.S. Bavdekar, R.R. Kasla, K.J. Raghunandana, S.Y Joshi and G.S. Hathi, 1994, 'Infant Feeding Practices in Bombay Slums', *Indian Pediatrics,* vol. 31, September, pp.1083–7.

Benjamin, Anoop I. and Prema Zachariah, 1993, 'Nutrition Status and Feeding Practices in Under 3 Year Old Children in a Rural Community in Ludhiana, Punjab, *Health and Population, Perspectives and Issues,* vol. 16, nos. 1 and 2, pp. 3–21.

Bharadwaj, A. K., D. Nayar, S. Ramachandran and Umesh Kapil, 1997, 'Assessment of Iodine Deficiency in District Bikaner, Rajasthan', *Indian Journal of Maternal and Child Health*, vol. 8, no. 1, pp. 18–20.

Bhat, B. Vishnu and M. Ravikumara, 1996, 'Perinatal Mortality in India: Need for Introspection', *Indian Journal of Maternal and Child Health,* vol. 7, no. 2, pp. 31–3.

Bhatia, V., H. M. Swami, M. Bhatia and S.P.S. Bhatia, 1999, 'Attitude and Practices Regarding Diarrhoea in Rural Community in Chandigarh', *Indian Journal of Pediatrics,* vol. 66, pp. 499–503.

Bhattacharjee, J., Devadethan and R.S. Sharma, 1994, 'Acute Paralytic Poliomyelitis in Delhi, 1975–1992', *Indian Journal of Pediatrics*, vol. 61, no. 2, pp. 167–72.

Bhattacharjee, J.R.S. Sharma, K.K. Datta and T. Verghese, 1991, 'Acute Respiratory Infection and its Control (in Under Five Children), New Delhi: National Institute of Communicable Diseases.

Bihari, V., S.K. Rastogi, B.N. Gupta, T. Hussain, N. Mathur, P.N. Mahendra, S. Srivastava, and N. Garg, 1992, 'Occupational Morbidity among Children Employed in Brassware Industry', *Indian Pediatrics*, vol. 29, February, pp. 195–201.

Booth, Beverley E. and Manorama Verma, 1992, 'Decreased Access to Medical Care for Girls in Punjab, India: The Roles of Age, Religion and Distance', *American Journal of Public Health*, vol. 82, no. 7, pp. 1155–7.

Booth, Beverley E., Manorama Verma and R.S. Beri, 1994, 'Fetal Sex Determination in Infants in Punjab, India: Correlations and Implications', *British Medical Journal* , vol. 309, 12 November, pp. 1259–61.

Bose, A.B., 1980, 'Welfare of Children in Need of Care and Protection', in *Profile of the Child in India,* New Delhi: Ministry of Social Welfare.

________, 1992, *The Disadvantaged Urban Child in India*, Innocenti: UNICEF International Child Development Centre.

Burra, Neera, 1986, 'Glass Factories of Firozabad, II, Plight of Child Workers', *Economic and Political Weekly,* 22 November, pp. 2033–6.

________, 1987, 'Exploitation of Child Workers in Lock Industry of Aligarh', *Economic and Political Weekly*, 11 July, pp. 1117–21.

________, 1991, *Child Labour in the Gem Polishing Industry in Jaipur,* Noida: National Labour Institute.

________, 1992, *Child Labour in the Pottery Industry of Khurja*, Noida: National Labour Institute.

Central Bureau of Correctional Services (CBCS), 1971, *Begging by Children: How Many of Them are Kidnapped*? New Delhi: Department of Social Welfare.

Central Bureau of Health Intelligence (CBHI), 2000, *Health Information India, 1997 & 1998,* New Delhi: Ministry of Health and Family Welfare.

Chandrashekar, Shalini, R.S. Phaneendra Rao, B.K. Chakladar, Lalitha Krishnan and N.S. Nair, 1998, 'Perinatal Mortality in a Rural District of South India', *Indian Journal of Pediatrics*, vol. 65, pp. 709–15.

Chhabra, P., S. Garg, S.K. Mittal, L. Satyanarayan, M. Mehra and N. Sharma, 1993, 'Magnitude of Acute Respiratory Infections in Under Fives', *Indian Pediatrics*, vol. 30, November, pp. 1315–19.

Chunkath, Sheela Rani and V.B. Athreya, 1997, 'Female Infanticide in Tamil Nadu: Some Evidence', *Economic and Political Weekly,* 26 April, pp. WS 21–8.

CINI, 1996, *Abuse of Children as Part of Commercialised Vice*, Village Daulatpur (District 24 Parganas, West Bengal): Child in Need Institute.

Clow, A.G., 1926, *Indian Factory Legislation: A Historical Survey,* Calcutta: Government of India, Central Publication Branch.

Comptroller and Auditor General of India (CAG), 1985, *Report for the Year Ended 31 March 1984, Union Government (Civil), Ministry of Social Welfare*, Delhi: Controller of Publications.

________, 1990, *Report for the Year Ended 31 March, 1989, Union Government (Civil), Integrated Child Development Services*, Delhi: Controller of Publications.

________, 1998, *Report for the Year Ended 31 March 1999, no. 3 (Civil), Government of West Bengal*, Calcutta.

________, 1999, *Report for the Year Ended 31 March 1999, no. 3 (Civil), Government of National Capital Territory of Delhi*, Delhi.

________, 2000a, *Report for the Year Ended 31 March 1999, no. 3 (Civil), Government of Assam.*

________, 2000b, *Report for the Year Ended 31 March 1999, no. 3 (Civil), Government of Himachal Pradesh*, Shimla.

________, 2000c, *Report for the Year Ended 31 March 1999, no. 3 (Civil), Government of Kerala.*

________, 2000d, *Report for the Year Ended 31 March 1999, no. 3 (Civil), Government of Orissa*, Cuttack.

_______, 2000e, *Report of the Comptroller and Auditor General of India for the Year Ended March 1999, Union Government (Civil), Performance Appraisals, no. 3 of 2000*, New Delhi.

Das Gupta, Monica, 1987, 'Selective Discrimination against Female Children in Rural Punjab, India', *Population and Development Review,* vol. 13, no. 1, pp. 77–100.

Datta, K.K., Shibani Bandopadhyaya, K.K. Khanna and K. Banerjee, 1993, 'Epidemiological Features of Cholera Outbreak in Delhi in 1988, *Journal of Communicable Diseases*, vol. 25, no. 2, pp. 57–61.

Dave, P. N., 1988, *Achievement Under Project PECR* , New Delhi: National Council of Educational Research and Training.

Dayal, R., R. Prasad, M.N. Misra, K. Kalra, D.N. Pandey, P.P. Mathur and R.S. Dayal, 1986, 'Are Delinquents Born or Made?' *Indian Pediatrics,* vol. 23, August, pp. 627–33.

Debabrata, Roma, 1997, *The Lost Childhood,* New Delhi: National Commission for Women.

Deivanayagam, N., K. Nedunchelian and K.G. Kamala, 1991, 'Neonatal Tetanus: Observations of Antenatal Immunisation, Natal and Immediate Postnatal Factors', *Indian Journal of Pediatrics,* vol. 58, pp. 119–22.

Deivanayagam, N., S. Sivarathinam and V. S. Sankaranarayanan, 1987, 'Morbidity and Mortality Pattern of the Hospitalized Children at Madras City', *Indian Journal of Pediatrics*, vol. 54, pp. 733–7.

Department of Education, 1995, *Budgetary Resources for Education 1951–52 to 1993–4*, New Delhi: Ministry of Human Resource Development, Government of India.

_______, 1997a, *Annual Report, 1996–7*, New Delhi: Ministry of Human Resource Development, Government of India.

_______, 1997b, *Report of the Committee of State Education Ministers on Implications of the Proposal to Make Elementary Education a Fundamental Right*, New Delhi: Ministry of Human Resource Development, Government of India.

_______, 1998a, *Annual Report, 1997–8*, New Delhi: Ministry of Human Resource Development, Government of India.

_______, 1998b, *Three Years' of DPEP and Learners' Achievement*, New Delhi: Ministry of Human Resource Development, Government of India.

_______, 1999, *Results of High School and Higher Secondary Examinations, 1995 and 1996*, New Delhi: Ministry of Human Resource Development, Government of India.

_______, 2000, *Annual Report, 1999–2000,* New Delhi: Ministry of Human Resource Development, Government of India.

Department of Salt, 1995, *Production and Availability of Iodised Salt: State-wise Profile*, New Delhi: Ministry of Industry, Government of India.

_______, 1997, 'Global Iodine Deficiency Disorder (IDD) Day', *Hindustan Times,* 21 October.

Department of Social Welfare, 1968, *Report of the Committee for the Preparation of a Programme for Children,* New Delhi: Government of India.

Department of Women and Child Development (DW&CD), 1994, *Child Prostitution: A Status and Action Report*, New Delhi: Government of India.

———, 1998, *India Nutrition Profile*, New Delhi: Government of India.

D'Lima, Hazel and Rima Gosalia, 1989, '*Situation Analysis of Street Children in the City of Bombay*, Bombay: College of Social Work.

Deshpande, J.M., V.K. Rao, S.S. Nadkarni, J.P. Bhatia and J.J. Rodrigues, 1995, 'An Evaluation of Cold Chain in Maharashtra and Karnataka State by Potency Testing of Field Samples of Oral Poliovirus Vaccine', *Indian Journal of Medical Research*, vol. 102, August, pp. 60–5.

Dharmalingam, A. 1993, 'Female Beedi Workers in a South Indian Village', *Economic and Political Weekly*, 3 July, pp. 1461–9.

Dhawan, S., P.K. Singhal and D.K. Taneja, 1988, 'Diarrhoeal Beliefs and Practices among Rural Mothers in Delhi', *Indian Pediatrics*, vol. 25, February, pp. 125–37.

Directorate General of Health Services (DGHS), 2000, *Bulletin of Rural Health Statistics in India*, New Delhi: Ministry of Health and Family Welfare, Government of India.

Dubey, Meenal, 2000, 'Suspected of Theft, Girl 8 Battered, Starved and Killed', *Hindustan Times*, 10 June.

Dutta, K.K., Shibani Bandopadhyaya, K.K. Khanna and K. Banerjee, 1993, 'Epidemiological Features of Cholera Outbreak in Delhi in 1988', *Journal of Communicable Diseases*, vol. 25, no. 2, pp. 57–61.

Dwivedi, S., G. Singh, M. Singh, R. Saran, A.K. Srivastava, and K. Kapoor, 1995, 'Medico-Social Factors Affecting Vitamin A Deficiency among Children', *Health and Population: Perspectives and Issues*, vol. 18, no. 1, pp. 27–36.

Economic and Political Weekly, 1986, 'Farcical Legislation', 15 November, p. 1965.

Fakhir, S., Ira Srivastava, P. Ahmed and S.S. Hasan, 1993, 'Prevalence of Xeropthalmia in Pre-School Children in an Urban Slum', *Indian Pediatrics*, vol. 30, May, pp. 668–72.

Finkelhor, David, 1994, 'The International Epidemiology of Child Sexual Abuse', *Child Abuse and Neglect*, vol. 18. no. 5, pp. 409–17.

Forum Against Sex Determination and Sex Pre-Selection, 1992, 'Using Technology, Choosing Sex', *Development Dialogue*, vols. 1–2, pp. 91–102.

Ganesh, Amita, 1995, 'Childhood Sexual Abuse of Girls', *My Name is Today*, vol. 3, nos. 1 & 2, pp. 23–5.

Garai, R. and A.K. Chakravarthy, 1980, 'Measles in a Rural Community', *Indian Journal of Public Health*, vol. 24, pp. 150–4.

Gattani, P. L. and N.E. Nimale, 1998, 'Low Birth Weight and Maternal Risk Factors: A Case Control Study at Government Medical College Hospital, Aurangabad, Maharashtra', *Indian Journal of Community Health*, vol. 4, no. 1, pp. 30–42.

Geetha, S. and M. Swaminathan, 1996, 'Nutrition Status of Slum Children of Mumbai: A Socio-Economic Survey', *Economic and Political Weekly*, 6 April, pp. 896–900.

Gelles, Richard J. and Ake W. Edfeldt, 1986, 'Violence Towards Children in the United States and Sweden', *Child Abuse and Neglect*, vol. 10, pp. 501–10.

George, K.N., 1975, 'Child Labour in the City of Madras', National Seminar on Employment of Children, 25–8 November, New Delhi: National Institute of Public Cooperation and Child Development.

George, Sabu, Rajaratnam Abel and B.D. Miller, 1992, 'Female Infanticide in Rural South India', *Economic and Political Weekly,* 30 May, pp. 1153–6.

George, Sabu and R.S. Dahiya, 1998, 'Female Foeticide in Rural Haryana', *Economic and Political Weekly*, 8 August, pp. 2191–8.

Ghosh, A.,1992, *Street Children of Calcutta: A Situational Analysis,* Noida: National Labour Institute.

Ghosh, Joydeep, 1997, 'The Black Hole of Bhiwandi', *Business World*, 25 December–7 January, pp.148–50.

Ghosh, S., P.G. Sen Gupta, S.K. Mondal, B. Manna, S.N. Sikder and B.K. Sirkar, 1997, 'Risk Behavioural Practices of Rural Mothers as Determinants of Childhood Diarrhoea', *Journal of Communicable Diseases*, vol. 29, no. 1, pp. 7–14.

Ghosh, Shanti, T. K. T. S. Ramanujacharyulu, Vijaya Hooja, and Santha Madhavan, 1979, 'Mortality Patterns in an Urban Birth Cohort', *Indian Journal of Medical Research*, vol. 69, April, pp. 616–23.

Gilada, I.S., 1990, 'Devdasi System: Link between Religious Cult and Sexual Exploitation', in *Prostitutes and their Children*, Delhi: Central Social Welfare Board.

Goldman, J.D.G. and Usha P. Padayachi, 1997, 'The Prevalence and Nature of Child Sexual Abuse in Queensland, Australia', *Child Abuse and Neglect*, vol. 21, no. 5, pp. 489–98.

Gomber, Sunil, D.K. Taneja and Kamla Mohan, 1996, 'Awareness of Pulse Polio Immunisation', *Indian Journal of Pediatrics*, vol. 63, pp. 99–103.

Gopalan, C., 1983, 'The National Goitre Control Programme—A Sad Story', *NFI Bulletin,* Nutrition Foundation of India, July.

________, 1993, 'Combating Vitamin A Deficiency: Need for a Revised Strategy', in *Recent Trends in Nutrition*, ed. C. Gopalan, New Delhi: Oxford University Press.

________, 1994, 'Low Birth Weight: Significance and Implications', in *Nutrition in Children: Developing Country Concerns*, H.P.S. Sachdev and Panna Choudhury, eds., New Delhi: Maulana Azad Medical College.

Gordon, John E., Sohan Singh and John B. Wyon, 1965, 'Causes of Death at Different Ages by Sex and by Season in a Rural Population of the Punjab, 1957–1959: A Field Study', *Indian Journal of Medical Research*, vol. 53, September, pp. 906–17.

Goswami, Omkar and Manoj K. Narula, 1998, 'Heart of Darkness', *Business India*, 26 January–8 February, pp. 58–68.

Government of India, 1931, *Report of the Royal Commission on Labour in India*, Calcutta: Central Publication Branch.

________, 1946, *Labour Investigation Committee: Main Report,* Delhi: Manager of Publications.

________, 1991, *Report of the National Commission on Rural Labour*, New Delhi: Ministry of Labour.

Government of West Bengal, 1992, *Report of the Education Commission,* Calcutta.

Govinda, R. and N.V. Verghese, 1991, *Quality of Basic Education Services in India: A Case Study of Primary Schooling in Madhya Pradesh*, New Delhi: National Institute of Educational Planning and Administration.

Guha Roy, S., Sudhir K. Mitra and Surja S. Roy, 1995, 'Evaluation of Attainment Level of Primary Students: The West Bengal Example', in *School Effectiveness and Learning Achievement at Primary Stage,* New Delhi: National Council of Educational Research and Training.

Gupta, J.P. and Indira Murali, 1989, *National Review of Immunisation Programme in India*, New Delhi: National Institute of Health and Family Welfare.

Gupta, K.M., 1995, *Learning Achievement of Primary School Children in Reading and Mathematics: Baseline Assessment Study of Five Districts of Chhatisgarh Region of Madhya Pradesh, India*, New Delhi: National Council of Educational Research and Training.

_______, 1996, 'Teachers Performance in Mathematics and Reading Test', *Indian Educational Review,* vol. 31, no. 1, pp. 92–104.

Gupta, Meena, 1994, 'Special Problems of Enforcement of Child Labour Laws and Regulations', *Awards Digest: Journal of Labour Legislation*, vol. 20, July–December, pp. 27–31.

Gupta, Piyush, M.V. Murali and Alka Seth, 1998, 'Epidemiology of Diarrhoea in Urban Slums', *Indian Pediatrics*, vol. 35, pp. 147–51.

Gupta, S.C., 1986, 'Sex Preference and Protein Calorie Malnutrition', *Journal of Family Welfare,* vol. 32, no. 3, pp. 59–64.

Gupta, S.D., R. Sharma, O.P. Gupta and S. Joshi, 1979, 'A Study of Feeding Patterns in Rural Pre-school Children', *Indian Journal of Pediatrics,* vol. 46, pp. 232–6.

Gurudeva, R.K., A.K. Gargye, S.B. Singh, V.J. Rajput and H.L. Tiwari, 1982, 'Infant Feeding Patterns in Rewa', *Indian Journal of Pediatrics,* vol. 49, pp. 815–18.

Gurung, Madhu, 2000, 'Demographic Danger Signals', *Frontline*, 22 January–4 February, pp. 71–4.

Handa, Sanjeev, Bhushan Kumar and Sarla Malhotra, 1995, 'Sexually Transmitted Diseases in Children following Sexual Abuse', *Indian Journal of Sexually Transmitted Diseases,* vol. 16, pp. 56–9.

Hindustan Times, 2000, 'Child Abuse Cases on the Rise', 11 June.

Hirve, S.S. and Bela R. Ganatra, 1994, 'Determinants of Low Birth Weight: A Community Based Prospective Study', *Indian Pediatrics*, vol. 31, October, pp. 1, 221–5.

Hobbs, Christopher J. and Jane M. Wynne, 1986, 'Buggery in Childhood—A Common Syndrome of Child Abuse', *Lancet,* 4 October, pp. 792–6.

_______, 1987, 'Child Sexual Abuse—An Increasing Rate of Diagnosis', *Lancet,* 10 October, pp. 837–41.

IMRB, 1993, *CDD WATSAN Study: An All India Report on the Study Carried Out in 15 Districts*, Delhi: Indian Market Research Bureau.

India Today, 1996, 'Daylight Theft', 15 November, p. 163.

Indian Council of Medical Research (ICMR), 1984, *Studies on Pre-School Children*, New Delhi.

_______, 1989a, *Epidemiological Survey of Endemic Goitre and Endemic Cretinism*, New Delhi.

_______, 1989b, *Evaluation of the National Nutritional Anemia Prophylaxis Programme*, New Delhi.

________, 1990a, *An Assessment Study of Coverage and KAP of Immunisation Programmes in Different States of the Country*, New Delhi.

________, 1990b, *Collaborative Study on High Risk Pregnancies and Maternal Mortality*, New Delhi.

________, 1990c, *A National Collaborative Study of Identification of High Risk Families' Mothers and Outcome of their Offspring with Particular Reference to the Problem of Maternal Nutrition, Low Birth Weight, Perinatal and Infant Morbidity and Mortality in Rural and Urban Slum Communities*, New Delhi.

________, 1991, *Evaluation of Quality of Family Welfare Services at Primary Health Centre Level*, New Delhi.

________, 1994, *A Multi-Centre Collaborative Study on the Care of Mothers and Infants with a Comprehensive MCH Care Package Utilising High Risk Approach Strategy at Primary Health Centres*, New Delhi.

Institute for Research in Medical Statistics, 1991, *Methodological Investigations on Surveys of Immunisation Coverage*, New Delhi: Indian Council of Medical Research.

International Institute for Population Sciences (IIPS), 1995, *National Family Health Survey, 1992–3*, Bombay.

________, 2000, *National Family Health Survey NFHS-2*, Bombay.

Iyer, Nandini R., 1999, '9 Yr. Old Boy Tortured', *Statesman*, 20 December.

Jangira, N.K., 1994, 'Learning Achievement of Primary School Children in Reading and Mathematics', in *Research Based Intervention in Primary Education: The DPEP Strategy*, New Delhi: National Council of Educational Research and Training.

Jangira, N.K., Ajit Singh and S.K.Yadav, 1994, 'Teacher Policy, Training Needs and Perceived Professional Status', in *Research Based Interventions in Primary Education: The DPEP Strategy*, New Delhi: National Council of Educational Research and Training.

Jeevan Raksha Parishad, 1997, *A Study of Women and Girls in Prostitution in Orissa: Their Needs, Problems and Prospective*, Bhuvaneshwar.

John, T.J., A. Joseph, T.I. George, Janaki Radhakrishnan, Rajdayal, P.D. Singh and Kuryan George, 1980, 'Epidemiology and Prevention of Measles in Rural South India', *Indian Journal of Medical Research*, vol. 72, August, pp. 153–8.

Joshi, S.K., U. Sharma, P. Sharma, S.S. Pathk, S. Sitaraman and C.R. Verma, 1994, 'Health Status of Carpet Weaving Children', *Indian Pediatrics*, vol. 31, May, pp. 571–4.

Juyal, B.N. 1993, *Child Labour in the Carpet Industry in Mirazpur—Bhadohi*, New Delhi: ILO–CLASP.

Kakker, S., A. Hooda, R. Jain, A.C. Kapoor and Vidyasagar, 1987, 'Nutrition Status of Pre-school Children in Rural Hissar', *Indian Journal of Nutrition and Dietetics*, vol. 24, pp. 204–8.

Kapil, Umesh and Deepika Nayar, 1997, 'Status of Salt Iodisation and Iodine Deficiency in Selected Districts of Different States of India' (personal communication).

Kapil, Umesh, Nandini Saxena and D. Nayar, 1996, 'Evaluation of National Programme for Prevention of Nutritional Blindness and National

Nutritional Anemia Prophylaxis Programme in Selected States of India', *Health and Population: Perspectives and Issues*, vol. 19, no. 1, pp. 19–28.

Kapoor, Aditi, 1993, 'Playing with Hot Glass for Rs. 30 a day', *Times of India*, 26 March.

Katiyar, G.P., P.K. Jaiswal, D.C.S. Reddy and K.N. Aggarwal, 1988, 'Interactions between Xeropthalmia and Morbidity among Under Five Rural Children', *Indian Pediatrics*, vol. 25, October, pp. 939–45.

Kaur, Manmeet, 1993, 'Female Foeticide: A Sociological Perspective', *Journal of Family Welfare*, vol. 39, no. 1, pp. 40–3.

Kaushik, S.L., V.R. Parmar, N. Grover and R. Kaushik, 1998, 'Neonatal Mortality Rate: Relationship to Birth Weight and Gestational Age', *Indian Journal of Pediatrics*, vol. 65, pp. 429–33.

Kempe, C.H., 1978, 'Sexual Abuse: Another Hidden Pediatric Problem', *Pediatrics*, vol. 62, no. 3, pp. 382–9.

Khadi, P.B., J. Khateeb and M.S. Patil, 1996, 'Development of Rural Girl Children—A Bias', *Indian Journal of Maternal and Child Heath*, vol. 7, no. 1, pp. 24–7.

Khan, M.E., 1990, 'Breast Feeding and Weaning Practices in India', *Asia Pacific Population Journal*, vol. 5, no.1, pp. 71–88.

Khatu, K.K., A.K.Tamang and C.R. Rao, 1983, *Working Children in India*, Baroda: Operations Research Group.

Kielman, A.A., C.E. Taylor, Cecile De Sweemer, I.S. Uberoi, H.S. Takulia, Norah Masih and S. Vohra, 1978, 'The Narangwal Experiment on Interactions of Nutrition and Infections: II, Morbidity and Mortality Effects', *Indian Journal of Medical Research*, vol. 68 (supplement), December, pp. 21–41.

Koen, M.C., M.S. Lemson, V.S. Sampathkumar and R. Abel, 1992, 'Prevalence of Anemia Among Pregnant Mothers in a Rural South Indian Population', *Journal of Obstetrics and Gynaecology of India*, vol. 42, pp. 743–6.

Kothari, Smithu, 1983, 'There's Blood on Those Matchsticks: Child Labour in Sivakasi, *Economic and Political Weekly*, 2 July, pp. 1191–202

Krishnakumar, Asha, 1995, 'Reprehensible by any Name: Children in Beedi Industry', *Frontline*, 17 November, pp. 86–8.

________, 1998, 'Scanning for Death', *Frontline*, 18 December, pp. 109–12.

________, 1999, 'Foeticide Unlimited', *Frontline*, 19 November, pp. 97–8.

________, 2000, 'Children Still at Work', *Frontline*, 29 April, pp. 40–2.

Kulashreshtha, M.K. and R. Sapru, 1991, 'The Ability of Paramedical Functionaries and Anganwadi Workers to Prepare and Demonstrate Sugar-Salt and ORS Solution to Beneficiary Mothers', *Health and Population: Perspectives and Issues*, vol.14, nos. 3 and 4, pp. 131–5.

Kulkarni, Manu N., 1997, 'Tackling Child Abuse', *Economic and Political Weekly*, 28 June, pp. 1522–3.

Kulkarni, S.S., 1970, *All India Survey of Achievement in Mathematics*, New Delhi: National Council of Educational Research and Training.

Kumar, Avdesh, Neena Gulati, C.S. Aggarwal, S.K. Rasamia and Kusum Sahgal, 1994, 'An Epidemiological Profile of Gastro-Enteritis Deaths in Delhi State', *Journal of Communicable Diseases*, vol. 24, no. 3, September, pp. 156–9.

Kumar, Seema, 2000, 'They Don't Live Off the Highway Anymore', *Hindustan Times*, 16 July.

Kumar, Sanjiv, L.M. Nath and V.P. Reddaiah, 1989, 'Factors Influencing Prevalence of Breast Feeding in a Resettlement Colony of New Delhi', *Indian Journal of Pediatrics*, vol. 56, no. 3, pp. 385–91.

Kushawaha, K.P., G.P. Mathur and O. Prakash, 1987, 'Infant Feeding Practices of Peri-Urban Areas of Gorakhpur', *Indian Pediatrics*, vol. 24, October, pp. 895–901.

Lal, R.B., V.K. Srivastava and R. Chandra, 1996, 'A Study of Spectrum of Iodine Deficiency Disorders in Rural Area of Uttar Pradesh', *Indian Journal of Public Health*, vol. 40, no. 1, pp. 10–12.

Laskar, Bahrul Islam, 2000, 'Child Labour in Aligarh Lock Industry, *Economic and Political Weekly*, 12 February, pp. 510–13.

Levine, Ruth E., Harry E. Cross, Sheena Chhabra and Hema Viswanathan, 1992, 'Quality of Health and Family Planning Services in Rural Uttar Pradesh: The Client's View', *Demography India*, vol. 21, no. 2, pp. 247–65.

Lobo, J., V.P. Reddaiah, S.K. Kapoor and L.M. Nath, 1987, 'Epidemiology of Measles in a Rural Community, *Indian Journal of Pediatrics*, vol. 54, no. 1, pp. 261–5.

Maheshwari, A.N. and V.P. Gupta, 1998, *Mathematics Learning in Government Primary Schools*, New Delhi: National Council of Educational Research and Training.

Makhija, K., G.V.S. Murthy, S.K. Kapoor, and J. Lobo, 1989, 'Socio-biological Determinants of Birth Weight', *Indian Journal of Pediatrics*, vol. 56, no. 5, pp. 639–43.

Malin, A.S. and R.W. Stones, 1988, 'Nutritional Anemia in the Urban Poor: A Community Based Study of Under Fives in an Indian Slum', *Journal of Tropical Pediatrics*, vol. 34, October, pp. 257–9.

Mandke, B.V., R.M. Pawar, D.D. Naik, V.P. Torne and A.M. Naiksatam, 1990, 'Review of Poliomyelitis in Bombay, 1982–1989: Observations on the Improved Immunisation Programme', *Indian Journal of Public Health*, vol. 34, no. 4, pp. 200–8.

Mandke, V.B., R.M. Pawar, D.D. Naik and S.D. Salgaonkar, 1994, 'An Outbreak of Poliomyelitis in the Marathwada Region of Maharashtra State: 1990', *Indian Pediatrics*, vol. 31, September, pp. 1091–3.

MARG, 1996, *Within the Four Walls: A Profile of Domestic Violence*, New Delhi.

Marla, Sarma, 1981, *Bonded Labour in India*, New Delhi: Biblia Impex.

Mehra, Jyoti, 1996, *Reducing Risk Behaviour related to HIV/AIDS, STDs and Drug Abuse among Street Children*, New Delhi: Ministry of Welfare, UNDCP, UNICEF and NACO.

Mehta, Prayag, 1983, 'Mortgaged Child Labour of Vellore', *Mainstream*, vol. 3, September, pp. 15–34.

Mendiratta, Vibhu, Vijay Kumar, R.C. Sharma and R.V. Koranne, 1996, 'STD Profile of Children', *Indian Journal of Sexually Transmitted Diseases*, vol. 17, no. 1, pp. 1–3.

Menezes, Sara, 1998, 'Schools of Scandal', *Outlook*, 9 March, pp. 33–4.

Menon, Venu, 2000, 'Innocence Betrayed', *Outlook*, 10 April, p. 30.

Ministry of Health and Family Welfare, 1985, *Towards Universal Immunisation*, New Delhi: Government of India.

Ministry of Health and Family Welfare, 2000, *Annual Report, 1999-2000*, New Delhi: Government of India.

Ministry of Labour, 1969, *Report of the National Commission on Labour*, New Delhi: Government of India.

________, 1979, *Report of the Committee on Child Labour*, New Delhi: Government of India.

________, 1987, *National Policy on Child Labour*, New Delhi: Government of India.

________, 1991, *Report of the National Commission on Rural Labour*, New Delhi: Government of India.

Ministry of Rural Areas and Employment, 1997, *Report of the Committee to Identify 100 Most Backward and Poorest Districts in the Country*, New Delhi: Government of India.

Ministry of Social Justice and Empowerment, 2000, *Annual Report 1999–2000*, New Delhi: Government of India.

Misra, G.P. and P.N. Pande, 1992, *A Study of Child Labour in Glass Industry, Firozabad*, Lucknow: Giri Institute of Development Studies.

Misra, R.K., 1995, *Preliminary Report on the Child Labour in the Saree Industry of Varanasi*, Varanasi: Human Rights Cell, Banaras Hindu University.

Mittal, Pallavi, 1997, 'Despite Ban, Many Clinics in City Do Sex Determination Tests', *Times of India*, 26 August.

Mohammed, Siraj, 1999, 'Mid-Day Meal or Poison', *Hindustan Times*, 5 March.

Mohan, Madan, 1989, *National Survey of Blindness, India: Report*, New Delhi: All India Institute of Medical Sciences.

Mohandas, M., 1980, 'Beedi Workers in Kerala: Conditions of Life and Work', *Economic and Political Weekly*, 6 September, pp. 1517–23.

Mukerji, Debashish, 1998, 'Brothel Buster', *The Week*, 25 January, pp. 32–7.

Mukherjee, K.K., 1997, *Girl Child Prostitution in India*, New Delhi: National Commission for Women.

Mukherjee, K.K., Tapan K. Daripa and Madhuri Mukherjee, 1997, *Girl Child Prostitution in Rajasthan*, New Delhi: National Commission for Women.

Mukherjee, K.K. and Deepa Das, 1996, *Prostitution in Metropolitan Cities of India*, New Delhi: Central Social Welfare Board.

Mukherjee, Mandipa, 1996, 'Female Infanticide Still Rampant', *Current*, 14–20 December, p. 6.

Nagaraj, V.K., Umesh Kapil and D. Nayar, 1997, 'Breast Feeding and Weaning Practices among Under Three Year Children Belonging to Under Privileged Communities in Two Districts of Haryana', *Indian Journal of Community Health*, vol. 3, no. 1, pp. 116–20.

Nagi, B.S., 1997, *Coverage Evaluation of the Child Survival and Safe Motherhood Programme in India*, New Delhi: Council for Social Development.

Naidu, Ratna and D. Parthasarathy, 1992, *Child Labour in Slate Industry*, Hyderabad: Department of Sociology, University of Hyderabad.

Nanda, Aswini Kumar, Sukhvinder Singh and Rajesh Aggarwal, 1993, 'Sex Detection Test: Death before Birth—A Study of Awareness and Acceptance in Seven Districts of North India', *Man and Development,* December, pp. 30–45.

Narain, J.P., 1987, 'Epidemiology of Acute Respiratory Infections', *Indian Journal of Pediatrics,* vol. 54, no. 2, pp. 153–60.

Narain, J.P. and K.B. Banerjee, 1989, 'Measles in India: Epidemiology and Control', *Indian Journal of Pediatrics,* vol. 54, pp. 261–5.

Narayan, Hemendra, 1997, 'Food Meant for Poor Feed to Cows', *Statesman,* 7 April.

National Human Rights Commission (NHRC), 1996, *Annual Report 1995–6*, New Delhi.

National Commission for Women, 1996, *Societal Violence on Women and Children in Prostitution,* New Delhi.

National Council of Applied Economic Research, 1994, 'Child Labour in Carpet Industry', *Margin*, vol. 27, no. 1, pp. 54–70.

National Council of Educational Research and Training (NCERT), 1982, *Fourth All India Educational Survey,* New Delhi.

________, 1992, *Fifth All India Educational Survey*, vols. 1 and 2, New Delhi.

________, 1994, *Attainments of Primary School Children in Various States,* New Delhi.

________, 1998, *Sixth All India Educational Survey*, vols. 1–7, New Delhi.

National Crime Records Bureau (NCRB), 2000, 2001, *Crime in India, 1998, 1999*, New Delhi.

National Institute of Communicable Diseases (NICD), 1986, *Diarrhoeal Diseases Status in Urban and Rural Areas of India*, New Delhi.

________, 1988, *Combined Surveys of ARI, Diarrhoea and EPI*, New Delhi.

________, 1999, *Epidemiological Investigation of an Outbreak of Measles in Badaun District, Uttar Pradesh, Executive Summary*, New Delhi.

National Institute of Nutrition, 1991, *Report of Repeat Surveys 1988–90*, Hyderabad: National Nutrition Monitoring Bureau.

________, 1996, *Nutritional Status of Rural Population: Report of NNMB Surveys, Additional Tabulations*, Hyderabad: National Nutrition Monitoring Bureau.

National Institute of Urban Affairs (NIUA), 1989, *Profile of the Urban Poor: An Investigation into their Demographic, Economic and Shelter Characteristics,* New Delhi.

National Labour Institute (NLI), 1991, *Child Labour in the Gem Polishing Industry in Jaipur*, Noida.

________, 1992a, *Child Labour in the Brassware Industry of Moradabad,* Noida.

________, 1992b, *Child Labour in the Lock Industry of Aligarh*, Noida.

________, 1992c, *Working Children of the Pottery Industry of Khurja*, Noida.

________, 1993, *Child Workers in the Carpet Weaving Industry of Jammu and Kashmir*, Noida.

National Sample Survey Organisation (NSSO), 1997, *Economic Activities and School Attendance by Children of India*, Fifth Quinquennial Survey, NSS Fiftieth Round 1993–4, New Delhi.

________, 1998, *Attending an Educational Institution in India: Its Level, Nature and Cost*, NSS Fifty-second Round, July 1995–June 1996, New Delhi.

Nayyar, Mohammed R. and M. Rajasekhar, 1998, 'Sex Related Risk Behaviour

Patterns among Street Children', *Contemporary Social Work*, vol. 15, October, pp. 49–57.

Nirbhawne, Neelu, Jayashree Kanojia, V. S. Toddywalla, Shahnaz Patel, S. Bedrabet, B.N. Saxena, S. Datte and L. Gaur, 1996, 'The Indian Couples and Gender Preferences for their Offsprings', *Journal of Obstetrics and Gynaecology of India*, vol. 46, April, pp. 175–9.

Operations Research Group (ORG), 1993, *Child Labour in Diamond Industry of Surat City*, Baroda.

________, 1993, *Child Labour in the Slate Pencil Industry of Mandsaur District, Madhya Pradesh*, Madras.

________, 1996, *Evaluation of Non-formal Education Programme in Lok Jumbish Project*, New Delhi.

Pachauri, Pankaj, 1988, 'Rajasthan, a Murderous Tradition', *India Today*, 31 October, pp. 35–9.

Pandav, C.S., N. Kochupillai, M.G. Karmarkar, K. Ramachandran, P.G. Gopinath and L.M. Nath, 1980, 'Endemic Goitre in Delhi', *Indian Journal of Medical Research*, vol. 72, July, pp. 81–8.

Pandey, A. and A.K. Chakraborty, 1996, 'Undernutrition, Vitamin A Deficiency and ARI Morbidity in Under Fives', *Indian Journal of Public Health*, vol. 40, no.1, pp. 13–15.

Pandey, Rajendra, 1991, *Street Children of India: A Situation Analysis*, Allahabad: Chugh Publications.

Panicker, Rita, 1998, 'Street Children and Drug Abuse in India', in *South Asia Drug Demand Reduction Report*, New Delhi: UNDCP, Regional Office for South Asia.

Panicker, Rita and Kalpana Desai, 1993, *Street Girls of Delhi: Case Studies*, Noida: National Labour Institute.

Panicker, Rita and Parveen Nangia, 1992, *Working and Street Children of Delhi*, Noida: National Labour Institute.

Parashar, Utpal, 1998, 'Village that Throbs in its Red Light Womb', *Hindustan Times*, 19 April.

Patel, Renu B., 1989, 'Care of Low Birth Weight Babies in Slums', *Indian Journal of Pediatrics*, vol. 56, no. 2, pp. 231–7.

Patil, B.R., 1985, 'Brick Kiln Workers in Greater Bangalore', *Indian Journal of Labour Economics*, vol. 27, no. 4, pp. 301–9.

Patkar, Priti, 1991, 'Girl Child in Red Light Areas', *Indian Journal of Social Work*, vol. 52, no. 1, January, pp. 71–80.

Patnaik, Sarat Kumar, 1991, 'Acute Respiratory Infection in Children: A Survey of East Godavari District of Andhra Pradesh', *Journal of Communicable Diseases*, vol. 23, no.1, pp. 34–7.

Patwari, A.K., S. Aneja, R.N. Mandal and D.N. Mallick, 1988, 'Acute Respiratory Infections in Children: A Hospital Based Report', *Indian Pediatrics*, vol. 25, July, pp. 613–17.

Peace Trust and SAVE, 1997, *Child and Adult Labour in Garment Export Industry of Tirupur, Dindigul and Tirupur.*

Phillips, W.S.K., 1992, *Street Children of Indore: A Situational Analysis*, Noida: National Labour Institute.

Planning Commission, 1972, *Report of the Committee on Pre-School Feeding Programmes,* New Delhi.

_______, 1980, *Report of the Task Force on Nutrition Policy, Planning and Implementation for the Sixth Plan, 1980–85*, New Delhi.

_______, 1990, *Employment: Past Trends and Prospects for 1990s*, New Delhi.

Prabhakara, G.N., P.V. Aswath, C. Shivaram and A.N. Viswanath, 1987, 'Infant Feeding Patterns in Slums of Bangalore', *Indian Pediatrics*, vol. 24, October, pp. 895–8.

Prasad, K.N., R.S. Phaneendra Rao and A. Sujatha, 1994, 'Birth Weight Pattern in Karnataka', *Indian Pediatrics*, vol. 31, July, pp. 836–9.

Pratinidhi, A.K., V.S. Bapat and Usha Shah, 1984, 'Magnitude of Vitamin A Deficiency in Primary School Children of Sirur: A Chronically Drought Affected Area', *Indian Journal of Pediatrics*, vol. 51, pp. 423–6.

Premrajan, K.C. and D.K. Srinivasan, 1991, 'Child Health Care: Is There a Gender Difference?', *Journal of Family Welfare*, vol. 37, no. 4, pp. 27–31.

Prerana, 1995, 'A Study on Girl Children in Prostitution in Kamathipura, Mumbai', in *Child Prostitution, The Ultimate Abuse*, New Delhi: UNICEF.

PROBE, 1999, *Public Report on Basic Education in India*, New Delhi: Oxford University Press.

Programme Evaluation Organisation, 1999, *Evaluation Study of Functioning of Community Health Centres*, New Delhi: Planning Commission.

Pushkarna, Vijaya, 1993, 'Female Foeticide', *The Week*, 1 August, pp. 36–42.

Pushpamma, P., P. Geervani and N. Laxmi Devi, 1982, 'Food Intake, Nutrient Adequacy and Anthropometry of Adolescents in Andhra Pradesh', *Indian Journal of Medical Research*, vol. 75, January, pp. 61–7.

Radhakrishnan, M.G., 1997, 'Moulding a New Destiny', *India Today*, 15 May, pp. 86–7.

Rajaretnam, T., 1992, 'Female Infanticide among Pramalaikallars of Tamil Nadu', *Social Change*, vol. 22, no. 3, pp. 93–101.

Ramachandran, K.V. and V.A. Deshpande, 1964, 'The Sex Ratio at Birth in India by Regions', *Milbank Memorial Fund Quarterly*, vol. 42, no. 2, pp. 84–95.

Raman, L., A.B. Pawashe and B.A. Ramalakshmi, 1992, 'Iron Nutritional Status of Pre-School Children', *Indian Journal of Pediatrics*, vol. 59, no. 2, pp. 209–12.

Ramanamma, A. and Usha Bambawale, 1980, 'The Mania for Sons: An Analysis of Social Values in South Asia', *Social Science and Medicine*, vol. 14 B, no. 3, pp. 107–10.

Ramamoorthy, Mohan, 1998, 'A District in Distress', *Business India*, 26 January, pp. 124–8.

Randall, Dana V., 1996, 'Spotting a Paedophile', *The Week*, 4 August, pp. 38–9.

Rao, K.S., R.D. Pilli, A.S. Rao and P.S.Chalam, 1999, 'Sexual Lifestyle of Long Distance Lorry Drivers in India: Questionnaire Survey', *British Medical Journal*, vol. 318, 16 January, pp. 162–3.

Rao, Shobha and Leena Karkhanis, 1993, 'Differential Patterns of Malnutrition among Kindergarten Children in Pune City', *Indian Journal of Medical Research*, vol. 98, June, pp. 129–35.

Rathee, S., A. Khosla, Neerja Sharma and R. Garg, 1987, 'Pregnancy Outcome in Severe Anemia', *Journal of Obstetrics and Gynaecology of India*, vol. 37, no. 4, pp. 478–80.

Ravindran, Nirmala, 2000, 'Temples of Doom', *Savvy*, June, pp. 98–100.

Ray, S.K., A.B. Biswas and S. Kumar, 1997, 'A Comparative Study of Household Food Security and Nutritional Profile of Under Five Children in a Rural and an Urban Community of West Bengal', *Indian Journal of Public Health*, vol. 42, no. 4, pp. 136-47.

Reddaiah, V.P., J. Lobo, S.K. Kapoor and L.M. Nath, 1988, 'Comprehensive Rural Health Services Project, Ballabhgarh: Trends in Under Five Mortality', *Indian Journal of Pediatrics*, vol. 55, no. 2, pp. 287–94.

Reddy, N., 1992, *Street Children of Bangalore: A Situational Analysis*, Noida: National Labour Institute.

Reddy, Vindodini and K. Satyanarayana, 1991, 'Nutritional Status of Indian Girls', in *Proceedings of the Workshop on Improving Young Women's Health and Development*, Srinagar, March 1989, New Delhi: Indian Council of Medical Research.

Registrar General, 1983, *Survey on Infant and Child Mortality, 1979*, New Delhi.

Registrar General & Census Commissioner, 1971, 1981, 1991, 2001, *Census of India*, different census volumes, Delhi: Controller of Publications.

Registrar General & Census Commissioner, 1993, *Census of India, 1991, Final Population Tables: Paper 2 of 1992*, New Delhi: Controller of Publications.

Registrar General, India, 1996, *Population Projections for India and States, 1996–2016, Report of the Technical Group on Population Projections Constituted by the Planning Commission*, New Delhi.

________, 1998, SRS Based Abridged Life Tables 1990–94 and 1991–5, Delhi: Controller of Publications.

________, 2000, Survey of Causes of Death (Rural), 1997, New Delhi.

Risbud, A.R, S.R. Prasad, S.M. Mehendale, N. Mawar, N. Shaikh, U.B. Umrani, S.S. Bedekar and K. Banerjee, 1994, 'Measles Outbreak in a Tribal Population of Thane District, Maharashtra', *Indian Pediatrics*, vol. 31, May, pp. 543–51.

Roy, Panchali, Prabir Kumar Sen, K.B. Das and A.K. Chakraborty, 1991, 'Acute Respiratory Infections in Children Admitted in a Hospital of Calcutta', *Indian Journal of Public Health*, vol. 35, no. 3, July September, pp. 67–70.

Roy, Samir and P.S. Chakravorty, 1992, 'Maternal and Perinatal Outcome in Severe Anemia', *Journal of Obstetrics and Gynaecology of India*, vol. 42, pp. 743 7.

Rozario, M.R., 1988, *Trafficking in Women and Children in India*, New Delhi: Uppal Publishing House.

Russell, Diana E.H., 1983, 'The Incidence and Prevalence of Intrafamilial and Extrafamilial Sexual Abuse of Female Children', *Child Abuse and Neglect*, vol. 7, pp. 133–46.

Sachar, R.K., J. Verma, S. Dhawan, Ved Prakash, A. Chopra and R. Adlaka, 1990, 'Sex Bias in Health and Medical Care Allocation', *Indian Journal of Maternal and Child Health*, vol. 1, no. 2, pp. 63–5.

Sachar, R.K., J. Verma, V. Prakash, A. Chopra, R. Adlaka and R. Sofat, 1990, 'Sex Selective Fertility Control: An Outrage', *Journal of Family Welfare*, vol. 36, no. 2, June, pp. 30–5.

Sachdev, Radhika, 1999, 'All Work and Little Pay', *Hindustan Times*, 18 May.

Saiyidain, K.G., J.P. Naik, S. Abid Hussain and Gopesh Kumar Ojha, 1966, *Compulsory Education in India; Progress of Compulsory Education in India*, Delhi: Universal.

Sampathkumar, V. and R. Abel, 1993, 'Xeropthalmia in Rural South Indian Children', *Indian Pediatrics*, vol. 30, February, pp. 246–8.

Sample Registration System, 1970–98, *Annual statistical reports on fertility and mortality*, New Delhi: Registrar General India.

Samuel, G.E. Rupert, J.P. Gupta and V.S. Wadhwa, 1992, 'Satisfaction and Utilisation of Primary Health Care Service Facilities in Karanataka', *Health and Population: Perspectives and Issues,* vol. 15, nos. 3 and 4, pp. 140–52.

Sanlap, 1996, *The Past, The Present,* Calcutta.

Sarma, Marla, 1981, *Bonded Labour in India: National Survey on the Incidence of Bonded Labour—Final Report*, New Delhi: Biblia Impex.

Saxena, Rashmi, 1996, 'The Young and the Damned', *The Week*, 4 August, pp. 40–2.

Sehgal, Rajiv, R.K. Sachar, J. Verma, Ved Prakash, Anil Goyal and R.K. Soni, 1990, 'Unwanted, Unwelcome and Unborn—The Female Foetus', *Journal of Maternal and Child Health,* vol. 1, no. 4, October–December, pp. 144–5.

Sekar, Helen R., 1993, *No Light in their Lives: Girl Child Labour in the Match Industry of Sivakasi*, Noida: National Labour Institute.

Sen, Amartya and Sunil Sen Gupta, 1983, 'Malnutrition of Rural Children and the Sex Bias', *Economic and Political Weekly,* Annual Number, pp. 855–64.

Sen Gupta, P.G., B.K. Sircar, S. Mondal, D.N. Gupta, S. Ghosh, and S.P. De, 1997, 'Epidemiological Profile of Acute Diarrhoeal Diseases of a Cohort of Rural Under Five Children: A Three Year Longitudinal Observation', *Indian Journal of Public Health*, vol. 41, no. 3, pp. 79–81.

Seshadari, Shekhar, 1995, 'Sexual Abuse of Boys: Report and Findings', *My Name is Today,* vol. 3, nos. 1 and 2, pp. 21–2.

Shah, Anupama and Sarita Taneja, 1991, 'What do Male and Females of Delhi City Think about Female Foeticide', *Journal of Family Welfare,* vol. 37, no. 2, June, pp. 28–39.

Shankar, Jogin, 1990, 'Causes of Continuation of Devdasi System: Strategies of Eradication and Rehabilitation', in *Prostitutes and their Children,* New Delhi: Central Social Welfare Board.

Sharma, Aradhana, 1997, 'Child Abuse: Safest Crime for the Perpetrator', *Statesman*, 8 June.

Sharma, A.K. and G.U. Qureshi, 1997, 'Juvenile Delinquency: Psychological and Medico-Legal Profile', *Journal of Forensic Medicine and Toxicology,* vol. 14, no. 1, pp. 1–4.

Sharma, M., S. Sen, B. Ahuja and K. Dhamija, 1990, 'Paralytic Poliomyelitis 1976–1988: Report from a Sentinel Centre', *Indian Pediatrics,* vol. 27, February, pp. 143–50.

Sharma, S.K., G.P. Mathur, Sudershan Kumari, M. Yadav, J. Rai, D.N. Mullick and A.K. Dutta, 1987, 'Xeropthalmia in Pre-School Children', *Indian Pediatrics,* vol. 24, August, pp. 645–50.

Shukla, Snehlata, 1974, 'Achievements of Indian Children in Mother Tongue (Hindi) and Science', *Comparative Education Review*, vol. 18, no. 2, pp. 237–47.

Sidhu, Sarda, 1996, 'Incidence of Anemia Among Scheduled Caste Pre-School Children of Punjab', *Indian Journal of Maternal and Child Health*, vol. 7, no. 3, pp. 76–7.

Singh, Jagvir, Ashok Kumar, R.N. Rai, Shashi Khare, D.C. Jain, Rajesh Bhatia and K.K. Datta, 1999, 'Widespread Outbreak of Measles in Rural Uttar Pradesh, India, 1996: High Risk Areas and Groups', *Indian Pediatrics*, vol. 36, March, pp. 249–56.

Singh, J.P., D. Halder, Sudershan Kumari, M. Yadav, J. Rai, D.N. Mullick and A.K. Dutta, 1988, 'Mortality Characteristics of Neonates with Birth Weight above 2000g', *Indian Pediatrics*, vol. 25, February, pp. 179–83.

Singh, Jagvir, Kaushal Kumar, D. Bora, Uma Chawla, N.C. Bilochi, R.S. Sharma, M.L. Kapur, Suresh Kumar, B.K. Aggarwal, J.K. Dhaon and K.K. Dutta, 1992, 'Epidemiological Evaluation of Oral Polio Vaccine Efficacy in Delhi', *Indian Journal of Pediatrics*, vol. 59, pp. 321–3.

Singh, Jagvir, R.S. Sharma and T. Verghese, 1994, 'Measles Mortality in India: A Review of Community Based Studies, *Journal of Communicable Diseases*, vol. 26, no. 4, pp. 203–14.

Singh, Meharban, 1986, 'Hospital Based Data on Perinatal and Neonatal Mortality in India', *Indian Pediatrics*, vol. 23, August, pp. 579–84.

_______, 1988, 'Strategies to Reduce Perinatal and Neonatal Mortality', *Indian Pediatrics*, vol. 25, June, pp. 499–509.

Singh, Meharban, A.K. Deorari, R.C. Khajuria and V.K. Paul, 1991, 'Perinatal and Neonatal Mortality in a Hospital, *Indian Journal of Medical Research*, vol. B94, February, pp. 1–5.

Singh, Meharban and V.K. Paul, 1988, 'Strategies to Reduce Perinatal and Neonatal Mortality', *Indian Pediatrics* , vol. 25, June, pp. 499–509.

Singh, M.P. and Sushila Nayar, 1996, 'Magnitude of Acute Respiratory Infections in Under Five Children', *Journal of Communicable Diseases*, vol. 28, no. 4, pp. 273–8.

Singh, Musafir, V.D. Kaura and S.A. Khan, 1980, *Working Children in Bombay*, New Delhi: National Institute of Public Cooperation and Child Development.

Singh, Padam, 1991, *Methodological Investigations on Surveys of Immunisation Coverage*, New Delhi: Institute for Research in Medical Statistics.

Singh, Sohan, John E. Gordon and John B. Wyon, 1962, 'Medical Care in Fatal Illnesses of a Rural Punjab Population: Some Social, Biological and Cultural Factors and their Ecological Implication', *Indian Journal of Medical Research*, vol. 50, no. 6, November, pp. 865–80.

Sinha, Indrani and Staff of Sanlaap, 1997, *A Study of Child Prostitution in West Bengal*, New Delhi: National Commission for Women.

Sinha, Raka, 1991, 'Rohtak Rampage: Alarming Female Foeticide', *Savvy*, July, p. 38.

Sircar, B.K., B.C. Deb, P.G. Sen Gupta, S. Mondal, D.N. Gupta, S. Sarkar, S.N. Sikder, S. Ghosh, N.C. Saha and S.C. Pal, 1991, 'An Operational Study on Implementation of Oral Rehydration Therapy in a Rural Community of

West Bengal, India', *Indian Journal of Medical Research*, vol. 93, September, pp. 297–302.

Social and Rural Research Institute, 1993, *CDD-WATSAN Study*, New Delhi: Indian Market Research Bureau.

Sokhey, Jotna, 1991, 'Elimination of Neonatal Tetanus, 1995', *Journal of Communicable Diseases*, vol. 23, no. 1, pp. 1–10.

Sokhey, Jotna and Kim Farley, 1990, *Vaccine Coverage Evaluation Surveys, 1987*, New Delhi: Ministry of Health and Family Welfare.

Sridhar, S., Lata Desai and Pankaj Shahi, 1991, 'Women's Health in Rural Gujarat—SEWA Rural's Experience', in *Proceedings of the Workshop on Improving Young Women's Health and Development*, New Delhi: Indian Council of Medical Research.

Srinivasan, Viji, 1992, 'Death for the Female: Foeticide and Infanticide in Salem District', *Frontline*, 9 October, pp. 82–5.

Srivastava, S.P. and N.P. Nayak, 1995, 'The Disadvantaged Girl Child in Bihar: Study of Health Care Practices and Selected Nutritional Indices', *Indian Pediatrics*, vol. 32, August, pp. 911–13.

Statesman, 1995, '10 Children Killed in Cracker Factory Explosion', 12 September.

Subrahmanyam, S. and R. Nageswara Rao, 1995, 'Gender Bias in Nutrition: Some Issues', *Journal of Family Welfare*, vol. 41, no. 3, September, pp. 1–9.

Sujatha, K., 1995, 'Effectiveness of Tribal Teachers: A Study of Single Teacher Schools in Tribal Areas in Andhra Pradesh', in *School Effectiveness and Learning Achievement at Primary Stage*, New Delhi: National Council of Educational Research and Training.

Sundar, Ramanami, 1994, 'Household Survey of Health Care Utilisation and Expenditure', *Margin*, vol. 26, July and September, pp. 865–74.

Sundaram, J., B.K. Sugunammanni and T. Chandrasekhar, 1997, 'Goitre Prevalence in Karnataka', *Indian Journal of Community Health*, vol. 3, no. 1, pp. 98–105.

Sunday Observer, 1997, 'Children of a Lesser God', 26 January–1 February.

Talukdar, B., B. Rath, H.P.S. Sachdev and R.K. Puri, 1994, 'Declining Trend in Tetanus Hospitalisation', *Indian Pediatrics*, vol. 31, July, pp. 849–51.

Times of India, 1993, 'Child Beaten to Death', 15 July.

________, 2000, 'Eight Year Old Girl Tortured and Battered by Surat Couple', 25 February.

Trivedi, C.R. and D.V. Mavlankar, 1986, 'Epidemiology of Low Birth Weight in Ahmedabad', *Indian Journal of Pediatrics*, vol. 53, no. 6, pp. 795–800.

UNICEF, 1995, *Child Prostitution: The Ultimate Abuse, Report on the National Consultation on Child Prostitution*, New Delhi.

________, 1998, *State of the World's Children*, New York: Oxford University Press.

Varma, A.P., 1994, 'Child Labour in India: An Overview', *Awards Digest, Journal of Labour Legislation*, vol. 20, nos. 7–12, pp. 1–16.

Varma, Mira and Anuradha Goel, 1993, 'Nutrition Status of Rural Children in

Some Districts of East Rajasthan', in *Quest for Excellence: A Development Panorama,* Jaipur: Social Welfare Department.

Vasanthi, G., A.B. Pawashe, H. Susie, T. Sujatha and L. Raman, 1994, 'Iron Nutritional Status of Adolescent Girls from Rural Areas and Urban Slums', *Indian Pediatrics*, vol. 31, February, pp. 127–31.

Venkatramani, S.H., 1986, 'Vested Interests', *India Today,* 15 July, p. 60.

________, 1986, 'Born to Die', *India Today,* 15 June, pp. 26–33.

Verma, I.C., Rose Joseph, Kusum Verma, Kamal Buckshee and O.P. Ghai, 1975, 'Prenatal Diagnosis of Genetic Disorders', *Indian Pediatrics*, vol. 12, no. 5, pp. 381–5.

Verma, M., J. Chhatwal and Gurmeet Kaur, 1998, 'Prevalence of Anemia Among Urban School Children of Punjab', *Indian Pediatrics*, vol. 35, October, pp. 1181–6.

Vidyasagar, R., 1991, 'The Lost Childhood: In the Sweatshops of Sivakasi', *Frontline,* 31 August, pp. 54–60.

Vijayalakshmi, S., 1984, *Working Conditions of Children Employed in Unorganised Sector: A Study in Sivakasi*, Madras: Centre for Social Research.

Vijayagopalan, S., 1993, *Child Labour in Carpet Industry: A Status Report,* New Delhi: National Council of Applied Economic Research.

Vinod Kumar, M.P., 1998, 'Children of a Lesser God', *Business India*, 9–22 February, pp. 115–22.

Viswanathan, Hema and Jon E. Rohde, 1990, *Diarrhoea in Rural India,* New Delhi: Vision Books.

Wadhwa, Soma, 1995, 'Lambs to the Slaughter', *Outlook,* 18 October, pp. 42–4.

________, 1998, 'For Sale: Childhood', *Outlook*, 23 February, pp. 78–80.

________, 2000, 'Class Struggle', *Outlook*, 10 April, pp. 50–60.

Women's Work and Child Development Network (WWCDN), 1995, *The Impact of Women's Work on Child and Maternal Health—A Summary Report*, New Delhi.

Wyon, John B. and John E. Gordon, 1971, *The Khanna Study: Population Problems in Rural Punjab,* Cambridge, Mass: Harvard University Press.

Yadav, R.J. and Padam Singh, 1999, 'Nutritional Status and Dietary Intake in Tribal Children of Bihar', *Indian Pediatrics*, vol. 36, January, pp. 37–42.

Yadav, S.K. 1994, *District Primary Education Programme, Madhya Pradesh, Malwa Region—A Summary*, New Delhi: National Council of Educational Research and Training.

Zargar, Abdul Hamid, Javid Amin Shah, Bashvi Almad Laway, S.R. Masoodi, N.A. Shah and Mohammad M. Mir, 1996, 'Goitre Survey in School Children in Kupwara (Kashmir Valley), *Indian Pediatrics,* vol. 33, March, pp. 248–9.

Zodpey, S.P., S.G. Deshpande, and N.D. Vasudeo, 1996, 'Breast Feeding Practices in a Tribal Community of Melghat Region in Maharashtra State', *Indian Journal of Public Health*, vol. 40, no. 4, pp. 120–5.

Index